Media and Political Violence

edited by

Hillel Nossek
College of Management Academic Studies, Israel

Annabelle Sreberny
SOAS, University of London

Prasun Sonwalkar
University of the West of England, Bristol

 HAMPTON PRESS, INC.
CRESSKILL, NJ 07626

Printed in the United States of America

Library of Congress Cataloging-in-Publication Data

Nossek, Hillel
    Media and political violence / Hillel Nossek, Annabelle Sreberny,
    Prasun Sonwalkar.
        p. cm.
    Includes bibliographic references and index.
    ISBN 1-57273-728-X (casebound) -- ISBN 1-57273-729-8 (paperbound : alk
    paper)
    1. Violence in mass media. 2. Violence--Press coverage. 3. Mass media--
    Political aspects. I. Sreberny, Annabelle. II. Sonwalkar, Prasun. III. Title.

    P96.V5N67 2007
    303.6--dc22
                            2006035053

Hampton Press, Inc.
23 Broadway
Cresskill, NJ 07626

CONTENTS

Introduction   1
    Hillel Nossek, Annabelle Sreberny, Prasun Sonwalkar

PART I   MEDIA AND POLITICAL VIOLENCE—THEORETICAL PERSPECTIVES

1   The Media and International Conflict: 23
    A Theoretical Overview
    Howard Tumber

2   Our News and Their News: The Role of National   41
    Identity in the Coverage of Foreign News
    Hillel Nossek

3   The Deictic of Mediated Violence: Public Intellectuals,   65
    Journalism and Some Problems of Pronoun-ciation
    Annabelle Sreberny

PART II   LONG BEFORE SEPTEMBER 11—MEDIA COVERAGE OF POLITICAL VIOLENCE—SOME HISTORICAL PERSPECTIVES

4   When Worlds Collide: Reporting the Realities   83
    of Hiroshima
    Stuart Allan

5   The Bosnian War in Spain: The Media's Representation   97
    of a Distant Violent Conflict
    Teresa La Porte

6   Media Functioning During a Violent International   119
    Crisis: Differences Between Elite and Popular Press
    Coverage of American Policy in Bosnia (1992-1995)
    Yaeli Bloch-Elkon & Sam Lehman-Wilzig

7   National Perspective in Foreign News Coverage: 143
    Australian Reporting of French Nuclear Testing
    in the Pacific
    Peter Putnis

PART III   SEPTEMBER 11 AND 21ST CENTURY VIOLENCE: NEW MODES OF REPRESENTATION?

8   Is All the News Ours? Political Violence, 161
    September 11 and the War on Iraq
    Dan Berkowitz
9   Round Up the Usual Suspects: Some Radical 183
    Implications of Indonesian and Euro-American
    Media Coverage of "Terrorist" Attacks
    Mark Hobart
10 Visions of Terror: On the Use of Images in the Mass 211
    Mediated Representations of the Bali Bombing
    Richard Fox
11 Disturbing the Banality of Journalism: Political Violence, 247
    Gujarat 2002 and the Indian News Media
    Prasun Sonwalkar
12 Terrorism and the Media: Does the Weapon Matter 269
    to the Coverage?
    Hillel Nossek

PART IV   RECENT WARS, CURRENT CRIES

13 "They" Shocked, "We" Saw: Psychological Operations 307
    in Operation Iraqi Freedom, 2003
    Philip M. Taylor
14 Framing Gender in Afghanistan and Iraq: 325
    Unveiling the Gaze of Empire
    Rashmi Luthra
15 The Power of Myths: The War on Terror 341
    and Military Might
    Justin Lewis
16 The Pornography of Barbarism of the 355
    Self-reflecting Sign
    Paul Taylor

About the Authors 373
Author Index 377
Subject Index 385

Introduction

Hillel Nossek

Annabelle Sreberny

Prasun Sonwalkar

The peaceful prospects of the late twentieth century did not last long. There had seemed to be a moment in the early 1990s that heralded a new era of international relations and the possibility of a period of greater peace. With the disintegration of the USSR and the end of the Cold War, the world's major faultline of conflict had cracked. The stability of the world's biggest democracy and its dynamic economic engine, the argument that democracies do not fight each other and the idea of a "democracy dividend" all gave rise to the belief that the world was moving into a new era in which conflict between and within nations could be solved by peaceful negotiation and democratic process. Economic, social and cultural trends such as globalization and multiculturalism were seen as contributing factors to these peaceful visions. The media's role in dismantling the regimes under the Iron Curtain was well documented and analyzed, and its prospective role in the anticipated new peaceful world could not be ignored.

These peaceful prospects were rapidly shown to be pipe dreams. The first decade of the "new era" saw the Gulf War in 1991, the contentious internal and international wars in the Balkans and especially the war in Bosnia, the first *Intifada* in the Middle East, and the murder of Yitzchak

Rabin, prime minister of Israel, by an Israeli Jew in order to prevent the implementation of the Oslo peace accord. The new millennium was met by the second *Intifada* in the Middle East. Terrorist events in many countries, including in New York on September 11, 2001, followed by acts in Madrid on March 11, 2004, and London on July 7, 2005, prompted a declaration by the United States (and its coalition) of the new "war on terror." This was rapidly extended to the promotion of democracy by any means necessary, producing the internationally visible (if still not well-documented) wars in Afghanistan and Iraq. Ongoing conflicts in Peru, the Congo, Sierra Leone, Sudan, Indonesia and elsewhere have affected even greater numbers of people, yet these are not so visible on most television screens. Neighbors were not very neighborly. India and Pakistan played nuclear brinksmanship and China rattled the tranquillity of Taiwan. Protests against the development of nuclear weapons, environmental issues, and antiglobalization often became violent, while violence penetrated further into the heartland of democratic stability with political assassinations in Norway and the Netherlands. Cartoons, instead of promoting laughter, triggered the burning of embassies. All of these events, and many others, indicate that the prospects for a new era of world peace were at least premature.

The role of the media in covering violent events and moments of conflict has become more and more crucial, aided by the new technologies developed during the recent period. These include direct broadcast satellite transmission from the field, cellular and satellite phones allowing direct reporting from battlefields and the expansion of access to the Internet, which now functions as a mass medium, evident in the massive recourse to it on September 11. The reduction in size and the simplification in use of new media technologies and better connectivity to the Internet allow people on the battlefield, as well as bystanders, to become journalists. One interesting example was SalamPax, the blogger from Baghdad, who regularly recorded his version of Gulf War hostilities and whose blog was syndicated by mainstream media.

The so-called "CNN effect" was suggested right after the Gulf War when Pentagon-orchestrated "news pools" and "embedded journalists" seemed to put in doubt the future role of journalists in the field and cancel out the effect of new media technologies on the coverage of various kinds of political violence. Echoing Fukuyama, Katz (1992) even proposed "the end of journalism." Yet both history and journalism keep on being re-formed and remade. Many books and articles written after September 11 tried to convey a similar message, that the world and the media would never be the same again. We wish to question the unthinking West-centrism in the unquestioned position that dares to define "the world" and "the media" so readily, and also to question whether the coverage of political violent events is really different after 9/11?

The contributors to this book review and critique existing theoretical frameworks for the study of media and political violence and suggest some new approaches and trajectories for research. They include rich, empirically grounded case studies of instances of mediated violence and try, often tentatively, to compare the evidence in order to understand whether there are any common patterns to be found in mediated coverage of political violence presented as domestic and foreign news around the world.

Given the number and range of violent events, we are subject to the same kind of critique as analysts make of the media: why include these events, and not others? Deliberately, we do not cover the ongoing political violence between the Israeli government and the Palestinians; this has spawned its own copious literature and therefore is not included here. Nor do we present material on the political violence in South America, nor on the post–Cold War conflicts in the new independent states that emerged from the former Soviet Union. Such locales deserve attention and remain projects to be taken up in the future by us and others.

We came to the project with our own national and professional backgrounds. Hillel Nossek brings a longitudinal analysis of terrorism and the media inflected by the experience of living all his life in a country where terrorism is an ever-present issue. Annabelle Sreberny has long been interested in deconstructing public/private boundaries in social analysis; in this book she focuses on commentary by public intellectuals rather than on professional news product. Prasun Sonwalkar is an Indian journalist with experience of covering political violence in South Asia for over two decades, who infuses his current academic writing with insights from the field.

We now review some general theoretical issues in regard to the mediated coverage of political violence and then offer a brief taste of each chapter.

WHAT IS POLITICAL VIOLENCE? TOWARDS A CONSENSUAL OPERATIONAL DEFINITION

Political violence has several definitions and meanings. Legal, political, psychological and moral theories all offer definitions, and social scientists also offer definitions for use as tools in empirical research. Political violence—in other words, violence in a political context—is a broad terrain encompassing a wide spectrum of behaviors and events, ranging from terrorism and war to political protest. All involve some form of conflict and some kind of political goal. Political violence also carries a message, which is why media coverage is important for those behind it, both as an end in itself and as a means to other ends. This is very clear in the case of protest, but also pertinent with regard to terrorism (Picard, 1993). Indeed, the symbolic dimensions of terrorism are often preferred as its definition; for example, as Wilkinson argues: "It (terrorism) is used to create and exploit a climate of fear among a wider target group than the immediate victims of the violence, and to publicize a cause . . ." (Wilkinson, 2000, p. 12).

The term "terrorism" is usually used in reference to politically motivated violent acts that are aimed against states and governments. This type of terrorism is labelled "terrorism from below." The other type that is so labelled are acts of politically motivated violence that are executed by governments directly on their own citizens, or indirectly by using non-state organizations to inflict acts of terror on other states. This is labeled "state terrorism" or "terrorism from above." State terrorism is used to describe acts of violence that are executed by a government to elicit fear in order to consolidate its power and deter groups from trying to initiate revolution. Furthermore, it seems that the kind of actions used by governments that adopt terrorism as a tool for achieving their internal or external political aims are very often similar to those used by terrorist groups that act against states. In both types of terrorism there are acts of extreme violence that include civilians (noncombatants) as victims in order to create deep fear and anxiety in large publics in the name of a political agenda (Norris, Kern, & Just, 2003).

In this book we discuss terrorism of the first type only—that is terrorism from below—and leave out the second one—terrorism from above—for a separate discussion in another context.

THE NEWSWORTHINESS OF POLITICAL VIOLENCE

The assumption that media flock to cover acts of violence has been and remains a powerful mantra within media studies The study of media coverage of political violence has a long history. The belief that such coverage may have an effect on governments and audiences—keeping conflicts alive or helping resolve them—sustains media research that seeks to better understand media treatments and outcomes. However, it seems that not all events that researchers define as political violence are regarded as such by the media, even if they meet the criteria for "newsworthiness"—that is, they possess elements of drama, negativity, tragedy/pain, and so forth (Kelly & Mitchell, 1984; Nossek, 1990, 1994; Weimann & Brosius, 1991). The assumption has been punctured by arguments that some violence is more-newsworthy than other similar events (Sonwalkar, 2004). Thus, media become implicated within the very definition of "events of political violence," bringing some to public attention and not others. The debate needs to be engaged again to explore if, when, and why violence becomes newsworthy.

NEGATIVITY—OR "VIOLENCE"— AS A KEY VARIABLE

One longstanding argument has been that violence exemplifies negativity, which is long established as a major news value anything that disrupts the ordinary flow of life. Following the seminal study by Galtung and Ruge (1965) regarding the structure of foreign news coverage, subsequent studies have persisted in their efforts to map the factors that define an event as "news" generally and, more particularly, as "foreign news." A recent American study found that in foreign news coverage of disasters, there was a clear link between the number of dead, the size of the tragedy, and both the decision to cover it and the extent of coverage of the event. The factor of an event's distance from the United States was found to be marginal in these decisions (Van Belle, 2000). To this discussion, Harcup and O'Neill (2001) have contributed a map of the news factors that influence coverage selection. The ten factors they identified include a fresh presentation of some of the factors that were conceptualized by Galtung and Ruge, including negativity, celebrity, audience relevance, and follow up. They also suggest that another significant factor is the newspaper agenda—that stories are covered that suit the specific media organization's agenda (Harcup & O'Neill, 2001).

JOURNALISTS AS "PROFESSIONALS" OR PATRIOTS

The focus on news factors is naturally linked to conceptions of journalists and editors as "gatekeepers" responsible for news selection and for producing the media view of social reality. The selection process is a complex one and takes place at several levels. The journalist does not function solely on the basis of personal preference, but obeys a set of professional practices and standards. S/he does not function in isolation, but within a media organization with its own priorities which operates in a matrix with other organizations. The single media organization is itself part of a wider social organization, the institution of the media, which enjoys reciprocal relations with other social institutions and is subject to their influence. Hence, as Shoemaker neatly observed ". . . none of these actors—the individual, the routine, the organization, or the social institution—can escape that fact that it is tied to and draws its sustenance from the social system' (Shoemaker, 1991, p. 75).

Perceptions of the journalistic profession are relative, influenced by historical and cultural traditions and defined by political, economic, and social contexts. Wei, Weaver, and Johnson (1996) examined journalists' attitudes towards professional values, perceptions, and functions in a comparative Russian-American study, and discovered that the perception of the profession is a relative concept that is influenced by various historical and cultural traditions and defined by the political, economic and social context. Neither the latter study nor Weaver and Wilhoit's (1996) book fully address the question of how journalists see their function in terms of national interests. This question is addressed, albeit indirectly, by the Glasgow University Media Group's (1985) study of the British media coverage of crisis situations, which supported the hypothesis that the politico-social context— essentially, the way journalists see national interest—influences their perception of their role. They wrote:

> The Falklands experience revealed conflicts of principle and interest. The right to the free flow of information in a democratic society was set against the need for censorship in the interests of the war effort. The right to present different points of view about the issue was set against a call to speak for the "national interest."

Their analysis indicates that it is precisely in the context of foreign news that we find voices that are out of sync with the government's position. According to the Glasgow group, this was possible when "Britain's immediate interests are not seen as threatened" (1985, p. 5). The group also notes that a desire to win the war and to be seen as supporting "our" patriotic effort links most of the British journalists and government sources. From this perspective, international acts of violence that (seem to) hail or threaten the nation will be seen as necessarily newsworthy, will be covered a great deal, and will be reported on with the usual caveat of objectivity loosened for a moment.

NEWS AS A HOMOGENIZED PRODUCT VS. LOCAL INFLECTIONS

Perhaps the most profound bias built into foreign news reporting is that resulting from the local "glasses" that news "gatekeepers" wear. Cohen, Levy, Roeh, and Gurevitch (1995) employ the metaphor of "a global news room" to describe a situation whereby a relatively small number of journalists act as gatekeepers, coordinating the flow of news. But these same "global" journalists must preserve their local cultural identity in order to continue communicating with their audiences, and they cover foreign societies from the perspective of their home society. One can regard this as a two-stage process in which, during the first stage, foreign news undergoes a process of localization, which may be observed in the emphasis on relevance to national interests. In the second stage, localization is evident in the adaptation of news content to individual and community spheres of interests rather than those of national or supra-national interest (Nossek, 2000). One reason for this is the attempt to tailor reports to the local audience (Gurevitch, Levy, & Roeh, 1991). One should bear in mind that different criteria affect audiences' preferences regarding news—some are universal, for example, the criteria of the importance of the country covered, whereas others are local, for example, the tourism connection for economically prosperous countries (Youichi, 1995).

GLOBAL VERSUS LOCAL DEFINITIONS

Within global news agencies, journalists decide which events will be of interest to far-flung audiences and media systems in various regions of the world. Paterson (1999) suggests a counterargument based on a comparison of images of two events supplied by two major news agencies and the images of the events broadcast by 27 television stations (the two events were France's nuclear test on Mururoa and the protest demonstrations in Tahiti in 1995). Paterson argues that the news agencies' main role, and the reliance of broadcast organizations worldwide on their material, greatly affects which news stories are broadcast. He maintains that, indeed, the larger, well-established broadcasting networks will tend to cover foreign news from the local angle, whereas the smaller broadcasting companies tend to give their audiences the story supplied by the agencies—with the "global" angle.

Paterson identifies four approaches used by television stations regarding agency inserts: they use large amounts of news agency footage, leading to a consensus on the kind of material used by broadcasters and agencies; they rely more on news agency editing than local editing, which also explains the use of agency frameworks; they use stories that seem closest to the importance already ascribed to them by the broadcasting bodies; and as noted above, the less well-established organizations exhibit greater dependency on news agency material than the larger ones (Paterson, 1999). Due to the reliance of smaller broadcasters on images supplied by the agencies, Patterson suggests that the stories that are broadcast to different audiences are the same because they use the same footage supplied by the agencies. However, simply using the same images does not guarantee identical coverage. Although television coverage relies on pictures, it also relies on the analysis that accompanies the pictures, the story positioning in the program, and the studio announcer's comments. Thus comparisons have to examine the story as it was broadcast in its entirety.

THE RELATIONSHIP BETWEEN MEDIA
AND TERRORIST VIOLENCE

The relationship between the mass media and insurgent terrorism against western democracies is a vastly debated and much studied question (Norris, Kern, & Just, 2003; Paletz & Schmidt, 1992; Schmidt & de Graaf, 1982; Tuman, 2003), despite the manufactured and erroneous sense that it developed anew in 2001. In the aftermath of September 11, one question is whether the event heralded new strategies in the terrorism arsenal (e.g., use of nonweapons such as airplanes as tools for terrorist attacks) or new threats (anthrax spores or radioactive materials). And would such acts herald new relationships with the media or would the coverage be just more of the same?

Not only do the weapons seem to have changed but also the communication technologies, changing the relations between the perpetrators of political violence and the media. Those responsible for terrorist activities perceive the media as an important means for achieving their ends, and their actions take place with an eye toward media attention. A survey of different media throughout the world indicated a number of elements that affect media coverage of terrorist events; for example, the location of the event, the identity of the victims, and the identity of the perpetrators (Weimann & Winn, 1994). Such actors' control of the media agenda is disproportionate to their real strength as a result of their efforts to tailor their activities for media requirements. In the context of reciprocal terrorism-media relations and other political violent acts, governments also come to play a key role.

When faced with terrorist attacks or other violent acts for political ends, governments often try to enlist media cooperation. On its part, the media usually accedes (Carruthers, 2000). A critical view of such cooperation sees the enlistment of the media as an outcome of cooperation between military, political, and media elites in order to construct a world picture designed to reinforce their existing power (see, for example, Chomsky & Herman, 1979; Gitlin, 1980; Glasgow University Media Group, 1985; Hallin, 1989; Kellner, 1992). Taking a different perspective, it has been maintained that it is necessary to restrict media coverage of terrorist events as part of the battle to eradicate terrorism (Kingstone, 1995). Even American media representatives, usually wedded to First Amendment principles, have said that they do not rule out entirely the possibility of government-imposed restrictions on the coverage of terrorist events (Martin & Draznin, 1991).

The media are not unselective in their coverage of terrorist events. The selection process may be seen as a two-stage process involving a decision to cover a particular story and a decision as to how much coverage it should receive and for how many days or weeks it will be covered (Weimann & Brosius, 1991). Beyond the classic news factors that might influence how terrorist events are covered, other local criteria have been suggested. For example, Simmons and Lowry (1990) established a link between the political orientation of perpetrators, the level of American involvement, and what names the American press gave to the perpetrators.

A somewhat different political focus on news media coverage of protest movements suggests that the absence of coverage cannot be ascribed simply to news factors. The protest's content and political context influence whether there is any news coverage or not. Analyzing protest events that were covered as domestic news, Oliver and Maney (2000) collected data from one city that revealed the interaction of the political process, news value, and news routine factors in news coverage of protest versus other events. Protests about legislative issues received the most coverage. Controlling for issue type, protest forms were covered less when the legislature was in session, whereas other forms (largely ceremonies and speeches) were covered more. Yearly variations in coverage rates of nonlegislative protests distorted the apparent shape of the protest cycle. Other predictive factors include size, police involvement, conflict, counterdemonstrators, amplified sound, Monday event, religious sponsorship (negative), and annual or holiday events.

If the political context is what influences whether there is coverage or not, we can speculate that the picture might be similar for foreign news, where the political context is at the level of the nation state, so that news factors may not provide an adequate explanation of coverage. We need to examine the content of the protest or act of political violence in the national context as a factor that can explain why and how an event is defined as news and how it is covered. Indeed, Nossek, in his chapter in this volume, found empirical support to that assumption in the differential coverage that the same events received in different counties by elite newspapers that are all advocates of professional journalism.

The question of domestic news versus foreign news also concerns the way political violence and terrorism are covered. The media tend to cover terrorist events based on cultural and geopolitical factors, producing the prominence of "local" terrorism (Nossek, 1990). Thus, not only is the media's selection process influenced by different factors, but so is the type of coverage. Kelly and Mitchell (1981, in Barnhurst, 1991, p. 129) found that both *The New York Times* and *The Times*, London, ignored some 44 per-cent of the incidents of international terrorism that occurred between 1968 and 1974 (based on a comparison of press coverage and factual records). The two papers disregarded most of the terrorist incidents that took place in South America. In contrast, these newspapers gave Palestinian terrorism at the time nine times as much coverage (although, in terms of quantity, the ratio between events was only twice as large). At times, the preference for one story over another is indicative of regional or local political preferences.

GOVERNMENTS AS INITIATORS OF POLITICAL VIOLENCE

Governments may be the initiators and perpetrators of political violence. A comparison of U.S. coverage frameworks in two similar events—the shoot-ing down of the Iranian plane by the U.S. army in 1988 and the downing of a Korean plane by the Soviet army in 1983—highlighted a number of differ-ences (Entman, 1991). The KAL victims were humanized in the verbal and visual messages; for example, labelling the victims as "innocent human beings" and "loved ones," which encouraged identification with them. The Iran Air victims were mentioned much less, the information less centered on their humanity and less likely to evoke empathy. The media's emphasis on Soviet guilt and denial of American guilt was somehow predetermined. The United States was seen as less morally responsible for the fate of the Iranians than the Soviet Union was for the KAL passengers. In the light of his find-ings, Entman concluded that official White House, Pentagon, and U.S. Foreign Office sources greatly influenced which frameworks were chosen for media coverage (Entman, 1991, p. 25).

A subsequent study of American foreign news coverage of human rights and political violence before and after the Cold War showed that countries considered important during the Cold War era were the object of consider-able journalistic attention in 1985, and that this declined significantly with the end of the Cold War. In general, it was found that *The New York Times* gave more extensive coverage to countries with which the United States was involved either politically or militarily (Caliendo, Gibney, & Payne, 1999). Another study, by Grundmann, Smith, and Wright (2000), found differences in the coverage of the Kosovo war between three leading newspapers in dif-ferent European countries; differences in content and coverage perspective were dictated by national agendas and the contexts in which the newspaper operated. Another American study distributed questionnaires to a sample of daily newspaper editors nationwide and showed similar results. Regarding foreign news, it was found that most editors focus on security and national interests. The editors believed that the most important factors were threats against the United States, world peace, and U.S. involvement. When the editors' positions were examined in light of their political leanings, the more conservative editors were found to evaluate foreign news from an American perspective and focus on elements of importance to the United States (Chang & Lee, 1992). The factors outlined above work to produce narrow, ethnocentric communication maps due to local editing considerations that stress the coverage of countries that are deemed to be geographically, politically, or culturally close (Sreberny & Stevenson, 1999).

Television news has a tendency to present social conflicts at the height of their intensity, consistent with its predilection toward the dramatic and unusual. According to studies about the rationale of news, the criterion of proximity—geographical, political, and/or cultural—is important with regard to the decision "to cover or not to cover," as well as to the type of coverage. It has also been suggested that as part of the effort to maintain the social status quo, remote conflict is often presented as more complex than local conflict; this way, public attention can be diverted away from local problems, which serves the existing power system (Cohen, Adoni, & Bantz, 1990). Additionally, in addition to the formal constraints placed on the media by their governments, the media enlist of their own accord in the war against terrorist organizations by adopting an establishment perspective; as Carruthers has argued (2000, pp. 195-196):

> In what is often not, in fact, a state of war, many Western news organizations have often seemed all too willing to present arms against terrorism, encouraged or bullied by governments which regard any dissent as tantamount to treason. . . . Insufficient displays of "patriotism" in the war against terrorism have resulted in formal restrictions being imposed on the media. But generally overt censorship has been an infrequent—because unnecessary—last resort of dubious effectiveness.

The many differences in the American networks' coverage of the intifada and their coverage of the Gulf War confirm this argument. The various coverage frameworks indicate that a different kind of media treatment is used in the case of "our" war as opposed to the case of "their" war. Journalists, it appears, prefer not to acknowledge the dilemma that arises at such times, when loyalty to their own side takes precedence over professional loyalty (Liebes, 1992). Another study (Cohen, Adoni, & Nossek, 1993) demonstrated that the 1980s intifada was covered differently by Israeli television than by European and American television networks because the conflict was perceived as an internal Israeli matter. These differences concerned the way the complexity of the conflict was presented and opinions of how possible it was to resolve—domestic conflict being presented as less complex than external conflicts. The Gulf War was covered differently by different newspapers around the world. Different emphases were discovered in the coverage of the war by French, German, Japanese, and American papers, as each paper related to the war from a different viewpoint (Kaid, Harville, Ballotti, & Wawrzyniak, 1993).

Differences in the coverage of terrorist events are chiefly the result of differences in the authors' cultural backgrounds. One of the most productive ways to analyze news is to treat it as myth (Bird & Darbenne, 1988). The function of the news as a story (Darnton, 1975; Roeh, 1989) and the reiteration of myths has been identified in earlier studies and has also been applied to the analysis of terrorist events (see, for example, Lule, 1988a, 1988b). One study (Nossek, 1994), which examined the Israeli media coverage of terrorist attacks between 1968-1978, demonstrated how the media utilized such events to convey the master narrative of the establishment of Israel as a result of the Holocaust and Zionism as a framework for understanding the events and to consolidate attitudes toward them. A similar study in the United States showed how terrorist events in Israel are used to transmit the foundational myth of the conquest of the west (Berkowitz, 2001). A comparison of the coverage of such events in different countries can show the various ways in which they are used to convey local cultural myths (Berkowitz & Nossek, 2001).

All these indicate coverage of terrorist events and political violence from a local point of view. The local point of view does not just influence how these events are covered, but actually how they are defined as "news." Foreign news is not only covered from the local angle; it is also defined from this perspective. The journalist who follows a set of professional norms does this within the narrower framework of his or her membership in a certain nation state, which has not lost its place or function even in the era of globalization. The key issue here is the extent to which the nation-state still represents the journalist's main frame of social reference when covering political violence and terrorism, superseding the normative professional frame of reference. The accumulating evidence suggests that the decision whether to cover a story is decided mostly by this primary bond and only secondarily by the normative professional frame. Once the story has been selected, the coverage will highlight the professional aspects, the news framework, and the cultural frame.

ORGANIZATION AND CONTENT OF THE BOOK

This book is organized in four parts. The first presents some theoretical perspectives that help shed light on the main question of whether there are any common patterns of coverage of political violence in the media, what their determinants might be, and what the potential effects are on all actors, including the initiators of violence for political aims, the governments involved—whether as law-and-order enforcers or initiators of political violence of their own—the media themselves, and the publics at large. This mapping of the issue allows us to put the question of a post-September 11 effect in a broader research context and ask if those common features did really change in the actual coverage of September 11. Finally we ask where do we go in the aftermath of September 11, which brings us to the wars in Afghanistan and Iraq, and to the question, does coverage of new kinds of political violence change after September 11.

The chapter by Howard Tumber, "The Media and International Conflict," opens Part I with a review of the theoretical and empirical literature that focuses mainly on the issue of media coverage in relation particularly to wars and groups that have no states, suggesting the contours of a new theoretical framework needed in the post–Cold War period of globalization, in which wars over territory become less prominent but the rise of nonstate actors more central. He concludes his arguments by suggesting that the new relationships between media and international conflict are based on a shift from "states without enemies" (Giddens, 1994, p. 235) to the threat of "enemies without states" of the new milieu (Webster, 2003, p. 61). Globalization's negative effects in creating inequality, competition, and exclusions on a global scale has strengthened fundamentalisms of different sorts (because they can provide certainty in an uncertain world), and terrorist, absolutist groups operating beyond national borders (i.e. Al Qaeda) become the new political actors. Media also now plays a key role in "information warfare" (Webster, 2003), which seeks its legitimacy in the name of democracy itself rather than in national interest. Public support for interventions aiming to protect human rights becomes essential and the media play a key role in these processes. Media are, on the one hand, the key vehicle of "perception management," creating public approval of contemporary conflicts, while, on the other, they play a key role in identifying and exposing abuses on human rights, even instigating intervention.

Nossek suggests in the second chapter that in spite of all these changes the role of the nation state is still crucial to the understanding of the role of the media in covering international political conflicts as well as intranational political violence. He argues that there is an inverse relationship between professional news values and the national identity of journalists and editors. Expressed as a rule, this could be stated as "the more 'national' the report is, the less 'professional' it will be"; that is to say, the closer the reporters/editors are to a given news event in terms of national interest, the further they are from applying professional news values. This claim is presented in the form of a flow diagram and is investigated using qualitative content analysis of the coverage of four events in three different countries' elite newspapers (United States, Britain and Israel).

Annabelle Sreberny's chapter, the third in Part I, takes the isssue of addressivity a step further with a discourse analysis of deictics, especially the use of "we" and "them" in the Commentary pieces from British newspapers, suggesting the public frameworks used by British intellectuals to make sense of September 11 and the ongoing power of national belonging and cultural identification. She concludes her chapter as follows:

"The doxic, toxic, truth, is that 'we' do think of 'ourselves' as different from them and the content of that we/they divide remains quite fixed, and post 9/11 even reinforced. 9/11 showed that both the realities, and the theorizing, around 'compassion fatigue' and 'states of denial' and indifference to 'distant suffering' are profoundly Westcentric constructions. Writing about 9/11 has revealed the difficulties we currently experience in trying to determine the inside and the outside, who we are and who they are."

The chapters in Part II present analyses of the media/violence relationship from a variety of different points in time and location. Stuart Allen's chapter provides some comparative historical frame with an analysis of the coverage of the U.S. bombing of Hiroshima and its aftermath. He concludes that, by the end of 1946, the paradoxical logics of nuclearist discourses were fast becoming fused into official justifications for not only maintaining but for radically exacerbating the threat of human extinction in the interests of national security. This prefigures, in an ominously exact fashion, the claims by Lewis in his chapter about the exaggeration of "terrorist threat" by hegemonic powers as a justification for twenty-first-century war and violence.

The chapters by Teresa La Porte and by Yaeli Bloch-Elkon and Sam Lehman-Wilzig add to the comparison by Nossek and present an analysis of the Bosnian war from a number of points of view, especially focusing on incidents during 1995. La Porte's focus is on the Spanish press; her main argument is that the concept of "political violence" present in each nation's media is no more than a reflection of the way in which it is understood by the society, shaped according to historical experience and day-to-day reality. Bloch-Elkon and Lehman-Wilzig examine U.S. press in relation to the multiple phases of the Bosnian crisis—onset, escalation and de-escalation—and they point to strong and significant correlations between the media's main attitudes and the sundry crisis phases, indicating the mutable functions of the press during the crisis.

The chapter by Peter Putnis also analyzes events in 1995, this time the coverage of the Mururoa nuclear tests in the Australian media, and his analysis supports the contention that press coverage arises from an interaction of an interpenetration of domestic, regional, and global concerns. The event, as covered in the Australian press, became predominantly an Australian story because of Australian actors in the field and, even more so, because Australia itself became a stage for reaction and protest. From a French colonial perspective Mururoa was French territory. But for the Australian press this was an event in "our region" in which Australia had a particular interest and the French were the "foreigners."

The chapters in Part III deal directly with the coverage of September 11 and other nonstate political violence, or look at September 11 as a reference point for the analysis of coverage of other events. The chapter by Dan Berkowitz shows how news ownership drives coverage of events that is consonant with American values, with little perspective lent to other positions. Whether or not there were opposing viewpoints about the World Trade Center attack or the Iraq War, to challenge American ideology in such threatening situations would place media in an awkward position of appearing unpatriotic and unsupportive and their counterideological positions would appear to cleave national unity, potentially turning the public against the news media. To the question "is all the news ours?" Berkowitz suggests that when an occurrence presents a clear ideological threat, the answer is yes.

Mark Hobart analyzes the coverage of September 11 in the Indonesian media and the attack on Bali in the U.K. media. He asks how media scholars themselves are positioned and suggests that a taken-for-granted Westcentrism means that reporters and academics alike continue to round up the usual suspects. Richard Fox focuses on the visual representations of the Bali bomb, providing a rich textual analysis inflected by Barthes and Zizek to explore why, following 9/11, there was a sense that "we wanted to see it again and again."

The chapter by Prasun Sonwalkar adds a different kind of conflict to the volume by dealing with the role of the media in a local, religious and ethnic conflict, the events in Gujarat, 2002, widely dubbed as India's first riot in the satellite TV era, but was more like a pogrom in the one-sided attacks on Muslims. He analyzes the serious questions faced by journalists in such a situation and argues that the moment marked a departure in the way the Indian media approached communal clashes and highlighted the disjuncture between the news cultures of the English-language and the non-English news media.

Nossek's second chapter asks a different, and important, kind of question, "Does the weapon matter to the coverage?" He answers through an analysis of coverage of two events where there was a threat to use weapons of mass distraction, or unconventional weapons, and suggests that the impact of the media coverage of terrorist threats to use unconventional weapons may be more effective than the use of the weapons themselves, and calls for a new frame to cover such events.

Part IV deals with the aftermath of September 11 and includes chapters on the coverage of the wars in Afghanistan and Iraq. Philip Taylor examines a different form of communication, psychological operations, during the war in Iraq. He argues that the battle for hearts and minds was not just confined to the Iraqi people but was also directed at world opinion because, for the power elite in Washington, the 2003 war in Iraq was the second battle of the "war" against terrorism (Afghanistan being the first). The war was seen in Washington as being as much a struggle for the moral high ground in the global information space as it was to secure command and control of the battlefield, and there may be a further sea change in the development of information operations to secure what is referred to as full-spectrum dominance.

Rashmi Luthra compares coverage of the Afghanistan and Iraq wars to make visible the ideological work that goes into the construction of news frames consonant with U.S. foreign policy. Gender was and is a particularly useful trope because it served as a convenient dividing marker between the West and Islam, between "civilization" and its supposed absence, and she argues that the ideological work of the press involves, among other mechanisms, making visible certain continuities and ignoring others among potentially infinite connections that can be made.

Examining British Media coverage of Iraq, Justin Lewis argues that one of the most important political consequences of the "war on terror" is that it played a key role in sustaining a political climate in which substantial public resources were and are allocated to military purposes. Echoing Allen's argument about Hiroshima, Lewis suggests that the excessive coverage given to the war on terror bears little relation to the actual risks posed by international terrorism. The media coverage and the resulting public debate failed to interrogate the subsequent myth that military spending can be used to fight terrorism, so Lewis concludes that the war on terror works to provide political cover for a new neo-imperialist approach to military expenditure.

Paul Taylor closes the book with another analysis of images, this time the images of American soldiers torturing Iraqi prisoners in jail. He contextualizes Bin Laden within a string of key Islamic hate-figures that previously included the Ayatollah Khomeini, and who all have in common being bracketed within a discourse of evil, fulfilling the role that Baudrillard describes of the Manichean demiurge who creates the evil illusions against which God and goodness avail themselves. Taylor suggests that a big danger for the West is if the hate figures begin to play this role self-consciously and trigger the West's own deeply embedded form of evil, of which Abu Ghraib was a vivid manifestation.

Thus, although the events of September 11, and subsequent arguments and mythologies run across many of the chapters, there is also a longer history and wider geography of comparative analysis of political violence at work in the book. The twenty-first century is already filled with political violence of historically recognizable forms as well as dreadful new kinds, and this book will not be the last word on the subject. But we hope that its rich mix of empirically grounded studies, including nuanced textual analyses and varied theoretical approaches, offer some new ways of thinking about old questions as well as some new questions to ask about the subject.

REFERENCES

Barnhurst, K.G. (1991). The literature of terrorism — Implications for visual communication. In O.A. Alali & K.K. Eke (Eds.), *Media coverage of terrorism* (pp. 112-137). Newbury Park, CA: Sage.

Berkowitz, D. (August, 2001). *The Middle East as wild west: News of terrorism in Israel through an American lens.* Washington, DC: AEJMC Annual Conference.

Berkowitz, D. & Nossek, H. (2001). Myths and news narratives: Toward a comparative perspective of news. *Ecquid Novi, 22,* 41-56.

Bird, E. & Darbenne, W.R. (1988). Myth, chronicle and story. In J.W. Carey (Ed.), *Media, myths and narratives* (pp. 313-328). England: Penguin.

Caliendo, S.M., Gibney, M.P., & Payne, A. (1999). All the news that fit to print? *New York Times* coverage of human-rights violations. *The Harvard International Journal of Press/Politics, 4*(4), 48-69.

Carruthers, S.L. (2000). *The media at war.* New York: St. Martin Press.

Chang, T. & Lee, J. (1992). Factors affecting gatekeepers' selection of foreign news: A national survey of newspaper editors. *Journalism Quarterly, 69,* 554-561.

Chomsky, N. & Herman, E. (1979). *After the cataclysm: The political economy of human rights,* 2. Nottingham: Spokesman Books.

Cohen, A. A., Adoni H., & Bantz, C. (1990). *Social conflict and television news.* Newbury Park, CA: Sage.

Cohen, A. A., Adoni, H., & Nossek, H. (1993). Television news and the intifada: A comparative study of social conflict. In A.A. Cohen & G. Wolfsfeld (Eds.), *Framing the intifada: People and media* (pp. 116-141). Norwood, NJ: Ablex.

Cohen, A.A., Levy, M. R., Roeh, I., & Gurevitch, M. (1995). *Global newsrooms, local audiences: A study of the Eurovision news exchange.* London: John Libbey.

Darnton, R. (1975). Writing news and telling stories. *Deadalus, 104,* 175-193.

Entman, R.M. (1991). Framing U.S. coverage of international news: Contrasts in narratives of the KAL and Iran air incidents. *Journal of Communication, 41*(4), 6-27.

Galtung, J. & Ruge, M.H. (1965). The structure of foreign news. *Journal of Peace Research, 2,* 64-91.

Giddens, A. (1994). *Beyond left and right.* Cambridge: Polity.

Gitlin, T. (1980). *The whole world is watching: The mass media in the making and unmaking of the new left.* Berkeley: University of California Press.

Glasgow University Media Group. (1985). *News about war and peace.* Milton Keynes & Philadelphia: Open University Press.

Grundman, R., Smith, D., & Wright, S. (2000). National elites and transnational discourses in the Balkan War: A comparison between the French, German and British establishment press. *European Journal of Communication, 15,* 299-320.

Gurevitch, M., Levy, M. R., & Roeh, I. (1991). The global newsroom: Convergences and diversities in the globalization of television news. In P. Dahlgren & C. Sparks (Eds.), *Communication and citizenship: Journalism and the public sphere* (pp. 195–216). London and New York: Routledge.

Hallin, D.C. (1989). *The uncensored war: The media and Vietnam.* Berkeley: University of California Press.

Harcup, T. & O'Neill, D. (2001). What is news? Galtung and Ruge revisited. *Journalism Studies, 2,* 261-280.

Kaid, L.L., Harville, B., Ballotti, J., & Wawrzyniak, M. (1993). Telling the Gulf War story: Coverage in five papers. In B.S. Greenberg & W. Gantz (Eds.), *Desert Storm and the mass media* (pp. 86–98). Cresskill, NJ: Hampton Press.

Katz, E. (1992). The end of journalism: Notes of watching the war. *Journal of Communication, 42*(3), 5-13.

Kellner, D. (1992). Television, the crisis of democracy and the Persian Gulf War. In M. Raboy & B. Dagenais (Eds.), *Media, crisis and democracy: Mass communication and the disruption of social order* (pp. 44-62). London and Newbury Park, CA: Sage.

Kelly, M. J. & Mitchell, H. T. (1984). Transnational terrorism and the western elite press. *Political Communication and Persuasion, 1*(3), 269-296.

Kingstone, S. (1995). Terrorism, the media and the Northern Ireland conflict. *Studies in Conflict and Terrorism, 18,* 203-230.

Liebes, T. (1992). Our war/their war: Comparing the Intifada and the Gulf War on U.S. and Israeli television. *Critical Studies in Mass Communication, 9*(1), 44-55.

Lule, J. (1988a). The myth of my widow: A dramatic analysis of news—Portrayal of a terrorist victim. *Political Communication and Persuasion, 5,* 101-120.

Lule, J. (1988b). *Symbolic sacrifice:* New York Times *coverage of the TWA 847 hijacking.* Boston: Emerson College, Terrorism and the Media Research Project.

Martin, L. J. & Drazin, J. (1991). Broadcast gatekeepers and terrorism. In Y. Alexander & R.G. Picard (Eds.), *In the camera's eye: News coverage of terrorist events* (pp. 121-130). New York: Brassey's (U.S.).

Norris, P., Kern, M. & Just, M. (2003). Introduction: Understanding crisis coverage. In P. Norris, M. Kern, & M. Just (Eds.), *Framing terrorism: The news media, the government and the public* (pp. 3-23). New York and London: Routledge.

Nossek, H. (1990). *Terrorism and the media.* Doctoral dissertation, Hebrew University, Jerusalem.

Nossek, H. (1994). The narrative role of the Holocaust and the state of Israel in the coverage of salient terrorism events in the Israeli press. *Journal of Narrative and Life History, 4,* 119-134.

Nossek, H. (2000, March). *Foreign news and the construction of reality: Between the Mondial and Mondo Cane.* Leicester, UK: Conference on International news in the 21st Century, Center for Mass Communication Research.

Oliver, P. E. & Maney, G. M. (2000). Political processes and local newspaper coverage of protest events. *American Journal of Sociology, 106*(2), 463-505.

Paletz, D. L. & Schmid, A. P. (1992). *Terrorism and the media.* Newbury Park, CA: Sage.

Paterson, C. A. (1999). Agency source influence on television foreign reporting: Case of Mururoa and Tahiti. *Asia Pacific Media Educator, 7,* 16-36.

Picard, R. (1993). *Media portrayals of terrorism* (pp. 10-23). Iowa: Iowa State University Press.

Roeh, I. (1989). Journalism as storytelling: Coverage as narrative. *American Behavioral Scientist, 33*, 162-168.

Schmid, A. P. & De Graaf, J. (1982). *Violence as communication: Insurgent terrorism and the Western news media.* Beverly Hills, CA: Sage.

Shoemaker, P. J. (1991). *Gatekeeping.* Newbury Park, CA, and London: Sage.

Simmons, B.K. & Lowry, D.N. (1990). Terrorists in the news, as reflected in three news magazines, 1980-1988. *Journalism Quarterly, 67*, 692-696.

Sonwalkar, P. (2004) Out of sight, out of mind? The non-reporting of small wars and insurgencies. In S. Allan & B. Zelizer (Eds.), *Reporting war: Journalism in wartime* (pp. 206-223). London and New York: Routledge.

Sreberny, A. & Stevenson, R. (1999). Comparative analysis of international news flow: An example of global media monitoring. In K. Nordenstreng & M. Griffin (Eds.), *International media monitoring* (pp. 55-72). Cresskil, NJ: Hampton Press.

Tuman, J. (2003). *Communicating terror: The rhetorical dimensions of terrorism.* Thousand Oaks, CA: Sage.

Van Belle, D.A. (2000). *New York Times* and network TV news coverage of foreign disasters: The significance of the insignificant variables. *Journalism & Mass Communication Quarterly, 77*, 50-70.

Weaver, D. H., & Wilhoit, G. C. (1996). *The American journalist in the 1990s: U.S. news people at the end of an era.* Mahwah, NJ: Erlbaum.

Webster, F. (2003). Information warfare in an age of globalization. In D. K. Thussu & D. Freedman (Eds.), *War and the media* (pp. 57-69).Thousand Oaks, CA: Sage.

Wei, W., Weaver, D. H., & Johnson, O. V. (1996). Professional roles of Russian and U.S. journalists: A comparative study. *Journalism and Mass Communication Quarterly, 73*(3), 534-48.

Weimann, G. & Winn C. (1994). *The theater of terror: Mass media and international terrorism.* New York and London: Longman.

Weimann, G. & Brosius, H. B. (1991). The newsworthiness of international terrorism. *Communication Research, 18*(3), 333-354.

Wilkinson, P. (2000), *Terrorism verses democracy: The liberal state response.* London: Frank Cass.

Youichi, I. (1995, June). *A study of psychological factors of international information flows: News and TV programs.* Portoroz, Slovania: IAMCR conference.

PART I

MEDIA AND POLITICAL VIOLENCE

Theoretical Perspectives

Chapter 1

The Media
and International Conflict

A Theoretical Overview

Howard Tumber

When looking at any area of media production or representation the relationship between communication and international conflict is one of the most complex and fast changing. Apart from taking into account definitions of war and conflict, any analysis has to consider not only the manner in which media produce and represent conflict but also the role the media may play in both conflict exacerbation and conflict resolution. The general drivers of globalization and new communications technology together with the more specific events of the September 11, 2001 terrorist attack on the World Trade Center and the recent wars in Afghanistan (2002) and Iraq (2003) have led to a reappraisal of the nature of security and a re-evaluation of the role of the media.

The role of technology is seen, particularly by news organizations, as a growing problem in the coverage of conflict and war. BBC journalist Nik Gowing has been ubiquitous in his warnings to news organizations and governments about the new dangers. "Today there is no escaping digital cameras—they are present at every trouble spot and capture every disaster. It is no longer just journalists who produce images and distribute them around the world. Nowadays many of the pictures that document events such as the aeroplane attacks on the Twin Towers or terrorist bombings are taken by private individuals. Modern gadgets such as laptops, mobile phones and radio telephones allow these images to be transmitted at lightning speed in 'real time' around the globe. This represents a huge challenge to governments. Crimes that contravene human rights laws and military attacks can hardly be kept secret anymore and this puts governments and the armed forces under enormous pressure" (http://www.britischebotschaft.de/en /news/events/nik_gowing.htm).

According to Gowing, the media's responsibilities have also changed. Today's high-speed technology means that decisions have to be made quickly. On the one hand television channels want to spread news as speedily as possible, but photographic and film material also has to be authenticated. "One mistake can destroy your credibility." Forgers and terrorist organisations have also been making use of modern techniques for a long time to further their goals (http://www.britischebotschaft.de/en/news/events/nik_gowing.htm).

DEVELOPING CONCEPTUAL APPROACHES

The difficulty of building theory when analyzing the media and international conflict is that definitions of the nation state and hence definitions of "international" conflict become problematic. Early definitions of conflict regarded it as the product of disagreement on national and international levels and the emergence, settlement, or abolition of conflict rested on the communication among different parts, with the news media being one of the most important channels (Arno, 1984, p. 1). The underlying, implicit or explicit, assumption was that the clearer the communication between the parties, the easier it would be to resolve the conflict. The emphasis on open communication channels dominated the writing on international relations during the 1940s and 1950s. Lack of knowledge and the stereotypical representation of the conflicting parties were identified as a decisive obstacle towards the resolution of conflicting interests. It was argued that the efforts of social management and social engineering should be directed towards the facilitation of communication channels among the antagonists (Coser, 1984, pp. 17-18).

The same line of argument was pursued by a different, more sophisticated tradition during the 1960s and 1970s. Habermas (1971) followed this path and argued that enlightened, rational communication can be the panacea for human exploitation, ignorance, and repression. In all these accounts, conflict was the product of distorted communication. At the same time, however, some theorists pioneered the argument that ignorance may actually result in the minimization of conflict (Rule, 1978, p. 136, cited in Coser, 1984, p. 21).

In more recent accounts, the media have been viewed not only as a communication channel, but an important player in themselves. Whereas previously the media was regarded as playing a neutral role as a channel for communication between government(s), leader(s), and public (Davidson, 1974), more recent studies see the media as more closely intertwined with the social, political and cultural structure. The media are viewed not simply as a tool in the hands of conflicting parties but as a major player in their own right (Arno, 1984, p. 11; see also Wolfsfeld, 2003, 2004).

The central role of the media in the production and management of conflict can take two forms: either as "making" conflict—that is, scandal—or, in contrast, operating as the public sphere assisting in the resolution (Arno 1984, 2-3). In the first case, the media are implicated in conflict disputes by treating them as individual cases; in the second, the media play a more structural role. The structural or the individual disposition towards a conflict also affects the media access granted to the conflicting parties. Access to media in certain contexts is based on the presupposition of the legitimacy of all individual parties involved, aiming at the resolution of the conflict. In other cases however, conflict is portrayed in structural rather than individual terms, and access may be restricted to the view that is regarded as the only legitimate one (Arno 1984, p. 5).

Mowlana (1984) identified four key approaches to international communications: idealistic-humanistic, proselytizing, economic, and political, the latter three known collectively as strategic. In all four the "communications revolution" is viewed as a means of institutional and industrial growth, rather than as a new way of human interaction that poses new challenges (pp. 29-30, 32).

These approaches have not escaped criticism. The idealistic-humanistic approach sees the media as the channel that brings together people and nations in order to facilitate a deeper understanding and to promote peace and assist conflict resolution. This approach has been heavily criticized on a number of fronts. Firstly, it fails to recognize the impossibility of the objective transference of values and information. Information is decoded within a changeable and highly subjective individual framework that is modified according to a wide range of social influences. Secondly, the ideals of international peace and world community are also subject to a variety of interpretations that make international consensus impossible. As a result, any dominant ideas that do not have a universal consensus will not escape the charges of ideological imperialism. Thirdly, the equation of international agreement with international good may result in the adoption of the proposed system as the only alternative, thus rejecting any alternative proposals. Fourthly, idealist demands rest on the premise that human beings are rational and this rationality leads them to the pursuit of the human good. If, however, we accept that human beings do not always act as rational agents and are often irrational or emotional in their choices and pursuits, then the idealist expectations become unattainable (Mowlana, 1984, pp. 27-29).

The first of the strategic approaches—political proselytization—emphasizes the manipulative potential of the media. Communications are viewed one way, structured by some central authority, aimed at legitimization of specific frameworks of understanding reality (via myths or clichés) and the propagation of certain ideological positions. The emphasis here is on the authoritarian/totalitarian character of the media. The generated distrust towards the international media, however, rests on the false assumption of manipulation. Even if international media are guilty of not promoting peaceful resolutions, this does not necessarily imply that they consciously promote rivalry and conflict among nations.

The second strategic approach—information as economic power—views the media as operating in a more subtle way, with the focus shifting towards the economic organization of the media as manifested in development projects, conglomerate economic activity, marketing, and technological innovation. This approach supports the "cultural imperialism" argument of domination of peripheral countries by Western culture, enabling the control of the developing countries by Western power centers.

The third strategic approach—political power of information—regards information as a value-free commodity. The examination of the international media and their products reveals the concentration of the means of production residing in a few countries, resulting in cultural domination. Both this political power approach and the economic power approach regard information as international resource (like oil) and as a currency in international bargaining. Nevertheless, information is a much more complex resource and its effects on social, economic, and political development are far-reaching (for further discussions of these approaches see Mowlana, 1984, pp. 27-29).

In recent times most discussion about international communications has centered on the economic and political, with work centered on the debates on the free flow of information (see Mosco, 1996; Mowlana 1997; UNESCO, 1982); modernization theory (see Lerner 1958; Schramm, 1964); dependency theory and cultural imperialism (see Boyd-Barrett, 1977; Galtung, 1971; Varis 1985); critical theory, hegemony, and propaganda (see Gramsci, 1971; Herman & Chomsky, 2002); and public sphere (Habermas, 1989). More recently, work on the information society and globalization has attempted to theorize the emergent global information society from the view of the promotion of global markets and liberal democracy (Fukiyama, 1992), the spread of modernity (Giddens, 1990), and media concentration and ownership (McChesney 1999, 2004).

All these various conceptual approaches have looked at international communications rather than at the media and international conflict.

DEFINITIONS OF WAR AND TERRORISM

In order to approach an understanding of the coverage of contemporary conflicts, it is important to trace changes in contemporary warfare. Although war is not a new phenomenon, the twentieth century experienced war as mass phenomenon, a constant theme of media coverage (Carruthers, 2000, p. 1). After the Second World War, a number of "smaller" conflicts, classified under a variety of labels, led to the questioning of the conventional categorization of conflict (Gray, 1997, p. 156). The concept of "total war," appropriate for the characterization of the First and Second World Wars, because they involved the mobilization of entire national populations, both civilians and military, seemed inadequate for conflicts such as in Bosnia, Rwanda, Kosovo, the Gulf War and the Falklands (Carruthers, 2000, pp. 1-2; Taylor, 2002, p. 130; Tumber, 2002). Although national populations may not be physically engaged in these wars, all civilians have become "witnesses of war" due to the technological progress of the mass media. Furthermore, although the actual battles remain limited, contemporary wars have a "total" impact on society: they redefine gender relationships, they affect the economy and they become part of the political discourse (Carruthers, 2000, p. 2, Gray, 1997, pp. 22-23; Taylor, 1997, p. 33).

There is also a further confusion. The distinction between "our wars" and "other people's wars" is blurred. The media coverage of "our wars" ("our troops" fighting alongside "our allies" against the enemy) and "other people's wars" (wars that do not involve our armies or do not involve us as allies of one side of the conflict) is fundamentally different in relation to the degree of engagement (Taylor, 1997, p. 130). In the first case, the media coverage supports "our" side, and the audiences' emotional involvement is much greater. In the second case, the coverage and the media involvement is more detached. Although the distinction between "ours"/"theirs" is not totally irrelevant, the dividing line between "theirs" and "ours" in many cases is blurred (see also Carruthers, 1998, 2000). The war in former Yugoslavia, for example, did not start as a war between Yugoslavia and NATO. NATO's intervention, justified on humanitarian grounds, was the intervention of a "neutral" power mediating between the opposing sides. Nevertheless, the Western reporting during the wars in Yugoslavia was predominantly anti-Serb (Taylor, 1997, p. 130). It was clear by the time of the NATO intervention in Kosovo that the Serbian side was perceived as the enemy of the NATO forces and the conflict had become "our war." Similarly, the Taliban/Northern Alliance was "their" conflict, a conflict distant and irrelevant to U.S. and Western society. After September 11, however, it became the U.S. war on terrorism, and only then did information about the Taliban/Northern Alliance conflict become a major subject for the Western media (Tumber, 2002).

One reason for the increasing attempts to place any military action within the political discourse of one's nation is the increasing realization that political preparation and political justification at home play an important role in winning over public opinion. The important decisions that define the outcome of any war action are not taken only at the field of battle but increasingly in the political arena (Gray 1997, pp. 169-170). The reporting of "other people's wars" may be less engaged until the dominant political discourse for whatever reason is transformed and "their war" becomes "ours."

Nossek's (2004) example of the NATO bombardment of Bosnia illustrates that despite the definition of the conflict as "their war," the selection of sources in *The New York Times* came largely from within the United States (Pentagon and Washington), thus giving the coverage an American angle. In another example, the coverage of the car bomb outside a Jewish school in Lyon in September 1995 was defined by *Ha'aretz* as a terrorist act against "us" with references and links to Jewish history. The *New York Times* and the *London Times*, in contrast, did not give a prominent place to the event and reported it in "nonrelational" terms. Nossek concludes that a divergence exists across national newspapers in their definition of politically violent events and in the manner and extent to which the stories are covered. Despite the political, social, and technological changes of recent decades, the coverage of political violence "remains a product of the existing framework of nationhood" (Nossek, 2004, pp. 354-364).

TERRORISM

A further characteristic of modern-day war is the blurring between terrorism and war. Despite the "smart" weapons and the "distant" targets, terrorism brings war back home. As a dominant form of international conflict, terrorism rejects civilian immunity and agreed upon warfare conventions, thus accelerating emotional responses (Carruthers, 2000, pp. 163-164). The September 11th attack, due to its aim and proximity for the Western World, put the traditional conceptions of warfare under question.

In the twenty-first century, political violence has become the primary means to communicate political messages, and terrorist attacks have taken a leading position in world news since the beginning of the new millennium. A number of experts have warned that we are moving towards a period of increased terrorist activity (Kupperman & Kamen, 1989, cited in Nacos, 2002, p. 21). Terrorism may not be a new phenomenon, but in contrast to the terrorist attacks in the 1970s and 1980s, political violence has now become a serious problem for the targeted countries (Laqueur, 1987, cited in Nacos, 2002, p. 21). As early as the end of the 1960s, the concept of "international terrorism" became a common currency, classifying together groups as diverse as the Red Army Faction in Germany (Baader-Meinhof), the Palestine Liberation Organization (PLO), and the Tupamaros in Uruguay. During this period, the common method of looking at international terrorism was by trying to connect the phenomenon with the Soviet Union. This led to the simplification of the terrorist objectives. Furthermore, it linked the terrorist phenomenon to the Left. In the early 1980s, the American government adopted this view as the main orthodoxy; at the same time, violent repressive regimes that were "friendly" towards the "Free World Order", although "authoritarian", were not associated with terrorism. The disappearances and tortures in Latin America during the Carter administration were evaluated as less bad than armed struggles against oppressors. Similarly, the U.S. interventions in Nicaragua and El Salvador were justified as part of the struggle against international communism. During the 1980s in Britain, the preoccupation with the IRA and the intensification of industrial struggles, led to a number of authoritarian changes within the state apparatus (Schlesinger, Murdoch, & Elliott, 1983, pp. 3, 6, 14).

The collapse of the Soviet Union did not diminish the importance of terrorism, although it did create a new political environment within which terrorism operated. Terrorism has become a major issue in the post–Cold War era, and Nacos (2002) identifies a number of reasons: first, the collapse of the Soviet Union may have fostered anti-American political violence, whereas previously it was able to restrain countries that belonged to the Eastern bloc or were affiliated to it, thus keeping terrorism beneath a certain threshold. Furthermore, the existence of the Soviet Union limited the scale of countert-errorist attacks by Western states. Second, the end of the old world order unleashed a number of religious and nationalist forces that emerged from the new states formed following the breakdown of the Soviet Union. In particular, the religious groups engaged in political violence were prepared to engage in terrorist attacks that were not bound to the moral imperatives of groups like the Red Brigades in Italy or the German Red Army Faction (Nacos, 2002, pp. 21-26).

These changes were assisted by a number of developments in the communications environment. Previously closed channels of communication were opened up making terrorism a much more attractive proposition; the developments of new communication technologies, such as the Internet and satellite, delivered a wider public space, larger audiences, and new means of publicity for terrorist groups; and the shift of media markets towards an increased number of mergers and acquisitions created the possibility of not only national, but international or even global coverage. As news organizations moved towards a more market-driven profit-oriented character, the dividing line between entertainment and "hard" news started to blur, making the terrorist incidents an attractive opportunity for drama, tragedy, shock, and panic (Nacos, 2002, pp. 27-29; Schlesinger et al., 1983).

One of the main problems in any conceptual reappraisal of terrorism and media is the definition of terrorism. The origins of the term can be traced to the Latin word *terrere,* meaning "to trample," and it was widely used by the Jacobins during the French Revolution. The word travelled across the channel, and in Britain, Burke used the word in the *Reflections on the Revolution in France* in order to discredit the Revolution and to highlight the threats it implied for England. The recourse to violence that exceeds the prescribed norms and rules of war or battle has remained as the core of the term. The use of violence originating from the nation-state has remained marginal within the use of the term, although a systematic analysis of the latter forces a distinction between "terrorism from above", referring to the coercive practices of the state, and 'terrorism from below,' when the groups practicing violence are outside the dominant sociopolitical structures (Nacos, 2002; pp. 16-17; Tuman, 2003; pp. 1-5).

Some definitions are confined to a limited number of violent activities exercised by small groups rather than mass or collective acts, thus excluding state-based terrorism (Crenshaw, 1995, cited in Tuman, 2003, p. 5; Herman & O'Sullivan, 1989, p. 214; Nacos, 2002). Others emphasize the use of the term by state institutions in order to differentiate between illegitimate violence against the state and legitimate violence from the state itself (Olivera, 1998, cited in Tuman, 2003, p. 6). The use of the term "terrorist" as opposed to "guerrilla" or "freedom fighter" implies that the act is illegitimate and criminal. While the state apparatus has an interest in delegitimizing its enemies, their opponents try to legitimize their armed struggles by presenting the violent attacks as part of the "liberation struggle" (Schlesinger et al., 1983, p. 1). As a consequence, the notion of legitimacy is a key concept in most definitions, where implicitly or explicitly some normative standard separates terrorism from acceptable uses of violence that obey "humanitarian rules" (Tuman, 2003, p. 6).

Even more synthesized definitions, like that of Jenkins (1984), who tried to bring together the most common components of many definitions, have problems overcoming degrees of ambiguity. Jenkins' suggestion that relates terrorism to the use of political violence is too broad, if it is acknowledged that all wars involve violence and have a political element. Furthermore, the terms "violence" and "political," on which the definition is based, are themselves quite broad terms (Tuman, 2003, pp. 11-12).

Schmid (1983) offers a more comprehensive and complex definition. "Terrorism is an anxiety-inspiring method of repeated violent action, employed by (semi-) clandestine individual group or state actors, for idiosyncratic, criminal or political reasons, whereby—in contrast to assassination—the direct targets of violence are not the main targets. . . . Threat- and violence-based communication processes between terrorist (organization), (imperilled) victims, and main target (audience(s), turning it into a target of terror, a target of demands or a target of attention, depending on whether intimidation, coercion or propaganda is primarily sought" (Schmid, 1983, p. 70, see also Tuman, 2003, pp. 13-14). Even this definition, however, although more inclusive, can also be dismissed if the concept of state terrorism is rejected (Tuman, 2003, p. 15).

State and international bodies assign terrorism to clandestine or subnational agents or groups that direct their activities against the state, government, or international organizations. They thus exclude "terrorism from above" while at the same time targeting all forms of political dissent by including, for example, environmental groups such as Greenpeace in their definitions (Tuman, 2003, pp. 6-9).

One undisputed dimension of terrorism, however, is its symbiotic relationship with channels of mass communication. Without these channels terrorism would be confined to the limited circle of those affected by terrorist violence, but with the assistance of the media it can reach a wide, even global, audience. Extensive news reporting and public attention, even if the actual identity and the motives of the terrorist remain unknown, has already made cases of "propaganda of the deed" highly successful (Nacos, 2002, pp. 8-10; Schlesinger et al., 1983; Tuman, 2003, p. 120).

It is unsurprising that both news and entertainment media share a fascination with terrorism. News media, both print and broadcast, frame their stories in terms of conflict. This allows them to offer events that carry the potential of sensationalism, dramatization, shock, and fear. In almost all cases of terrorist violence the prerequisite of "public interest" is by definition already present. As the demand for increasingly more dramatic and "bloody" events guarantees increased coverage, the threshold for a successful terrorist attack is also raised (Nacos, 2002, pp. 28-29; Schlesinger et al., 1983, p. 12; Tuman, 2003, pp. 119, 135-136). The centrality of communications for terrorism has also led to increased sophistication on the part of the terrorists. As a deviant branch of political communication professionals, terrorists try to bypass the mediators (journalists) by actively engaging in their own broadcast production. The Bin Laden tapes, for example, although amateur by Western standards, are relatively sophisticated in terms of their rhetoric, targeting an Arab as well as a global audience (Tuman, 2003, pp. 136-137). Furthermore, the choice of Al Jazeera may indicate a logic that operates on the "exclusivity" lines that Western political candidates have capitalized on for decades. The bypassing of traditional media by various groups reached a gruesome pinnacle recently with the use of internet broadcasts to show the beheading of hostages in Iraq.

SOURCES

The role that "terrorist" groups play or the relationship they have with the media can be looked at in the wider context of sources.

In his study of the U.S. media and the Vietnam War Hallin (1986) argued that the way the media report events is closely tied to the degree of consensus among the political elite, the "sphere of consensus" as he labels it. Hallin's view contrasts with the conservative analysis of the media at that time as "anti-establishment" institutions that were "undermining the authority of governing institutions" (Hallin, 1994, p. 11). The explanation for the media's "volte face" in its support for/rejection of the war was grounded in "commitment to the ideology and the routines of objective journalism" (1986, pp. 63-69). Up to 1967 there was relatively little disagreement among the policy elite, and reflecting this official viewpoint did not "seem to violate the norms of objective journalism" (1994, pp. 52-53). However, during the period 1963-1967 reporters in Vietnam itself were being given accounts of the war by officers serving in the U.S. military that were not compatible with the largely optimistic accounts coming out of Washington; during this period, both versions of how the war was going were reported (1986, pp. 38-39).

The gradual breakdown of the national security consensus and the cold war ideology among the political elite, together with the concern over the conduct of the war, was reflected in the coverage by the news media. The media were able to respond to the growing strains and divisions within the foreign policy elite by producing far greater amounts of critical news coverage "without abandoning objective journalism for some activist and anti-establishment conception of their role. As opposition to the war moved into the mainstream, the news media reflected this movement of debate into the sphere of legitimate controversy." The media reflect the prevailing pattern of political debate: "when consensus is strong, they tend to stay within the limits of the political discussion it defines; when it begins to break down, coverage becomes increasingly critical and diverse in the viewpoints it represents, and increasingly difficult for officials to control" (1994, pp. 53-55).

It is evident that as policy debate moves from the "sphere of consensus" to the "sphere of legitimate controversy," governments and administrations become concerned at the possible loss of control over the news agenda. Censorship and flak consequently become prominent features of their response to the increase in media activity as journalists begin to question government statements and become more sensitive to other official and nonofficial viewpoints (Hallin, 1994, p. 71; see also Morrison & Tumber, 1988, p. 228).

A similar formulation of source behavior to account for media-government relations is Bennett's (1990) "indexing hypothesis": "Mass media news professionals, from the boardroom to the beat, tend to 'index' the range of voices and viewpoints in both news and editorials according to the range of views expressed in mainstream government debate about a given topic" (1990, p. 106). According to the hypothesis, nonofficial sources only appear in news stories when their opinions are "already emerging in official circles." The possibility of contention among official sources is acknowledged, and this is sometimes reflected in the news media, but when that institutional opposition collapses, even if public opinion is opposed to a particular policy, the volume of opposition in news and editorials is indexed accordingly. In effect the news media revert to the established line at the expense of the democratic ideal (1990, p. 113).

Wolfsfeld's (2003) political contest model is a variation on this theme but he concentrates on the role the media may play not just in the coverage of a conflict but in its possible resolution. He argues that the ability of powerful sources to manage the news tends to vary over time and circumstance, with the key variable being the degree of monopoly of the information environment. Wolfsfeld's formulation echoes part of the critique of primary definition provided by Schlesinger and Tumber (1994) in which they demonstrated how some powerful sources declined in importance over time. Wolfsfeld uses the analysis of sources to examine the extent to which the press becomes an active agent in a given conflict rather than a passive conveyor of political information. His hypothesis is that the "news media are more likely to play an independent role when the powerful lose control because it allows the weaker side a better platform for the promotion of its frame of the conflict and increase the probability for third parties to intervene" (2003, p. 228). His argument has similarities to Hallin's analysis, which looked at the changes in coverage in relation to the behavior of sources. Many studies have looked at the role of media in conflict resolution and foreign policy more generally (see, for example, Cohen, 1986; Davidson 1974; Entman, 2004; Gilboa, 1998; O'Heffernan, 1993; Weiman, 1994).

Wolfsfeld looked mainly at the media as a whole rather than at the individual journalist. In exploring the coverage of three military interventions that won bipartisan support in Washington, Mermin (1996) concurs with the indexing hypothesis but adds an amendment to the effect that the major media are doing something to maintain the illusion of fulfilling the journalistic ideals of balance and objectivity. What the news media present as subject to question and debate "is the *ability of the government to achieve the goals it has set*. When there is no policy debate in Washington, reporters may offer critical analysis *inside the terms of the apparently settled policy debate*, finding a critical angle in the possibility that existing policy on its own terms might not work" (1996, p. 182; italics added).

Focusing on this "critical angle" helps to explain the perception among politicians and business leaders that journalists are overly independent and critical of government and also to illustrate that there is a significant element of present-day conflict in the news.

To fulfil the idea of independent, balanced coverage when official sources are united behind a particular policy, journalists attempt to fill the void "by finding conflicting possibilities in the efforts of officials to achieve the goals they have set" (Mermin, 1996, p. 191).

The accepted norm is that reporters should have a neutral role in reporting conflict. Based on their professional values they are supposed to avoid bias and strive for objectivity, thus refraining from advocating or defending the position of either side. This perspective, however, does not assist with understanding the reality and the dynamics of covering a conflict. The mere presence of media may alter the behavior of conflicting parties even unintentionally. Thus it has been argued that in the case of Bosnia, the presence of reporters prevented or postponed atrocities (Botes, 1996, p. 6). Alternatively, the negative reporting of a conflict can potentially influence public opinion and policy. In some cases, there is a tendency to report international conflict by dividing the international community in two camps. The international and national media approach conflict through the dichotomization and demonization of one side and the whole reporting is overtly dramatized (Tehranian, 1996, p. 3).

The journalist can become the third party, a role that is legitimately reserved for conflict mediators rather than reporters. It is true that there are certain similarities between conflict resolvers and journalists: they both start by outlining the main components of the conflict; who are the involved parties, the origin of the dispute, the underlying problems. Furthermore, like the mediators, they try to stay neutral while presenting all sides accurately and fairly. Finally, like the mediators, reporters try to predict the future course of the conflict and evaluate possible resolutions. It is not uncommon that journalist's attempt to get to the "heart of the conflict" may lead to "reframing," a standard process in conflict resolution, where the conflicting parties identify their shared problems that led to the conflict. Within this picture, the media become forums of direct or indirect exchange of viewpoints and debate over possible avenues toward conflict resolution. Radio talk shows, television discussion programs and round tables, all could play a peacemaking role as mediating forums (Botes, 1996, p. 7; Tehranian, 1996, p. 3).

The similarities, however, should not be overemphasized. Unlike conflict mediators, journalists' professional aims and objectives are quite different and are subject to different constraints. As employees of news organizations, they produce a commodity that's supposed to generate profit. Conflict sells, and the overemphasis on extreme positions, violence, and simplification of the conflict increases the value of their commodity. It follows that their interest in conflict focuses on the high points of the dispute, dramatic or violent incidents, events that can be interpreted as focal points in the course of the conflict. In contrast, conflict resolvers follow the whole progress of the conflict. The difference between conflict resolvers and journalists is very apparent in relation to their attitude towards secrecy. Whereas the former try to maintain privacy in order to facilitate discussion, the journalists, by invoking the right of the public to know, attempt to break secrecy, thus often bringing themselves in direct conflict with the mediators (Botes, 1996, pp. 7-8).

CONCLUSION

Rojecki synthesises the range of studies on the media and international conflict into three general theoretical responses to the new political environment (2002, p. 4). The first views a continuation of hegemonic control, albeit using a number of new strategies; the second features elite dissensus as the basis of its explanatory framework, and the third alters "the balance of power to the media from the elites who find the absence of the cold war frame to demonise enemies and thus to invoke the patriotism that once could be counted on to rally public opinion" (2003, p. 4). September 11 and the consequent war on terror suggest that the "gap" in this third perspective has been filled, leaving the first two, which essentially are variations of the old Marxist/pluralist formulations, albeit more developed with more sophistication.

Webster (2003) argues that a radical shift has occurred between previous wars and contemporary ones. This shift is the product of a changing sociopolitical environment captured under the term "globalization". First, globalization processes have enormous consequences on a symbolic level, creating greater diversity and differentiation (Tomlinson, 1999). A second feature of globalization is the changing role of the nation-state, which becomes less exclusive and self-contained. Finally, the advancement of democratization around the globe (Eley, 2002) creates new needs for legitimization of political processes and a greater concern about human rights abuses (Webster, 2003, p. 65; see also Tumber & Webster, 2006).

These three changes have a great impact on media and conflict. In relation to cultural globalization, the media become the main channel of this spread of information, through 24-hour news broadcasting (CNN effect) and a constant flow of entertainment and information. Within this context, war has a dominant position, due to its inherent newsworthiness. At the same time, however, the relationship between media and war is a paradoxical one expressed in the role of the journalists. At one level they are driven by an ethical commitment to reporting war, and at the same time they are deeply cynical about the sources. Secondly, the diminishing role of the nation-state (through crossover ownership of capital, open markets and transnational decision centers) creates what Giddens called "states without enemies" (Giddens, 1994, p. 235). Wars over territory become less prominent, but at the same time the world is far removed from achieving global peace. Globalization has negative effects, too, creating inequality, competition, and exclusions on a global scale. As a consequence, fundamentalisms of different sorts are strengthened (because they can provide certainty in an uncertain world) and terrorist, absolutist groups operating beyond national borders (i.e., Al Qaeda) become the "enemies without states" of the new milieu (Webster, 2003, p. 61). Finally, Information Warfare, as Webster terms it, seeks legitimacy in the name of democracy itself rather than national interests. Public support for interventions aiming to protect human rights becomes essential, and the media play a key role in these processes. On the one hand, they are the key vehicle of "perception management", creating public approval of contemporary conflicts. On the other, they play a key role in identifying and exposing abuses on human rights, even instigating intervention (Webster, 2003, pp. 64-65; see also Tumber & Webster, 2006).

What is needed then is a conceptual approach that acknowledges the globalization process; American exceptionalism; the decline of the nation state; the increasing concentration of media ownership; 24-hour news; the development of the internet and the bypassing of traditional journalistic forms (we are all journalists now); the rise of fundamentalism; new social movements; new diasporas, communities, and identities; and the role of news sources. An impossible task? Maybe, but certainly a necessary one in understanding the nature of the relationship between the media and international conflict.

REFERENCES

Arno, A. (1984). Communication, conflict, and storylines: The new media as actors in a cultural context. In A. Arno & W. Dissanayake (Eds.), *The news media in national and international conflict*. Boulder and London: Westview.

Bennett, L. W. (1990). Toward a theory of press-state relations in the United States. *Journal of Communication, 40,* 103-125.

Botes, J. (1996). Journalism and conflict resolution. *Media Development, 4.*

Boyd-Barrett, O. (1977). Media imperialism: Towards an international framework for the analysis of media systems. In J. Curran, M. Gurevitch, & J. Woollacott (Eds.), *Mass communication and society*. London: Edward Arnold.

Carruthers, S. L (2000). *The media at war*. Basingstoke: Macmillan.

Cohen, Y. (1986). *Media diplomacy: The foreign office in the mass communications age*. London: Frank Cass.

Coser, L. A. (1984). Salvation through communication? In A. Arno & W. Dissanayake (Eds.), *The news media in national and international conflict.* Boulder and London: Westview.

Crenshaw, M. (Ed.). (1995). *Terrorism in context.* University Park: Penn State University Press.

Davidson, W. P. (1974). *Mass communications and conflict resolution.* New York: Praeger.

Eley, G. (2002). *Forging democracy: The history of the left in Europe, 1850-2000.* Oxford: Oxford University Press.

Entman, R. (2004). *Projections of power; framing new, public opinion, and U.S. foreign policy.* Chicago: University of Chicago Press.

Fukuyama, F. (1992). *The end of history and the last man.* London: Hamish Hamilton.

Galtung, J. (1971). A structural theory of imperialism. *Journal of Peace Research, 8,* 281-317.

Giddens, A. (1990). *The consequences of modernity.* Cambridge: Polity.

Giddens, A. (1994). *Beyond left and right: The future of radical politics.* Cambridge: Polity.

Gilboa, E. (1998). Media diplomacy: Conceptual divergence and applications. *Harvard International Journal of Press/Politics, 3,* 56-75

Gramsci, A. (1971). *Selections from the prison notebooks* (Q. Hoare & G. Nowell-Smith, Eds. & Trans.). London: Lawrence and Wishart.

Gray, H. C. (1997). *Postmodern war: The new politics of conflict.* London: Routledge.

Habermas, J. (1971). *Toward a rational society: Student protest, science & politics.* London: Heinemann Educational.

Habermas, J. (1989). *The structural transformation of the public sphere.* Cambridge: Polity.

Hallin, D. C. (1986). *The "uncensored" war: The media and Vietnam.* Oxford: Oxford University Press.

Hallin, D. C. (1994). *We keep America on top of the world.* London: Routledge.

Herman, E.S., & Chomsky, N. (2002). *Manufacturing consent.* New York: Pantheon.

Herman, E.S., & O'Sullivan, G. (1989). *The "terrorism" industry: The experts and institutions that shape our view of terror.* New York: Pantheon.

Jenkins, B. (1984, November). *The who, what, where, when, and why of terrorism.* Paper presented at the Detroit Police Department Conference on Urban Terrorism, Detroit, MI.

Kupperman, R., & Kamen, J. (1989). *Final warning: Averting disaster in the new age of terrorism.* New York: Doubleday.

Laqueur, W. (1987) *The age of terrorism.* Boston: Little, Brown.

Lerner, D. (1958). *The passing of tradional society: Modernising the Middle East.* New York: Free Press.

McChesney, R. W. (1999). *Rich media, poor democracy.* Champaign: University of Illinois Press.

McChesney, R. W. (2004). *Problem of the media. The U.S. communication politics in the twenty-first century.* New York: Monthly Review Press.

Mermin, J. (1996). Conflict in the sphere of consensus? Critical reporting on the Panama invasion and the Gulf War. *Political Communication, 13*(2), 181-194.

Morrison , D. & Tumber, H. (1988). *Journalists at war.* London: Sage.

Mosco, V. (1996). *The political economy of communications: Rethinking and renewal.* London: Sage.

Mowlana, H. (1984). Communication, world order, and human potential: Towards an ethical framework. In A. Arno & W. Dissanayake (Eds.), *The news media in national and international conflict.* Boulder and London: Westview Press.

Mowlana, H. (1997). *Global information and world communication: New frontiers in international relations* (2nd ed.). London: Sage.

Nacos, B. L. (2002). *Mass-mediated terrorism.* Lanham, MD: Rowman and Littlefield.

Nossek, H. (2004). Our news and their news. The role of national identity in the coverage of foreign news. *Journalism, 5*(3), 343-368.

O'Heffernan, P. (1993). Mass media and foreign policy. In R.J. Spitzer (Ed.), *Media and public policy.* Westport, CT: Praeger

Olivero, A. (1998). *The age of terror.* Albany: State University of New York Press.

Rojecki, A. (2002). Media and the new post–Cold War movements. In E. Gilboa (Ed.), *Media and conflict.* Ardsley, NY: Transnational.

Rule, J. B. (1978). *Insight and social betterment.* New York: Oxford University Press.

Schiller, H. (1976). *Communication and cultural domination.* New York: International Arts and Sciences Press.

Schiller, H. (1992). *Mass communications and American empire.* New York: Westview.

Schlesinger, P., Murdoch, G., & Elliott, P. R. (1983). *Televising terrorism: Political violence in popular culture.* London: Comedia.

Schlesinger P., & Tumber, H. (1994). *Reporting crime: The media politics of criminal justice.* Oxford: Oxford University Press.

Schmid, A. P. (1983). *Political terrorism: A research guide to concepts.* New Brunswick, NJ: Transaction Press.

Schramm, W. (1964). *Mass media and national development: The role of information in developing countries.* Stanford, CA: Stanford University Press.

Taylor, P. (1997). *Global communications, international affairs and the media since 1945.* London: Routledge.

Taylor, P. (2002). *War and the media: Propaganda and persuasion in the Gulf War.* Manchester: Manchester University Press.

Tehranian, M. (1996). Communication and conflict. *Media Development, 4.*

Tomlinson, J. (1999). *Globalisation and culture.* Cambridge: Polity.

Tuman, J. S. (2003) *Communicating terror. The rhetorical dimensions of terrorism.* London: Sage.

Tumber, H. (2002). Reporting under fire. In B. Zelizer & S. Allan (Eds.), *Journalism after September 11.* London: Routledge.

Tumber, H., & Webster, R. (2006). *Journalists under fire: Information war and journalistic practices.* London: Sage.

UNESCO (1982). *Culture industries: A challenge for the future of culture.* Paris: United Nations Economic, Social and Cultural Organisation.

Varis, T. (1985). *International flow of television programmes. Reports and papers on mass communication, no. 100.* Paris: UNESCO

Webster, F. (2003). Information warfare in the age of globalisation. In D. K. Thussu & D. Freedman (Eds.), *War and the media.* London: Sage.

Weimann, G. (1994). Can the media mediate? Mass mediated diplomacy in the Middle East. In G. Ben Dor & D. Dewitt (Eds.), *Confidence building measures in the Middle East.* New York: Westview.

Wolfsfeld, G. (2003). The role of the news media in unequal political conflicts: From the 1987 *intifada* to the 1991 Gulf War and back again. In N. Palmer (Ed.), *Terrorism, war, and the press.* Teddington, UK: Hollis.

Wolfsfeld, G. (2004). *Media and the path to peace.* Cambridge: Cambridge University Press.

Chapter 2

Our News and Their News

The Role of National Identity in the Coverage of Foreign News*

Hillel Nossek**

This chapter examines the case of political violence as foreign news, as it provides the best example of what news theories consider the essence of news in general and foreign news in particular. I start by presenting two viewpoints on the question of how foreign news is defined and covered. The first view sees foreign news as a product of professional journalistic definitions and internal (media outlet) constraints, and the second sees foreign news as a product of external factors—political, economic, and technological. If the recent developments in media technology and the changes in international relations, economics, and the professional training of Western journalists override journalist and editor identification with their own nation state, then we should find similarities in the coverage (selection and presentation) of stories involving political violence by the Western (elite) media. However, if a journalist applies a national frame of reference to an event

*Thanks are due to my devoted research assistant Ronie Kolker for the data collection and analysis and to Ruth Freedman for the English translation and editing.
**A previous version of this chapter was published under the same title in *Journalism*, 2004, 5, 343-368.

41

involving political violence, then the coverage of the event (if it is covered at all) will vary accordingly.

Before journalists submit their reports on political violence in the international arena, they first define whatever has happened either as a specific type of political violence—for example, war, terrorism, political assassination, rioting, or violent demonstrations—or as violence with no political characteristics—for example, a bomb explosion, violent clashes, and so forth. Once a journalist has defined what has happened as a specific type of political violence, a second definition is immediately required, when the journalist must decide whether the event that s/he is covering is "our war" or "theirs," "our terrorism" or "theirs," and so forth. Thereafter, professional norms become subordinate to the national identity of the reporting correspondent. The journalist's definition of an event—as "ours" or "theirs"—determines whether the event is selected by the journalist and editor as news and how it will be covered (the suggested flow of decisions by the journalists and editors appears later as a flow diagram).

In order to substantiate the suggested flow of decisions, a qualitative content analysis was carried out on the coverage of four foreign news events in three countries: the United States, Britain, and Israel. The four events were categorized as "political violence" based on three factors: (1) the nature of the event, (2) its aim, and (3) who was targeted. The empirically tested theory discussed here can help our study of the coverage of September 11 and subsequent events such as the wars in Afghanistan and Iraq and aid us in understanding how events were and still are covered as foreign news and, specifically, how political violence is covered as foreign news. I conclude by explaining why the existing viewpoints do not offer a complete answer to the question of why foreign news coverage has not changed despite the multiple, far-reaching changes of the late twentieth century.

THEORETICAL FRAMEWORK AND LITERATURE REVIEW

Globalization and Foreign News Flow

As a result of globalization trends and the emergence of supranational or global media corporations, conflicting claims have arisen regarding the effects of world media flow. According to cultural imperialism proponents, the flow is in one direction, whereas global culture advocates argue the flow is in several directions (Sreberny-Mohammadi, 1991). Whatever the case, the broad consensus among researchers since the 1980s is that because of developments on the world media map and the growth of new media technologies, a reassessment of foreign news flow is needed (Fenby, 1986; Gonzenbach, Arant, & Stevenson, 1992; Stevenson & Cole, 1984a). Apparently, although news organizations use new technologies to communicate information, they nevertheless tackle foreign news from a local angle (Fenby, 1986). Other researchers support this claim (Caliendo, Gibney, & Payne, 1999; Chang & Lee, 1992; Golan & Wanta, 2003; Nossek, 2000; Sreberny & Stevenson, 1999; Stevenson & Cole, 1984a, 1984b; Stevenson & Gaddy, 1984).

In addition to this research, which has explored the effect of these changes on the world map with respect to editing considerations, it is also worth considering other arguments and results relating to the limited impact of globalization. The reason is that one should not totally ignore the role of the nation state, which, although it has lost its status, still affects the environment in which the media institutions function—either through legislation or on a social and cultural level (Curran & Park, 2000; Nossek & Adoni, 1996, forthcoming). Furthermore, the "CNN effect" ascribed to global networks and TV channels has, in fact, been identified as limited and dependent on administration policy: policy changes ultimately lead to alterations in news coverage and media impact alters according to the tenor of foreign policy (Livingstone, 1997).

The arguments relating to the absence of change in the nature of foreign news and the continuing presence of domestic editing considerations are, I believe, inextricably linked to the role of the nation state. Support for this is found in Tunstall's (1977) early insights. Tunstall argued that despite the import and export of news and other communication products and because of the dominant position of American media organizations in the world, every country has three media levels: international, local-ethnic, and national, which exist side by side. The national media is a kind of hybrid consisting of domestic news combined with international news, which, according to Tunstall, will become the most important and dominant of the three levels.

Foreign News—Journalists and Editors as Local "Gatekeepers"

As with news theory, which is divided into groups such as news values and functional, critical, and normative professional models (Gans, 1979; Gitlin, 1980; Nossek, 1990), foreign news research also proposes several key arguments, which I briefly describe and analyze.

A basic concept in foreign news studies suggests that journalists and editors are responsible for news selection and refers to them as "gatekeepers." Accordingly, journalists apply a set of norms to their professional practice. Journalists work for media organizations, which have their own priorities, operate in a network of other organizations, and are part of a larger social organization, namely the institution of the media, which interacts with, and is affected by, other social institutions. Shoemaker's (1991, p. 75) description of the process is the most comprehensive: "none of these actors—the individual, the routine, the organization, or the social institution—can escape that fact that it is tied to and draws its sustenance from the social system." In the case of foreign news, part of the process is also that a relatively small number of journalists act as the gatekeepers, coordinating the flow of foreign news (Cohen, Levy, Roeh, & Gurevitch, 1995).

When we analyze how the gatekeepers function regarding foreign news coverage, we realize that the broader cultural-domestic environment that influences their professional work cannot be ignored. Normative professional theory sees this environment as one of the internal or external forces that shape the news. Accordingly, the journalist's domestic viewpoint is inseparable from his or her professional norms and considerations. Galtung and Ruge's (1965) seminal study was the first to point out that the news journalists deliver is shaped by a mixture of both internal and external constraints.[1]

In their study (also based on Galtung and Ruge), Westerståhl and Johansson (1994) highlight the relationship between news and ideology in news reporting. Subsequent studies have also sought to map the features and factors that render an event newsworthy. These studies suggest that a country's local editing preferences call for coverage of countries sharing a geographical, political or cultural affinity (Chang & Lee, 1992; Rosengren, 1974; Sreberny & Stevenson, 1999; Wu, 2000). Thus, we find evidence of cultural filtering in the context of foreign news coverage (Stevenson & Cole, 1984a). Even Paterson (1999), who makes claims in his study for an external factor effect (the reliance of international broadcasting organizations on material from large news agencies greatly affects which news stories are broadcast), found that the bias in foreign news coverage produced by established broadcasting networks is usually consistent with the foreign policy of the network's government. Studies of the coverage of terrorism in the foreign news support these observations of a domestic culture filter (Simmons & Lowry, 1990; Van Belle, 2000; Weimann & Winn, 1994). In fact, it is possible to refer to the prominence of "local" (domestic) terrorism (Nossek, 1990).

According to normative professional theory, the domestic filter is considered as a professional requirement, which it is incumbent on journalists to apply when addressing their particular audience (Cohen et al., 1995; Gurevitch, Levy, & Roeh, 1991; Nossek, 2000; Youichi, 1995). Critical approaches to the study of news also examine the question of domestic bias in foreign news coverage but see this as indicative of collaboration among the social elites in an effort to preserve the status quo. The critical approach thus regards the bias as consonant with the interests of the government of the nation state. The Glasgow University Media Group study (1985), which examined press coverage in a crisis situation, the Falklands War, also supports the idea that the politicosocial context and journalists' understanding of their nation's interests will influence their role perception.[2] Critical theory researchers, like their professional theory colleagues, believe that one cannot separate professional considerations from the domestic/national climate in which the journalist functions.

Foreign News: Journalists and Editors as Universal Human Rights "Gatekeepers"

According to the radical-democratic critique, the media serve "social ends" despite the tension that exists between such ideological ends and professional journalistic values (Herman & Chomsky, 2002). The "propaganda model," which comprises economic and political news "filters," suggests that in order for journalists to survive, they must be able to adapt to the system's demands. "The media are indeed free—for those who adopt the principles which the social ends demand" (Herman & Chomsky, 1988, p. 304). Journalists generally handle any tensions between their journalistic values and the need to meet national ends by having a belief system such as patriotism. Inevitably, there are exceptions and journalists who lack the "right attitude" earn themselves labels like "irresponsible" and "ideological."

Studies of journalists' role perceptions indicate a close but also distinct relationship between a journalist's professional attitudes and domestic-cultural attitudes. Shamir's (1988) study on the role perceptions of Israeli journalists serving the quality press found that a high percentage was ready to place the nation's morale and image, as well as a broad definition of the national interest, before their own professional values: more than half the study sample felt they needed to consider the country's morale. Furthermore, the journalists in the sample found no contradiction between freedom of the press and social responsibility. This points to a perception of national interests that are not in conflict with professional attitudes. Similar conclusions were reached by Wei, Weaver, and Johnson (1996), whose study examined journalists' attitudes to professional values, perceptions, and roles, in a comparative Russian–American study. They found that journalists adopt a relative view of their profession influenced by various historical and cultural traditions and defined by their political, economic, and social environment. These studies appear to support Herman and Chomsky's (1988) claim that journalists are willing to concede professional norms to national interests. In fact, however, their findings show that journalists' behavior is actually context dependent.

Earlier research studies show that not only is media news selection affected by domestic factors but that the nature of the coverage is also affected by such factors (Entman, 1991; Grundmann, Smith, & Wright, 2000;

Kaid, Harville, Ballotti, & Wawreyniax, 1993). Thus, it is possible to present the same data in different ways (Roeh & Cohen, 1992). One important example of this can be found in the study by Cohen, Adams, and Bantz, (1990) of television news coverage of social conflict. The many differences in American network coverage of the intifada and their coverage of the Gulf War are further evidence of this. The nature of the coverage shows that the media treat an event differently depending on whether the conflict is internal (i.e., whether it concerns the media's nation state) or external (it does not concern the media's nation state) (Cohen, Adoni, & Nossek, 1993; Liebes, 1992). Moreover, in the news coverage of terrorism, different myths are woven into the coverage depending on the degree of affinity with the audience culture (Berkowitz & Nossek, 2001; Nossek, Berkowitz, & Gavrilos, 2003).

Political Violence as Foreign News:
A Case Study

Political violence has several definitions and meanings. This is due to differences in viewpoint and interpretation. Legal, political, psychological, and moral theories all offer definitions, and social scientists offer definitions for use as tools in empirical research. Political violence or, in other words, violence in a political context is a broad definition encompassing a wide spectrum of behaviors and events, ranging from terrorism and war to political protest, and all involving some form of conflict. Political violence is invariably employed by a person or group with a political goal opposing a government or political rival. Political violence also carries a message, which is why media coverage is important for those behind it, both as an end in itself and as a means to other ends. This is very clear in the case of protest but also pertinent with regard to terrorism (Picard, 1993). References to this appear in other empirical definitions of terrorism, such as Wilkinson's (2000, p. 12): "It (terrorism) is used to create and exploit a climate of fear among a wider target group than the immediate victims of the violence, and to publicize a cause."

The media's function in covering terrorism is, as already mentioned, important to the terrorist, the government, the audience, and the media. However, it seems that not all events that researchers define as political violence are regarded as such by the media even if they meet the criteria for "newsworthiness"—for example, drama, negativity, tragedy, pain, and so forth (Kelly & Mitchell, 1984; Nossek, 1990, 1994; Weimann & Brosius, 1991).

Furthermore, analysis of the impact that factors relating to news value have on the coverage of protest movements shows that we cannot ascribe a lack of coverage simply to these factors. A triangular relationship exists between protest, politics, and the media, whereby news coverage of protest is shaped by political factors and journalists' professional routines. The grounds and political context for the protest determine whether it attracts news coverage (Oliver & Maney, 2000). Oliver and Maney analyzed protests that were covered as domestic news. If the political context is what determines whether a protest receives coverage, one could speculate that the same might apply to foreign news. In the case of foreign news, because the political context is on the level of the nation state, news factors cannot adequately explain why a protest on foreign soil received or did not receive coverage. We need to place the protest or other act of political violence in a national context in order to explain why an event is defined as news and how it is covered.

To summarize: although proponents of the professional and critical theories of foreign news coverage do not distinguish between bias of a cultural, political, and national nature and general professional considerations, radical critique sees them as separate dimensions. Thus, journalists can choose whether to adopt a universal professional perspective or a domestic national one. It is with this question of the tension between the two perspectives that my argument is concerned.

I wish to argue that, as in the professional approach mentioned earlier, journalists and editors "wear a pair of domestic glasses" when dealing with foreign news. These glasses, however, are not an inseparable part of the professional considerations they apply. Like the radical critique, I maintain that journalists and editors have two distinct "frames" regarding foreign news coverage—a national "frame" and a professional "frame." I believe that the frame that the gatekeepers apply is dependent on several factors: (1) the type of event (some form of political violence, namely war, terrorism, political assassination, etc.); (2) the location of the event (is the locality relevant to the domestic politics and foreign policy or international relations of the journalist and media's nation state?); and (3) the event context (the timing of the event and its local and international context). The definition of an event is, therefore, dictated by these three variables and by the domestic-national "glasses" worn by the gatekeepers. Only when the event is defined as either "ours" or "theirs," can the journalist decide whether to apply a professional or a national-patriotic "frame" when covering the event.

This argument can be displayed and analyzed using a flow diagram of the gatekeepers' decision-making processes vis-à-vis the coverage of political violence (see Figure 2.1). To answer the research question, that is, which factors dictate the nature of foreign news coverage given to political violence, the article poses five questions. These questions are based on the theoretical literature and empirical studies regarding definitions of news and foreign news and the coverage of political violence and terrorism in the news. The five questions are:

1a. Is the political violence that one country defines as news also news in another country?

1b. What do the similarities and differences in the coverage of political violence by the media tell us about the definition of news?

2. How does the type of event and its location affect whether it is defined as news?

3. Do all events of a certain type anywhere in the world receive the same coverage or are some events only defined as news if they happen in certain places?

4. What is the relationship between the party responsible for political violence, the target of the violence, and the definition of an event as news and newsworthy?

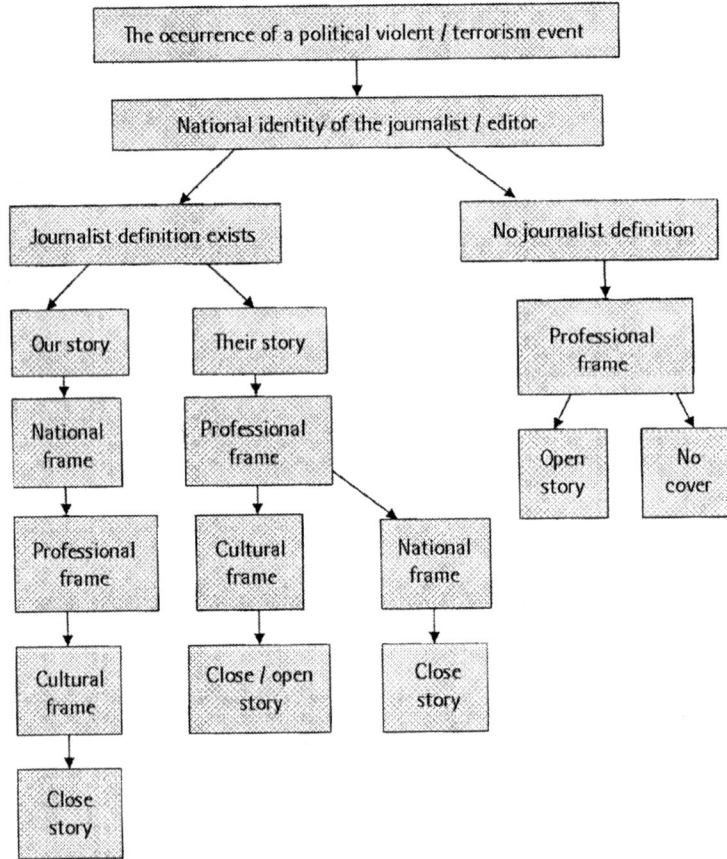

FIGURE 2.1. The Process of Decision Making by Journalists and Editors of Political Violence and Terrorism as News.

5. How does the new media environment, that is, global television and the internet, affect how foreign news is defined?

METHODOLOGY

To study the research argument and research questions empirically, the study used data formerly collected for a large study of foreign news conducted in September 1995. One reason why the data are relevant today is that they relate to the mid-1990s and can, therefore, offer us insights into the impact of global trends on foreign news. Another reason is that the process of data collection enables us to investigate how different countries covered the same event, while controlling all other relevant variables apart from the national identity of the media professionals reporting the event. Thus, the data could be treated as quasi-experimental, that is, as an approximation of laboratory conditions.

I also had the aim of examining different types of events along an axis of political violence (with protest at one end and war at the other). The vehicle that presented itself was a study initiated by the International Association for Media and Communication Research (IAMCR) that examined foreign news coverage in some 40 countries, using the same time frame (see Sreberny & Stevenson, 1999; Wu, 2000). The type of foreign news coverage studied fulfilled two of my criteria; namely they provided (1) a variety of events involving political violence over a short period, and (2) no differences in the political and international context that might affect the results.

The following events, which took place in the first two weeks of September 1995, were chosen for the study:

Event 1: NATO bombardment of Bosnia. On 5 September 1995, in an attempt to force the Serbs to end the siege on Sarajevo and withdraw their heavy artillery, NATO bombers attacked Serbian army emplacements in Bosnia. On 14 September 1995, America sent Assistant Secretary of Defense Richard Holbrook to discuss a peace agreement with Serbian president Slobodan Milosevic on behalf of the Bosnian Serbs. The NATO attacks drew fierce criticism from Russia and, on 12 September 1995, the U.S. Deputy Secretary of State was sent to Moscow to calm matters. This event fits the definition of war, being an armed conflict between ethnic groups involving their armies and intervention by military forces of sovereign states (Carruthers, 2000).

Event 2: Explosion at Jewish school, Lyon, France. On 7 September 1995, a car bomb exploded close to the gate of the Jewish school in Lyon, minutes before 700 pupils left their classrooms at the end of the day.

Fourteen people were wounded in the explosion, among them three children; a delay in the bell signaling home time prevented greater tragedy. The explosion was one of several attacks on French Jewry. The event is defined as political terrorism—the bomb was planted by an oppositional group fighting a government: its purpose was not simply to injure the schoolchildren but to reach a larger target audience with a specific message (Nossek, 1990; Picard, 1993; Wilkinson, 2000).

Event 3: Nuclear test by France in the Pacific. France conducted a series of mid-ocean nuclear tests in the Mururoa area of the South Pacific, the first detonated on 5 September 1995. President Chirac's decision to hold the tests sparked a wave of protest across several countries, led by countries in the region, namely Australia and New Zealand. Protest demonstrations were also organized on the island of Tahiti by environmentalists and members of the Polynesian independence movement to protest against French rule. Serious damage was caused to property on the island, occasioning a police response. French soldiers were dispatched to the area. The demonstrations on Tahiti are defined here as violent political protest, both because of the type of action (disturbing the public peace) and the character of the instigators (movements for independence) acting against the establishment (Sprintzak, 1995; Tarrow, 1983).

Event 4: Bomb explosion at the BBC bureau, Srinigar, Kashmir. On 7 September 1995, a bomb exploded in the BBC bureau in Srinigar. Three people were injured in the blast, including the BBC regional correspondent. A television cameraman who was wounded in the incident died later of his wounds. Several other attacks in the region by pro-Pakistan Kashmiri separatists took place at about the same time, including the kidnapping of several Western hostages. The incident is also defined here as political terrorism due to the nature of the incident and its goals. This case is an interesting example of journalists' involvement, this time as a direct victim of the act.

CHOOSING THE MEDIA

To investigate the research questions, newspapers regarded as "elite" or "quality press" and as the finest models of Western journalism were chosen. The decision to focus on printed rather than on broadcast media resulted from the fact that, in an era of advanced communication technologies, newspapers still provide a basis and model for professional journalistic norms across all media. Another relevant parameter of the quality press is the prominence it gives to foreign news, in particular political and international news.

Newspapers from the United States, Britain, and Israel were chosen because these are countries with an indirect national connection to some events and no direct connection to others. It is important to note that none of the incidents occurred in any of the selected countries, which means that they should all be foreign news for the three countries. The following newspapers were selected: *The New York Times*, *The Times* (London), and an Israeli newspaper, *Ha'aretz*. All three newspapers are considered elite, veteran, and prominent publications in their field. *The New York Times* and *The Times* are regarded as role models for newspapers worldwide (Tunstall, 1977, p. 28) and *Ha'aretz* is considered quality press in Israel (Roeh, 1994).

For each event, each of the newspapers was scoured for several days, searching for relevant news items. Because the French nuclear test and the war in Bosnia were not isolated incidents but ongoing operations, the analysis focused on "climactic" events as far as possible. In contrast, because the car bomb outside the Jewish school and the explosion at the BBC office in Kashmir were isolated incidents, the newspapers were only searched on the first day of coverage, that is, the day after the incident. Table 2.1 displays the number of items found on the dates relevant to the various events. The total number of items for a given event provided the data on which the findings were based.

TABLE 2.1. Data Description

HA'ARETZ	THE TIMES	NEW YORK TIMES	DATE OF SEARCH (1995)	NEWSPAPER / EVENT
6	7	8	13–15 Sept.[a]	NATO bombardment of Bosnia
5	1	1	8–10 Sept.[b]	French nuclear tests in Mururoa
4	5	4	6–8 Sept.[c]	Car bomb explosion at Jewish school, Lyon, France
—	2	—	8–10 Sept.[d]	Bomb planted in BBC offices in Srinigar, Kashmir

[a]Days that were climactic in terms of American involvement.
[b]Here, too, we chose the 'climactic' event—immediately after the first test, as protest internationally and on Tahiti grew more intense.
[c]This one-time event was checked from the first day to the last day of coverage.
[d]Another one-time event but in this case, when the newspapers were first examined for the Kashmir explosion, we found that the story had not been covered. The search for items was, therefore, extended until 15 September.

QUALITATIVE CONTENT ANALYSIS METHOD

The first factor to be evaluated was the journalistic definition of the coverage. This was chosen because not all acts of terrorism or political violence are newsworthy, that is defined as news. To qualify as newsworthy, an event requires drama: injury to civilians and damage to property is simply not enough (Nossek, 1990). Nevertheless, the coverage of a dramatic type of event does not guarantee that the media definition will coincide with the observational research definition of the type of event. Thus, this criterion concerns how the newspaper defines the story—as war, terrorism, freedom fighting, bombardment, an explosion, and so forth.

Roeh and Cohen's (1992) research, which defines "openness" and "closedness" in television news items, was chosen as the basis for this research criterion. Their discussion of the application of professional considerations versus the application of the national viewpoint brought new criteria to the analysis of journalistic definitions of newsworthiness. When we examine the definitions of "openness" and "closedness," we see they can also be applied to the press, as in this study. According to Roeh and Cohen (1992), journalists use three kinds of rhetoric in their writing: (1) objective rhetoric, (2) fact-based rhetoric, and (3) neutral rhetoric. Whether a news story is "open" or "closed" will depend on the type of rhetoric used.

From this analysis, we can obtain the following criteria for deciding whether a news story is "open" or "closed":

- Balance: Is only one position presented? Does the rival viewpoint get the same amount of exposure?
- Fact/commentary: Is the report fact or partly commentary?
- Neutrality: Is the coverage biased toward one of the parties or does it maintain objectivity and avoid partiality?
- Labels: Are the adjectives emotive or neutral? Labels can indicate the journalistic professional frame (Entman, 1991).
- Historical references: Does it link the event to past events in the report text, with source citations?

Other criteria for professional definitions of newsworthiness and for indicating how open or closed the coverage was were added to the examination:

- Scope of coverage: How many items on the news pages were devoted to the subject? How many days did the coverage last?
- Prominence: Where were the items located—front pages or inside pages? (Nossek, 1990). Position in a newspaper is a criterion for measuring newsworthiness (Servaes, 1991). According to the liter-

ature, if a story has a more national frame of reference, it will generally be defined as domestic news as opposed to foreign news and vice versa.

- Story source: Who supplied the newspaper with the story? Where is the source of the story located? This criterion is important both for measuring the newsworthiness of an event and as a factor affecting the news frame of the story (Servaes, 1991, p. 32).
- Information sources: Who are the parties referred to directly or indirectly in the story as sources of information, that is, secondary sources? Who are the story's spokespersons (direct and indirect)? The choice of sources is important in terms of the frame of coverage (Liebes, 1992).
- Emphases: Which aspects of the story are highlighted in the report? What is the story's main point/main themes?

In summary: how open or closed a story is depends on how balanced and factual its presentation. Thus, the fewer historical allusions and emotive labels there are, and the greater the variety of sources, the more open the story will be and vice versa.

FINDINGS

To understand the relationship between the journalistic definition of an event and its coverage, the findings have been summarized according to each newspaper's coverage of each event.

Story 1: The NATO bombardment of Bosnia

All newspapers defined the NATO bombardment of Bosnia as part of a regional war. This appears to be a case of "their" war, because the theater of conflict is the Balkans and because it involves local actors—Bosnians, Serbs, Croatians, the UN, and NATO. On closer scrutiny, however, a different position can be detected in the story. Thus, while the war is actually "their" war, the story in essence addresses issues of concern to "our" country.

The New York Times

Analysis of *The New York Times* coverage shows that even though the war is indeed "theoretically" their war, it is nevertheless "our" war when we identify the sources of information for the story and where those sources are, in fact, located. Thus, we find that, whereas the story contains information sent from the theater of war, it is actually being reported from inside the United States. American sources such as the Pentagon and Washington are widely used. That the event is not only "theirs" but "ours" too is evident from the coverage components: the coverage is extensive—both the scope and duration—and although an obvious journalistic frame of reference renders the story "closed," the American national angle affects the way in which it is "closed." This can clearly be seen from the way America's involvement and the Russian stance are described. The text describes the antagonistic Russian stance, and the commentary leaves little room for uncertainty: Russia is depicted as having lost her influence at the end of the Cold War and her stance is interpreted as an attempt to recoup international standing. The agreement reached with the help of American mediation is represented as an American diplomatic victory, which gains in stature against the background of failed attempts to reach agreement. Emphasis on the NATO attack and the refugee problem draws attention to how important American involvement is. Reference to the Second World War stresses the picture of America as Europe's savior and ally, whereas references to the Communist regime in the region carry associations with the Cold War and imply that the United States is a force for good. This is evident from the use of expressions like "military forces," "peace initiatives" and "war criminals." In the war context, America stands ready to help countries that have managed to banish the Communist gloom. As mentioned earlier, defining the bombardment as part of the war makes the news story closed (due to the abundance of commentary, the lack of balance and neutrality, and the use of historical allusions). However, the additional journalistic definition of the story as "ours" is what dictates how it is closed.

The Times

The Times also awarded the story extensive coverage. Here too, the news items were very prominent, although the extent and prominence of the coverage was less than in The New York Times. Although the journalistic definition (as war) is similar to that seen in The New York Times, because Britain is less involved in the war, the story is more open (the reporting is factual, more balance is evident among the various positions and there is a wider variety of sources—UN officials, Western diplomats, senior American officials, Bosnian and Croatian government representatives, local Bosnians). The British paper puts a lot of emphasis on the Russian–American angle. This can be seen from the fact that the report is from the paper's Washington and Russian correspondents. In the British paper, the American-mediated agreement is viewed more skeptically. The refugee issue is also covered, though the British paper talks about their return home following the local army's victory. Compare this with *The New York Times*, where the report stresses the flight of the refugees. At first glance, the story appears to be open: relatively factual, relatively balanced reporting, no emotive historical references, and more use of neutral labels (Bosnian army, Croatian forces). However, the concluding commentary is skeptical over the American involvement and stresses the local nature of what is happening: this is "their" war and we don't need to interfere in it and make it "ours."

Ha'aretz

Ha'aretz, the Israeli paper, also covered the subject relatively extensively. However, unlike the other papers, *Ha'aretz* used Western news agencies (Reuters, AP, and AFP), whose reports quoted similar sources to those referred to in the other two papers. This indicates a decision not to dispatch a correspondent to the region and shows the paper's attitude to the war as "theirs." Also relevant is the low profile given to the story, compared with the other two papers, where it was very prominent. *Ha'aretz* too defined the event as war and covered it in a relatively factual, balanced way. It interprets Russian opposition to the NATO attack as reflecting a keenness to re-establish her influence abroad. This interpretation resembles the opinion of *The New York Times* and shows the reporting country's attitude toward the dispute between the United States and Russia. The paper's historical reference to the Gulf War reflects a relatively pro-American stance. Accordingly, American intervention is important for restoring order, a theme that is emphasized by the use of such terms as "Western Alliance" and "peace initiative." References to matters not mentioned in the other papers, namely to neo-Nazis and Muslim states (mentioned despite their obvious lack of relevance to Israel), are indirect references to the Gulf War coverage frame, a war into which Israel was dragged unwillingly and America stood by her. The story in *Ha'aretz* is ostensibly "open," though some of its elements serve to "close" it and point to a perception of the United States as an ally in crisis, which explains why *Ha'aretz* emphasizes the American position.

Story 2: French nuclear test in the Pacific

The second story that gained wide coverage in all three papers was the French nuclear test in the Pacific and the wave of protest in response. Both *The New York Times* and *The Times* were not satisfied with defining the event as a protest; they made the struggle for Tahitian independence a significant element of that protest. Both papers covered this story widely—both over time and in quantity. The story was covered by correspondents in Tahiti and Paris.

The New York Times

The New York Times carried items on this story on the inside pages, hence the story's main definition as foreign news. The coverage, however, does not remain "open": it makes no reference to France's position, only to the protests from the various countries, the struggle for Tahitian independence, and reports of ensuing chaos and police violence. Much of the commentary addresses France's international reputation, which was undermined following widespread criticism of French policy and action from other countries. *The New York Times* describes the test as an attempt by France to boost her international standing. Historical references to Hiroshima reflect an "our" position on the subject, despite its classification as foreign news.

The Times

The Times defined the story in terms of protest and the struggle for independence. The story had more coverage and even greater prominence than in *The New York Times*. The paper also carried items on the story on its first pages, showing that it too had embraced the story as "ours." This explains the closed nature of the coverage, which was marked by considerable editorial commentary and emphasis on the threat to French colonial rule in the region and France's isolation in the international arena. References to France's colonial past appear in the commentary and historical references are made. France is accused of forcibly trying to quash the call for independence, of taking an anachronistic approach to decision making, and of trampling the sovereignty of other states in the region. Criticism inside France regarding the decision is also reported, highlighting the lack of balance.

This story, which ostensibly has no bearings on Britain, is clearly closed because of how *The Times* defined it. The fact that *The Times* reported the events as local protest against an outside power fits in with British attitudes on the subject of nuclear testing. The emphasis on France's isolation (in both *The Times* and *The New York Times*) is clearly seen from the wide platform given to the various countries involved and the absence of a French side to the story. Note that both newspapers reported their own government's official reaction to the event. Both American and British government responses were extremely muted, even neutral. For example, Britain's Prime Minister referred to it as a French domestic affair. Given the official responses, it is interesting that the coverage is so closed and nonneutral. This highlights the fact that the newspaper's national viewpoint is based on a definition of the event that is not necessarily consistent with the government position.

Ha'aretz

Ha'aretz covered the event extensively, though not as much as the other papers. It also published the story on the front page, although confining it to smaller pieces at the end of the page. Note, that in contrast to *The New York Times* and *The Times*, which both had correspondents in Tahiti, *Ha'aretz* mainly relied on news agencies for news about the island. *Ha'aretz* also defined the event slightly differently. Although it was defined as protest—that is, protest by both nearby countries and environmentalists, there was considerable emphasis on the test itself. Because the subject was a nuclear test, the coverage was relatively closed. France was presented as power seeking and its position received less coverage than the protests of the countries opposing the test. However, the coverage was factual and more balanced than the coverage in either *The Times* or *The New York Times*. It was also relatively neutral, as it did not describe the Tahitian protestors with much sympathy. In fact, the environmentalists' actions are portrayed as lacking in seriousness, which somewhat "opens" the story. Although *Ha'aretz* refers to Israel's official response together with that of other countries, it mostly defines the event as "theirs." The reporting is closed because the event is defined as a nuclear test, which itself rules out the possibility of it being "ours." Here, historical references to Hiroshima and Nagasaki contribute to the emphasis on the definition of the event as a nuclear test.

The remaining events in this analysis—the explosion at the Jewish school in Lyon and the bomb at the BBC bureau in Kashmir—clearly show how the journalistic definition has a pronounced effect on the frame (professional or national) in which the events are reported.

Story 3: The car bomb outside the Jewish school in Lyon

The car bomb outside the Jewish school in Lyon was defined as terrorism by both *The New York Times* and *Ha'aretz*. *The Times* did not define the incident as terrorism, which meant that its coverage was "open" in every respect: the report was very factual; there was no reference to who planted the bomb; and almost no reference to those wounded in the attack.

The New York Times coverage was relatively open: the report was factual and its lack of prominence shows that it had been defined as foreign news (its profile in *The Times* was also low, that is, it was similarly treated as foreign news there). Both papers published just one item about the attack, which was covered by their Paris correspondent, and both used French sources (*The Times* quoted just one source, *The New York Times* had several). The definition of the event as "terrorism" gave the coverage a closed dimension. However, there was no emphasis on the injured party, apart from a single, isolated reference to the Jewish context, which made the item relatively neutral. This is substantiated by the two sources quoted: the Rabbi of Lyon and an Islamic organization. *The Times'* report was "clean" and neutral; there was no standpoint, emphasis, or use of labels and attributes.

The coverage in *Ha'aretz* was completely different (even though the attack was covered by a correspondent in Paris using only French sources). The attack was clearly defined as terrorism—specifically, terrorism against Jews—hence its prominence. Because the paper defined the incident as "our" terrorist attack (an attack on us), the report is very closed. We see this from the emphasis on Jewish community sources, the imbalance of the report, the use of epithets like "Algeria's most bloody terrorist organization," "an armed Islamic group," "terrible tragedy," and, above all, its references and links to recent and ancient Jewish history. (Note that the other papers contained no historical references.)

Story 4: Explosion at the BBC offices in Srinagar, Kashmir

This case demonstrates clearly the impact that the definition of an event has on its coverage. *The Times*, the only paper out of the three that covered the event, did not define it as terrorism. Thus, the explosion was foreign news only and had little prominence. The scant coverage (two items) was "open"—that is, factual, in that it adhered to the details and did not present the sides to the argument. However, the paper used the event as the peg for a story about the challenges facing journalists in that region. This angle, which another item takes even further, examined the problems journalists encounter when trying to do their professional work. The report explained that threats against journalists made objective coverage a problem and terrorized correspondents in the region. Here we have a position that clearly relates to the journalist as a professional individual, alongside absolute neutrality regarding the actual blast. We can speculate that because this event was not defined as terrorism, the other papers decided not to cover it.

DISCUSSION

With regard to the research questions, we can summarize the study findings as follows: Is the political violence that one country defines as news, also news in another country, (RQ 1) and what do the similarities and differences in the coverage of political violence by the media tell us about the definition of news?

We found that the three national, quality newspapers, examined did not define every event of political violence the same way. This divergence can also be seen in the way in which the story is covered and the extent to which it is "closed." Once an event has been defined as war, terrorism, or violent protest, the question is: is it "our" event or "theirs"? However, when an event is defined as neither theirs nor ours, its coverage remains "open" and it conforms to the professional criteria for defining foreign news coverage. The best example of this is the coverage of the explosion in Kashmir. From this incident, we see that not all acts of political violence are necessarily defined as news, which corroborates Nossek's (1990) finding.

How does the type of event and its location affect whether it is defined as news (RQ 2)? In contrast to earlier studies, we found that the location of an event was not especially relevant to defining an event as news. The professional frame and criteria that make an event news (see Galtung & Ruge, 1965, for example) only go part of the way towards explaining how the event location and type of event affect whether it is defined as news or not, but do not account at all for the frame of the coverage. The present findings demonstrate that the national frame can answer this question. The criterion of relevance, too, which can explain why an American paper covered the war in Bosnia (American involvement) but not the explosion in India, does not explain why, for example, the paper took a particular stance in its coverage of the events in the Pacific. This points to the existence of a national frame, which stems from the definition of the event as an event involving protest against the colonialist behavior of a significant country. The popular explanation in the literature on the subject of the press adopting and reflecting a governmental position fails to account for the closed coverage of the nuclear tests because the actual report states that the American administration avoided taking a clear position, whereas the paper actually adopted a national stance in spite of its government's position.

Do all events of a certain type anywhere in the world receive the same coverage (RQ 3) or are some events defined as news only if they happen in certain places? The findings also demonstrate that only some political violence and terrorism become foreign news. Once again, the key lies in the predefinition of the event as a certain type of political violence and if this event then is "ours" or "theirs" according to the national frame adopted by the reporter and the editorial board for the coverage of the event. Differences in the coverage of the attack on the BBC bureau in Srinigar and the Jewish school in Lyon illustrate this very clearly. However, this contrasts with the popular argument that an act of terrorism guarantees the perpetrators automatic publicity and ultimately serves their ends. With Lyon and Srinigar, neither the terrorists' demands nor the political background to their action received any publicity—apart from a bit of conjecture by the reporting journalists themselves.

What is the relationship between the party responsible for political violence, the target of the violence and the definition of an event as news and newsworthy (RQ 4)? From the findings, we see that the victim and the target that he or she represents have an influence on the coverage and the nature of the coverage. However, as we saw, the perpetrator has no control over whether an event will receive any publicity and certainly no control over its content and nature. This can clearly be seen from the analysis of the demonstrations against France's nuclear tests and with regard to the bomb attacks in Lyon and Srinigar.

How does the new media environment, that is, global television and the internet, affect how foreign news is defined (RQ 5)? As Paterson (1999) argued, and Fenby (1986) before him, it is generally assumed that such wide access to new technologies will most likely lead to uniformity in reporting. According to the study findings, regarding the quality press at least, the global character of sources has no bearing on consistency in reporting. Thus, according to the analysis of the findings relating to the coverage of the four events by the three newspapers, it is empirically valid to claim that the definition of an event as belonging to the frame of war, terrorism, or other type of political violence is responsible for its definition as foreign news. The definition of an event as political violence causes the reporter and editorial board to adopt a stance and define the political violence as "theirs" or "ours." Because an event is defined as theirs or ours, it is then covered as either an open story or a closed one. I suggest that the reason for this distinction is that the national position takes precedence over professional norms whenever an event is defined as "our" political violence and that the professional frame of reference takes precedence whenever political violence is defined as "theirs" or is not framed as a specific type of political violence (e.g., war, terrorist attack, violent protest, etc.).

These findings complement earlier ones concerning the selection of events and their presentation as foreign news. The present findings show that the national identity of journalists and editors influences definition during the selection of political violence as news. This overrides Western journalistic professional norms, which previous research has shown to dominate the selection and presentation of foreign news (Sreberny & Stevenson, 1999). The national frame is an addition to the journalistic news frames and cultural frames, which mainly explain the domestication and localization of stories (Berkowitz & Nossek, 2001; Nossek et al., 2003). At least in terms of political violence and terrorism, this frame exists and is extremely obvious. It precedes all other frames and dictates which line the coverage will take and which other journalistic and cultural frames will be selected. In light of the findings, we can theorize that this frame exists in foreign news coverage of other kinds of events—it is very evident in sport (Nossek, 2000) and perhaps in other types of events as well.

Based on their study of domestic news, Oliver and Maney (2000) have argued that political context is what influences news coverage. We can, therefore, speculate that, in a broader sense, this context can affect whether an event is defined as news in the domestic arena as well as with respect to foreign news. Indeed, earlier studies of journalists' professional perceptions offer support for this idea and conclude that the professional viewpoint is a relative concept defined by its social, economic, and political context (Glasgow University Media Group, 1985; Shamir, 1988; Wei et al., 1996). To examine this question specifically, further study is needed to address the methodological issue of how to isolate these attitudes for journalists whose professional definitions prevent them from directly relating to national frames of reference, which take precedence over professional frames of reference, at least in cases where the government of their nation state is somehow involved in some kind of political violence.

Regarding the technological changes to global communication, we can further theorize that when dealing with such events, Internet coverage is structured according to the national ties of whoever built and edited the Web site. The way even non-institutional or anti-institutional Web sites covered Israel's Operation Defensive Shield might at least give an indication of this. Naturally, these claims must be empirically founded and be appropriate for future research examination. A future study of this nature should also investigate the impact of the internet on the attitudes of journalists working for the traditional media, both from the point of view of their use of sources and in terms of their address to their target audiences—that is, knowing they are no longer a unique source of information and news.

Despite the spectacular changes in the world of global communication, the role of the nation state has not ended. Further to the arguments presented by Livingstone (1997) and by Curran and Park (2000), the results of this present study teach us that regardless of the changes on the political, economic, and communication map at the end of the twentieth century, when it comes to politics and international relations, foreign news is still a product of the existing frameworks of nationhood. The tragedy of 9/11 and its aftermath is a dramatic and clear example of political violence and terrorism gaining extensive coverage throughout the world. Use of the model presented here to examine the news coverage of these events and their aftermath can help to shed further light on the questions raised in this chapter.

NOTES

1. For a fresh, more contemporary discussion of some of Galtung and Ruge's points, see also Harcup and O'Neill (2001).
2. Another support for this claim can be found in American studies that examined American media behavior during the Vietnam War (Gitlin, 1980; Hallin, 1989)

REFERENCES

Berkowitz, D. & Nossek, H. (2001) Myths and news narratives: Toward a comparative perspective of news. *Ecquid Novi, 22*, 41–56.

Caliendo, S. M., Gibney, M. P. & Payne, A. (1999). All the news that is fit to print? *New York Times* coverage of human-rights violations. *The Harvard International Journal of Press/Politics, 4*(4), 48–69.

Carruthers, S. L. (2000). *The media at war.* New York: St. Martin Press.

Chang, T. & Lee, J. (1992). Factors affecting gatekeepers' selection of foreign news: A national survey of newspaper editors. *Journalism Quarterly, 69*, 554–561.

Cohen, A. A., Adoni, H. & Bantz, C. (1990). *Social conflict & television news.* Newbury Park, CA: Sage.

Cohen, A. A., Adoni, H. & Nossek, H. (1993). Television news and the intifada: A comparative study of social conflict. In A. A. Cohen & G. Wolfsfeld (Eds.), *Framing the intifada: People and media* (pp. 116–141). Norwood, NJ: Ablex.

Cohen, A. A., Levy, M. R., Roeh, I. & Gurevitch, M. (1995). *Global newsrooms, local audiences: A study of the eurovision news exchange.* London: John Libbey.

Curran, J. & Park, M. J. (2000). Beyond globalization theory. In J. Curran & M. J. Park (Eds.), *De-Westernizing media studies* (pp. 3–18). London: Routledge.

Entman, R. M. (1991). Framing US coverage of international news: Contrasts in narratives of the KAL and Iran air incidents. *Journal of Communication, 41*(4), 6–27.

Fenby, J. (1986). *The international news services.* New York: Schoken.

Galtung, J. & Ruge, M. H. (1965). The structure of foreign news. *Journal of Peace Research, 2,* 64–91.

Gans, H. J. (1979). *Deciding what's news.* New York: Pantheon.

Gitlin, T. (1980). *The whole world is watching: Mass media in the making and unmaking of the new left.* Berkeley: University of California Press.

Glasgow University Media Group (1985). *War and peace news.* Milton Keynes/Philadelphia: Open University Press.

Golan, G. & Wanta, W. (2003). International elections on the US network news: An examination of factors affecting newsworthiness. *Gazette: The International Journal for Communication Studies, 65,* 25–40.

Gonzenbach, W. J., Arant, M. D. & Stevenson, R. L. (1992). The world of US network television news: Eighteen years of international and foreign news coverage. *Gazette: The International Journal for Communication Studies, 50,* 53–72.

Grundmann, R., Smith, D. & Wright, S. (2000). National elites and transnational discourses in the Balkan war. *European Journal of Communication, 15,* 299–320.

Gurevitch, M., Levy, M. R. & Roeh, I. (1991). The global newsroom: Convergences and diversities in the globalization of television news. In P. Dahlgren & C. Sparks (Eds.), *Communication and citizenship: Journalism and the public sphere* (pp. 195–216). London: Routledge.

Hallin, D. C. (1989). *The uncensored war: The media and Vietnam.* Berkeley: University of California Press.

Harcup, T. & O'Neill, D. (2001). What is news? Galtung and Ruge revisited. *Journalism Studies, 2,* 261–280.

Herman, E. S. & Chomsky, N. (1988). *Manufacturing consent & the political economy of the mass media.* New York: Pantheon.

Kaid, L. L., Harville, B. Ballotti, J. & Wawrzyniak, M. (1993). Telling the Gulf war story: Coverage in five papers. In B. S. Greenberg & W. Gantz (Eds.), *Desert storm and the mass media* (pp. 86–98). Cresskill, NJ: Hampton Press.

Kelly, M. J. & Mitchell, H. T. (1984). Transnational terrorism and the Western elite press. *Political Communication and Persuasion, 1*(3), 269–296.

Liebes, T. (1992). Our war/their war: Comparing the intifada and the Gulf War on U.S. and Israeli television. *Critical Studies in Mass Communication, 9*(1), 44–55.

Livingstone, S. (1997). *Clarifying the CNN effect: An examination of media effects according to military intervention.* Research Paper R-18. Cambridge, MA: The Joan Shorenstein Center for Press/Politics, John F. Kennedy School of Government, Harvard University.

Nossek, H. (1990). *Terrorism and the media.* Doctoral dissertation, Hebrew University, Jerusalem.

Nossek, H. (1994) The narrative role of the holocaust and the state of Israel in the coverage of salient terrorist events in the Israeli press. *Journal of Narrative and Life History, 4,* 119–134.

Nossek, H. (2000). *Foreign news and the construction of reality: Between the mondial and mondo cane.* Paper presented at the Conference on International News in the 21st Century, March. Leicester, UK: Centre for Mass Communication Research.

Nossek, H. & Adoni, H. (1996). The social implications of cable television: Restructuring connections with self and social groups. *International Journal of Public Opinion Research, 8,* 51–69.

Nossek, H. & Adoni, H. (forthcoming). The global village, the nation state and the ethnic community: Audiences of communication and boundaries of identity. In M. Blondheim & R. Watson (Eds.), *The Toronto School of Communication Theory: International perspectives.* Jerusalem: Magnes, Hebrew University Press.

Nossek, H., Berkowitz, D. & Gavrilos, D. (2003). *Journalism as social practice in crisis: Restoring identity through mythical newswork.* Paper presented at the ICA Annual Conference, San Diego, CA.

Oliver, P. E. & Maney, G. M. (2000). Political process and local newspaper coverage of protest events: From selection bias to triadic interaction. *American Journal of Sociology, 106,* 463–505.

Paterson, C. A. (1999). Agency source influence on television foreign reporting: Case of Mururoa and Tahiti. *Asia Pacific Media Educator, 7,* 16–36.

Picard, R. (1993). *Media portrayals of terrorism.* Ames: Iowa State University Press.

Roeh, I. (1994). *Acheret al tikshoret* [Different media]. Israel: Reches. (In Hebrew)

Roeh, I. & Cohen, A. A. (1992). One of the bloodiest days: A comparative analysis of open and closed television news. *Journal of Communication, 42*(2), 42–55.

Rosengren, K. E. (1974). International news: Methods, data and theory. *Journal of Peace Research, 11,* 145–156.

Servaes, J. (1991). European press coverage of the Granada crisis. *Journal of Communication, 41*(4), 28–41.

Shamir, J. (1988). Israeli elite journalism: Views on freedom and responsibility. *Journalism Quarterly, 63,* 589–594.

Shoemaker, P. J. (1991). *Gatekeeping,* Newbury Park, CA: Sage.

Simmons, B. K. & Lowry, D. N. (1990). Terrorists in the news, as reflected in three news magazines, 1980–1988. *Journalism Quarterly, 67,* 692–696.

Sprintzak, E. (1995). *Alimut politit be'Israel* [Political violence in Israel]. Jerusalem: Jerusalem Institute.

Sreberny, A. & Stevenson, R. (1999). Comparative analysis of international news flow: An example of global media monitoring. In K. Nordenstreng & M. Griffin (Eds.), *International media monitoring* (pp. 55–72). Cresskill, NJ: Hampton Press.

Sreberny-Mohammadi, A. (1991). The global and the local in international communication. In G. Curran & M. Gurevitch (Eds.), *Mass media and society* (pp. 118–138). London: Edward Arnold.

Stevenson, R. L. & Cole, R. R. (1984a). Issues in foreign news. In R. L. Stevenson and D. L. Shaw (Eds.) *Foreign news and the new world information order* (pp. 5–20). Amesa: Iowa State University Press.

Stevenson, R. L. & Cole, R. R. (1984b). Patterns of foreign news. In R. L. Stevenson & D. L. Shaw (Eds.), *Foreign news and the new world information order* (pp. 37–62). Ames: Iowa State University Press.

Stevenson, R. L. & Gaddy, G. D. (1984). "Bad news" and the third world. In R. L. Stevenson & D. L. Shaw (Eds.), *Foreign news and the new world information order* (pp. 88–97). Ames: Iowa State University Press.

Tarrow, S. (1983). *Struggling to reform: Social movements and policy change during cycles of protest.* Occasional Paper No. 15. Western Societies Program. Ithaca, NY: Cornell University.

Tunstall, J. (1977). *The media are American. Anglo-American media in the world.* London: Constable.

Van Belle, D. A. (2000). *New York Times* and network TV news coverage of foreign disasters: The significance of the insignificant variables. *Journalism & Mass Communication Quarterly, 77,* 50–70.

Wei, W., Weaver, D. & Johnson, O. V. (1996). Professional roles of Russian and U.S. journalists: A comparative study. *Journalism & Mass Communication Quarterly, 73,* 534–548.

Weimann, G. & Brosius, H. B. (1991). The newsworthiness of international terrorism. *Communication Research, 18,* 333–354.

Weimann, G. & Winn, C. (1994). *The theater of terror: Mass media and international terrorism.* New York & London: Longman.

Westerståhl, J. & Johansson, F. (1994). Foreign news: News values and ideologies. *European Journal of Communication, 9,* 71–89.

Wilkinson, P. (2000). *Terrorism versus democracy: The liberal state response.* Portland, OR: Frank Cass.

Wu, H. D. (2000). Systemic determinants of international news coverage: A comparison of 38 countries. *Journal of Communication, 50*(2), 110–130.

Youichi, I. (1995). *A study of psychological factors of international information flows: News and TV programs.* Paper presented at the International Association for Media and Communication Research Conference, June, Portoroz, Slovania.

Chapter 3

The Deictic of Mediated Violence

Public Intellectuals, Journalism and Some Problems of Pronoun-ciation*

Annabelle Sreberny

The extension of the nation-state system is said to be one of the key processes of globalization (Giddens, 1990). The "nation and the state are each other's projects" (Appadurai, 1990), and contemporary manifestations of national belonging—from flags to anthems, invented traditions and symbols (Hobsbaum & Ranger, 1983), sporting events and political rituals—have become banal signifiers of a taken-for-granted but always re-asserted national identity.

One of the most obvious yet often unremarked modes in which this national positioning is established is through the routine deixis of mediated address, the "little words" (Billig, 1995, p. 11) such as "we" and "us" that invite readers and viewers into a shared position.[1] Deixis is a form of rhetorical pointing that anchors sentences to certain aspects of their contexts of utterance. For example, "now" refers to the time of the utterance; "here" to its place; and pronouns ("I," "you," "we") ground the sentence in the immediacy of the speaker and the addressee (Harre, 1991). Billig (1995, p. 94) suggests the importance of being "linguistically microscopic":

---

*This chapter draws on material published in Sreberny (2002).

> The crucial words of banal nationalism are often smallest: "we," "this" and "here," which are the words of linguistic "deixis." . . . Beyond conscious awareness, like the hum of distant traffic, this deixis of little words makes the world of nations familiar, even homely.

As an obvious example, "We, the people" as a foundational slogan of America doesn't need to define itself or the limits of its inclusivity: it is preknown.

That media maintain and naturalize nationalist consciousness is well understood (Billig, 1995, p. 10). One of the most obvious forms of nationbuilding content can be found in the undisguised nationalism of broadcast sports commentary, when all attempts at objective positioning collapse. But a more diffuse invocation of the nation runs through much media output. As Billig argues (1995, p. 11), "all the papers, whether tabloid or quality (*sic*), and whether left- or right wing, address their readers as members of the nation." Such a process seems to occur in every nation and is not just a manifestation of the British media; in the main, media "present news in ways that take for granted the existence of a world of nations" (*ibid*). When such language is used to refer to the audience, presumably playing again on the basis of a pre-given national identification, the audience may well not be physically present but exists as "imagined" (Hartley, 1992; echoing Anderson's [1983] notion of the nation itself as an "imagined community").

Discourse manifests power relations on the ground, what Billig refers to as a "syntax of hegemony." That can be found within nationalist discourse when a particular version of the language becomes privileged as "the national language," or when a specific locale (the capital) or specific interests (a political party) speak in the name of all, in "the national interest." A form of linguistic and political metonymy takes place, where a part claims to represent the whole.[2]

Going beyond a banal nationalism, deixis can also privilege a more global set of power relations, and political rhetoric may well seek to address a more global "we." This is a further level of movement that sees a national "we"—or a modern, Western "we"—becoming elided with a more totalizing, universalizing position; "'our' particular interests can appear as the interests of universal reason" (Billig, 1995, p. 88). Political language can function in this way. For example, Bush's rhetorical trope "whoever is not with us, is with the terrorists" implies an "us" that is not just Americans but rather the "coalition of the willing" or even "the entire free world" in which, by implication, terrorists have no place. Media language also makes such claims. For example, the television presenter Jonathan Dimbleby in a BBC program ostensibly examining the causes of terrorism (October/November 2004) started by claiming that "the events of 9/11 shocked and outraged us all; and everyone else." The "us" in the sentence seems to refer to the British audience. The claim of "everyone else" is clearly far too big, because it presumably cannot by definition include the terrorists themselves nor the growing numbers of people whom Dimbleby proceeds to find and present to "us," the British viewers, who have sympathy with the broad political position exemplified by al Qaeda.

One of the useful, if crude, functions of binary formulations such as "us and them" is the projection of everything bad on to the "other." This is also a very early kind of individual response to ambivalent feelings, usefully analyzed by the post-Kleinian school of Object Relations in which the self is seen as foundationally constituted through imaginative encounters with the other (Klein, 1957). Intersubjective understanding is built in the baby's experiential, affective encounters with the (m)other, generating powerful feelings of love and hate that are managed only by splitting them off from the self and reducing them to good or bad objects—the bad mother, bad breast, paranoid-schizoid position. With good enough (m)othering, a more mature position, that of the depressive, develops in which bad parts of the self are reintegrated, clearer boundaries are established between self and other, and a richer, more ambivalent and more adult understanding is reached.

Trauma can produce a regression to the earlier psychological position. To paraphrase Winnicott (1971, p. 114), trauma implies a break in life's continuity, so that primitive defences organise to defend against a repetition of "unthinkable anxiety" or a return of the acute confusion that might disintegrate the nascent ego structure. Thus, one response to trauma might be regression to an earlier less integrated psychological stage. The paranoid-schizoid defences include excessive splitting, omnipotent thinking, and denial. All hostility/badness is offloaded on to the other. Bush's early political rhetoric readily invites such a reading as can the U.S. government and media's refusal to have any sense of the global anger and political hurt that might have led to September 11 and the difficulty of even entertaining the question "why do they hate us?" or seeing this as a politically motivated act.

From a more sociological perspective, Norbert Elias recognized that the content and definition of a "we" may change over an individual lifetime, through the individual life-process:

> One's sense of personal identity is closely connected with the "we" and "they" relationships of one's group, and with one's position within those units of which one speaks as "we" and "they." Yet the pronouns do not always refer to the same people. The figurations to which they currently refer can change in the course of a lifetime, just as any person does himself. This is true not only of all people considered separately, but of all groups and even of all societies. Their members universally say "we" of themselves and "they" of other people, but they may say "we" and "they" of different people as time goes by. (Elias, "What is Sociology" p. 128, quoted by Mennell 1992, p. 265)

For Elias, identity is awareness of belonging to a group, but this awareness changes over time as increasing social interdependence produces more
complex layers of we-image in people's habitus; hence "habitus and identification, being related to group membership, are always—and in the modern
world where people belong to groups within groups within groups—multi-
layered" (Mennell, 1994, p. 177).

The spatial metaphor of the "inside-outside" also functions within
international relations theory, in relation to the nation-state system (Walker,
1993). 9/11 mobilized this structure in two ways. One was the peculiar
nature of the actors, the "terrorists," who could not be readily configured
within the nation-state system and whose use of violence and implied politics posed a challenge to the very nature of that system. This, of course, produced the confusion about how to name the response to the event, given that
"war" can only be declared against a state; later on, it "allowed" the United
States to fudge the Geneva Convention in terms of treatment of prisoners.
The second way was in the instant synecdochic collapse of the entire world,
or the global system, into America as its heart. Thus, for example, an attack
on the United States.was also an attack on "us" in Britain, as Blair rapidly
suggested, or on the "entire free world" (wherever/whatever that is).

There was yet a third moment of deictic usage—beyond the syntactic
hegemony of the national or the global—that both echoed but also complicated these first two forms (a sedimented nationalism and a globally
extending universalism). It reflected a moment of collective uncertainty
where the deictic categories make new and unclear claims or try to (re-
)establish commonality and cultural closeness when this appeared to be
threatened or ruptured. I intend to use responses to 9/11 in select pieces of
British press content to explore this third position, which manifested neither a simple sedimented nationalism nor a syntactic hegemony but a crisis
of identity and invocation of emergent collective identifications in response
to the events.

DIFFERENT KINDS OF DISTANCE:

Media popularizers such as Cairncross (2001) have triumphantly proclaimed
the "death of distance" brought about by the fall in cost and the increase in
capacity of all forms of communication over long distances. But many critical media scholars and social analysts have revealed a harsher reality; the
immovability of the news audience in relation to events far away, to death at
a distance. The literature on international news and audience reactions to
that has been filled with metaphors of "compassion fatigue" (Moeller, 1999),
"states of denial" (Cohen, 2001), and a general lack of concern about "distant suffering" (Boltanski, 1999).

But for the most part, the news violence rarely happens to "us," the Western media audience. This supposition was challenged by the Balkans conflict, ominously close to the Western European "us" but also the locale where many different fault lines of othering can be brought into play. Many Western urban locales (e.g. Belfast, London, Madrid) *have* experienced sporadic political violence. But clearly *the* event that shattered the illusion of Westerners as "distant" from the victims of violent politics experienced as news events was 9/11, watched by a global television audience of millions. One of the central outcomes of September 11 was to draw a line, not in sand but in many minds, between "us" and "them" and to establish the crude binaries of "syntactic hegemony" supported by political rhetoric and media compliance that supported military adventures in Afghanistan and Iraq and continue to threaten Iran and other countries. But the first responses were more open, more ambivalent, and harder to read. Here, then, are some crucial issues of pronoun-ciation.

JOURNALISM AFTER SEPTEMBER 11: EMOTION AND ATTACHMENT?

Journalists were severely challenged in their ability to impose sense on the event, resorting often to simple narrative formats. The manner in which the event took over the airwaves and dominated the papers in itself signified massive crisis and a new hierarchy of significance that downplayed on-going conflicts. The event's sheer scale and surprise prompted a breakdown of the usual journalistic frameworks and a scramble for interpretation. How could journalists help interpret the event if the experts could not agree? How could audiences think about this event? For a moment, the event was represented as a massive global trauma implicating everyone. The event seemed to demand, and quickly spawned, new or renewed genres of writing: the eye-witness account; the final messages to and the tearful stories of those left behind. There were instant expert opinions and rapid code histories. The everyday, taken-for-granted norms of journalism were shaken, in rushed opinion and emotion, and an affective public sphere evolved. The balance seemed to shift between the ordinary work of journalism and a kind of extraordinary writing that people seemed to need to write and others to read—writing as catharsis, writing trauma out of ourselves, trauma talk.

In Britain, it seemed as though there was awareness, at least in parts of the liberal media, about the problem of Islamophobia; a new range of voices was invited onto television and radio discussion programs and into the pages of the press. Many programs worked hard to find speakers from Muslim communities and solicit the opinions of Muslims, including, in

March 2002, a wide-ranging series of television programmes *Muslim and British* produced for Channel Four.

The Guardian and its Sunday sister *The Observer* have a long history of publishing both regular columns and also occasional think-pieces by writers who are not part of its regular staff, which contribute to a lively public debate about controversial matters. This media space is one of the few available to public intellectuals to articulate a range of positions. It is key to my regular readership of these papers and, at least anecdotally, this is true for many others. Starting immediately after September 11, articles were published from a range of well-known and respected writers and commentators, some filed from New York or taken from U.S. newspapers, and others posted from further afield. The list of authors included Martin Wollacott, Saskia Sassen, Ian McEwan, Simon Schama, Rana Kabbani, Ian Buruma, Arundhati Roy, Christopher Hitchins, Anne Karpf, Caryl Philips, Salman Rushdie, Blake Morrison, Ahdaf Souief, Ziauddin Sardar, Polly Toynbee, Gary Younge, Yusuf Islam, Edward Said, Pete Hamill, Katie Roiphe, Larry Elliot, Darryl Pinkney, and others. Constructed not as experts on Islam, terrorism, or military ordinance, they were regarded as independent writers and thinkers voicing personal, often emotional, responses. *Guardian* editor Alan Rusbridger said of this writing "some of it is raw, some controversial, some prescient, some overtaken by subsequent information or events."

This was affective writing within serious newspapers in Britain, a culture less inclined to overt expressions of emotion than the United States (although the emotional public reactions to the death of Diana triggered interesting public debate; see Blackman & Walkerdine, 2001). This was not regular column material, nor was it written by regular columnists, but this writing deserves serious consideration for a number of reasons. These public intellectuals—serious, thoughtful, critical, creative—do not represent the voices of hegemony, but they do show how the process of hegemony is internalized. In their rapidly written and emotionally expressive form, these voices reflect something of the collective unconscious, of the anxieties and mistrust as well as the shared understandings and attachments that sudden trauma summons up. They thus revealed something of "ourselves," but just which selves is what I want to tease out.

Another element that makes this writing worthy of attention is that the collective outpouring of grief and fear reversed the usual pattern of indifference. Part of the deep shock of 9/11 was that "we" had become the object of violence, not its perpetrator. In this case, instead of indifference, there was over-identification, with British media coverage showing an instant identification with New Yorkers. Many international writers and commentators were somehow merged with Americans in a cultural geography of attachment. This is partly an effect of America as the global universal, an indication of the internalization of a steady drip-feed of hegemonic values. In

Britain, there was also a deep sense of cultural proximity, "our" familiar and much loved New York of the movies, television, tourism, Americans as people very like "us". Then there was the sheer unexpectedness of the event, and the attendant difficulty in understanding it, as well as a generalized anxiety by big-city dwellers that they could be next. All of this fostered an unusually emotive response to this event in many places, which was clearly expressed through these articles.

What is intriguing about this material are its repetitive themes. The texts abound with notions of collective identity at the same time that there is confusion about the collectivity, its nature and whom it encompasses. There seems to be also confusion about the audience, about whom one was writing for, and why one was writing, confusion about who "we" are. At issue, then, in these writings is the almost visceral, unthought-of, unquestioned location of some of these authors, the semiconscious groupishness that lurk in their minds, and thus perhaps in "ours."

ISSUES OF PRONOUN-CIATION: WHO DO "WE" THINK "WE" ARE?

What follows is a detailed commentary on three texts. These stood out from a plethora of pieces for the most sustained and repeated use of deictic signifiers that were taken to be transparent and meaningful to the middle-class British readership being addressed.

The first two are by well-known British writers, white and middle-class. Martin Amis is the author of many novels including *The Information* and *London Fields*; a recent autobiography, *Experience;* and a collection of writing, *The War Against Cliché*. He published an article on September 18 (http://www.guardian.co.uk/Archive/Article/0,4273,4259170,00.html) entitled "Letter from London," immediately invoking some far-off unnamed recipient, presumably the United States itself, playing with Alistair Cook's familiar "Letter from America." Amis started with the change brought about by the second plane. Before that, it was simply "the worst aviation disaster in history." But the second plane "galvanised with malice, and wholly alien, meant the end of everything." And he continued, "for us, its glint was the world flash of a coming future." Who are this "us"? City-dwellers? Britons? Westerners, thus eliding the invitation of the title? Amis then recounted in detail the events of the morning, over-stating the perpetrators' intentionality, as did so many of the early commentators, by underscoring that the global real-time media audience was planned and the perpetrators knew the twin towers would implode. Because he was not there, he appropriated the experience of "my wife's sister" who stood on Fifth Avenue and

Eleventh Street at 8:58 a.m. under the flight path of one of the planes, and cut back to another "we," a presumed modern city-dweller or airpane-spotting nerd: "We have all watched aeroplanes approach, or seem to approach a large building. We tense ourselves as the supposed impact nears, even though we are sure that this is a parallax illusion, and that the plane will cruise grandly on."

The twin towers "flail and kick" as they came down, and Amis talked of the "demented sophistication" of the suicide killers who belonged in a different psychic category: "Clearly, they have contempt for life. Equally clearly they have contempt for death." "We should know our enemy." Here the division was not complicated, a simple binary echoing that of Bush. These people are quite unlike "us," who implicitly both love life and revere death. The stereotype of the callous Oriental who devalues life lurks dangerously close, and the body counts against the West are too easily forgotten in both the political rhetoric and Amis's commentary.

Then Amis slipped back to a British "we": American parents will feel their inability to protect their children, "but we will also feel it." So although the event was over there, in America, its impact shattered British parental illusions about their abilities to protect their children. We share your fate. He then allowed himself imaginings of even worse scenarios, involving biological, chemical, and nuclear weapons. The slip back into binary processing summons up our own paranoid tendencies. He talked of how difficult it would be for Americans to realize that they are hated, because "being right and being good support the American self to an almost tautologous degree," and an adaptation of national character is needed. This sounded like the criticism of a close friend, as perhaps only a Brit can say to a Yank, the patronizing hierarchy of colonialism.

However, "on the other side," reflexively acknowledged in the phrase "the world suddenly feels bipolar," even more fundamental change was required: "We would have to sit through a renaissance and a reformation, and then await enlightenment. And we're not going to do that." This proclaimed a crude and obvious Eurocentrism, with the assumption that "they" represent the entire Muslim world that needs to replicate the Western historical process. The Briton was safely camped back in "the US-led side," which doesn't have the patience to wait for change over there. So his rhetorical "what are we to do?" is given a clear answer: "violence must come; America must have catharsis," thus appearing both empathetic and justificatory. But "we would hope that the response will be, above all, non-escalatory." Here, the "we" is really "he," his own opinion, which appears for the first time in the first person, a kind of Eliasian reversal. Did speaking as "I" simply feel too lonely? Was the "we" a retreat into some kind of collective security? Amis actually offered a novel idea, that the Afghanis not be bombarded with missiles but with consignments of food, a practice that was indeed followed during the Afghan war, even if the contents were ready meals for GIs and not the rice that Afghanis eat.

In the final paragraph, Amis then suggested that "our best destiny, as planetary cohabitants" is the development of "species consciousness—something over and above nationalisms, blocs, religions, ethnicities." And Amis tried to apply this: "Thinking of the victims, the perpetrators, and the near future, I felt species grief, then species shame, then species fear." Thus, in a literary but convoluted manner, Amis finally addressed the very nature of collectivities and what "we" all share in common, and he did so in a voice that sounded much like Elias's civilizational reach extending over old boundaries. To do this, Amis detoured through at least eleven ambiguous usages of "we" that suggest a profound disturbance to a clear identity position.

Deborah Moggach is also a prolific novelist whose titles include *To Have and To Hold*, *Tulip Fever*, and *Final Demand*. Her piece (October 27th) was entitled "Cares of the World—How Should Individuals Respond At A Time Of Crisis?" (http://www.guardian.co.uk/Archive/Article/0,4273,4286332,00.html).

Yet, in her first sentence, instead of the individual "I" of the title, an uncertain groupishness was invoked: "In these strange times, we've all become hypochondriacs, charting our symptoms day by day." Overly dramatic, instead of drawing this particular reader in, this sentence triggered instead the internal response "no, I have not." In a three-page article she used "we" no less than twenty-six times (let alone "our" and other derivatives) in often vague invocations of audience segments to be inferred from the sentence or line of argument. Deixis works when it is clear, when the meanings are well-established; as with Amis, the mixed direction of pronoun use suggests the confusion of the moment. For example, "We're all caught up in the same narrative and we're learning together—both about our own psyches and about things of which a few weeks ago we were entirely ignorant." If this was supposed to invoke the nation, it presumed that "we" knew little before about Islam, or Middle East politics, thus constructing the national audience as essentially Christian and white. There was no sense of a multicultural nation.

A similar tone was struck in the next paragraph: "We're stupefied by the bizarre nature of it all—for instance, that somebody who can't spell penicillin can send the whole of America into panic; that even with our sophisticated media and a thousand TV channels, the one thing we can't see is what we're doing in Afghanistan." Here the "other," the culprit whose name is not spoken, is seen as illiterate, quite opposite to his construction by Amis as a highly prescient structural engineer. But the commonality was recourse to the simple personification that helped politically drive the adventure into Afghanistan: Al Qaeda is Osama bin Laden (as Iraq is Saddam, as Iran was Khomeini). Synecdoche and personalization are common tropes of journalistic practice (see, for example, Zelizer's 1992 detailed exposition in relation-ship to the Kennedy assassination); that they run so powerfully through these individual columns shows how hard it is even for the most imaginative of writers to think "outside the frame." That individualized pieces of writing should echo the dominant political frames of the day is perhaps not a surprise; but "we" (academics?) don't often get a chance to see this happening so clearly.

Moggach's theme was about "our own helplessness," exacerbated because "we cannot identify the enemy." This echoed arguments from within International Relations about the blinkered nature of state-centric politics (Walker, 1993): if this was not a nation acting, then what was the political animal with whom "we" had to deal?

But the helplessness here was not really political; it was writers unable to write, Moggach admitting that she would be paralyzed if she were in the middle of a writing project. Part of her problem was the ever-shifting story: "And the process of bereavement we've all (*sic*) been going through has its rhythms too: already we are different people from the stunned TV audience watching the towers explode, from the people a day later who flinched when a plane passed overhead, from the people a week later in a state of shock and sadness. We can hardly recognise those early selves, let alone the selves that preceded them and went about their daily business before September 11." This evoked a dramatic overidentification with the events in New York. What was interesting in Moggach's piece was that the ties that bind "us" were never articulated but presumed, a simplistic elision into Westerners, English-speakers, metropolitan city-dwellers, middle-class, white. But again, if "we" was multicultural Britain, then how sustainable was the presumption that "we" were more moved by this event than by the numerous other violent episodes happening around the world during this period?

The risks of everyday life particularly upset Moggach, and so the piece shifted gear to the personal: "we went to a cinema in Piccadilly only to find that it was full. So we changed our plans and went to another." Here the "we" is presumably family and/or friends; again, the felt lack of need to explain is significant. There had been rumors of an attack on London, and the chance and randomness of modern life was suddenly acutely felt but almost immediately denied: "fanatics need hold no terror for us because it's always been like this. Ultimately they are as helpless as we are. Chance can conspire against us, but it can also save our lives." Here is a more ambigu-ous "us," possibly still personal but evoking the national. Moggach enter-tains no political rationale for the events of 9/11, and here in the piece she erases its existence as a motivated act. Instead, acts of nature and acts of fanatics are all incoherently random. "And in these peculiar and most inter-esting days, perhaps there's a comfort in that." An odd kind of fatalism settles in, one more in tune with fundamentalist teleology than modernist sentiment, a reduction to the helplessness described in the text.

The third and last text was an editorial comment from the *Observer*, the Sunday twin of *The Guardian*, which produced a special supplement "9/11 Six Months On" (10 March 2002) http://www.guardian.co.uk/Archive/Article/0,4273,4286332,00.html.

Again, "we" was used twelve times in a short column. The article began: "The moment the first plane hit the first tower we wanted to know: Why had this happened? What would the future bring? Who was safe?" But exactly who experienced this epistemophilic drive? All Westerners? All Britons? All *Observer* readers? The *Observer* staff? The Editor manifesting the royal "we"? Clearly the invitation was that the readers of this issue read themselves into this position. But the column recognized the passing of time and the fading urgency of the questions. "Because the centre held. Things did not fall apart. Chaos was not unleashed upon the world" (making obvious waves toward Yeats, Achebe, and the Bible). The powerful fear that gripped "us" in mid-September subsided. And "our" world was not altered so radically:

> We are not at war. Bombs are not exploding on the streets of British cities. There is no blackout. There are no no-go zones. We go to work, we go out, we go home, we take holidays, we sleep and we eat. And when we look out of the window we can see, with our own eyes, what appears to be a simple truth. Life as we know it did not end of September 11.

This was a fascinating paragraph for a number of reasons. At the time of its writing, some two hundred Royal Marines were based in Afghanistan, a fact noted lower down on the very same page. And although perhaps not formally at war, the Western military machine was still very much involved in violent incidents inside Afghanistan. Because "we" Britons were safe in our cities, that did not make the Afghans safe in theirs, and not declaring this a war, politically or discursively, allowed for weasel maneuvers. There was also accumulating evidence that British Muslims felt less at ease than before September 11, not least because of the domestic violence and bigotry unleashed against them, yet their experience did not seem to factor into this account. From a different tack, the economic downturn, rising unemployment, and the negative impact on aviation and travel from September 11 all raised doubt as to whether or not all middle-class *Observer* readers were getting to work or taking holidays. And yet there emerged an important distinction between the early rhetoric surrounding the event and a more tempered perspective now, six months later, underscored in a critical recognition of "the dramatic extension of American military might across the globe."

The "we" of Western modernists appalled at this outrage splits back into its national constituencies.

The over-easy elision of all Britons into the social and economic mores of *Observer* readers is harder to swallow. Indeed, further down the column, recognition was made of "subtle changes to our culture, our politics, our lifestyles," yet what these changes are was not clarified or explored. The column ended by suggesting that "the questions we (Britons? Observer journalists? Middle-class Observer readers?) were asking six months ago—about Islam, (are no readers Moslem?) security, the law, globalization, poverty, business, America, international finance—are as important now as they were then. And the answers are more important than ever." To that one might add many other important questions, about ethical foreign policy, about new strategies for the Middle East, the global arms race, or Britain's role in Europe vis-à-vis the United States.

CONCLUSION

The importance of the Amis and Moggach pieces is the sense they gave of ordinary (British) responses to events. Oddly, if each had been written in the singular personal pronoun, there would have been less to say about them. It is precisely the claims to shared experience that they made through their shifting "we" that was problematic. Their very rawness and immediacy provided a powerful indication of the way discourses about the self and feelings are imbricated with hegemony, how political discourses are taken up in private imaginings, here made public. If regular fact-based journalism helps configure and confirm our views of the world, the Comments pages filled by writers shows the extent to which these views have been taken up. In this sense Rorty (1989) is correct to point us to a wider range of voices, including the fictional, that all partake of a conversation about the nature of politics. It is ironic that two novelists, who summon up the contingency of social life in their fictional work, inhabit a far more rigidified socioscape in their personal voices.

I recognize a contradiction between the demand for a more affective public sphere, or one that better balances head and heart in human affairs, and a quick dismissal of its content. It was positive for *The Guardian* to solicit and publish such writing, and indeed its Comments pages remain relatively open and discursive. The authors, too, took risks in publishing such raw material. Being critical about such texts is a way of taking them seriously and accepting their role in a more open universe of journalistic forms. It seems important to accept the validity of affect but also to challenge its origins.

In all cases, the act of splitting off refused a relational politics. For Amis and Moggach, the "other" was fanatical, mad, "evil," but nothing to do with "us." It seems that in times of trauma, there is a powerful need to invoke the "we," to reclaim trust and build attachment. However, Sennett (1998, pp. 136-138) has called it "the dangerous pronoun" and describes how the "we" of attachment to community can also become the defensive weapon for self-protection. Additionally, Elias helps to recognize the shifting "others" that a culture and individuals experience over the course of time. Both Amis and Moggach moved back and forth through a register of "we" constructions, multiple yet inexplicitly articulated connections to others, neither a simple national consciousness nor always a "syntax of hegemony," although that deictic register was certainly apparent at times.

The particular nature of 9/11 summoned up the ambivalences of the nation-state system and its difficulties in fully addressing nonstate actors. Over time, also, the over-identification with America/New York gave way to a more detached and critical discussion, with different national interests and political cultures recovering their voice. Indeed, in Britain, the political environment in early spring of 2002 was one of growing anti-American sentiment, a long way from the universalization of American grief of only six months before. *The Observer's* position reclaimed the British audience, albeit in a problematic construction of its own.

The discursive structuring of affect and attachment implied an ethics, what is allowed to happen to others and to us. This suggests that Baumann's challenge remains:

> [A] post-modern ethics would be one that readmits the Other as a neighbour, as the close-to-hand-and-mind, into the hard core of the moral self . . . an ethics that restores the autonomous moral significance of proximity; an ethics that recasts the Other as the crucial character in the process through which the moral self comes into its own. (Baumann, 1993, p. 84)

The challenge is one of recognition. These articles suggest not only the difficulty of beginning to think of "the terrorist" in this way but, more urgently perhaps, the ongoing difficulty of recognizing our own neighbors, some "others" who live next door, as people with whom some things are shared but who may also have different yet equally valid constructions of the world.

The voices of Amis and Moggach might be taken to represent "our" British common sense that is deeply impregnated with cultural categorizations and they repeat the deeper "civilizational" divides that Western audiences have been invited to inhabit for a very long time. The doxic, toxic, truth, is that "we" do think of "ourselves" as different from "them" and the content of that we/they divide remains quite fixed, and post 9/11, even reinforced. 9/11 showed that both the realities and the theorizing, around "compassion fatigue" and "states of denial" and indifference to "distant suffering" are profoundly Westcentric constructions. Writing by British public intellectuals about 9/11 reveals the difficulties "we" currently experience in trying to determine the inside and the outside and the constructions used to define who "we" are and how "we" think about "them."

NOTES

1. This particular mode of deictics draws upon the specific set of categories and patterns of use of British English; exploration of the deixis of non-European languages that often use more differentiated and complex modes of address would be fruitful.
2. This appears to work in a manner opposite to Barthes' (1973) argument of "exnomination" whereby the characteristics of the speaker are not announced, a possibly more subtle linguistic usage. But, of course, one practice does not rule out the other.

REFERENCES

Appadurai, A. (1990, Spring). Disjuncture and difference in the global cultural economy. *Public Culture, 2*(2), 1-24.

Anderson, B. (1983). *Imagined communities*. London: Verso.

Barthes, R. (1973). Myth. In R. Barthes, *Mythologies*. London: Paladin.

Baumann, Z. (1993). *Post-modern ethics*. Cambridge: Polity.

Billig, M. (1995). *Banal nationalism*. London: Sage.

Blackman, L. & Walkerdine, V. (2001). *Mass hysteria*. Houndmills, Basingstoke, Hampshire, UK & New York: Palgrave.

Boltanski, L. (1999). *Distant suffering*. Cambridge: Cambridge University Press.

Cairncross, F. (2001). *The death of distance*. Boston: Harvard Business School Press.

Cohen, S. (2001). *States of denial*. Cambridge: Polity.

Giddens, A. (1990). *The consequences of modernity*. Stanford: Stanford University Press.

Harre, R. (1991). The discursive production of selves. *Theory and Psychology, 1*, 51-64.

Hartley, J. (1992). *Teleology*. London: Routledge.

Hobsbaum, E. & Ranger, T. (1983). *The invention of tradition*. Cambridge: Cambridge University Press.

Klein, M. (1957). *Envy and gratitude and other works*. London: Hogarth.

Mennell, S. (1992). *Norbert Elias*. Dublin: University College Dublin Press.

Mennell, S. (1994). The formation of we-images: A process theory. In C. Calhoun (Ed.), *Social theory and the politics of identity.* London: Blackwell.

Moeller, S. D. (1999). *Compassion fatigue.* London: Routledge.

Rorty, R. (1989). *Contingency, irony, solidarity.* Cambridge: Cambridge University Press.

Sennett, R. (1998). *The corrosion of character.* New York: W. W. Norton and Co.

Sreberny, A. (2002). Trauma talk: Reconfiguring the inside and the outside. In B. Zelizer & S. Allen (Eds.), *Journalism after September 11.* London: Routledge.

Walker, R. B. J. (1993). *Inside/outside: International relations as political theory.* Cambridge: Cambridge University Press.

Winnicott, D. W. (1971). *Playing and reality.* City: Pelican.

Zelizer, B. (1992). *Covering the body: The Kennedy assassination, the media, and the shaping of collective memory.* Chicago: University of Chicago Press.

PART II

LONG BEFORE SEPTEMBER 11— MEDIA COVERAGE OF POLITICAL VIOLENCE

Some Historical Perspectives

Chapter 4

When Worlds Collide

Reporting the Realities of Hiroshima

Stuart Allan

> Words can be just as destructive as any weapon.
>
> Charles W. Sweeney, U.S.A.F. (Ret.), participant in the
> atomic bombings of Hiroshima and Nagasaki (1997)

In this so-called post–Cold War age, nuclear weapons are widely credited with having helped to "keep the peace" for over sixty years. Certain preferred discourses regarding how this peace was ostensibly achieved in the Second World War are well known, and seemingly above dispute by reasonable people. To this day the decisive role attributed to the atomic bomb in bringing the war to a close is readily reaffirmed across an array of popular media contexts. Not only do these discourses register in news and documentary texts, they have also been taken up and re-inflected in novels, cinema, television drama, pop songs and school textbooks, among other media (see Bartter, 1988; Bird & Lifschultz, 1998; Boyer, 1985; Halleck, 1998; Newman, 1999; Weart, 1988). It is my contention, however, that these nuclearist discourses recurrently help to legitimize, to varying degrees, a normalized rationality of political violence.

Typically, nuclearist discourses about the atomic destruction of Hiroshima and Nagasaki adhere to a remarkably consistent narrative frame from one media context to the next. Usually taken for granted is the claim that the atomic bombings were undertaken reluctantly, but with the confident expectation that they would bring about a quicker end to the conflict. Japanese military, political, and religious elites, it is alleged, would never have agreed to the U.S. government's terms of surrender otherwise. The atomic bomb, by this logic, deserves to be credited with saving thousands of Allied soldiers' lives by making the potential invasion of mainland Japan unnecessary. This narrative frame, invoked as self-evident "common sense" by President Harry Truman and his officials at the time, was only rarely called into question in a sustained manner in the months following the war (Boyer, 1985; Lifton & Mitchell, 1995). One opinion survey after another asserted that among members of the U.S. public, "the great majority felt that the bombs had been justly used (and a substantial minority were sorry that more had not been dropped before the Japanese had a chance to surrender)" (Weart, 1988, p. 107). Voices seeking to challenge the morality of Truman's fateful decision to allow the bombings, then, routinely found themselves positioned as being outside of the ideological limits of the apparent "nuclear consensus."

My aim in this chapter is to contribute to the difficult work of rendering problematic the "common sense" imperatives informing efforts to construct this "nuclear consensus" in the immediate aftermath of the atomic bombings. Specifically, attention will focus on two particularly consequential journalistic engagements with the human suffering associated with the atomic bombings. It will be shown that the reportage of Wilfred Burchett for the London *Daily Express*, and that of John Hersey for the *New Yorker* magazine, profoundly challenged the nuclearist assumptions underpinning the proclaimed rationality of officially sanctioned truth-claims.[1] Of particular importance here, I shall argue, was the extent to which their reports helped to give voice to the experiences of the *hibakusha* (literally, "explosion-affected persons") still alive in the shattered city of Hiroshima. In attempting to draw the world's attention to their plight, both Burchett and Hersey endeavored to place a human face on official statistics regarding the atomic obliteration of the city's inhabitants. In so doing, their writings contributed to the eventual emergence of a counternarrative over the years, namely one that sought to redefine the atomic bombings as horrific acts of political violence.

THE ATOMIC PLAGUE

The headline of *The New York Times* on 7 August, 1945, spanning the width of the front-page, declared:

FIRST ATOMIC BOMB DROPPED ON JAPAN;
MISSILE IS EQUAL TO 20,000 TONS OF TNT;
TRUMAN WARNS FOE OF A 'RAIN OF RUIN'

Beneath several subtitles, the news item—filed by Sidney Shalett and date-lined Washington, 6 August—began with the lead:

> The White House and War Department announced today that an atomic bomb, possessing more power than 20,000 tons of TNT, a destructive force equal to the load of 2,000 B-29's and more than 2,000 times the blast power of what previously was the world's most devastating bomb, had been dropped on Japan.
>
> The announcement, first given to the world in utmost solemnity by President Truman, made it plain that one of the scientific landmarks of the century had been passed, and that the "age of atomic energy," which can be a tremendous force for the advancement of civilization as well as for destruction, was at hand. (*The New York Times*, 7 August 1945)

No details regarding the bombing's effects were presented in the account. "What happened at Hiroshima is not yet known," Shalett noted, before quoting an unnamed source from the War Department that it "as yet was unable to make an accurate report" because "an impenetrable cloud of dust and smoke" had "masked the target area." In the absence of information about Hiroshima, the news item turned to the first test of the atomic bomb in New Mexico, three weeks earlier, to describe "this terrible new weapon."

In the following days, Hiroshima—and with it Nagasaki, following its obliteration—promptly receded from newspaper headlines. Indeed, *The New York Times* reporting of the "atom bomb loosed on Nagasaki" on 9 August was overshadowed by the Soviet Union's declaration of war on Japan, which received far more extensive coverage. While press attention about the atomic bombings waned, much of that which did appear was driven by press releases from the War Department.[2] Typically these items focused on such matters as the history of the Manhattan Project, the design and manufacture of the bombs, and the biographical details of those closely involved. Much was also made of the possible industrial applications of "the basic power of the universe," with many news items heralding the "new era of power" to be ushered in by atomic (or "cosmic" in some accounts) energy. For U.S. military officials anxious to sustain what was evidently overwhelming public approval for the atomic bombings, then, the question of how best to "manage" news reports about the horrific aftermath of the attacks was difficult to resolve. Given that in all likelihood it would be just a matter of time before Western journalists attempted to visit the devastated cities, a decision was taken to organize a carefully screened group of four

U.S. journalists who could be trusted to reproduce faithfully official definitions of the realities they would confront.

On 3 September, this authorized delegation of U.S. reporters (along with an official censor) was flown into Hiroshima from Washington. The reporters were from the *New York Herald Tribune, The New York Times,* the *Associated Press,* and *United Press,* respectively, along with photographers from the U.S. Strategic Bomb Survey. The Pentagon ensured that members of the team would be accompanied at all times by military spokespeople and press officers, who determined what the reporters were able to see and provided them with an array of papers outlining the facts of the situation in accordance with the government's perspective. Moreover, the Manhattan Project's deputy commander, Brigadier General Thomas D. Farrell, together with a group of its physicists, were on hand to explain the scientific principles involved in the atomic bomb technology. Only some of the reporters were experienced war correspondents, thereby making the task of ensuring their co-operation that much easier to achieve. Evidently little effort was made to resist the controlling influence of the officials shepherding them around the ruins of Hiroshima, not least because the promise of their guaranteed "scoop" hung in the balance.

The "official line" on Hiroshima from Washington revolved around the perceived necessity of restricting reportage to the technological achievement of the atomic bomb itself, especially with regard to its tremendous destructive power on the urban infrastructure. Each member of the authorized delegation of reporters had been brought to Hiroshima in order to "report on the devastating power of America's new war-winning weapon," a task that most appeared content to fulfil. Certainly this appeared to have been the case with W.H. Lawrence of *The New York Times.* His first report, "Visit to Hiroshima Proves It World's Most-Damaged City," appeared in the 5 September edition of the newspaper. It described, at times vividly, the terrible scale of the destruction in the "flattened, rubble-strewn" city. It is Lawrence's second report, datelined Tokyo, 12 September 1945, that is more telling, however:

NO RADIOACTIVITY IN HIROSHIMA RUIN

Army Investigators Also Report Absence
Of Ground Fusing—68,000 Buildings Damaged

By W.H. Lawrence (By Wireless to The New York Times)

Brig. Gen T.F. Farrell, chief of the War Department's atomic bomb mission, reported tonight after a survey of blasted Hiroshima that the explosive power of the secret weapon was greater even than its inventors envisaged, but he denied categorically that it produced a dangerous, lingering radioactivity in the ruins of the town or caused a form of poison gas at the moment of explosion. . . .

He said his group of scientists found no evidence of continuing radioactivity in the blasted area on Sept. 9 when they began their investigations, and said it was his opinion that there was no danger to be encountered by living in the area at present. . . .

"The physical destruction in the target area was practically complete," he reported. "The scene was one of utter devastation. The total number of destroyed and damaged buildings was 68,000, or somewhere between 80 and 90 per cent of all buildings in the city. . . ." (*The New York Times*, 13 September 1945)

Radioactivity, Lawrence reports Farrell as stating, had occurred only "in a limited area whose geographical extent he would not estimate," and "this exclusively at the moment of the explosion." Farrell's insistence that that was "no evidence of continuing radioactivity in the blasted area," like his assertion that there was no danger for those living in the area, passed unchallenged by Lawrence.[3]

Also arriving in Hiroshima on 3 September, however, was Wilfred Burchett, an Australian journalist in the employ of London's *Daily Express* newspaper. Self-described as a "maverick" who regarded the activities of the "select party of housetrained reporters" with some contempt, Burchett intended to file a report from the epicentre below where the bomb exploded. To do so, he knew all too well, was to openly defy official restrictions. Still, in his words, he "reported what I had seen and heard, while [Lawrence] sent back a prefabricated report reflecting the 'official line'" (Burchett, 1983, p. 17). Anger and resentment over Burchett's presence from both the officials and rival reporters, however, ensured that he was refused transport back to Tokyo with the U.S. Air Force charter aircraft. Similarly, his request that a copy of his report be passed on to his *Daily Express* colleague at press headquarters in Tokyo was also denied by an official. Little did he know, moreover, that further steps would be taken to block his efforts to report on what he had witnessed in Hiroshima. As Burchett (1983, p. 16) later observed, "I had no inkling that in writing what I did, I was taking on the US military and political establishment."

News accounts like those prepared by the members of the authorized press delegation demonstrated to Burchett just how far his own reporting had strayed from the "official line." Indeed, as he wrote, "I was forced to recognize the existence of an official policy to suppress accurate reportage of the terrible after-effects of nuclear war" (1983, p. 9). Certainly the realities of life in Hiroshima after the atomic attack, as he witnessed them, bore little resemblance to the depictions typically presented elsewhere in the newspaper press. Burchett's own dispatch from 3 September (bylined "Peter" rather than Wilfred), published by the *Daily Express* two days later, took up most of the front page and a large portion of a page within. It began as follows:

THE ATOMIC PLAGUE

"I Write This as a Warning to the World"
DOCTORS FALL AS THEY WORK
Poison gas fear: All wear masks
Express Staff Reporter, Peter Burchett

In Hiroshima, thirty days after the first atomic bomb destroyed the city and shook the world, people are still dying, mysteriously and horribly—people who were uninjured in the cataclysm—from an unknown something which I can only describe as the atomic plague.

Hiroshima does not look like a bombed city. It looks as if a monster steamroller has passed over it and squashed it out of existence. I write these facts as dispassionately as I can, in the hope that they will act as a warning to the world.

In this first testing ground of the atomic bomb I have seen the most terrible and frightening desolation in four years of war. It makes a blitzed Pacific island seem like an Eden. The damage is far greater than photographs can show.

When you arrive in Hiroshima you can look around for twenty-five and perhaps thirty square miles you can see hardly a building. It gives you an empty feeling in the stomach to see such man-made destruction. . . . (*Daily Express*, 5 September 1945)

The newspaper account continued with a description of the damage in the remains of the city. Burchett described how the police chief of Hiroshima took him, along with the local manager of the Japanese news agency *Domei*, to visit those hospitals still able to treat survivors of the attack:

In these hospitals I found people who, when the bomb fell, suffered absolutely no injuries but now are dying from the uncanny after-effects.

For no apparent reasons their health began to fail. They lost appetite. Their hair fell out. Bluish spots appeared on their bodies. And then bleeding began from the ears, nose and mouth.

At first, the doctors told me, they thought these were the symptoms of general debility. They gave their patients Vitamin A injections. The results were horrible. The flesh started rotting away from the hole caused by the injection of the needle. And in every case the victim died.

That is one of the after-effects of the first atomic bomb man ever dropped and I do not want to see any more examples of it. . . .

The counted dead number 53,000. Another 30,000 are missing which means certainly dead. In the day I have stayed in Hiroshima, 100 people have died from its effects. They were some of the 13,000 seriously injured by the explosion. They have been dying at the rate of 100 a day. And they will probably all die. Another 40,000 were slightly injured. (*Daily Express*, 5 September 1945)

These figures, as Burchett (1983) later acknowledged in his book *Shadows of Hiroshima,* were provisional, based on information from the police at the time that would later be revised upwards of 130,000. "At the time," he pointed out, "there was obviously no way of estimating how many victims lay under the ashes nor how many would die soon after from the effects of radiation" (1983, p. 121).

The U.S. military's reaction to Burchett's report had far-reaching repercussions. Burchett attributed the delay of nine days in *The New York Times'* publication of Lawrence's account from Hiroshima to how "the nuclear chiefs and their public relations men fumbled with their gears, eventually deciding to mount a counter-offensive to disprove the existence of radiation sickness or any causes of death other than blast and burns" (1983, p. 44). The official denial of Burchett's report (dismissed as "Japanese propaganda") was quickly followed by a declaration making Hiroshima off limits to journalists. Back in Tokyo, Burchett was taken to a U.S. Army hospital for tests, where it was found that his white corpuscle count was down, attributed by the hospital authorities to the antibiotics he had used to treat a knee infection. A drop in white corpuscles, he later learned, "is a typical phenomenon of radiation sickness" (1983, p. 23). Burchett speculated that the real reason he was taken to a military hospital so promptly was to ensure that he was isolated from other journalists who might have reported his descriptions of the "atomic plague" as he had witnessed it. In any case, when he was discharged from the hospital, he discovered that his camera with its full roll of photographs taken in Hiroshima had been stolen. To make matters worse, he was then informed that U.S. General MacArthur had withdrawn his press accreditation and issued an order for his immediate expulsion from Japan (an action which Burchett was later able to have rescinded).

New restrictions were placed on all Allied journalists, including a revised press code that imposed prior censorship on any item concerned with the human aftermath of the atomic attacks. Evidently this prohibition curtailed the publication of reports discussing how to treat survivors suffering from atomic bomb–related symptoms. It also served to halt news about the *hibakusha* emerging from Nagasaki. There George Weller of the Chicago *Daily News* had slipped away from his military escort on a guided tour elsewhere to board a train to the city to see for himself what had happened (like Burchett, he later expressed his dismay with the other reporters — "the conformists" — covering only officially approved stories; cited in Lifton & Mitchell 1995, p. 50). The only Western reporter in the city, he filed a lengthy news account, including observations made in hospitals about the dead and dying (taking due care to avoid, in his words, "all horror angles"). This report, duly forwarded by Weller to MacArthur's press headquarters in Tokyo for clearance and transmission, was never to appear in print.

A NOISELESS FLASH

"At exactly fifteen minutes past eight in the morning, on August 6, 1945, Japanese Time, at the moment when the atomic bomb flashed above Hiroshima, Miss Toshiko Sasaki, a clerk in the personnel department of the East Asia Tin Works, had just sat down at her place in the plant office and was turning her head to speak to the girl at the next desk." So begins John Hersey's (1946) journalistic account, titled "Hiroshima," which made up the entire issue of the weekly *New Yorker* magazine for 31 August, 1946. The opening paragraph continues, identifying five more residents of Hiroshima and describing what they were doing at the precise moment of the atomic cataclysm. Introduced, in turn, are Dr Masakazu Fujii, a physician reading his newspaper on a hospital porch; Hatsuyo Nakamura, a widowed seamstress looking out of her kitchen window; Father Wilhelm Kleinsorge, a German priest reading a Jesuit magazine; Dr Terufumi Sasaki, a young doctor walking the corridors of a hospital carrying a blood specimen; and the Reverend Kiyoshi Tanimoto, a pastor of the Hiroshima Methodist Church unloading a handcart full of objects that required safekeeping from a possible air raid.

The lives of each of these individuals immediately before, during and after the explosion of the atomic bomb over their city constitute the principal focus of Hersey's account. Adopting a journalistic style which calmly details facts virtually bereft of emotional comment—far too calmly, in the opinion of some critics—he succeeds in the considerable achievement, as one historian writes, of "transforming the subhuman 'Japs' of wartime propaganda back into Japanese: human beings who loved their children, bled when they were cut, and spent their time in life's ordinary routines" (Boyer, 1985, p. 208). Commissioned by the *New Yorker* to prepare the essay for publication to mark the passing of a year from the time of the atomic attack, Hersey spent three weeks interviewing as many of the surviving *hibakusha* as he could manage. In electing to interweave the voices of six of them into the "Hiroshima" essay, the necessary conditions were at last being created whereby their solemn testimonies could be heard by members of the U.S. public. Reactions among readers of the *New Yorker* immediately sparked a nationwide controversy that led, in turn, to the essay being re-released in book form, in which it promptly became a best-seller. "Hiroshima" was also read in several installments over the ABC radio network, subsequently winning the Peabody award for the outstanding educational broadcast of 1946.

Much of the "Hiroshima" essay is devoted to documenting the desperate struggle of the *hibakusha* to grasp the incomprehensible magnitude of the city's obliteration. Each of the six individuals interviewed by Hersey attempted, in his or her own way, to come to terms not only with the death of over one hundred thousand of their city's inhabitants, but with his or her own survival. As Hersey (1946, p. 2) observes:

> They still wonder why they lived when so many others died. Each of them counts many small items of chance or volition—a step taken in time, a decision to go indoors, catching one streetcar instead of the next—that spared him. And now each knows that in the act of survival he lived a dozen lives and saw more death than he ever thought he would see.

The *pikadon* or "flash-boom" of the atomic bomb occurred at 8:15 am as it detonated about 1,800 feet above the courtyard of Shima Hospital (so timed to increase the radius of the blast). The central section of the city was full of people beginning their morning routines, with many more, including thousands of school children, working to raze houses in order to prepare firebreaks in the event of an incendiary attack. An air raid alert about an hour earlier had been called off following the departure of a B-29 (a weather plane), so few paid much attention to three more B-29s approaching the city. The searing white flash of the detonation was blinding, for many people literally so, and for those near the epicentre evidently soundless. A firestorm was ignited that swept through what was left of the city (due to the convection set up by the blazing wreckage), sparing little in its path. "Boiling dust" and smoke were lifted into the air, returning in the form of radioactive "black rain" as the smoldering ruins of Hiroshima were plunged into darkness (Feis, 1966; Powaski, 1987; Rhodes, 1986).

"Why is it night already?" the children were asking. "Why did our house fall down? What happened?" These questions, Hersey (1946, p. 19) writes, were difficult for Hatsuyo Nakamura to answer. Equally bewildered by what "had happened (had not the all-clear sounded?), [she] looked around and saw through the darkness that all of the houses in her neighbourhood had collapsed" (1946, pp. 19-20). Meanwhile Dr Masakazu Fujii was discovering that the remnants of his hospital had been overturned into the Kyo River. Nearby, at the Red Cross Hospital, Dr Terufumi Sasaki was the only doctor situated there to escape injury. According to the evidence gathered by Hersey, it was becoming all too apparent why so many of Hiroshima's citizens would not receive the treatment they required to live: "Of a hundred and fifty doctors in the city," he writes, "sixty-five were already dead and most of the rest were wounded. Of 1,780 nurses, 1,654 were dead or too badly hurt to work" (1946, p. 24). The Red Cross hospital's patients were dying by the hundreds, their wounds left untended. At least ten thousand more victims were making their way to the hospital, widely regarded as the best in the city. Dr Sasaki, having replaced his missing glasses with those belonging to a now incapacitated nurse, set about attempting to alleviate suffering as best he could. Moving his way through the hospital corridors, he tried to develop some sort of treatment strategy for those he encountered: "Wounded people supported maimed people; disfigured families leaned together" (1946, p. 25). Crushed into a suffocating crowd, people wept and cried for help.

Outside the *hibakusha* staggered through the debris of Hiroshima in states of extreme shock. The Reverend Kiyoshi Tanimoto had been working near the outskirts of the city at the time of the explosion. Fearful for both his family and his church, he was one of the very few survivors to be making his way into the worst affected area. It seemed to him that every person he met along the way had been hurt in some manner:

> The eyebrows of some were burned off and skin hung from their faces and hands. Others, because of the pain, held their arms up as if carrying something in both hands. Some were vomiting as they walked. Many were naked or in shreds of clothing. On some undressed bodies, the burns had made patterns—of undershirt straps and suspenders and, on the skin of some women (since white repelled the heat from the bomb and dark clothes absorbed it and conducted it to the skin), the shapes of flowers they had had on their kimonos. Many, although injured themselves, supported relatives who were worse off. Almost all had their heads bowed, looked straight ahead, were silent, and showed no expression whatsoever. (Hersey, 1946, p. 29)

Briefly reunited with his family, Tanimoto then proceeded to make his way toward his church in order to help care for the people of his Neighborhood Association. Pausing to collect water in a basin to help relieve the thirst of the victims around him, he realized that he could help by ferrying people across a river away from the worst of the still-burning fires. Tragically, few of his efforts were successful: in one case, for example, he "reached down and took a woman by the hands, but her skin slipped off in huge, glovelike pieces" (1946, p. 45). Struggling to lift "the slimy living bodies" out of the water so as to carry them up the slope of the riverbank, Tanimoto kept repeating to himself, "These are human beings" over and over again.

Early the next day a Japanese radio broadcast provided a short announcement acknowledging the atomic assault: "Hiroshima suffered considerable damage as the result of an attack by a few B-29s. It is believed that a new type of bomb was used. The details are being investigated" (cited in Hersey, 1946, p. 49). Father Kleinsorge, like the city's other survivors, was too busy coping with the bomb's aftermath to be listening to the short-wave set. Using a bottle and a teapot, he was doing his best to fetch water for the wounded. Moving through the woods "he saw there were about twenty men, and they were all in exactly the same nightmarish state: their faces were wholly burned, their eyesockets were hollow, the fluid from their melted eyes had run down their cheeks" (1946, p. 51). Guessing that they must have had their faces upturned toward the source of the explosion, Kleinsorge noticed that their "mouths were mere swollen, pus-covered wounds, which they could not bear to stretch enough to admit the spout of the teapot" (1946, p. 52). Drawing the stem out of a large strand of grass, he quickly fashioned a straw for them to drink the water, before attempting to instill in them the hope that medical attention would be forthcoming. Whether or not these men eventually joined the thousands of inhabitants of the city who perished, Kleinsorge would never know for certain.

One year after the atomic attack, the future appeared grim for each of Hersey's six interviewees. In the concluding section of his essay, he writes: "Miss Sasaki was a cripple; Mrs Nakamura was destitute; Father Kleinsorge was back in the hospital; Dr Fujii had lost the thirty-room hospital it took him many years to acquire, and had no prospects of rebuilding it; Mr Tanimoto's church had been ruined and he no longer had his exceptional vitality" (1946, p. 87). Opinions among the group members about the use of the atomic bomb were not unanimous, although Hersey (1946, p. 87) points to their shared sense of pride in "the way they and their fellow survivors had stood up to a dreadful ordeal." In what can only be regarded as an extreme understatement, however, he observes that the "lives of these six people, who were among the luckiest in Hiroshima, would never be the same" (1946, p. 87).

EMERGING FROM THE SHADOWS

Life for the *hibakusha* in the years since the atomic attacks on Hiroshima and Nagasaki has been extremely difficult. Most have lived listless, broken lives, enduring medical symptoms that usually include chronic weakness and periods of intense lassitude (often making steady employment impossible). The lingering effects of radioactivity continue to this day, including in the bodies of those who were unborn in August 1945 but whose mothers were exposed to the after-effects. These people are prone to diseases and malformations (most notably leukemia and other cancers, microcephaly, tuberculosis, liver cirrhosis, and myopia, among many others) to a significantly higher extent than is prevalent in adjacent areas (see also Committee for the Compilation of Materials, 1981; Lifton, 1967). Compounding the ongoing tragedy of these medical conditions was the stigmatization of the *hibakusha* by those fearful of being somehow contaminated (literally or by association) in their presence. The Japanese Government refused to "recognize" the afflicted, choosing instead to ignore their pleas for assistance, in part because it "did not want to find itself saddled with anything like moral responsibility for heinous acts of the victorious United States" (Hersey, 1946, p. 92).[4]

In the United States, due in no small part to the efforts of journalists like Burchett and Hersey, official rationalizations regarding the use of the atomic weapons—and the denial of the existence of atomic radiation—were gradually undergoing more careful scrutiny. Still, the broad parameters marking the normative limits of public debate about the atomic attacks had largely taken shape by 1946. A particularly salient feature of popular perceptions, as discerned impressionistically by various opinion surveys, was the near-absence of publicly expressed remorse. Time and time again, these surveys claimed to show that the vast majority of American citizens considered the invention of the atomic bomb to have been a welcome development, hailing its use as a means to save the lives of Allied soldiers (see Hogan, 1996; Lifton & Mitchell, 1995). Examinations of media coverage during this period find little evidence of sustained critiques being presented, and where voices of dissent were advanced (even in such limited form as "letters to the editor" in newspapers) they often engendered extraordinarily hostile reactions (see Bird & Lifschultz, 1998; Boyer, 1985; Hammond, 1997; Weart, 1988). Such challenges to the emergent imperatives of what was rapidly evolving into a "nuclear consensus" among military, political, economic, scientific—and journalistic—elites were typically branded as being disloyal and unpatriotic, if not outright immoral, in their opposition.

By the end of 1946, then, the paradoxical logics of nuclearist discourses were fast becoming fused into official justifications not only for maintaining but for radically exacerbating the threat of human extinction in the interests of national security. The organizing tenets of what would evolve into a fully fledged doctrine of "nuclear deterrence" were being consolidated in ideological terms, not least on the front pages of the world's newspapers. Meanwhile, the shadows of the *hibakusha*, scorched into the ground of Hiroshima and Nagasaki by thermal flashes of radiation, slowly faded from view.

NOTES

1. Wilfred Burchett was born in Melbourne, Australia in 1911. His work as a freelance journalist began in 1940 in New Caledonia, a French colony in the Pacific, before he moved on to China, where he became a correspondent for the *Daily Express* of London. After the war, he lived and worked in several countries, including North Vietnam, Cambodia, the Soviet Union, and France. He died in Sofia, Bulgaria, in 1983. John Hersey was born in Tientsin, China in 1914. His family returned to the U.S. in 1925. He later studied at Yale, and worked as a secretary to Sinclair Lewis, before becoming a correspondent in the Far East for *Time* magazine. During the war, Hersey also wrote for *Life* magazine and the *New Yorker*. Afterwards, he turned to writing fiction in the main. He died in Florida in 1993.

2. A month after the attack on Pearl Harbor, the War Department (an executive department of the U.S. government, later renamed the Department of Defense) announced the accreditation of 115 correspondents to report news of developments in the Pacific area of operations. "All correspondents accredited to US forces," as Desmond (1984, p. 238) observes, "were required to wear officers' uniforms, minus insignia of rank, but with a green brassard on the left arm designating the wearer as a 'War Correspondent.'" Each and every dispatch prepared by correspondents was subjected to official censorship prior to publication or broadcast. The Manhattan Project was the top-secret initiative, headed by U.S. General Leslie R. Groves, to build an atomic bomb. An international team of physicists and engineers was involved at several sites. The construction of the bomb took place under the direction of Robert J. Oppenheimer at Los Alamos, New Mexico. The first atomic bomb was detonated nearby, close to Alamogordo, on 16 July, 1945.

3. Similarly pertinent here was the previous day's edition of the *The New York Times*, as it included a delayed report from Lawrence's colleague (and near-namesake) William L. Laurence. The front-page story, headlined "US ATOM BOMB SITE BELIES TOKYO TALES," reported on Laurence's visit to the "atomic bomb range" in New Mexico where the "first atomic explosion on earth" had taken place on 16 July, 1945. In addition to listening to the "expert testimony" of atomic scientists, member of group of newspaper journalists and photographers witnessed for themselves the "readings on radiation meters carried by a group of radiologists" on the test site. Such evidence, Laurence reported in the account, provided "the most effective answer today to Japanese propaganda that radiations were responsible for deaths even after the day of the explosion, Aug. 6, and that persons entering Hiroshima had contracted mysterious maladies due to persistent radioactivity" (*The New York Times*, 12 September, 1945). More specifically, it was the absence of radioactivity at the testing range, Laurence maintained, that allowed the U.S. Army "to give the lie to these [Japanese] claims" about lingering radiation in Hiroshima and Nagasaki. Nowhere in this account is mention made of the fact that Laurence himself had been covertly working with the U.S. War Department.

   Laurence was effectively on loan from *The New York Times*, at the request of General Groves, to be the Manhattan Project's official military spokesperson regarding pertinent events in the atomic bomb's development. For four months he wrote under conditions of strictest secrecy, which only began to be lifted the morning of 7 August, when news of the bombing of Hiroshima was announced. "The world's greatest story was being broadcast," Laurence (1947) later recalled, "and mine had been the honor, unique in the history of journalism, of preparing the War Department's official press releases for world-wide distribution. No greater honor could have come to any newspaperman, or anyone else for that matter" (1947, p. 187; see also Laurence, 1946).

4. The numbers of the *hibakusha* would later expand to include those affected by the testing of a hydrogen bomb on the Bikini Atoll in the Marshall Islands by the United States military on 1 March, 1954. Radioactive ashes covered a Japanese fishing boat, named "Lucky Dragon," situated some 160 kilometers from the detonation. One member of the crew reportedly died soon after, and the others were stricken with radiation sickness. Vast expanses of the fishing areas were declared

off limits. Public outrage in Japan over this event helped to intensify the pressures being brought to bear on their government for improvements in the living conditions of the hibakusha. Since the 1970s, the organization of the *hibakusha* and their representatives into a national movement has led to their demands for fairness being addressed to a much improved, if still inadequate, extent.

REFERENCES

Bartter, M.A. (1988). *The way to ground zero: The atomic bomb in American science fiction.* New York: Greenwood Press.

Bird, K. & Lifschultz, L. (Eds.). (1998). *Hiroshima's shadows.* Stony Creek, CT: Pamphleteer's Press.

Boyer, P. (1985). *By the bomb's early light: American thought and culture at the dawn of the atomic age.* New York: Pantheon.

Burchett, W. (1983). *Shadows of Hiroshima.* London: Verso.

Committee for the Compilation of Materials on Damage Caused by the Atomic Bombs in Hiroshima and Nagasaki. (1981). *Hiroshima and Nagasaki: The physical, medical, and social effects of the atomic bombs.* London: Hutchinson.

Desmond, R.W. (1984). *Tides of war: World news reporting, 1931-1945.* Ames: University of Iowa Press.

Feis, H. (1966). *The atomic bomb and the end of the World War II.* Princeton, NJ: Princeton University Press.

Halleck, D. (1998). Perpetual shadows: Representing the atomic age. *Wide Angle, 20*(2), 70-76.

Hammond, P. (Ed.). (1997). *Cultural difference, media memories: Anglo-American images of Japan.* London: Cassell.

Hersey, J. (1946/1989). *Hiroshima.* New York: Vintage Books.

Hogan, M.J. (Ed.). (1996). *Hiroshima in history and memory.* Cambridge: Cambridge University Press.

Laurence, W.L. (1946). *Men and atoms.* London: Hodder and Stoughton.

Laurence, W.L. (1947). *Dawn over zero: The story of the atomic bomb.* London: Museum Press.

Lifton, R.J. (1967). *Death in life: The survivors of Hiroshima.* London: Weidenfeld and Nicolson.

Lifton, R.J. & Mitchell, G. (1995). *Hiroshima in America.* New York: Avon.

Newman, K. (1999). *Millennium movies: End of the world cinema.* London: Titan.

Powaski, R.E. (1987). *March to Armageddon: The United States and the nuclear arms race, 1939 to the present.* New York: Oxford University Press.

Rhodes, R. (1986). *The making of the atomic bomb.* New York: Touchstone/Simon and Schuster.

Sweeney, C.W., with Antonucci, J.A. & Antonucci, M.K. (1997). *War's end: An eyewitness account of America's last atomic mission.* New York: Avon.

Weart, S.R. (1988). *Nuclear fear: A history of images,* Cambridge, MA, and London: Harvard University Press.

Chapter 5

The Bosnian War in Spain

The Media's Representation of a Distant Violent Conflict

Teresa La Porte

APPROACHING THE CONCEPT OF POLITICAL VIOLENCE

There is a general consensus of opinion on what political violence is: it is when force is used to put pressure on the ruling authority with the aim of favoring interests of a political nature. However, this general definition allows for many clarifications and approaches. The relationship established between violent groups and the mass media and the dominance of one over the other is also open to interpretation. In this introduction the assumptions on which this research is based will be briefly outlined.

Most of current research literature identifies political violence with terrorism (Morrison et. al., 1999). However, the definition that we will use as our reference also includes many other types of violence covering a wide range of acts: those carried out by the armed forces—war or armed attacks (Giddens, 1985; Shaw, 1991)—and demonstrations or public protests in which shop windows are broken or street furniture is vandalized (Clutterbuck, 1981).

Logically, the social groups who use violence do so in the belief that it is the most effective way of attaining their objectives. These can be accomplished either immediately and decisively by, for example, the military occupation of a territory during a war or by violence used to coerce the political institutions by means of protests or acts threatening public safety, allowing the weakest to confront the strongest. In the case of the war in Bosnia, which is the object of this study, the two strategies were combined: armed force was deployed to achieve military objectives together with pressure exerted on international bodies by means of direct attacks on an undefended civilian population.

In both cases, the effectiveness of the use of coercion on political decisions means that there is a huge temptation to use force in the defence of self-interest. As Schlesinger states: "Without doubt, the analysis of violence ought to be central in social and political analysis, for we cannot discuss the ultimate foundations of state power without recognising how coercion and the use of force articulate with political consent" (Schlesinger, 1991, p. 1).

In any of the situations referred to, the use of force has an undoubted public effect and awakens the interest and attention of the social environment where it happens. It is targeted at the political authority, but with the sure knowledge that it is observed by public opinion which by supporting or condemning the use of force helps to turn up the pressure. In terrorist acts this intention is clear. In armed conflicts the military objectives may be the first priority but, as was shown in Bosnia, international public opinion also has an important function.

THE COVERAGE OF POLITICAL VIOLENCE IN THE MEDIA

The political dimension of acts of political violence place them in direct relation with the media (Mowlana, Gerbner, & Schiller, 1992; Mueller, 1973; Zaller, 1992). Even though they are not the means by which political violence is expressed, the media have become an essential element for violent groups because they guarantee the presence of their interests in the public arena and they channel the pressure that is aimed at political power.

However, the media do not act simply as transmitters and may increase or minimize the effectiveness of a violent act according to how they treat the story. The media shape the public opinion's perception of events and their protagonists (Entman, 1989; Glasser, 1984; Rosen, 1993; Tuchman, 1978) with two fundamental decisions: selection of the news story and how it is reported.

The media's function as gatekeeper means that they determine which issues the public should know about. In international news this function is reinforced, because very often the citizen does not have access to any other sources apart from newspaper and television. This is the first barrier that groups who use violence as a means of political pressure must overcome: to make sure they are selected out of all of the day's events. If the aim of overcoming this difficulty is what causes the aggression and the scope of the terrorist attacks, then the violence must be greater when it is aimed at an international audience. This was demonstrated once again by the attacks on the World Trade Center in New York.

On the other hand, depending on how a story is presented, the media can confer legitimacy on a group or an act or, on the contrary, discredit the arguments put forward and the resources used to defend them. The most important factor influencing how the story is dealt with is the newsroom's corporate identity. A journalist's personal opinion may have an influence on the approach to the facts but it is the newsroom, the medium itself, that establishes how a long-term conflict will be covered. In reporting on this type of conflict it is often the case that it is not one journalist but several who write up the story on a daily basis (Canel & Piqué, 1997; Shoemaker & Reese, 1991; Splichal & Sparks, 1994; Weaver & Wilhoit, 1991).

When covering distant conflicts, what is revealing is the different treatment given by the media depending on the extent to which they wish to involve their audiences. Taking Shaw's classification as a guide, the media can restrict themselves to describing the conflict by providing a portrayal of the conflict or they can advocate greater involvement, such as, for instance, defending human rights (Shaw, 1996). As will be seen later on, in the Spanish press an example of each one of these cases can be found.

The groups that use violence as a form of politics prefer the media to encourage the audience's involvement. To the extent that an audience takes sides, the group's aim of exerting pressure on public organs is attained. A more passive position, that of a mere spectator, means there is less chance to force the political will in their favor.

In this chapter we will study the Spanish media's coverage of the war in Bosnia as a case of news on a violent political conflict. The news produced about the NATO bombing of Sarajevo, which aimed to break the Serbian forces' siege, will be examined in detail. This event was significant both politically and from a news perspective. In its political dimension it spelled the end of the war and, because of its special relevance, the way it was concluded would create a decisive precedent for the definition of international order. From the news perspective, the coverage was an example of the Spanish media's behavior during the conflict.

Although in describing the general characteristics of international news data from television was used, the main conclusions are the result of the study of the two newspapers with the highest circulation in Spain, *El País* and *El Mundo*.

Decisions taken by the media that are evaluated in this study are those related to the treatment of the news and not to news selection. The latter is not of particular interest in a study dealing with one specific event.

How news is treated reflects the editorial line adopted by the medium. The stand it takes on any issue is indiscriminately expressed in its straight informative news and the opinions expressed in columns and editorials, or in equivalent spaces on the radio and TV. Although in the first case the editorial line is reflected by how the journalist selects the different resources to construct a text, it is in the second in which the medium's opinion is found more explicitly expressed. In Spain, a newspaper's editorial page has an important influence on the shaping of the general public opinion because the audio-visual media take it as a point of reference (Diezhandino et al., 1994; Santamaría, 1997).

How the different treatments contribute to define either a medium's advocacy standpoint or a passive one of portrayal will be specifically evaluated. The results have been obtained from an analysis of the quantitative and qualitative content. The first describes the general behavior of the Spanish media in international news. The qualitative analysis aimed to find out the journalistic devices that define the medium's stance in the news content and opinion.

THE SOCIAL CONCEPT
OF "POLITICAL VIOLENCE" IN SPAIN

The concept of "political violence" present in each nation's media is no more than a reflection of the way in which it is understood by its society. And societies shape their ideas according to their historical experience and their day-to-day reality. For this reason, it is important to bear in mind every country's idiosyncrasies in order to know what extra element must be added to the general concept, or how to frame the significance that is commonly accepted in political science. From this point of view, the comparison of how the media perform in different nations is an extremely enriching one.

In Spain, as in the rest of the countries in Western Europe, violence in any form is an illegitimate expression of aggression, and its capacity to act as an instrument of social communication is not accepted. Therefore, it is also rejected as a means of obtaining political goals (Delgado Ruiz, 1998). The only accepted violence is the use of force by the state or by organs delegated this function by the state. And even in this case, as has been shown in the

Spanish public opinion's reaction to the government's position on the conflict in Iraq, this power has its limitations, and an armed intervention or a police action is only accepted when it is the last available option, always and only to defend individual and collective security in proportion to the threat (Alvira, 1992).

The terrorist attack in Madrid on 11 March 2004 increased the pacifism of Spanish society. The attack was perpetrated by a fundamentalist Islamic group related to Al Qaeda. Several bombs blew up in different trains at the Atocha railway station and two others near Madrid at 7.35 am, rush hour in Spain. One hundred ninety-two people were killed and more than 1,600 injured. It was the most terrible event to occur in Europe in recent times—worse than the 7th of July attack in London—and the behavior of Spanish citizens has been quite remarkable, following the general pattern that was mentioned above. The popular reaction in those days, manifested again a year later during the first anniversary of the disaster, has had two key notes: first, to prioritize assistance and support to the victims and their families; and second, to eliminate the possible motive of the attack, which seemed to be the presence of the Spanish troops in Iraq. It led to the defeat of the Popular Party at the general elections of that year and later, to the withdrawal of the army from Iraq. Neither the ordinary citizens nor the media stimulated any vengeful response. The only aim was peace at all cost.

Therefore, political violence is not legitimized in every case. Those who use these means are usually "the others," those who are on the outside of social opinion and thought. In the coverage the media give to any manifestation of this type there is a more or less explicit perception of a condemnation of the groups, individuals, or states that use force to defend their aims. The image of social exclusion is also reinforced.

As well as social consensus, historical experience is also important to understand society's stance on political violence. In present-day Spain's case it is important to remember that it is a country marked by two violent conflicts: the Spanish Civil War, which lasted from 1936 to 1939, and the terrorist acts perpetrated by the Basque independent group, Euskadi Ta Askatasuna (ETA). Both conflicts took place and take place in Spanish territory and were caused by internal tensions: the first was of a political and military nature and the second has nationalistic and secessionist causes. The Spanish society has had direct experience of violence produced by these two conflicts, a list to which the experience of fundamentalist Islamic terrorism can now be added as well.

With respect to the Spanish Civil War, it can be stated that today it lives on in the memory of the old, and for the younger people it is a historical event relived in its anniversaries. However, during Franco's regime it divided Spanish society for forty years. Although the peaceful transition to democracy showed that the Spanish had managed to overcome antagonisms, these feelings are still significant enough for political parties to make political capital of them during electoral campaigns. In any case, it is true to say that they are no longer violent and they seem to be to disappearing.

However, the terrorist conflict has constantly plagued Spanish society from the late 1960s. ETA's terrorist attacks and actions carried out by fringe supporters, such as the so-called *kale borroka,* are the most direct reference to public manifestations of violence with direct consequences for human life and property. These are violent acts carried out by supporters of ETA. They are usually carried out by young adults under 20, and their aim is violent street protest with the destruction of urban property.

The terrorist phenomenon is also the cause of confrontations that go beyond what are directly the result of the armed group's attacks. A good example of this is the conflict generated among the political forces themselves. Political parties are divided depending on the strategy they consider most effective to deal with this problem: the pro-independence parties favor establishing a dialogue prior to a ceasefire; the centralists or "pro-constitutionalists" refuse to consider any kind of negotiations until there has been a complete surrendering of arms. They are called "pro-constitutionalist" because they justify their position by arguing that they follow the political principles on nationalism and independence contained in the Spanish Constitution. Political parties that belong to this group are Partido Popular (PP) and Partido Socialista Obrero Español (PSOE).

Another important factor to complete the outline of characteristics that define the concept of political violence in Spain is that the Spanish have had no involvement in a foreign conflict in the twentieth century. A different matter has been their role in the last decade in aid missions carried out by international organizations of which Spain is a member during the war in Bosnia and Kosovo. The Spanish government's conduct with regard to the war in Iraq is an exception; and in any case, its support has been political rather than military. The Spanish army's participation has, once again, been limited to that of a humanitarian aid mission—as it is in Afghanistan right now. Even so, the presence in Iraq was still unacceptable, as the clamor for the withdrawal of the troops would prove.

It could be stated, then, that the general Spanish perception of armed conflicts is that they are no concern of theirs: the wars are other people's wars which foreign political actors decide and take part in and whose consequences have no direct effect on their country.

Precisely because of this, it is of special interest to analyze whether the media's behavior reinforces this perception of distance or if, on the contrary, they help to bring it closer to home. It would also be interesting to evaluate what is the medium's intention according to its editorial line: to involve citizens in the conflict or keep them on the sidelines as a mere spectator.

AN OVERVIEW OF THE SPANISH MEDIA
DURING THE BOSNIAN WAR

With regard to print media, there are a total number of 97 daily newspapers in Spain and 87 of these are of general news. In 1995, figures were slightly different: out of 88 daily newspapers, 76 were of general news (*Noticias de la Comunicación*, 1996, 1997 and 2002). Print media's readership is small when compared with the total Spanish population: only 32 percent read newspapers everyday. In 1995, the total daily distribution was a little over three million copies. This figure was almost the same in 2002 (3.2 million). There was, however, an increase in the specialized press: the daily sport newspapers' readership was 27 percent of the total newspaper readership and the financial newspapers had a share of 1.5 percent.

In Spain, the regional press is well regarded and is of a high quality with a significant readership. This shows the strength of the nationalistic trends characterizing Spanish society. To compete with these regional newspapers, most of the national newspapers also publish their own regional editions. This is the case with *ABC Sevilla, El País Barcelona, El Mundo El País Vasco*.

In the audiovisual market, there is the public television station, *Televisión Española* and three private channels: *Antena 3, Tele 5*, and *Canal +. Televisión Española* has two channels, *TV1* and *TV2*. There are also eight autonomic or regional channels, which depend on local institutions for their management and funding. There is also a wide range of local TV channels in response to the wish to defend and preserve the different cultures and languages that make up the nation as a whole.

The two principal news agencies are *EFE*, a public enterprise that until 1976 was the only Spanish news agency providing international news, and *Europa Press*, a private agency that started up an international section from the same date.

In the early 1990s Spanish audiences began to show more interest in international news. In 1991, 21 percent of the population claimed that they followed the international events on a daily basis. In 1995, this number had grown to 26 percent (Center of Research of Social Reality, 1995-1997). After a significant drop at the end of the 1990s, international news has regained past figures due to the events of September 11 and its consequences, such as the war in Afghanistan and the current crisis in Iraq.

Regarding new technologies, the increase in the cost of paper at the end of the 1980s had negative repercussions for the print media, forcing a reduction in the number of pages and a change in the sections design. However, it led to interest in promoting new technology. There have been significant efforts to incorporate it in the Spanish print and audiovisual media. Currently, all national and regional newspapers have on-line editions, and digital TV has also begun to be successful.

INTERNATIONAL NEWS
IN THE SPANISH MEDIA

International news coverage in the Spanish media reflects the same behavior as has been observed in the rest of Europe. In the study carried out in 1995,[1] the initial conclusion was that, at least to some extent, the "image of the world" transmitted by the media was an accurate reflection of Spain's place in the global context. This means that they are "Euro-centered" and "Western-centered" in the choice of topics and actors. The considerable interest in Latin America was also noted, showing typical conduct of European countries with regard to former colonial territories.

In the years after its transition to democracy, Spain has evolved in political, economic and social terms. This has had a significant effect on the development of its international relations. It has reinforced its position towards the United States and the European Union. Even though Spain still has enormous possibilities for widening its international scope, its status as a significant Euro-Atlantic nation has been sufficiently confirmed.

Regarding the definition of newsworthiness in Spanish newsrooms, a constant pattern in the selection of international events was observable. Although there are obviously events that in themselves merit coverage, meaningful indicators of Spanish newsrooms' preferences in covering an international event showed that sport and entertainment news items occurred more often than any other. The second most frequent topic was international economic news followed in third place by other countries' domestic political issues.

In the analysis of the most important countries reported, it was observed that Spain was considered the most important country in the greatest number of international stories (23%) followed by the United States (9.35%) and some of the European countries: France (7.6%) and Italy (4.1%). The European Union as an international organization was also mentioned (4%). During the period of study, Bosnia Herzegovina made up a significant 4.2 percent, reflecting the events that were taking place at the time. Spain's prominence is explained by the interest to focus the story on the involvement of the country or those aspects that affect the country.

There was a general disposition to narrate events through the voice of state officials who represent countries involved in news (33.2%), which, added to the percentage of the public sector (20%), yielded a total of 53.2 percent, slightly over half of the total data of news sources.

However, when sources were classified as either national or international, regardless of whether they were public or private, it can be seen that 63.6 percent of news had its origin in international entities. This means that foreign news was not concentrated on the activity of specific countries and a more transnational image of the world was promoted.

Private citizens appeared as main actors in a significant 23.5 percent of cases, but most of the news items were related to human rights issues, crime, sports, and entertainment, with political topics hardly featuring.

A distinctive feature of Spanish international news lies in its level of independence with respect to news sources. An analysis by frequencies indicates that for 44.5 percent of the news items studied, the source was a correspondent of the news medium: 11.1 percent were written in the newsroom; and 8 percent were obtained from EFE, the Spanish news agency. The single international news agency whose services were most frequently used was Reuters with 4.2 percent, followed by France Press (3.5%). Associated Press was the source of news items for only 0.5 percent of the cases registered. Regional or specialized news agencies were not mentioned, and the foreign media quoted were *The New York Times, Liberation, Le Monde, Le Figaro,* and *The Times.*

The Bosnian conflict was covered, as might have been expected, through officials from state (62.3%) or international organizations (20.8%). Only 5.2 percent of these news stories presented private citizens as main actors. These results indicate that for situations as critical as a war, the role of other main actors is reduced and limited to military and political authorities.

This trend is also shown through the analysis of the origin of news: 53.2 percent originated from the government. However, the media made a serious attempt not to rely just on the official version either by seeking information by themselves (they were the news source in 27.3% of the cases) or through citizens directly affected by the conflict (18.2%). This is a typical professional routine when dealing with long-running coverage.

With regard to the sources, international news agencies, mainly European, were used more often than correspondents. The percentage for "stringers" was higher for news about Bosnia than for any other event. As for datelines, half of the information came from former Yugoslavia (50%), mainly from Bosnia itself (40.8%). Quite frequently the information about the war came from European cities where peace talks or decisions relative to the deployment of military actions were taking place.

THE COVERAGE OF NATO'S BOMBING OF SARAJEVO IN 1995 AS AN EXAMPLE OF NEWS REPORTING ON THE BOSNIAN WAR IN SPAIN

The analysis is focused on the last phase of the Bosnian War, from May to September of 1995 when interventions by NATO and its allies were decisive in ending the conflict. On February 5, 1994, a Serbian bomb killed 68 civilians and injured several hundreds in a market of Sarajevo. Four days later, NATO posted an ultimatum demanding for an immediate withdrawal of the Serbian troops from Sarajevo and its surroundings. It was not obeyed and the NATO troops intervened, following United Nations recommendations. For the first time in its history, four Serbian planes were brought down. Afterwards NATO troops attacked on several other occasions. However, from May 1995 and especially during that summer, NATO launched the last offensive, bringing to an end the Bosnian war.

The following analysis derives from the coverage given by the two most important Spanish newspapers, *El País* and *El Mundo*. They represent divergent political positions and they also differ in their specific approach to covering the war in Bosnia (Canel, 1999).

El País, which follows a progressive-liberal line, was clearly in tune with the Partido Socialista Obrero Español (PSOE), the Socialist Spanish Worker's Party, which was in power during this time. Its pro-democratic and pro-European stance is a basic point of reference in the definition of public opinion at that time.

El Mundo defines itself as anti-imperialistic and anti-military, a radical defender of human rights and public liberties. It was the declared enemy of the then president, Felipe González, and it represented the opposition party's position—Partido Popular, conservative, centrist-right—although the newspaper itself claimed that its ideological space was centrist-left.

As has been previously pointed out, the analysis of the news on NATO's bombing of Sarajevo in 1995 is of interest because it presents the most significant characteristics of the coverage that had been given from the beginning of the conflict.

News on the Bosnian War: Reinforcement of the Audience's Attitude as "Spectator"

The Spanish media had no doubts in understanding the bombing as one more action in a war that had lasted for four years. The operation's objectives were military and the armed forces from both sides were the protagonists. The actors and possible political interests were not mentioned or given little prominence.

The general approach used towards the conflict was that it was an international issue: it only affected the Spanish people to the extent that Spain was a member of the international organizations involved in the conflict (NATO, EU, and UN) and, as such, it was the moment to debate issues related to the international order, such as the legitimacy of foreign intervention or national sovereignty. Even the detention of three Spanish observers by Serbian forces three days before the bombing of Sarajevo did not alter either the location of the news, which was in the international section, or the number of pages given to the rest of the conflict.

The two newspapers gave the event their full attention. They gave it greater importance than other actions in the conflict because of the significance of NATO's intervention but, above all, because they believed that this operation would mean the end of the conflict. The duration of the coverage (all the period analyzed), the extension in the number of pages (no less than two pages per day) and its location (front page and main news in the international section) show, however, a thorough coverage of events.

The coverage was carried out by reporters and special correspondents who had reported on the war from its outset. They were located in Washington, Brussels, Belgrade, and Ljubljana. For news coverage on Sarajevo itself, Naples (NATO bases are situated there), and Paris they used agency news, mainly Associated Press and Reuters. So the story sources were a combination of the places where decisions were made and where the events took place.

The most frequent news sources were the NATO high commands (chiefly R. Holbrooke and L. Smith). *El Mundo*, in keeping with its more liberal and pacifist character, gave greater importance to the UN spokespeople and observers, and they also used declarations from Yugoslavian television.

In any case, the treatment of the conflict as a whole showed clear support for the international organizations, especially NATO, in this specific action. *El País* did this by dedicating a smaller space to the conflict, always after the arguments presented by the Atlantic Alliance. *El Mundo*'s vision was more balanced, and the Serbian viewpoint appeared in all the news, but always in second place and rarely citing direct sources.

Neither one of the newspapers condemned NATO's armed intervention. *El País* justified it as a necessary measure to break the Serbian position; all the news stories reflected the fact that it was an exceptional decision and insisted that the objectives were primarily military.

El País and *El Mundo* did little interpretation of the news; information and opinion were clearly differentiated. The articles centered on the different incidents of the battles without making judgments or evaluations; the newspaper's opinion could be found in the editorial or featured columns. The language used by the two newspapers was neutral, impersonal, and with no literary concessions.

However, a certain evaluation was expressed in the pullouts and the headlines. *El Mundo* framed the coverage of the conflict under the title "The Balkans' Hornet's Nest" referring to the complicated historical development of this area of Europe. With this heading it marked an equidistant position from any of the diverse groups fighting in this war, while indicating a certain irrationality in the evolution of the confrontations. *El País* gave the conflict a more objective description: "War in the Balkans."

The coverage's emphasis has been evaluated bearing in mind the main issue developed in the text and the events to which the headlines referred. The conclusion arrived at, using these two co-ordinates, is that Spanish newspapers emphasized two aspects over the rest: the defiant resistance of the Serbians and NATO's inevitable intervention. Together with this generalized behavior, *El Mundo*'s specific interest in the war's humanitarian consequences both for the Croatians and the Serbs was significant; following its editorial line, the defence of the rights of the civil population meant that taking sides was not an option.

A Distant and Remote War

In Spain, the war in Yugoslavia was a war of "the others." The perception of this drawn-out conflict echoed the characteristic signalled at the beginning of the chapter: Spanish society in general does not feel involved in armed confrontations of this nature. The harshness of the situation was lamented, there was reaction to the violation of human rights, and the length of the war was regretted, but it was not given detailed attention, and public opinion was highly reluctant for its army to be involved in international operations. The Spanish people, although aware of the seriousness of the conflict in all its dimensions, adopted a passive role, one of spectator.

The media, specifically the two newspapers analyzed, reflected and were sometimes instrumental in provoking this attitude. This psychological distance was mainly the result of three professional conducts: the regularity with which the conflict was covered, where the news was located in the newspaper, and the general frame in which it was presented. The decisions adopted in these three aspects had an influence on the psychological distance with which the reader perceived the news, reinforcing the Spanish public opinion's position as spectator.

With regard to the regularity of the publication of news on the war, the following can be said. Once the first confrontations had occurred, news appeared only when the seriousness of events made it impossible to ignore them. Therefore, coverage was irregular, and only the most crucial moments of the war were reported. The effect of this discontinuity was highly negative for a complete understanding of events; added to the complexity of the war in itself was the difficulty in following it through a disjointed narrative. It was impossible for the reader to remember from one time to the next the names of the political and military actors, the places where the action was taking place, or the connection between one event and another. All of this brought about a distancing effect, a certain weariness at the repetition of incomprehensible news and, as a consequence, led to a lack of interest in the coverage of the conflict.

When the news about Yugoslavia was taken up again it was located in one specific place: the two newspapers reported it on their front pages and opened their pages with a special section with its own pullout. It stayed on the front page one or two days, and was then progressively relegated to the international section until, in less than a week, it disappeared altogether. (In *El Mundo* this section is found in the middle of the newspaper; *El País* opens with foreign news.) In the other cases, the news on the war in Yugoslavia took second place in the international section.

The newspapers sent special correspondents to cover specific events, such as an especially violent act or the intermediaries' negotiations on the ground, but they were hardly ever in the place of conflict (Julio Fuertes and Alonso Rojo from *El Mundo*). The usual procedure was to move the journalists to border zones such as Ljubljana and Belgrade (Francesc Relea from *El País*) or to cities that were home to the headquarters of the organizations involved: Washington (José María Calvo from *El País*), Brussels (J. Carlos González from *El País*).

The pullout is not just a graphic resource that highlights and unifies the news, but it contributes to providing the newspaper's first frame: it presents and frames news. The texts used in these titles are especially significant with respect to the effect of distance. As has been previously pointed out, *El Mundo* flagged its story on the war with the title "The Balkan Hornet's Nest," and *El País* referred to the conflict as "The Balkan War."

The use of the word "Balkan" has the connotations of a distant past because it is the name that was used to describe the group of provinces and principalities found in the peninsula of the same name during the Turkish empire. Even though it provided a certain context, a reference to Yugoslavia would have brought it much closer to home, historically and culturally. Also, the metaphor in the term "hornet's nest" underlined the area's constant and irrational chaos. It is a well-honed term often used by historians referring to the constant unrest in the area dating back to the thirteenth century.

In the media's representation of events, the silences and gaps are also of interest. Despite the potential for making comparisons with the problems of nationalism affecting Spain, neither of the two newspapers used the possible parallels as a reference. Even when the politicians themselves took the initiative, such as the case of some leaders' statements from the Basque Country, the newspapers only reported the speech without pursuing the line of argument.

Therefore, the unevenness of the reporting, where the news originated and the framing used in the publishing of the main news by the two newspapers meant that the conflict was presented as a far-off and distant event — an external issue, only affecting Spanish society and politics insofar as it affected the international community as a whole.

Bosnia Was Not the Center of Attention

The debate that captured the reader's attention was not so much the progress of the war but rather what function the international entities should perform in the new international order.

This approach, which would be justified by the event that is the object of this analysis—NATO's bombing to break the siege of Sarajevo—was a constant throughout the coverage of the whole conflict.

The explanation for this particular focus is found in the selection of news sources. In general terms it can be asserted that news about the conflict originated 80 percent of the times from official statements. Two thirds of those were issued by high-ranking officials, either state officials or experts of those international organizations involved in the war: United Nations, NATO, European Union, and the Council of European Security and Co-operation.

This type of source was used especially at the beginning of the conflict, which was an important moment for defining it. The Spanish media adopted the official international vision without subjecting it to any kind of scrutiny; this would be maintained throughout the whole process. In this sense, Spain's case corroborates Sadkovich's thesis that sources of an official nature end up by influencing the journalist's personal viewpoint (Sadkovich, 1998). As has been previously mentioned, this was a civil war caused by Milosevich's nationalist pretensions and his desire to create Greater Serbia. There was no room for any other hypothesis such as that of secession or the ancestral ethnic hatred present in all of the social groups of the former Yugoslavia.

The frequent use of international official sources not only determined the definition of the conflict but also the priority given to issues debated on this subject. This was the case in Spain where the media expressed opinions and debated issues that were of interest with regard to international organizations and ignored those that dealt strictly with the progress of the conflict. The issues about which the newspapers wrote editorials were the legitimacy of international intervention, the opportuneness of one or other organization being involved, the effectiveness of the proposed models of intervention, or the need to reform international law to adapt it to new situations. There was no mention of the official or non-official viewpoints of those taking part in the conflict, such as their perception of the problems, difficulties, and ways they could be solved. When they were asked for statements it was usually to get their reaction to the official international viewpoint.

El Mundo was the newspaper with a more varied viewpoint in dealing with the definition of the conflict and the issues involved. However, it never really managed to get away from the general coverage. It did not agree with the official version, but it argued about the same issues, which meant that its agenda was just as conditioned as the others'. Although it reported more than the other newspapers on citizens' or victims' testimonies, it was always from within the previously established framework. When any important event took place, such as the bombing of Sarajevo by NATO forces, *El Mundo* published statements broadcast on Yugoslavian television, permitting the reaction of those who had been attacked to be part of the chorus of voices that would judge the events of that day. However, this was a one-off occasion, and it was certainly not aimed at granting the Serbs their own voice in the Spanish media.

Divergent Editorial Lines

The media's influence in shaping public opinion on international issues is decisive. They usually reinforce a consensus that already existed, a latent social tendency that is activated and given shape when faced with a certain event. But at specific moments they can also modify a general feeling.

In the case of Spain, the editorial policy of the main newspapers performed this dual role. As has already been pointed out, the news coverage of the war contributed to maintaining the distance with which the Spanish public observed the conflict. But also, breaking through the traditional Spanish passivity, the media managed to provoke debate on the responsibility of international organizations to maintain world order and defend human rights with regard to the legitimacy of international intervention.

The place where this debate was apparent was in the editorial pages more than in the news sections, although the newspaper's line also had an influence on the newsroom routine. There was both agreement and divergence in the opinions put forward by the media selected for this analysis. As Zaller has pointed out when referring to political leaders, there are moments when the media coincide in their opinion and unify their message, creating public opinion that gives a unanimous response. At other stages of the conflict, the media diverge and provoke a polarization of public opinion, choosing two extreme positions (Zaller, 1992).

As in the United Kingdom (Shaw, 1996), the Spanish press has a special influence in shaping society's attitudes: even though they do not reach the public at large, their audience is, from the qualitative point of view, decisive, because the country's political and economic leaders form part of their readership.

The newspapers most closely analyzed, *El País* and *El Mundo*, are both illustrative of the effect pointed out by Zaller. In moments when the conflict was at its worst, the general agreement in condemning it and on the need for international intervention was plain to see; however, when the war had entered the halfway stage, *El País* backed the more official state position, considering foreign intervention as necessary, while *El Mundo,* in its pacifist line, argued for the conflict to be resolved internally without outside interference. This disagreement divided public opinion.

El País: The Legitimacy of an International Intervention[2]

El País condemned the cause of the conflict, which it attributed to Milosevich's expansionism in his bid to rebuild Greater Serbia. As far as the newspaper was concerned, no historical or political argument justified this aim. The newspaper constantly qualified Milosevich's acts as "cruel" and "criminal actions," which "correspond to the most strict communist tradition." It also condemned the means used in order to achieve it, which it did not hesitate to judge as the systematic violation of international law and of human rights. The direct victims of the conflict were the Serbian, Bosnian, and Croatian peoples and, indirectly, the credibility of the international organizations if they did not intervene in a decisive and effective way.

This approach justified its main editorial line: *El País* argued decisively for international intervention, backed by legislation that would cover the new threats to human rights. It was also reflected in the selection and treatment of the actors and issues with which the war was interpreted. Their most important characteristics are outlined below:

- International organizations, whose function in the beginning was neutral as mediators and arbiters of the conflict, would finally appear as the second contender in the war, practically replacing the Bosnians and the Croatians. Especially at the end of the conflict, confrontation was limited to one between the Serbian forces and the international institutions attempting to bring a solution to the situation. To give only an example, there is a significant opinion published at the end of the war, summing up the newspaper's position during the conflict: "In those places there are already many armed people hostile towards vehicles identified as belonging to the United Nations Peacekeeping Forces or other Western organisations. Serbian forces have opened fire at UN vehicles practically from the very beginning" ("Good luck in Sarajevo," 17 August 1995).
- Regarding consideration of contenders, its editorials often used terms that showed the strength of the international alliance, on the one hand, and the Serbs' isolation on the other. For instance, *El País* used expressions such as "international community" and "the West" to refer to NATO member nations' positions, stressing their consensus. There are also headlines specially significant in showing the perception about the Serbs: "Ultimatum to Serbian People" (10 February 1994); "A Message to Karadzic by Spanish

Airforce" (26 May 1995); "The Serbian Nightmare" (16 July 1995).

- It personalized the sides involved in the war, using political and military leaders' names so as to attribute the different political and military actions to them. It can be seen in some expressions, such as "Milosevic treats blue berets as enemies"; Milosevich, Mladic and Karadzic have promoted "a crusade against peace plans and against the whole international community" ("Fair Decision," 1 July 1995), and Spain "has the responsibility to defend the international community from challenges like Karadzic" ("Spain in Bosnia," 27 May 1995). According to the theory expounded by Iyengar and Simon, this resort to episodic storytelling through specific events and characters contributes to determining who are specifically guilty and provokes a desire in the audience to find immediate solutions. In contrast, general or thematic narration tends to attribute the causes of the situation to the social structures or the general system, reasons that do not move the public to act (Iyengar & Simon, 1997).

All of its coverage had an alarmist tone, as if it assumed the responsibility of preventing war-weariness caused by the length of the conflict and had to remind people of the seriousness of events (in expressions such as "bloody conflict" which holds "huge risks for those involved," "the way the conflict is going is extremely serious," "this is the greatest catastrophe for European security of the late twentieth century"). An alarmist tone led to pressure on the international political bodies, urging the adoption of an effective solution ("the worst of all possible scenarios—inactivity—is now happening in Bosnia" or "is the international community going to repeat what they did in Somalia: shamefully abandon Bosnian territory leaving the contenders to settle their differences with the use of force?) (among others "The Defeat of the United Nations," July 12th). The most frequently used device to promote this attitude was to alert its readers to future trouble-spots involving nationalism such Karadzic's challenge, lifting his behavior out of the specific context of the war and making a kind of political fiction of the consequences of not preventing such risks.

The newspaper underlined the importance of solidarity and responsibility as the underlying values of the new international order and made a clear case for the need to design a global policy overriding national interests. It argued for a clearly defined international law for regulating the use of force and for a commitment to the defence of international organizations. *El País* was of the opinion that the NATO intervention was an American intervention, not an "international community" initiative, and should have been considered as the lesser of two evils ("A Very Weak Peace Agreement," 9 October 1995; "A Little Victory," 31 October 1995).

The gravest danger this war presented was the international institutions' loss of credibility in their role as guarantors of world peace. In this sense, the newspapers considered that "Bosnia can mean (for the United Nations) the end of the authority to enforce a peace agreement" ("The Time of Truth," 27 July 1995).

This standpoint was shared by the Spanish Socialist government, which this newspaper supported. However, as is customary in its behavior, it did not give explicit backing to the government but rather provided arguments to support the same ideas defended by the government.

El Mundo: Reservations about International Intervention[3]

El Mundo's coverage of the conflict was less sustained than that of *El País*. It restricted itself to reporting the most important events in the war. This made it much more difficult to follow the conflict's development by reading this newspaper.

This newspaper understood the war as a conflict between nationalities caused by Serbia's rejection of Croatian and Slovenian self-determination. It was a war between different peoples who had lived together in an artificial state imposed by Serbia.

It considered both sides of the conflict equally as victims, without taking sides for one or another. It restricted itself to condemning certain behavior, regardless of who was involved. In this sense, the newspaper alluded frequently to the nationalist past of both Serbians and Croatians and recalled the "genocide" carried out by the Croatians in the Second World War ("The Balkans: Towards a Total War?," 5 August 1995) as well as the ultranationalistic propaganda of the Serbs in the years leading up to the conflict ("Bosnia: The Time of the Cannons," 8 August 1995). These historical references gave a balance to the treatment of the two sides. The pullout used for framing the news corroborated this tendency.

For this reason, it had its reservations with regard to international intervention: only at the most critical moments of the conflict did it consent to the NATO bombings by not voicing its opinions of dissent. The rest of its reporting would argue for the withdrawal of the "UN Blue Berets" and for the end of the embargo on the Bosnians. It claimed that "the peacekeeping operations are not applicable *urbi et orbe* but only where . . . contenders agree with them" ("The United Nations: Neither Black nor White Assessment," 27 June 1995)

Unlike *El País*, instead of international organizations, it used other sources with no political or military responsibilities such as NGO volunteers and civil associations. There was a greater variety in positions and opinions, although from the political point of view they were less relevant.

In *El Mundo* the term "international community" always appeared in quotation marks as if it questioned the entity or nature of this institution.

The term was used because all the media referred to it in this way, but the paper also made its skepticism clear. It did not hesitate to point out its "spectacular failures" or to describe its actions as "taking stabs in the dark" or "just playing to the gallery" ("A Promise of Peace," 15 December 1995).

The language tended to be colloquial, playing down the drama. This style reinforced the newspaper's stance as a simple observer, uninvolved in the conflict. It adopted phrases of common usage in Spanish speech: "We've got this war for quite a while to come yet"; the Serbs "have come to blows"; "This powder keg is going to explode again" ("Balkans, Farewell to the Mirage," 3 May 1995, among others).

In contrast to *El País*, and in line with the devices described, *El Mundo* did not refer to international solidarity nor did it understand that security should be conceived as global. On the contrary, it appeared to lean towards a local security, with each state responsible for solving its own problems ("Blue Berets: Time to Go Home," 11 May 1995). It did not give its backing to an international commitment led by the states at the heart of international organizations and criticized specific decisions: ". . . to keep the Bosnian embargo is an absurd contribution to worsen the situation" ("A Great Repugnance," 4 June 1995). It defended a multiple structure, with other actors able to take part and action limited to diplomatic mediation. *El Mundo*, in line with its pacifist idealism, rejected the idea that the use of force would have any utility, with the extreme exception of NATO's intervention in Sarajevo. In this case, it did not support the bombing but considered it "The Least Wrong of the Wrong Solutions" (headline of 31 August 1995).

The newspaper frequently made references to domestic politics, centering its attention on statements made by Spanish politicians on the war more than on the progress of the war itself. It turned an international news story into a national issue, in which domestic reactions were more important than the outside action. *El Mundo* was against Spanish intervention in Bosnia and used it against Felipe Gonzalez's government, asking for a law "to impede arbitrariness of a government that does not fulfil what it has promised" and qualified as "stupid deaths" the fifteen casualties in the Spanish force. ("Humanitarian Mission, an Impossible Mission," 28 May 1995).

CONCLUSION

The Spanish media's news coverage of the Bosnian war yields one clear conclusion: newspapers chiefly adopted a passive attitude that reinforced the Spanish public opinion's position as a mere spectator of the conflict.

The distance with which the conflict was viewed was increased by the irregularity in coverage, a secondary localization in the international section—except for especially critical moments—and the lack of historical references or of similarities drawn to Spanish problems, which would have brought the conflict closer to home culturally speaking. In addition, the approach adopted was the result of the priority given to official international sources: the newspaper's interest was more centered on the design of the new international order than on the war itself. The specific circumstances of the conflict were secondary, and the debate on the legitimacy of the intervention and the function that international organizations should carry out was what prevailed.

Both newspapers used certain devices that could have prompted calls from the readership for greater international intervention. The portrayal of the civilian population's suffering of which *El Mundo* made frequent use or the alarmist tone taken by *El País* seemed to want to provoke a reaction in public opinion. However, in themselves they were not enough to break down the Spanish readership's traditional passivity with regard to these conflicts.

NOTES

1. We have drawn the conclusions that will be presented here as a result of a quantitative content analysis of foreign news in four Spanish media over two weeks in September 1995. It was the Spanish contribution to the Foreign News Comparative Research that has been mentioned. The newspapers selected were *El País,* which has a national distribution and the highest circulation figures, and *La Vanguardia,* which is the biggest regional newspaper, published in Barcelona, but with a nationwide readership. The TV channels chosen were Televisión Española, the Spanish public television station and Antena 3, a commercial network, both for their evening newscasts. These two also hold the largest audience indices (see *Boletín de la Oficina de Justificación de la Difusión,* no. 49, May 1996 and Sofres, *CM Informe,* May 1996). The study is based on a total of 1,821 news items.

2. As mentioned, all quotations have been taken from editorials of *El País,* published between May to December of 1995. Some expressions do not have a specific quotation because they were repeated frequently.

3. All quotations have been taken from editorials of *El Mundo,* published between May to December of 1995. Some expressions do not have a specific quotation because were repeated frequently.

REFERENCES

Alvira, R. (1992). *Opinión pública, servicio militar y fuerzas armadas en España* [Public opinion, military service and armed forces in Spain]. *Política Exterior,* VI (26), 163-170.

Canel, M. J. (1999). *El País, ABC y El Mundo: Tres manchetas, tres enfoques de las noticias* [*El País, ABC* and *El Mundo:* Three mastheads, three approaches to news]. *ZER, 6,* 97-117.

Canel, M., & Piqué, A. (1997) Journalists for emerging democracies. The case of Spain. In D. Weaver (Ed.), *The global journalist.* Cresskill, NJ: Hampton Press.

Center of Research of Social Reality (1998). *La realidad social en España, 1995-1999* [The social reality in Spain, 1995-1999]. Madrid: CIRES.

Clutterbuck, R. (1981). *The media and political violence.* London: Macmillan.

Delgado Ruiz, M. (1998). *Discurso y violencia: La "fantasmización" mediática de la fuerza* [Discourse and violence: The media "phantomization" of the use of force]. *Trípodos, 6,* 55-68.

Diezhandino, P. et al. (1994). *La elite de los periodistas* [The journalists' elite]. Bilbao: Servicio Editorial de la Universidad del País Vasco.

Entman, R. (1989). *Democracy without citizens, media and the decay of American politics.* Oxford: Oxford University Press.

Giddens, A. (1985). *The nation-state and violence.* Berkeley: University of California Press.

Glasser, T.L. (1984, February). Objectivity precludes responsibility. *The Quill,* pp. 120-135.

Iyengar, S. & Simon, A. (1997). News coverage of the Gulf crisis and public opinion. *Communication Research, 20*(3), 365-383.

Morrison, D. et al. (1999). *Defining violence.* Luton: University of Luton Press.

Mowlana, H., Gerbner, G., & Schiller, H. (Eds.). (1992). *Triumph of the image: The media's war in the Gulf. A global perspective.* Boulder, CO: Westview.

Mueller, J. (1973). *War, presidents and public opinion.* New York: Wiley.

Noticias de la Comunicación [News on Communication], *153,* November, 1996; *164,* November, 1997; *220,* December, 2002.

Rosen, J. (1993, Winter). Beyond objectivity. *Nieman Reports,* pp. 48-53.

Sadkovich, J. J. (1998). *The U.S. media and Yugoslavia, 1991-1995.* Westport, CO: Praeger.

Santamaria, L. (1997). *Géneros para la persuasión en periodismo* [Genre for persuasion in journalism]. Madrid: Fragua.

Schlesinger, P. (1991). *Media, state and nation. Political violence and collective identities.* London: Sage.

Shaw, M. (1991). *Post-military society: Militarism, demilitarization and war at the end of the twentieth century.* Philadelphia: Temple University Press.

Shaw, M. (1996). *Civil society and media in global crisis. Representing distant violence.* London: Pinter.

Shoemaker, P. & Reese, S. (1991). *Mediating the message. Theories of influences on mass media content.* New York: Longman.

Splichal, S., & Sparks, C. (1994). *Journalists for the 21st century.* Norwood, NJ: Ablex.

Tuchman, G. (1978). *Making news.* New York: The Free Press.

Weaver, D., & Wilhoit, C. (1991). *The American journalist. A portrait of US news people and their work.* Bloomington: Indiana University Press.

Zaller, J. (1992). *The nature and origins of mass opinion.* Cambridge: Cambridge University Press.

Chapter 6

Media Functioning During A Violent International Crisis

Differences Between Elite and Popular Press Coverage of American Policy in Bosnia (1992–1995)

Yaeli Bloch-Elkon

Sam Lehman-Wilzig*

Already at the end of the nineteenth century, the sociologist G. Tarde (1969 [1898]) argued that the mass media had turned from being an institutional platform of opinions to a body that decides opinion. Although this view was somewhat of an exaggeration as later research found, there is no denying the strength of media influence in the modern age. They can act as central agenda-setters (McCombs & Shaw, 1993; Ruddock, 2001), create powerful images, excite emotions, reduce tensions, and present a battery of symbols that can rally the nation (Nossek, 2003; Paletz, 2002; Zaller, 2001). As an American army officer stationed in Bosnia put it, in response to a question by CBS's Dan Rather, his biggest fear was "saying the wrong thing to the media" (Moskos & Ricks, 1995, p. 7).

*This article is based on part of Dr. Bloch-Elkon's PhD dissertation: *The Press, Public-Opinion and Foreign Policy During an International Crisis: U.S. Policy in Bosnia (1992-1995)*, Dept. of Political Studies (Public Communications Program), Bar-Ilan University, Israel, 2003 (co-supervised by Prof. Lehman-Wilzig & Dr. Yehudith Auerbach).

The growth of mass communications in the twentieth century was accompanied by growing academic and research interest, especially in the United States, regarding the functioning and influence of the media (Ruddock, 2001). However, lacunae continue to exist, among them the issue of how mass media function during international *crises* in general, and *violent crises* in particular. Much research has been undertaken dealing specifically with war and the mass media, and somewhat less is available regarding the role of the mass media in foreign policy decision making during peacetime. Yet little exists on the topic of foreign policy crisis management and the media, despite the large number of such international relations phenomena in the contemporary era (Malek, 1996).

The present study will make a serious attempt to try and fill this untouched research niche by offering a comprehensive analysis of the media's functions during various phases of an international relations crisis. It will apply a familiar theory from the field of international relations (division of crisis phases) to the developing discipline of mass communication research, in order to achieve a better understanding of the media in times of crisis by examining the differences between types of newspaper. By applying media reports to an international crisis we seek to find links between crisis phases and press positions and frames.

THEORETICAL FRAMEWORK

Media-Government

Democratic regimes have a tendency to bask in the myth of a free press, but even in "open societies" the media serve the polity's control apparatus, consciously or not. On the one hand, most media organizations expect their representatives to cover government actions in one way or another. On the other hand, the universal temptation exists for governments to manipulate and control the media—especially true during crisis periods.

The amount and type of governmental supervision and control over the media depend in large part on the political/mass communications philosophy of each country at distinct points in time. Overall, the research literature has centered on five main, general, politico-philosophical approaches (McQuail, 1987; Siebert, Schramm, & Peterson, 1956). We shall focus here on the two that are relevant to this research:[1]

1. In the libertarian philosophy of government/press relations, also called the Free Press theory, the mass media best serve the public as an aggressive, independent, adversarial *watchdog* on govern-

ment actions. This approach assumes a high level of competition between the media themselves, tending to decrease editorial supervision of journalistic practice as well as leading to denial of public education as a prominent journalistic role (Serfaty, 1991).

2. Although the media might be formally and legally free, politico-cultural constraints can render their output highly supportive of the government. This approach can best be categorized as *mobilization*, whereby the media view their task more in terms of supporting the authorities and reinforcing national consensus. This is most widely found among developing nations, but it is also not unusual to see such *self*-mobilized journalism during times of crisis among otherwise libertarian-minded media caught in a "rally-round-the-flag" mentality (Holsti, 1996; Zaller & Chiu, 2000; Zelizer & Allan, 2002). Indeed, previous studies have found that most domestic mass media tend to support national foreign policy aims and goals, especially when the national interest is threatened, thereby acting as a source of "national integration" (Paletz, 2002; Schudson, 2002), that is, a unifying force behind government decisions/actions (Rivenburgh, 1996; Waisbord, 2002).

Situations like these, highlighting the complexity of journalism's public role and the range of press responses, are especially interesting (Arno, 1984; Holsti, 1996; Russett, 1990). However, one must note that it is hard to find in the literature a clear definition of what we call the "self-mobilized media." This approach is different from the "social responsibility" model (Siebert et al. 1956) that posits a degree of self-restraint for specific, localized, social reasons (e.g., protection of a crime victim's privacy), and which normally does not involve self-restraint regarding criticism of government policy. Moreover, it is not always clear for whom the media are mobilized: the constitutional regime, state, government, or specific interest groups. It seems that one can delineate two main roles of the press within the self-mobilization function: on the one hand, "rally-round-the-flag"—that is socionational consensus-building; on the other hand, "support of the government" for its policies and decisions in the conduct of the crisis.

MEDIA

Framing

An examination of the nature of media functioning leads to the question of framing, whereby journalists "package" the information in such a way as to present a specific reality in order to influence audience perceptions (Entman,

1991; Entman & Rojecki, 1993; Gitlin, 1977; Wolfsfeld, 1997). Such packaging usually involves a broad range of subjects, all of which are presented from the same *weltanschauung*, thereby limiting the full panoply of public discourse. As a result of such framing, not only is the issue presented in a preset fashion, familiar to the public and therefore "understandable" (Callaghan & Schnell, 2001; Durham, 1998; Eilders & Luter, 2000; Gamson & Herzog, 1999; Karim, 2002; Norris, 1997; Paletz, 2002), but also the very meaning of the news is changed (Bloch & Lehman-Wilzig, 2002; Kuypers, 1997; Putnam, Phillips, & Chapman, 1996; Scheufele, 1999).

The decision to raise the prominence of a particular subject, to choose and emphasize a certain image or word, to promulgate specific explanations and commentary regarding the reasons for—and consequences of—events, and the attempt to connect new stories with old ones, all contribute to the manufacture of news frames with a definite slant (Callaghan & Schnell, 2001; Entman, 1993; Gamson, 1992; Gitlin, 1980; Naveh, 2002; Nossek, 2003; Paletz, 2002; Tankard, 2001; Zaller, 1992). Such frameworks create a certain image of the world and set the public mood (Beaudoin & Thorson, 2002; Brown, 2001; D'Angelo, 2002; Iyengar & Simon, 1997). Thus, the framing concept has become a central component of journalism studies, especially those assessing media influence (Nossek, 2003).

PRESS TYPES

News frames differ, as one can imagine, from medium to medium. The tendency in print journalism has been to differentiate from the start between two groups: information journalism and narrative journalism. Relatively few newspapers, read by the highly educated elite are called "quality press." Their influence emanates from their audience being (by definition) quite influential. These papers are serious (most, but not all, to the point of being rather dry), viewing themselves as carrying the torch of social responsibility while acting as a political watchdog of democracy. The major emphasis is on "hard news," especially national security, foreign policy, the economy, and so forth, bringing to bear extensive background and wide-ranging commentary on the event/phenomenon (Paletz, 2002). In the literature one can even find a further subdivision of the elite press: the "quality press" functioning in open, liberal democracies; the "prestige press" found in closed, authoritarian regimes (Merrill, 1968). In any case, in the United States the quality press is the main source of foreign policy news through its excellent, wide-ranging coverage of overseas, as well as national, events (Beaudoin & Thorson, 2002; Mermin, 1999; Paletz, 2002). It has at its disposal a wide range of news sources independent of the government (Tifft & Jones, 1999) and draws its influence from its critical stance and lack of dependence on other institutions, governmental or otherwise.

On the other hand, the nonelite newspapers tend to be called "cheap," "yellow," "mass," "infotainment," with little or no feelings of social responsibility (Dahlgren & Sparks, 1992). They report more "soft news" on human interest subjects, on the "colorful" aspects of the news, through dramatic and entertainment literary and visual devices. Little intellectual effort is demanded of the reader—the reading experience is simple and enjoyable (Paletz, 2002). Literary antecedents of this approach are mythology and romance, emphasizing melodramatic and "human-interest" genres (Roeh, 1989). Specific techniques are colorful description (Bird, 2002), especially in headlines. The reader is enticed to "feel" the news, and the presentation is "camera"-oriented, inviting a "close-up" view of events (Dahlgren & Sparks, 1992). Unfortunately, despite its widespread popularity this entire press category suffers from profound research neglect, as very little serious literature on this type of journalism has been produced.

It has to be noted, though, that a strict differentiation between two archetypes is not altogether accurate, for thousands of papers around the world are what we would call "mass-popular" but not "yellow-sensational." The former produce real news and serious commentary, albeit short and simple. Moreover, the two archetypes do not always act in accordance with their usual approach; if the elite press has slowly begun to adopt some structural-format aspects of colorful journalism (e.g., more color photos and how-to columns), the popular press in times of crisis tends to offer more serious treatment of the issues at hand (Bird, 2002). There is one element in which no clear demarcation between the two types of paper can be made: political position. Both elite and popular newspapers can be found in either the Left or Right camps on a host of issues. However, a paper's political line can indeed influence the framing of its coverage by way of editing techniques, reportorial slant, unidimensional commentary, and the paper's daily, official, editorial take on the issues of the day.

The need for more in-depth examination and analysis of the differences between press coverage by type of paper regarding foreign policy, has become especially pronounced over the past two decades due to the huge expansion of the media and the increased amounts of information flowing from the field. The importance of the mass media is also related to the satiated and highly educated democratic public at large that no longer can be easily railroaded into supporting war. Thus, democratic governments are more dependent on public opinion (Foyle, 1999; Mueller, 1994; Paletz, 2002; Power, 2002; Powlick, 1995; Shapiro & Jacobs, 2000; Sobel, 2001), itself dependent on its major source of information—the mass media (Brody & Morin, 1991; Everts, 2000; Splichal, 1999; Jentleson & Britton, 1998; Malek, 1996; Page & Shapiro, 1992; Rogers & Dearing, 1988; Ruddock, 2001; Van

Belle, 2000; Zaller, 1992). Consequently, several experts recommend pursuing different research strategies. Ours is to examine newspaper frameworks regarding foreign policy, but to do this through the prism of different types of media.

GOVERNMENT—INTERNATIONAL CRISES

One can find definitions in the research literature of two levels of crisis: macro-objective and micro-subjective. From a systems perspective (macro), a crisis entails an event constituting a drastic change, influencing and destabilizing the international system (Brecher & Wilkenfeld, 1997; Young, 1968). From a psychological perspective (micro), focusing on the decision-making process, the foreign policy crisis is defined as a situation that is perceived as threatening one or more of the basic values; leaves finite time for response; and carries a high probability of involvement in military hostilities involving a heightened risk of violence (Brecher & Wilkenfeld, 1997).

The present study follows Brecher's (1993) categorization of four international crisis phases, regarding the extent of violence:

1. *Onset*, the precrisis period typified by change in the intensity of disruption between two or more states, a significant increase in the potential for violence, and threat perception by at least one of them.
2. *Escalation*, involving a significant increase in the severity of disruption and a growing probability of hostilities and use of military force between the parties. On the micro-level this is the peak of the crisis, with increased time pressure and growing probability of violence adding to the feeling of maximal threat.
3. *De-escalation*, characterized by reduction in hostile and violent interactions leading to accommodation and crisis termination.
4. *Impact*, occurring in the postcrisis period, which includes the consequences of a crisis. We omitted this phase from the research, because our study focuses on the functions of the media during a crisis and not afterwards.

These crisis phases and the various parts of the present research were applied to the Bosnian crisis (1992-1995). This was a product of the ongoing Yugoslavian conflict that turned into a crisis and then escalated into outright war (Brecher & Wilkenfeld, 1997). This crisis was one of the first extended, complex, and highly violent crises that American foreign policy makers had to deal with since the demise of the Soviet Union (Daalder &

Forman, 1999; Jentleson & Britton, 1998; Kanner, 2001; LoTempio & Eldred, 2000).

Sarajevo served for years as a sterling example of cosmopolitan culture—a combination of Eastern and Western Christianity, together with Islam. Yet the Bosnian War was characterized by great cruelty: mortar fire on unarmed civilian populations, concentration camps, mass rape, as well as the combined use of military, paramilitary, and guerilla warfare along with terrorism. All these destroyed the city, and in Bosnia as a whole 200,000 people were killed, an additional 180,000 were injured, and 3,000,000 were turned into refugees (Holbrooke, 1998; Power, 2002; Weiss, 1996). Throughout this international crisis the UN passed approximately thirty resolutions, applied sanctions, froze diplomatic relations, set up various peace conferences to discuss the tragedy, but no military intervention was forthcoming for the first two years of hostilities (Daalder, 2000; Daalder & Forman, 1999; Holbrooke, 1998).

As the world's sole superpower since the breakup of the Soviet empire in the late 1980s, the United States has had difficulty defining its international interests and central role in the new international (dis)order (Hass, 1997). The Bosnian case study can serve as an exemplar for understanding the policy of countervailing forces within the United States during the post–Cold War era (Bennet, Flickinger, & Rhine, 1997; Ullman, 1996). One should note that the Bosnian crisis was largely ethnic in character—precisely the type of conflict on the increase since the fall of the Soviet Union (Daalder & O'Hanlon, 1999; Saideman, 2001; Sarkees, Wayman, & Singer, 2003; Seib, 1997; Vuckovic, 1999)—with direct influence on the degree of superpower intervention as well as on media coverage.

RESEARCH DESIGN

Propositions

Before analyzing the position and frame of each newspaper during the crisis phases we offer two basic propositions through which we can detail the elite and popular press's functioning.

1. A link exists between crisis stage and the sundry papers' positions on the issue.
2. A link exists between crisis stage and the sundry papers' framing of the issue.

We are attempting a pioneering study in two senses: (a) *news framing and positions held* during foreign policy *crisis* (not war/peace); (b) distinguishing between *elite and popular press* functioning, for there is hardly any prior research that describes precisely what such press coverage will look like during each crisis stage.

Methodology

The complexity of the topic and lack of former integrative research required several steps to be taken in approaching the issue. We first mapped all the significant events of the crisis (*Keesing's,* 1992-1994; Reuters, 1995). The period under study was from June 1991 until November 1995—107 specific dates in all. Then we selected only those in which the United States was mentioned (initiating/reacting); thus, twenty-three main events formed the core sample of the study.

In order to examine the newspapers' positions and frames and compare the functioning of the press by type, we thought it preferable to perform a qualitative and quantitative content analysis of two elite and two popular newspapers. Of the former, we chose two of the leading U.S. papers (Merrill, 1995; Smith & Epstein, 2001; Vincent, 2000): *The Washington Post* (henceforth *WP*) and *The Wall Street Journal* (*WSJ*). We focused on commentary and editorial articles in order to analyze framing and positions taken, for these constitute the most important issues on the news agenda and reflect/influence to a large extent the public agenda (Grosswiler, 1996). In the elite press especially, these articles tend to be more critical of government policy than what is presented on the news pages. All daily issues were examined during the twenty-three specific events under scrutiny two weeks before and after each main event, in order to ensure that all relevant material was included.

The same type of analysis was carried out for the popular press. We chose *The Washington Times* (*WT*) and *USA Today* (*USAT*), in part because they cover the same geographic areas as the two selected elite newspapers. However, because of the different nature of the popular press, not to mention the reading practices of its audience, we felt that we had to use a different methodology in order to examine the papers' attitudes. The news headlines were analyzed for a few reasons. First, the readers of this type of paper tend to "scan" the headlines, which are usually quite descriptive, emphasizing the most interesting details from the text (Paletz, 2002), thus priming the audience by highlighting the "main" issue. It seems that most readers very infrequently read the entire text (Nir & Roeh, 1992) as it tends to have built-in redundancy with the headline, especially regarding overseas news. Furthermore, the commentary section is much less popular among these readers than it is for the elite press's more educated and "involved" readership. For the popular press we analyzed Bosnia-related news items for the 10-day period before and after the major events noted above, in order to cover all news related to the issue. Sixty such items were identified in WP and 64 in WSJ (altogether 124 articles), in addition to 139 from WT and 432 in USAT (altogether 571 news reports)—overall 695 items.

Inquiring into the positions and central frame used by the press required planning and developing different categories and various scales, which helped to describe and define the specific attitudes of the articles/news headline. Because the study is wide-ranging, several scales and categories were developed, of which two are directly relevant to the topic at hand: (a) the main position taken in the article/headline towards government policy (pro, pro with reservations, neutral, anti with reservations, anti). This scale has a constant range between its categories, enabling us to characterize the publications' general approach; and (b) the type of frame (security and world order, economic, humanitarian, domestic politics, or a combination of these). This scale was designed to define which main argument was emphasized in constructing the paper's main position. The examination of the articles and news headlines required a comprehensive and close reading in order to elicit the specific position and central frame of each news item (in the discussion section examples are provided based on these scales). Because our methodology involves a subjective element due to its qualitative components, we also tested for intercoder reliability.[2]

The scales were further divided into the first three central crisis phases as delineated earlier (Brecher, 1993), in order to examine how the press (elite and popular) functioned in each stage. The "Onset" phase included four dates, from April 6, 1992, to February 1, 1993, during which the United States did not offer to intervene diplomatically or militarily. The Escalation phase included sixteen dates from February 10, 1993 (when the U.S. offered to lend its diplomatic services for finding a peaceful solution to the Bosnian crisis), until June 1994. The third phase (De-escalation) included three dates running from October 5, 1995, until November 21, 1995 (Dayton Agreement). In addition, in several cases, in order to further substantiate the findings, the research material included a number of articles and interviews, appearing in different publications, written by senior government officials and media practitioners.

FINDINGS

As we can see from Table 6.1, dealing with the position of the press by crisis phases, the statistical test (contingency coefficient) proved unequivocally (highly significant) that the press's stance vis-à-vis government policy changes from (crisis) phase to phase.

Table 6.2 also clearly shows that the central frame put forward by the press undergoes significant change from one crisis phase to another. Thus, overall changes in the press's treatment of the conflict are strongly correlat-

TABLE 6.1. Position of All Four Newspapers by Crisis Phase

POSITION OF THE PRESS	CRISIS PHASES					
	PHASE 1		PHASE 2		PHASE 3	
	N	%	N	%	N	%
Pro	2	2	20	4.4	18	12.7
Pro with Reservations	13	13.5	78	17	21	14.8
Neutral-Balanced	25	26	131	28.7	30	21.1
Anti with Reservations	35	36.5	140	30.6	50	35.2
Anti	21	22	88	19.3	23	16.2
Total	96	100	457	100	142	100

$C = 0.171$ $p = 0.007$

TABLE 6.2. Framing of All Four Newspapers by Crisis Phase

POSITION OF THE PRESS	CRISIS PHASES					
	PHASE 1		PHASE 2		PHASE 3	
	N	%	N	%	N	%
Security and World-Order	50	52.1	303	66.3	84	59.1
Economic	0	0	8	1.7	6	4.3
Humanitarian	29	30.2	94	20.6	11	7.8
Domestic Politics	0	0	20	4.4	28	19.7
Combination	17	17.7	23	5	5	3.5
Other	0	0	9	2	8	5.6
Total	96	100	457	100	142	100

$C = 0.355$ $p = 0.000$

ed to the crisis phases, constituting a basis for pursuing the specific changes by newspaper type *through the three crisis phases.*

Table 6.3 shows the elite press to be quite highly critical of government policy during the first crisis phase: seventy-five percent of articles were critical. Indeed, during this phase not one single column was unequivocally supportive of government policy regarding the Bosnian crisis, and only a very few were conditionally supportive. On the other hand, the popular press displayed a much more moderate stance: most news items were conditionally critical or neutral vis-à-vis government policy. The second phase exhibited some decrease of elite press criticism, but almost half the columns (48.2%) were critical and none were totally supportive. In the popular press the largest categories during the second phase were neutral (31%) and moderately critical (30.8%). The highly critical items decreased 40 percent in relative terms and the completely supportive ones increased relatively by over 100 percent (in absolute terms over 1000%!). Thus, during the height of the crisis, the popular press was far more supportive and less critical than the elite press. During the third stage, elite press criticism dropped by about 50 percent, with neutral and supportive positions taking their place—and yet the largest category was still conditional criticism (40%). The popular press, on the other hand, increased the number of absolutely supportive items threefold, with a significant additional number being neutral, and yet here too the largest category remained conditionally critical (34%). Thus, overall, support for the government's actions increased in all the papers during the de-escalation phase of the crisis, but still a good measure of conditionally critical reportage and commentary was in evidence.

TABLE 6.3. Positions of the Elite Press and Popular Press by Crisis Phase

		CRISIS PHASES			
	PHASE 1		PHASE 2		PHASE 3	
POSITION						
Elite Press	N	%	N	%	N	%
Pro	0	0	0	0	0	0
Pro with Reservations	1	6.2	3	3.6	4	16
Neutral-Balanced	3	18.7	15	18	5	20
Anti with Reservations	7	43.8	25	30.2	10	40
Anti	5	31.3	40	48.2	6	24
Total	16	100	83	100	25	100
Popular Press						
Pro	2	2.5	20	5.4	18	15.4
Pro with Reservations	12	15	75	20	17	14.6
Neutral-Balanced	22	27.5	116	31	25	21.5
Anti with Reservations	28	35	115	30.8	40	34
Anti	16	20	48	12.8	17	14.5
Total	80	100	374	100	117	100

When we turn to the issue of news *framing*, as can be seen in Table 6.4, here, too, we find differences between the two types of press. In the first phase of the crisis, the elite press focused on two frames in equal measure: humanitarian and security (37.5% each) or a combination thereof (25%). The popular press, though, largely emphasized the security issue (55%), with humanitarian issues far behind (29%). In all the newspapers, other frames did not exist at this point. Things changed during the second phase: the elite press emphasized the humanitarian issue (50%), with security decreasing and for the first time economic (4.8%) and political (3.6%) issues emerging. The popular press went in a completely different direction: 74 percent of the items were framed in security terms, with the humanitarian issue dropping by 50 percent and domestic-political (4.6%) as well as economic (1%) frames beginning to rear their heads. In the third phase, the elite press significantly lowered the humanitarian frame, with the domestic-political frame taking up much of the slack (an eightfold increase)—equaling the security frame (28%). These two frames also appeared for the first time in combination with each other (the economic frame doubled its representation). In the popular press, despite some reduction the security frame still dominated (65.8%), with domestic politics increasing by a factor of four and economics by three and a half. In both elite and popular newspapers, the

TABLE 6.4. Framing of the Elite Press and Popular Press by Crisis Phase

	CRISIS PHASES					
FRAMING	PHASE 1		PHASE 2		PHASE 3	
Elite Press	N	%	N	%	N	%
Pro	0	0	0	0	0	0
Pro with Reservations	1	6.2	3	3.6	4	16
Neutral-Balanced	3	18.7	15	18	5	20
Anti with Reservations	7	43.8	25	30.2	10	40
Anti	5	31.3	40	48.2	6	24
Total	16	100	83	100	25	100
Popular Press						
Pro	2	2.5	20	5.4	18	15.4
Pro with Reservations	12	15	75	20	17	14.6
Neutral-Balanced	22	27.5	116	31	25	21.5
Anti with Reservations	28	35	115	30.8	40	34
Anti	16	20	48	12.8	17	14.5
Total	80	100	374	100	117	100

humanitarian frame ceased to be relevant at this phase of the crisis, as the process of ethnic cleansing and other atrocities had by and large ceased to occur in Bosnia.

DISCUSSION: MEDIA FUNCTIONS

Our findings clearly show significant—albeit not consistent—differences between the treatment of the Bosnian crisis by the American elite press as opposed to the popular press. The underlying reason for this seems to be the different news function that each type views as being paramount. Another possible factor underlying such differences could be the nature of their respective audiences, that is, the need for each type of newspaper to present the news and commentary in ways that resonate best with their respective audiences.

The first stage of the crisis (Onset), characterized by lack of U.S involvement, was marked by a relatively high level of criticism on the part of all the newspapers, but more so by the elite press. This is not unusual, as one would expect the elite press to be more involved in foreign policy matters and more willing to serve its watchdog function. The popular press tends to perceive itself less as a watchdog and more as a neutral reporter of the news. This may be in part due to the fact that its audience is broader and more heterogeneous politically and socially, so that being overly critical might well alienate sectors among its traditional readership.

The respective framing at this stage is also not completely surprising: the elite press emphasized to a greater extent the humanitarian problem of ethnic cleansing (this supports the findings of Grosswiler, 1996, and Malek, 1996, who also found greater stress on the humanitarian aspect among the elite press), given the greater interest of its audience on civil rights; the popular press had a more national security slant based on its broader audience's more fundamental interests.

The historical context of the Bosnian Crisis is also important to understanding the different frames of the two types of press. With the Cold War over just a few years earlier, the elite press needed to find a different slant for framing the international news, as its audience would no longer be moved by (or scared into) saber rattling. Given American history and values, the humanitarian frame strikes a deep resonance, especially for the Baby Boom generation brought up on civil rights and other "liberationist" ideologies. Moreover, for those steeped in international politics (readers of the elite press) it seems that it was becoming increasingly clear that although Big Wars were no longer in the cards, the world was increasingly suffering from low-intensity conflict (LIC, e.g., civil wars), most of which are based on ethnic cleavages. Thus, for the elite press (even the *WSJ*), humanitarian framing of the Bosnian crisis was not merely a particularistic matter but rather could be understood as the paradigm for conflict in the post–Cold War era, and as such more likely to strike a chord with the audience and concomitantly with the powers-that-be (Jentleson & Britton, 1998).

The popular press, however, could not so easily abandon the tradition-al national security frame that had served it so well for half a century—and even if it was capable of doing so, its broad (and less educated/knowledge-able) audience would certainly not be able to abandon the security news frame on such short notice, a mere two-three years after the fall of the Iron Curtain. Moreover, the general public (certainly, but not only, in a country with a deep streak of isolationism) usually does not tend to have much of an opinion—and certainly will not have a critical perspective—regarding its government's handling of foreign affairs unless (and until) the nation com-mits palpable resources (monetary or personnel). Thus, one can expect the popular press to remain relatively muted in its criticism of government for-eign policy during the first stage of a crisis.

Press criticism of the government's (mis)handling of foreign policy, especially when sounded from the pages of the elite press (by its very nature, read avidly by policymakers), can be quite influential in moving the government to reassess its policy. We make no argument here as to the exact measure of contribution on the part of elite press criticism to such change, but the first stage soon enough led the Administration to the second stage of crisis, Escalation—that is, greater American involvement—and press criticism also decreased somewhat as a result. Indeed, the elite press now criticized the administration not so much for what it was doing but rather for what it was not doing *enough of* regarding the ongoing violence in the area. In order to reinforce this humanitarian frame, the elite press began a semantic process of demonization, comparing the Serbs to "Nazi bad guys" and using such phraseology as "New Hitler," "Serb warlords," and "war criminals." Conversely, the Bosnians were characterized as "victims," "innocent people," and "refugees"—all of whom were undergoing "human suffering" in a "humanitarian disaster." The general situation itself was denoted as "law of the jungle," "genocide," "mass murder," and "systemat-ic slaughter."

The following *WP* editorial, published on April 23, 1993, was represen-tative of elite press framing during this period (our emphases):

> The feeling of **moral obligation** promoted by the new **Holocaust** Memorial Museum, coinciding with the **public outrage** generated by fresh **Serb brutalities** in Bosnia . . . in dealing with the issue of **Serb aggression**. . . . Belgrade and Bosnia Serbs have not bowed to repeated international condemnations . . . threatened **war crimes** trials. . . . It is time to stop the killing and **"ethnic cleansing."**

One can discern here that certain recognizable terms such as "Holocaust" were used to heighten the emotional impact of the news frame. Moreover, the American audience (as opposed, for example, to its French counterpart) is more attuned to a moral-humanitarian than to a "realpolitik" frame, especially when there is a need to overcome its traditional antipathy to overseas involvement, an isolationist position harking back to Washington's Farewell Address.

And yet, as we saw in the Findings section, the popular press continued to emphasize the national security frame. For example, a *USAT* news item (April 20, 1994), after a Serbian attack, was headlined: "New Sense of Urgency in Policy on Bosnia." Above and beyond the reasons noted earlier in this discussion, another possible explanation for the dichotomy between elite and popular press framing of the issue is the materialism/postmaterialism divide (Inglehart & Abramson, 1995). The popular press readership— less educated—is more heavily "materialistic" in the classic values sense (e.g., pre-eminence of security issues), whereas the elite press addresses a highly educated audience with a more postmaterialistic value system—for example, civil rights (Naisbitt, 1982). This is a function of the higher socioeconomic class moving up the Maslow pyramid from basic needs to "higher" needs such as self-expression. Political freedom and other similar abstract, liberal-humanistic concepts, usually speak more to those who no longer have to worry about their basic livelihood—by and large, the entire audience of the elite press. The popular press, most of whose audience is middle-to-lower class, still seeks stability and security, so that their papers' news frame will tend to concentrate on the security issue on the national (and personal) level. In short, it seems that each type of press speaks in an "ideological-value" language geared to the contemporary mentality of its respective audience.

How can one define popular press functioning (and to a very limited extent, elite press as well) at this second stage, in light of its growing support of government policy? With America becoming more heavily involved in the Bosnian crisis, even if not yet militarily, the press began a process of "self-mobilization," taking on in part the role of "rallying-round-the flag." With the nation's reputation as sole superpower "world policeman" being tested, the press began to restrain itself from taking an overly critical position that could cause a public backlash. When the national interest is on the line and danger exists for loss of (American) life in a violent situation, the press becomes much more of a consensus-manufacturing factor. This is especially true of the popular press with its broader-based audience and greater "patriotism."

However, the Bosnian case does suggest that this is not a hard and fast rule, for signs of criticism could still be found in the popular press as well at this stage. For instance, a *WT* news item (April 19, 1994) on the Serbian attack on UN troops was headlined: "Finger Pointing Takes Place of Action in Bosnia." The elite press, as well, did not exercise full restraint, that is, become fully self-mobilized. A possible explanation for this is that direct national interests were not at stake in the Bosnian crisis (other than America's reputation as sole world policeman), nor were American troops' lives in danger. Indeed, the criticism of Administration policy was that the country was not committing *enough* resources to the crisis:

> Suddenly, in the depths of August and the budget debate, the war in Bosnia has reached a crux. . . . Meanwhile, President Clinton is busy lobbying for his tax increase. . . . We would **certainly support anything that could be done to help the Bosnians**. . . . If the Clinton administration somehow decides to send the Air Force to Sarajevo, we hope that it's **part of some plan that could actually make a difference. So far the West has slipped further and further into this war, with no plan to bring it to an end.** (WSJ editorial, May 8, 1993, p. A 12; emphases ours)

It is clear, therefore, that among other things, the different levels of "rallying-round-the-flag" by the press will be determined by how serious the respective newspaper types view the crisis—and how involved their country has become in resolving the crisis de facto. In the Bosnian case, the crisis was indeed severe—for Bosnia and Central Europe, but was less so for the United States per se. Another element that is involved in the level of press support/criticism is the solidarity found within the ruling Establishment. Here, too, there were some disagreements between the Clinton Administration and the Republican leadership in the Senate, so that press criticism could not have been perceived as being "traitorous."

The third stage (De-escalation phase) presents an equally complex picture. On the one hand, the Administration succeeded in ending the conflict, thereby winding down the violence; on the other hand, the operative outcome was that American troops were heavily ensconced in Bosnia and probably staying there for awhile. Thus, the elite press evinced *both* a high level of support as well as strong criticism. For example, on October 13, 1995, towards the signing of the Dayton Accord, the *WSJ* issued an editorial "Drifting Into Bosnia" (p. A14):

> . . . . Now, the U.S. and NATO will seek to forge a permanent peace by intermediating between indicted war criminals and their victims. . . . In this exercise, 25,000 American troops would be just right, the Clinton Administration tells us. . . . The Bosnians' troop commitment plan betrays the **ad hoc nature of this administration's foreign policy.** Important commitments are made as part of a presidential **rhetorical exercise** or White House **improvisation**, unified by one principle: **Get Bosnia off the front pages until after November 1996.** . . . But it [e.g.

building the Bosnian army] can't be done with **U.S. troops as peace-keeping hostages** and it doesn't require 25,000 troops. . . . Sending U.S. combat troops into the middle of **somebody else's war** is a serious matter. Fighting troops are trained to fight, not to offer themselves **as targets for war criminal** Ratko Mladic's thugs. If this is to be the role of the U.S. troops Mr. Clinton is promising, Congress has every right, indeed responsibility, **to challenge the President.** . . . Not because we are turning isolationist, but precisely because we believe the American superpower has interests in and responsibilities to keep peace in the world. . . . **This need not require American ground troops.**

The popular press was more supportive overall in phase 3, but here too one can find criticism, albeit framed more in political and economic terms, that is, the consequences for the domestic political scene. For instance, a *WT* news item (November 25, 1995) after the Dayton agreement was headlined "Congress Will Ask why Bosnia Won't Be Rerun of Somalia." This criticism does not contradict its traditional role of cheerleader during a crisis, for the crisis was now basically over. As such, there was probably less need to frame the issues in foreign policy terms (where the action had died down); it was possible and even logical, to frame the issue in terms of *domestic* consequences that interested the general audience in any case. Moreover, with presidential elections approaching, it was obvious that the Administration's overall handling of the Bosnian issue needed to be placed within the general political context.

Overall, though, the press coverage during this latter crisis stage was more positive—a clear reflection of the successful conclusion of the whole affair. However, in comparing the level of praise/criticism between the two types of press, it is clear that each tends to what it views as its prime function. The elite press stressed the watchdog elements of policy critique; the popular press emphasized more the cheerleading approach towards consensus-building. Indeed, the "half" success (end of the war), "half" failure (American troops stuck in Bosnia) enables us to clearly see how each press type gravitates to its basic stance. As we have seen throughout this study, this is but a continuation of the general pattern: the elite press tends to be more critical than the supportive, popular press in all stages—with each type adding some supportive or critical flavor, respectively, in light of violent developments in the international arena.

CONCLUSION

This study offered a comprehensive look at the media's functioning, comparing two different types, during the multiple phases of an international crisis. The contribution of this research can be seen as both theoretical and practical. Theoretically, we tried to present an integrated outlook combining theories from different fields (international relations and mass communications) in order to explain the media's performance during an international crisis. In doing so, we hope to have made clearer the functioning of the press in foreign policy making, especially during a crisis period, where virtually very little research has been undertaken heretofore. Our basic conclusion is that the media seem to react to the government's foreign policy in a way that adapts to the "politico-philosophical" function of the press (by type) over the various phases of the crisis—in part due to the nature of each newspaper's audience (regarding the readers' educational/ knowledge background as well as their social value system), and, of course, also in relation to the nature of the crisis and its context.

On the practical side, several explanations were offered for the press's functioning during the crisis phases, in the hope that journalism practitioners, government official, and students will more clearly understand the function (position and framing) that the media can play in foreign policy. Hopefully, this will improve the media's coverage and analysis of international crises while enabling foreign policy makers to improve their dealings with the press, especially regarding ethnic conflicts that have come to dominate the international arena at the turn of the millennium.

Nevertheless, much work remains to be done in order to fully explore this complex topic. Future studies might look into different case studies with other elements to broaden our understanding of media functioning during international crises. Such elements might include different types of democratic regimes; a short-term crisis; a small state's foreign policy; other media, for example, electronic—again by type (public vs. private) and so forth. Additional studies should also try to focus on the most effective ways to examine and integrate knowledge from different disciplines while exploring the best methods for scrutinizing the enigma of influence.

As a modest initial exploration, we hope that the present study can be considered a useful first step along the road to a better understanding of how the media deal with what has become an increasingly important subject in both mass communications and international relations studies: press functioning during foreign policy crisis at different levels of violence.

NOTES

1. The three other approaches are: social-responsibility (located between the aforementioned two), authoritarian, and totalitarian. For elaboration see Siebert et al. (1956) for the original four; Hutchins (1947) on social responsibility; and McQuail (1987), for additional philosophical approaches.

2. The results for inter-coder reliability were highly supportive of coding consistency: regarding 'Position', Cronbach Alpha = .932; for the 'Frame' = .938.

REFERENCES

Arno, A. (1984). Communication, conflict and storylines: The news media as actors in a cultural context. In A. Arno & W. Dissanayake (Eds.), *The news media in national and international conflict* (pp. 1-16). Boulder: Westview Press.

Beaudoin, C. & Thorson, E. (2002). Spiral of violence? Conflict and conflict resolution in international news. In E. Gilboa (Ed.), *Media and conflict* (pp. 45-64). New York: Transnational Publishers.

Bennett, S. E., Flickinger, R. S., & Rhine, S. L. (1997). American public opinion and the civil war in Bosnia. *The Harvard International Journal of Press/Politics, 2*, 87-105.

Bird, E. S. (2002). Taking it personally: Supermarket tabloids after September 11. In B. Zelizer & S. Allan (Eds.), *Journalism after September 11* (pp. 141-159). New York: Routledge.

Bloch, Y. & Lehman-Wilzig, S. (2002). An exploratory model of media-government relations in international crises: U.S. Involvement in Bosnia 1992-1995. In E. Gilboa (Ed.), *Media and conflict* (pp. 153-169). New York: Transnational Publishers.

Brecher, M. (1993). *Crises in world politics: Theory and reality*. Oxford & New York: Pergamon Press.

Brecher, M. & Wilkenfeld, J. (1997). *A study of crisis*. Ann Arbor: The University of Michigan Press.

Brody, R. A. & Morin R. (1991, 31 March). From Vietnam to Iraq: The great American syndrome myth. *Washington Post*, p. B2.

Brown, R. (2001, February 20-24). *Foreign policy and the press revisited: From* The New York Times *to the internet.* Paper presented at the International Studies Association (ISA) annual meeting, Chicago, Illinois.

Callaghan, K. & Schnell, F. (2001). Assessing the democratic debate: How the news media frame elite policy discourse. *Political Communication, 18*, 183-212.

Daalder, I. H. (2000). *Getting to Dayton: The making of America's Bosnia policy*. Washington, DC: Brookings Institute.

Daalder, I. H. & Forman, M. B. G. (1999). Dayton's incomplete peace. *Foreign Affairs, 78*, 106-121.

Daalder, I. H. & O'Hanlon, M. (1999). Unlearning the lessons of Kosovo. *Foreign Policy, 116*, 128-140.

Dahlgren, P. & Sparks C. (1992). *Journalism and popular culture*. London: Sage.

D'Angelo, P. (2002). News framing as a multiparadigmatic research program: A response to Entman. *Journal of Communication, 52*, 870-888.

Durham, F. D. (1998). News frames as social narratives: TWA flight 800. *Journal of Communication, 48*, 100-117.

Eilders, C. & Luter, A. (2000). Research note: Germany at war: Competing framing strategies in German public discourse. *European Journal of Communication, 15*, 415-428.

Entman, R. M. (1991). Framing U.S. coverage of international news: Contrasts in narratives of the KAL and Iran air incidents. *Journal of Communication, 41*, 6-27.

Entman, R. M. (1993). Framing: Towards clarification of a fractured paradigm. *Journal of Communication, 43*, 51-58.

Entman, R. M. & Rojecki, A. (1993). Freezing out the public: Elite and media framing of the U.S. anti-nuclear movement. *Political Communication, 10*, 155-173.

Everts, P. (2000). When the going gets rough: Does the public support the use of military force? *World Affairs, 162*, 91-107.

Foyle, D. C. (1999). *Counting the public in presidents, public opinion and foreign policy.* New York: Columbia University Press.

Gamson, W. (1992). *Talking politics.* Cambridge: Cambridge University Press.

Gamson, W. A. & Herzog, H. (1999). Living with contradictions: The taken-for-granted in Israeli political discourse. *Political Psychology, 20*, 247-266.

Gitlin, T. (1977, 1 April). Spotlight and shadows: Television and the culture of politics. *College English*, 790-798.

Gitlin, T. (1980). *The whole world is watching.* Berkeley: University of California Press.

Grosswiler, P. (1996). The impact of media and images on foreign policy: Elite U.S. newspaper editorial coverage of surviving communist countries in the post–cold war era. In A. Malek (Ed.), *News media & foreign relations* (pp. 195-210). Norwood, NJ: Ablex.

Hass, R. N. (1997). *The reluctant sheriff.* New York: A Council on Foreign Relations Book (Brookings Institution Press).

Holbrooke, R. (1998). *To end a war.* New York: Random House.

Holsti, O. R. (1996). *Public opinion and American foreign policy.* Ann Arbor: The University of Michigan Press.

Hutchins, R. M. (Ed.). (1947). *A free and responsible press: A general report on mass communication: Newspapers, radio, motion pictures, magazines, and books.* Chicago: University of Chicago Press.

Inglehart, R. & Abramson, P. (1995). *Value change in global perspective.* Ann Arbor: University of Michigan Press.

Iyengar, S. & Simon, A. F. (1997). News coverage of the Gulf crisis and public opinion: A study of agenda setting, priming and framing. In S. Iyengar & R. Reeves (Eds.), *Do the media govern? Politicians, voters and reporters in America* (pp. 248-257). Thousand Oaks, CA: Sage.

Jentleson, B. W. & Britton, R. L. (1998). Still pretty prudent: Post-cold war American public opinion on the use of military force. *Journal of Conflict Resolution, 42*, 395-417.

Kanner, M. D. (2001, February 20-24). *Framing, risk, and interventions.* Paper presented at the International Studies Association (ISA) annual meeting, Chicago, Illinois.

Karim, K. H. (2002). Making sense of the "Islamic peril": Journalism as cultural practice. In B. Zelizer & S. Allan (Eds.), *Journalism after September 11* (pp. 101-116). New York: Routledge.

Keesing's Record of World Events (1992, 1993, 1994). R. East (Ed.). London: Longman (38: 38832-33, 38848-50, 38970-91, 39012-13, 39035-37, 39102-103, 39149-50, 39197-98, 39240; 39: 39277-79, 39327, 39374-75, 39425-27, 39469-70, 39516-19, 39563-65, 39603-606; 40: 39870-72, 39925-27, 40071-73).

Kuypers, J. A. (1997). *Presidential crisis rhetoric and the press in the post–cold war world*. Westport, CT: Praeger.

LoTempio, A. & Eldred, N. A. (2000, August 31). *When the camera never blinks: TV coverage of military conflict and the rally effect*. Paper presented at the American Political Science Association (APSA) annual meeting, Washington, DC.

Malek, A. (1996). "New York Times" editorial position and U.S. foreign policy: The case of Iran revisited. In A. Malek (Ed.), *News media & foreign relations* (pp. 224-245). Norwood, NJ: Ablex.

McCombs, M. E. & Shaw, D. L. (1993). The evolution of agenda-setting research. *Journal of Communication, 43*, 58-67.

McQuail, D. (1987). *Mass communication theory: An introduction*. London: Sage.

Mermin, J. (1999). *Debating war and peace*. Princeton, NJ: Princeton University Press.

Merrill, J. (1968, Spring). Global patterns of elite daily journalism. *Journalism Quarterly*, 99-105.

Merrill, J. (1995). *Global journalism*. New York: Longman.

Moskos, C. C. & Ricks, T. E. (1995). *Reporting war when there is no war: The media and the military in peace and humanitarian operations*. Cantigny Conference Series special report. Chicago: Robert R. McCormick Tribune Foundation.

Mueller, J. E. (1994). *Policy and opinion in the Gulf war*. Chicago: University of Chicago Press.

Naisbitt, J. (1982). *Megatrends: Ten new directions transforming our lives*. New York: Warner Books.

Naveh, H. (2002). The role of the media in foreign policy decision-making: A theoretical framework. *Conflict & Communication Online, 1*, 1-14.

Nir, R. & Roch, I. (1992). Intifada coverage in the Israeli press: Popular and quality papers assume a rhetoric of conformity. *Discourse & Society, 3*, 47-60.

Norris, P. (1997). *Politics and the press*. London: Lynne Rienner.

Nossek, H. (2003). Our news and their news: On the role of national identity in the definition of political violence and terrorism as news. *Nekudat Mifgash* (Israeli periodical), *A-1*, 75-116.

Paletz, D. L. (2002). *The media in American politics*. New York: Longman.

Page, B. I. & Shapiro, R. (1992). *The rational public: Fifty years of trends in American policy*. Chicago: University of Chicago Press.

Power, S. (2002). *A problem from hell*. New York: Basic Books.

Powlick, P. J. (1995). The sources of public opinion for American foreign policy officials. *International Studies Quarterly, 39*, 427-451.

Putnam, L. L., Phillips, N., & Chapman, P. (1996). Metaphors of communication and organization. In S. R. Clegg, C. Hardy, & W. R. Nord (Eds.), *Handbook of organization studies* (pp. 375-408). Thousand Oaks, CA: Sage.

Reuters (1995, December 15). Main events in former Yugoslavia. *Haaretz* [Israeli Daily Newspaper], p. A2.

Rivenburgh, N. (1996). Social identification and media coverage of foreign relations. In A. Malek (Ed.), *News media & foreign relations* (pp. 79-94). Norwood, NJ: Ablex.

Roeh, I. (1989). Journalism as storytelling, coverage as narrative. *American Behavioral Scientist, 33*, 162-168.

Rogers, E. M. & Dearing, J. W. (1988). Agenda-setting research: Where has it been, where is it going. In J. A. Anderson (Ed.), *Communication Yearbook 11* (pp. 555-594). Thousand Oaks, CA: Sage.

Ruddock, A. (2001). *Understanding audiences*. London: Sage.

Russett, B. (1990). *Controlling the sword*. Cambridge, MA: Harvard University Press.

Saideman, S. M. (2001, February, 20-24). *Is everything relative? Dyadic analyses of the international relations of ethnic conflict*. Paper presented at the International Studies Association (ISA) annual meeting, Chicago, Illinois.

Sarkees, M. R., Wayman, F. W., & Singer, D. J. (2003). Inter-state, intra-state, and extra-state wars: A comprehensive look at their distribution over time, 1816-1997. *International Studies Quarterly, 47*, 49-70.

Scheufele, D. A. (1999). Framing as a theory of media effects. *Journal of Communication, 49*, 103-122.

Schudson, M. (2002). What's unusual about covering politics as usual. In B. Zelizer & S. Allan (Eds.), *Journalism after September 11* (pp. 36-47). New York: Routledge.

Seib, P. M. (1997). *Headline diplomacy: How news coverage affects foreign policy*. Westport, CT: Praeger.

Serfaty, S. (1991). The media and foreign policy. In S. Serfaty (Ed.), *The media and foreign policy* (pp. 1-16). New York: St. Martin's Press.

Shapiro, R. Y. & Jacobs, L. R. (2000). Who leads and who follows? U.S. presidents, public opinion and foreign policy. In B. L. Nacos, R. Y. Shapiro, & P. Isernia (Eds.), *Decision making in a glass house* (pp. 223-246). New York: Rowman & Littelfield.

Siebert, F. F., Schramm, W., & Peterson, T. (1956). *Four theories of the press*. Urbana: University of Illinois Press.

Smith, J.Y. & Epstein, N. (2001, July 18). *Post*'s Katharine Graham Dies; Leading Voice in U.S. Journalism. *International Herald Tribune*, 1, 3.

Sobel, R. (2001). *The impact of public opinion on U.S. foreign policy since Vietnam*. Oxford: Oxford University Press.

Splichal, S. (1999). *Public opinion: Developments and controversies in the twentieth century*. Lanham, MD: Rowman & Littlefield.

Tankard, J. W. Jr. (2001). The empirical approach to the study of media framing. In S. D. Reese, O. H. Gandy Jr., & A. E. Grant (Eds.), *Framing public life* (pp. 95-106). Mahwah, NJ: Erlbaum.

Tarde, G. de (1969). Selection from *Logique sociale* (1898). In T. N. Clark (Ed.), *On communication and social influence; Selected papers*. Chicago: University of Chicago Press.

Tifft, S. E. & Jones, A. S. (1999, April 19). The Family. *The New Yorker*, pp. 44-52.

Ullman, R. H. (Ed.). (1996). *The world and Yugoslavia wars*. New York: The Council of Foreign Relations.

Van Belle, D. A. (2000). *Press freedom and global politics*. Westport, CT: Praeger.

Vincent, R. C. (2000). A narrative analysis of US press coverage of Slobodan Milosevic and the Serbs in Kosovo. *European Journal of Communication, 15*, 321-344.

Vuckovic, G. (1999). Promoting peace and democracy in the aftermath of the Balkan wars: Comparative assessment of the democratization and institution-building processes in Croatia, Bosnia and Herzegovina, and former Yugoslavia. *World Affairs, 162,* 3-10.

Waisbord, S. (2002). Journalism, risk, and patriotism. In B. Zelizer & S. Allan (Eds.), *Journalism after September 11* (pp. 202-219). New York: Routledge.

Weiss, T. G. (1996). Collective spinelessness: U.N. actions in the former Yugoslavia. In R. H. Ullman (Eds.), *The world and Yugoslavia wars* (pp. 59-96). New York: The Council of Foreign Relations.

Wolfsfeld, G. (1997). *Media and political conflict.* Cambridge: Cambridge University Press.

Young, O. R. (1968). *The politics of force.* Princeton, NJ: Princeton University.

Zaller, J. R. (1992). *The nature and origins of mass opinion.* New York: Cambridge University Press.

Zaller, J. R. (2001). Monica Lewinsky and the mainsprings of America politics. In L. W. Bennett & R. M. Entman (Eds.), *Mediated politics: Communication in the future of democracy* (pp. 252-278). Cambridge: Cambridge University Press.

Zaller, J. R. & Chiu, D. (2000). Government's little helper: U.S. press coverage of foreign policy crises, 1946-1999. In B. L. Nacos, R. Y. Shapiro & P. Isernia (Eds.), *Decision making in a glass house* (pp. 61-84). New York: Rowman & Littlefield.

Zelizer, B. & Allan, S. (Eds.). (2002). *Journalism after September 11.* New York: Routledge.

Chapter 7

National Perspective in Foreign News Coverage

Australian Reporting of French Nuclear Testing in the Pacific*

Peter Putnis

It is well established that foreign news is reported in the press of individual nations through what Fenby (1986, p. 4) called a "local prism." More controversial are questions of how this local perspective is constituted and how it should be valued. Seen through the lens of UNESCO's New World Information and Communication Order agenda, developed in the 1970s, the local prism was primarily associated with the negative notions of imbalance and distortion. The large variations in the geographic flow of news among countries and regions and the selective reporting of the developing world in the Western media were viewed as the outcome of a flawed global news distribution system. Others, including Fenby, have viewed the local prism as a matter of responsiveness in the selection and presentation of news to the demands of local audiences—that is, as a matter of response to local market forces.

More generally, the local character of foreign news coverage has been viewed as a matter of domestic cultural filtering and framing arising from the inevitable influence of cultural-domestic environments on journalists' pro-

*An earlier version of this chapter appeared in *Asia Pacific Media Educator*, 1998, No. 5, pp. 38-51.

fessional practice (Shoemaker, 1991). These influences are likely to be particularly marked when the national interest is implicated in the foreign events that are being covered.

Gurevitch, Levy and Roeh (1991) point out that foreign news content and presentation in national news services arises out of an interplay of convergent and divergent factors. They comment that "the tendency to 'domesticate' news stories may be regarded as a countervailing force to the pull of globalization . . . [as] . . . the 'same' events are told in divergent ways, geared to the social and political frameworks and sensibilities of diverse domestic audiences" (p. 207). The degree of convergence and divergence in the reporting of the "same" foreign news events across nation states is likely to vary according to many factors, some practical (e.g., degree of reliance on news agencies, access to sources) and others ideological (e.g., degree of national interest involved). Although some aspects of the local coverage might arise from news flow factors, particularly in circumstances of restricted access, others, particularly news framing (Entman, 1991), are likely to arise from the interaction of domestic and foreign concerns. The "domestic context" within which news events are reported is expressed through the use of established culturally salient news frames and narratives. As Gurevitch, Levy, and Roeh (1991, p. 207) put it, "the meaning of a concrete news story is always produced in the public sphere of culture, and in the framework of a relevant family-of-stories, already familiar to members of a given society." This chapter examines the process of localization and the construction of national perspective in news reporting through an analysis of Australian press coverage of a major international news event—France's controversial nuclear testing in the Pacific in 1995. These highly contentious nuclear tests and the protests they provoked made headlines around the world. At the same time, the fact that they were so contentious ensured that national interest played a major role in their media portrayal and interpretation.

The nuclear tests took place on the French Polynesian atoll of Mururoa situated in the Pacific midway between the coasts of Australia and South America and about 1,200 kilometers southwest of Tahiti. This isolated atoll, with a perimeter of 60 km, became France's test center in the early 1960s, after Algeria ceased to be an option following its independence in 1962. The establishment of the Pacific Test Center arose out of the imperatives of post–World War II French nuclear policy and was also an assertion of French colonial power in the Pacific.

France had acquired groups of islands in the South Pacific in the nineteenth century in the context of European imperial rivalry in the region and its ambition to build a "Greater France" through colonization. France, to a greater extent than most other colonial powers, resisted local independence movements and sought to maintain direct control over its colonies. Hence, when the need for a new testing site arose, it was in a position to have

Mururoa and its neighboring island of Fangataufa ceded to it for this purpose. France had embarked on the development of a nuclear arsenal in the late 1950s both for defence purposes and as a vehicle for securing France's status in world affairs. Atomic weapons "made France a power with which other nations had to contend" and were viewed as enhancing "French prestige" (Aldrich, 1993, pp. 306-307).

Between 1966 and 1992, 41 atmospheric and 138 underground tests were conducted. Testing was suspended in 1992 in response to growing international protest, particularly from nations of the South Pacific. However, to international disbelief, French President Jacques Chirac announced on 13 June 1995 that testing would resume and that eight tests would be conducted between September 1995 and May 1996. The decision provoked anti-nuclear protests around the world as well as trade boycotts, particularly in New Zealand, Australia, and Japan. It also gave renewed energy to independence movements among France's Pacific colonies. In the event, six of the eight tests were completed, with the last taking place on 27 January 1996. At that time France announced an end to all testing. In March 1996 it signed the Rarotonga Treaty, thus agreeing to the South Pacific being henceforth a nuclear-free zone.

Our focus is on media coverage of the first of this series of nuclear tests, which took place on 5 September 1995. We examine coverage of the test itself and associated events in the Pacific for the week of 4–9 September in two major Australian broadsheet newspapers, *The Australian* and the *Sydney Morning Herald*. News events reported during this week included demonstrations prior to the test, including the French seizure of a Greenpeace ship that had been heading towards Mururoa, the explosion itself, and demonstrations and riots in Tahiti that followed the test. In the six-day period 51 Mururoa-related stories appeared in *The Australian* and 53 in the *Sydney Morning Herald*.

In order to capture the multifaceted nature of national perspective, three ways of looking at the coverage are utilized in this analysis. In the first instance, Mururoa-related stories are viewed in relation to the total international news output of the two newspapers in the period. The prominence of South Pacific countries in relation to the overall Australian international news map is assessed. A comparative perspective to this analysis of prominence is introduced by examining the extent of Australian coverage in relation to that in the United Kingdom. This aspect of the study is limited to the traditional task of newsflow research of identifying and accounting for differences in the prominence given to foreign news events in the press of different nations. Secondly, the Australian press coverage itself is analyzed in terms of story type, main actors, story perspective, and sources. Here, the main interest is in what Gurevitch, Levy, and Roeh (1991, p. 206) label the "domestication of the foreign" as we consider ways in which a South Pacific event is transformed into an "Australian story." The third view examines the framing role of the South Pacific paradise narrative in the coverage. It is argued that this myth acted as a backdrop against which events were interpreted and that it ultimately inflected these interpretations in a way that supported the political status quo in French Polynesia, despite the violation of the test itself.

Each view contributes to a descriptive account of Australia's press coverage of Mururoa and to some extent, for example in the documentation of news sources and of the "authorised knowers" (Ericson, Baranek, & Chan, 1987, pp. 17-18) with respect to this event, allows us to explain the nature of the coverage. Each view also raises challenging issues about the reporting of international news events in a particular national context. The dominant way of addressing news-mediated relationships among countries has been via the notion of international news flow. Yet this linear notion of news flow between nations is clearly an inadequate model in this case, given the interpenetration of domestic, regional, and global concerns.

THE SOUTH PACIFIC IN THE INTERNATIONAL NEWS MAPS OF AUSTRALIA AND THE UNITED KINGDOM

The period of this particular study (4-9 September 1995) comprised part of the sample period for the international study "Foreign News and Global News Flows in the 1990s," for which the author coordinated the Australian data (see Putnis, Penhallurick, & Bourk, 1997).[1] The media chosen for the Australian data included *The Australian*, the nation's major national daily newspaper, and the *Sydney Morning Herald*, the most important daily of Australia's largest city. Data from this study enabled a comparison of the prominence given to the Mururoa test in the Australian and British press.

For this purpose, two broadly comparable data sets relating to the press of each country were constructed:

1. All items with a clear foreign or international element that appeared in *The Australian* and the *Sydney Morning Herald* for the period 4-9 September 1995—897 items in all.
2. All such stories in *The Telegraph* (U.K.) and *The Guardian* (U.K.) for the same period—1,013 items in all.

Of the Australian data set, 104 stories (or 11.6%) were related to the Mururoa test. In the British data set there were 54 stories (5.3%) related to Mururoa.

These two data sets were analyzed so as to determine the extent to which various countries were represented in the coverage of international news in Britain and Australia. For this purpose (following Putnis et al., 1997) a prominence measure was constructed by assigning simple mathematical values to country references: three points were awarded when a country was ranked as the most important country in a story, two points if it was the second most important, and one point if it was the third most important. Scores were then aggregated and the resulting totals aligned by adjusting the British data to match the size of the Australian data set.

This yielded Table 7.1, "Country Prominence Measure: Top 30 Countries."

TABLE 7.1. Country Prominence Measure: Top 30 Countries

AUSTRALIAN DATA SET		BRITISH DATA SET	
Country Name	Total Score	Country Name	Total Score
Australia	949	United Kingdom	1,026
United States	731	United States	565
France	367	France	311
United Kingdom	345	Europe	153
China	189	Germany	143
South Pacific/French Polynesia	154	Ireland	134
Japan	120	Bosnia-Herzegovina	99
United Nations	92	United Nations	93
New Zealand	90	China	91
Bosnia-Herzegovina	71	Italy	87
India	63	Russia	87
"World Community"/nations	52	South Africa	84
Russia	50	Spain	79
Indonesia	50	India	79
Canada	45	Japan	73
South Africa	43	South Pacific/French Polynesia	71
Germany	42	Australia	66
Hong Kong	37	EU	53
Malaysia	36	NATO	45
Europe	35	Canada	44
Vietnam	34	Belgium	40
Asia, in general	32	Pakistan	38
Spain	31	Sweden	36
Italy	30	Algeria	31
Israel	27	Austria	30
Papua New Guinea	26	Kenya	28
Sri Lanka	26	Iraq	27
Serbia	25	Denmark	27
South Korea	24	New Zealand	24
Pakistan	23	Serbia	23

Table 7.1 compares the international news priorities of Australia and Britain. We can note, for example, that in both data sets international news stories that feature the home country are most prominent. Furthermore, in the survey period the United States and France had similar prominence in both Australia and the United Kingdom, though one suspects that a greater proportion of the stories involving France could be accounted for by the Mururoa test in the Australian data than in the British data. Beyond the top few rankings the two patterns of country prominence in international news diverge significantly with regional interests coming to the fore. Significantly, Britain is 5.2 times more prominent in Australia than Australia is in Britain (see Sreberny, Putnis, Penhallurick, & Bourk, 1998, for further such comparative analyses).

For the purposes of this study two points can be drawn from Table 7.1:

1. The South Pacific/French Polynesian region was 2.2 times more prominent in the Australian press than in the British press. This reflects the relative prominence of the Mururoa story. As indicated earlier, the story accounted for 11.6 percent of the total international news coverage in the Australian data but only 5.3 percent in the British data. Such a differential is consistent with expectations with respect to regional bias in international news priorities (see, for example, Sreberny-Mohammadi et al., 1985), though it could also be influenced by the relative silence of the British Government in response to the French nuclear test when many other countries were protesting loudly.

2. Despite the fact that the Mururoa test was by far the single most newsworthy event of the week, the United States remained by far the most prominent country in the news overall. More generally, Table 7.1 illustrates the point that the influence of extraordinary events, like the Mururoa test, on the overall pattern of international news needs to be balanced against other more constant factors including the dominance of the United States in international news, the influence of traditional cultural links (e.g., Australia and Britain), and the pattern of international links in particular areas of news such as business (where Asia is prominent in the Australian media) and sport (where, for example, New Zealand is prominent in the Australian media). Another way of putting this is to say that virtually all of the coverage of the South Pacific region (except for that of New Zealand and Papua New Guinea) can be accounted for by Mururoa-related stories.

Our analysis thus far simply confirms that the relative prominence given to particular foreign news events—in this case the significantly greater prominence given to the Mururoa nuclear test in Australia than in Britain—

is one dimension of the local prism through which the world is seen by local media. "Regional bias" is a significant factor in this regard.

THE MURUROA TEST IN THE AUSTRALIAN AND THE SYDNEY MORNING HERALD

We now turn to a more detailed consideration of Mururoa-related stories that appeared in *The Australian* and the *Sydney Morning Herald* from 4-9 September 1995. In this six-day period 51 such stories appeared in *The Australian* and 53 in the *Sydney Morning Herald*. If we examine these bodies of text, separately and together, what characteristics and patterns of representation can be discerned?

It hardly needs saying that the coverage of the Mururoa-related events and their aftermath in the Australian press constitutes a very particular representation. The key players, or at least their prominence, in the Australian version of this drama, would be very different from those in the British, New Zealand, or Fijian versions. We would expect the range of interpretative frames and the respective weight given to them to vary greatly between the Australian version and the French version. There are also particular qualities associated with these events that lend themselves to the construction of multiple and competing articulations. The tests inevitably brought into play large cultural and ideological rifts; much of the news was constituted by various reactions to and commentaries on the tests which competed for editorial space; many of the reported events, such as the demonstrations in Papeete and the Greenpeace missions to Mururoa, were specifically designed to maximise media coverage of opposition to the tests; at the same time the French authorities sought to control media access so as to better project their own official version of the test, the visuals of which were presented to the media as a prepackaged (and pre-interpreted) video.

The Australian media's version of events grows out of many factors, some practical (e.g., where overseas correspondents were located), others related to the news values and priorities of journalists writing for an Australian audience, others related to the range of frames of interpretation available to journalists (or provided by sources), and still others arising from the mythologies and stereotypes evoked by these events.

Table 7.2 classifies the 104 stories appearing in *The Australian* and the *Sydney Morning Herald* according to story type. In the first instance, the fact that there were 104 relevant stories in the two newspapers in the six-day period (i.e., over 8 stories per day in each paper) should be remarked upon. This suggests not just the prominence of the story, but the way in which these newspapers construct their overall coverage in terms of multiple perspectives. There is no single story, no single angle, though there may, of

TABLE 7.2. Stories Relating to the Mururoa Test: *The Australian* and the
Sydney Morning Herald, 4/9/95 – 9/9/95

	THE AUSTRALIAN	SYDNEY MORNING HERALD	TOTAL
News stories—event focused	11	8	19
News stories—reaction, interpretation focused	25	17	42
Commentary/editorial	11	8	19
Letters	4	20	24
Total	51	53	104

course, be dominant ones. Rather, each issue of each newspaper characteris-
tically features various aspects of the story written by different, often specialized, journalists—science writer, environment writer, European correspondent, and so on.

It is noteworthy that only 19 of the 104 stories are event focused in the
sense that they are primarily concerned with describing an occurrence. The
other 85 are concerned with interpretation, commentary, and opinion.
Journalism, at least in the quality press, is less a depiction of events as such
than about what is said about them. As Tuchman (1978) pointed out, news
can be usefully seen as an ongoing communication among journalists and
influential sources. This, of course, raises the question of who does and who
does not get a say and what range of perspectives these sources offer.

Table 7.3 analyzes the named actors appearing in the 104 stories by role.
Only the first appearance of a particular actor in each story is counted.
Politicians made 204 separate appearances out of a total of 299 named actor
appearances. It is also noteworthy that Greenpeace workers made appearances on 20 separate occasions.

Table 7.4 analyzes the named actor appearances by the nationality of the
actor, where this is given. It is evident that in the Australian media construction of the story the drama is very much an Australian one as far as actors
are concerned. Australia has more actors in this version than any other
nation, including France. South Pacific actors make far fewer appearances
than Australian or French ones and in number only just exceed those in the
"Other European" category. As far as prominence of actors is concerned,
this is an Australian/French drama rather than a South Pacific one. The
South Pacific region provides both the stage for a physical expression of
French colonialism—the bomb itself—and a particular setting for an ongoing Eurocentric, but also global, discursive drama about nuclear weapons,
power politics, and the environment.

TABLE 7.3. Named Actor Story Appearances by Role

ROLE	NO. OF ACTOR APPEARANCES
Politician	204
Government and military officials	30
Experts (scientists and analysts not directly related to the event)	22
Greenpeace workers	20
Community/business leaders	19
Other minor actors	4
Total	299

TABLE 7.4. Named Actor Story Appearances by Country/Region

COUNTRY OF ACTOR	NO. OF ACTOR APPEARANCES
Australia	118
France	109
South Pacific	24
Other European	19
Asian	8
United States	5
New Zealand	5

A further insight into the nature of the Australian coverage is provided in Table 7.5 which analyzes the sources of the news stories as indicated in the acknowledgments given within the stories themselves. It is noteworthy here that the newspapers' own Australian-based correspondents provide, in each instance, the most stories. This reflects the focus in the coverage on Australian reaction and comment. Also noteworthy is the prominence of European perspectives in *The Australian's* coverage arising from the great use made of material supplied by the paper's European correspondent, coupled with syndication arrangements with London-based papers in the Murdoch group.

As was noted earlier, only 19 of the 104 stories in the data set were event focused; the other 85 involved interpretation, commentary, and opinion. The pattern of story perspectives, which doubtless reflects the range of main

actors in the stories, is presented in Table 7.6. If we discount the letters that
were nearly all "anti-France and/or pro-protest" we can note that 43 of the
remaining 80 news items (or 54%) were "anti-France and/or pro-protest,"

TABLE 7.5. News Sources of Mururoa-related Stories: *The Australian* and
Sydney Morning Herald 4/9/95–9/9/95. Maximum Two Sources
per Story

	THE AUSTRALIAN	SYDNEY MORNING HERALD	TOTAL
Own correspondent—Australia	26	20	46
Own correspondent—Papeete	14	6	20
Own correspondent—Europe	10	2	12
Agencies—General	5	2	7
AAP	2	-	2
AP	1	1	2
Reuters	2	1	3
Dow Jones	-	1	1
The Times	2	-	2
The Financial Times	1	-	1
Letter Writer	4	20	24
Editorial Writer	2	3	5

TABLE 7.6. The Pattern of Story Perspectives

	THE AUSTRALIAN		SYDNEY MORNING HERALD		NO. OF STORIES
	News Items	Letters	News Items	Letters	
Anti-France and/or Pro-Protest Perspectives Predominant	25	4	18	17	64
French Perspectives and/or Anti-Protestor Perspectives Predominant	5	-	7	1	13
Mixed Perspectives	11	-	7	1	19
Distinct Perspectives not Evident	6	-	1	1	8
Total	47	4	33	20	104

18 (or 23%) had mixed perspectives, and 12 (or 15%) had "French perspectives and/or anti-protestor perspectives predominant." Despite community outcry against the tests, the French perspective managed to get through quite strongly, particularly in European correspondent and agency reports. The use of global news sources ensured the presence of French perspectives beyond those presented by French government representatives in Australia.

Pacific Representations

Thus far the analysis has focused on the total set of Mururoa-related stories that appeared in *The Australian* and the *Sydney Morning Herald* in the week under study. It has demonstrated how an "Australian perspective" is constituted via a number of factors. With respect to type of story, stories concerned with interpretation, commentary, and opinion predominate. With respect to actor roles, politicians dominate. With respect to actor nationality, Australians are most prominent followed closely by the French, with South Pacific actors a very distant third. With respect to sources (in the sense of authors rather than actors), the coverage is largely produced by the newspapers' own correspondents. In relation to perspective, "anti-France/pro-protest" perspectives dominate.

We now turn to stories that specifically present a representation of the South Pacific as a particular kind of place, with respect to nature, culture, and political landscape, within which these events are staged. We address just one aspect of this representation—the role of the South Pacific paradise myth. It is argued that the Australian media's presentation of key events—the demonstrations, the test itself, the riots and their resolution—and their interpretation were inflected by the South Pacific paradise myth in a way that ultimately acted ideologically to support the political status quo. The notion that the paradise myth can act in this way is not a new one (see, for example, Chanter, 1998). But the way it works itself out in the context of the Mururoa tests is of particular interest, if only because the context of French nuclear testing seems to stretch the myth's conservative functionality to the limit.

The South Pacific paradise myth and the set of values and supposed lifestyles associated with it are an implicit and often explicit backdrop against which events and statements are interpreted. The myth itself is rarely interrogated. Rather, events, actions, and people are seen as either consonant with or violations of the myth.

The demonstrations in Papeete prior to the test were seen as consonant with the myth. They were "noisy and colourful demonstrations" (*The Australian*, 4 September 1995). The participation of Australian parliamentarians was presented almost as a kind of holiday jaunt, as in the following story of two New South Wales MPs:

MP prepares to surf into action
By Roger Maynard in Papeete

Armed with his surfboard and a letter of support from the NSW Parliamentary Speaker, Green MP Ian Cohen sailed out of Papeete yesterday to do battle with France.

Accompanying the veteran anti-nuclear campaigner was Labor Senator Tom Wheelwright and 10 other parliamentarians from as far afield as Japan and Italy.

They will spend the next 10 days at sea and hope to penetrate the 12 mile limit around Mururoa in an attempt to persuade the French Government to abort the resumption of its nuclear test program.
Mr Cohen, who earned his place in the history of anti-nuclear campaigning by riding his surfboard beneath the bows of a US warship in Sydney Harbour in 1986, hopes his board will come handy again this time.
He would not disclose his tactics short of confirming that he was prepared to take on the French navy in pursuit of his goal.

(*The Australian*, 5 September 1995)

The actions of the French against Greenpeace and the nuclear test itself were, of course, seen as violations of the myth. The rough tactics of the French military were highlighted. The test itself, which in Australian Prime Minister Paul Keating's words expressed "contempt for the countries and people of the region," was also an assault on nature. It turned "the placid waters of the Mururoa lagoon into white froth" (*The Australian*, 7 September 1995). As one letter writer put it:

Only the French could be in possession of a South Pacific coral atoll where it is always summer, the sea as clear as the air . . . and defile it by exploding the most horrific weapons of war there.

(*The Sydney Morning Herald*, 8 September 1995)

Yet there was a counterpoint to this view of the French as violators of paradise. For if the French could be projected as violators, so too could anti-colonial protestors and supporters of the Tahitian independence movement. In this latter narrative the French became not the violators but, indeed, the custodians of the myth.

Here it is relevant to note that in their own widely circulated and publicized video construction of the Mururoa test, the French sought to mobilize the paradise framework for their own ideological purposes. The French propaganda sought to resolve the contradiction between the paradise myth and its nuclear tests through a narrative of disruption followed by normality. The French projected themselves as minimizing "necessary" disruption by shortening the test series and assuring the world that these were the last tests, a position for which they got a great deal of publicity (and implicit credit) in the Australian press. The event itself was presented by the French in the genre of a travel video. As the *Sydney Morning Herald's* Andrew Byrne reported:

> The French military in the Tahitian capital presented the scene like a holiday travel video. The 31/2 minute recording, watched in silence by the tightly packed gathering, opened with shots of a sun-kissed golden beach, swaying palm trees and the sound of the Pacific Ocean as its waves broke gently on the sand . . . on the video there is a holiday feel as people are seen sitting on deckchairs waiting for the blast.

Byrne maintains a critical distance from the message of the video, commenting that despite the holiday images:

> The image the world will best remember from the film is the moment, a split second after the 20 kilotron device explodes, that the turquoise lagoon was transformed into a churning white mass.

And later:

> The final scene, in a crude attempt to convey normality on the island — reduced to swiss cheese by 30 years of nuclear blasting — is of apparently unconcerned staff riding mopeds and bicycles along a road.
>
> (*The Sydney Morning Herald*, 7 September 1995)

However, the video had, in large measure, done its work anyway. The headline to Byrne's article reads: "The Palms Swayed, the Sun Shone, the Lagoon Jumped." After this, we are led to believe, it was over.

Of course it wasn't over. The following day saw demonstrations and rioting in Papeete in what *The Australian* headlined as "Rebellion in Paradise" (9-10 September 1995). This so-called "rebellion," like the tests, was projected as a violation of the paradise myth. Indeed, *The Australian* (9-10 September 1995) editorialized: "It is the violence in Tahiti that has caught the world's attention in the aftermath of the test. It seems almost incongruous that this Polynesian holiday island should become the scene of such a confronting expression of anti-French sentiment." Why incongruous, one must wonder, given the true history of Pacific Islander exploitation behind the "coconut curtain" (see, for example, Alcalay, 1993)? While there were many reports suggesting that the French had, in the words of Australian Foreign Minister, "reaped what they had sowed" and should bear responsibility for the Tahitian riots, there was also a recurring and ultimately dominant theme that cast the independence movement, rather than the French, as the most serious threat to paradise. At the extreme, P.P. McGuiness of *The Sydney Morning Herald*, under the headline "Anti-Nuclear, Anti-Colonialism Protests Threaten Pacific's Stability" commented:

> It had to happen that the anti-nuclear testing hysteria would overlap with the smelly orthodoxy of anti-colonialism quite spectacularly in Tahiti, where a minority independence movement unleashed a wave of rioting, burning and looting in the name of protest against the French nuclear tests.

He goes on to suggest that "upheaval, violence, terrorism and eventual murderous indigenous dictatorship and poverty" are the realistic alternative to continuing French colonial rule (*Sydney Morning Herald*, 9 September 1996). The paradise myth, in the end, best served the interests of the French colonialists despite the violation of the nuclear test. Although independence leader Oscar Temaru's successful calls for the end of violence were also publicized, the French remained, in this phase of the drama at least, the prime custodians of the myth and the guardians of the stability and "normality" that protected it.

CONCLUSION

This analysis of the coverage of the first Mururoa test and associated events in the Pacific by *The Australian* and the *Sydney Morning Herald* suggests the limitations of the notion of news flow between nations as a way of understanding coverage of foreign news in national contexts. The event was in the Pacific, yet given the international resources of newspapers, news relating to the event came from sources around the globe. Although the event was in the Pacific the key player initiating the event was European. The event, as an international news event, inherited the complex relations of colonialism. The event was in the South Pacific, but the independent nations of the Pacific played only minor roles.

The analysis supports the contention that press coverage arises from an interaction of foreign events with domestic concerns. The event, as covered in the Australian press, became predominantly an Australian story because of Australian actors in the field and even more so, because Australia itself became a stage for reaction and protest. From a French colonial perspective Mururoa was French territory. But for the Australian press this was an event in "our region" in which Australia had a particular interest. The French were the "foreigners." The coverage (and the nature of the developing story) involved an interpenetration of domestic, regional, and global concerns.

NOTE

1. In the international study researchers from some forty countries analyzed the foreign news that appeared in their country's media for sample periods of 3-9 September 1995 and 17-23 September 1995. Each country participating selected at least three major media outlets (typically a minimum of two newspapers and a television station) and analyzed their foreign news content using procedures set down by the international study co-ordinators. All items judged to have a clear foreign or international element that appeared in each newspaper issue or television news edition were included. This comprehensive approach meant that items of all sizes, including brief one paragraph stories, were included, as were items on all topics. The selected stories were each coded in terms of twenty-six variables including prominence (with each story classified as being either major, medium, or minor), source (up to two sources per story), gender of correspondent, countries prominent in the story (with the possibility of indicating up to three countries per story scaled as "most important country," "second country" and "third country"), topic (up to three topic areas per story scaled as "main topic," "secondary topic no. 1," and "secondary topic no. 2" selected from twenty-four topic areas) and variables relating to the status and gender of the main actors in each story.

REFERENCES

Alcalay, G. (1993). Pacific island responses to U.S. and French hegemony. In A. Dirlik (Ed.), *What is in a rim?* (pp. 235-249). Boulder, CO: Westview.

Aldrich, R. (1993). *France and the South Pacific since 1940*. London: MacMillan.

Chanter, A. (1998). A better way forward: Research on media and violence in the Pacific. *Asia Pacific Media Educator, 4*, 8-23.

Entman, R.M. (1991) Framing U.S. coverage of international news: Contrasts in narratives of the KAL and Iran air incidents. *Journal of Communication, 41*(4), 6-27.

Ericson, R.V., Baranek, P.M., & Chan, B.L. (1987). *Visualising deviance: A study of news organisation*. Milton Keynes: Open University Press.

Fenby, J. (1986). *The international news services*. New York: Schocken Books.

Gurevitch, M., Levy, M.R., & Roeh, I. (1991). The global newsroom: Convergences and diversities in the globalization of television news. In P. Dahlgren & C. Sparks (Eds.), *Communication and citizenship*. London and New York: Routledge.

Putnis, P., Penhallurick, J., & Bourk, M. (1997). *Cultural crossroads: Australia's international news map and its significance*. Paper presented at the Cultural Crossroads Conference, Australian Key Centre for Cultural and Media Policy, Sydney.

Shoemaker, P.J. (1991). *Gatekeeping*. Newbury Park and London: Sage.

Sreberny, A., Putnis, P., Penhallurick, J., & Bourk, M. (1998). *Commonwealth, common knowledge?: The mutual news representations of Britain and Australia*. Paper presented to the International Association for Media and Communication Research Conference, Glasgow.

Sreberny-Mohammadi A. et al. (1985). *Foreign news in the media: International reporting in 29 countries*. Paris: UNESCO.

Tuchman, G. (1978). *Making news: A study of the construction of reality*. New York: The Free Press.

PART III

SEPTEMBER 11 AND 21ST-CENTURY VIOLENCE

New Modes of Representation?

Chapter 8

Is All the News Ours?

Political Violence, September 11, and the War on Iraq

Dan Berkowitz

On the face of it, news coverage of the September 11 World Trade Center attacks *and* the U.S.–led war on Iraq in March 2003 to unseat Saddam Hussein should both be "our news," the news of America. After all, *our* jet-liners flew into *our* tall buildings in *our* largest city. Similarly, *our* armed forces led the attack on Baghdad, using *our* fighting equipment and *our* troops.

But when examining news coverage of this political violence, the situation becomes much less straightforward. For national identity, some elements of each story shift to *them*, to *their* news. Yet, a larger, more important distinction looms when the us/them news dichotomy draws its shape from the initiator of the news. When the World Trade Center attack happened to *us* by *them*, American journalists needed to explain how our culture, our society was under threat. This act of terrorism was done to *us* by *them*, but they were largely excluded. To accomplish this journalistic task, American journalists needed to depart from their professional norms and shift to a mythical, storytelling mode of newswork. This mythical news-work mode could affirm the notion that although our way of life had been threatened by something horrid and completely unimaginable, our values and traditions would nonetheless survive, because it was the right and just outcome.

In contrast, when America stepped out on a limb to take on—almost single-handedly—what it perceived as a threat to that very same identity—what the Bush administration dubbed an "axis of evil" in Iraq—reporting shifted quickly back toward traditional professional modes of journalism. Moving to this more fact-based, "impartial" style of journalism allowed news media to assert a national identity as leaders of the "just." News, within this journalistic form, would draw much less from storytelling and lean more toward an aura of authority and authenticity through the presentation of straightforward facts. Or so it would seem.

For *us*, the World Trade Center attack was terrorism, whereas for the unseen *other*, the attack was an attempt to restate the values of a different way of life under threat. For *us*, the attack on Iraq appears to be the opposite—it was the right thing to do, a necessity to preserve *our* American lifestyle and its values, yet for *them*, for many of the Iraqis, our attack represented unbridled terrorism, a war on national identity; America should have minded its own business.

This chapter, then, builds on others in this book, and especially on the work of Nossek (2001), to examine news coverage from two particularly notable days that appeared in one particularly notable newspaper. Specifically, the chapter applies its theoretical framework to *The New York Times* coverage from September 12, 2001—the day after the World Trade Center attack—and from March 20, 2003—the day after the United States launched its attack on Baghdad. The chapter applies qualitative textual analysis methodology to explore the richness and nuances of coverage, to interrogate journalistic conventions of that coverage, as well as journalistic efforts at mythical storytelling. By this analysis of two sharply contrasting events of political violence, the chapter begins to zero in on yet another dimension of "our news and their news."

CONCEPTUAL FOUNDATION

If news about political violence involves telling stories about the interface between two societies (and their clash in beliefs), then this news can be viewed as representing those differences in ideological terms (Altschull, 1995; Berkowitz & TerKeurst, 1999; Lichtenberg, 2000). News must state and restate a society's dominant values while labeling the values of the opposing society as deviant (Hall, 1982). By making the case this way, journalists straddle the fence between *professional* norms and *societal* ones (Hallin, 2000). And they need to accomplish their work while also being matter-of-fact about it, without raising an awareness that could possibly compromise their professional promises. An economic outcome is at stake for the media organization, one that weighs in significantly for the journalistic outcome (Golding & Murdoch, 2000; Herman & Chomsky, 1988). In recent times, journalists have faced this challenge when covering Vietnam War protests in the 1960s and 1970s (e.g., Gitlin, 1980), the 1991 Desert Storm Gulf War (e.g., Greenberg & Gantz, 1993), the 1993 bombing of the World Trade Center, and the 1995 bombing of the Alfred P. Murrah Federal Building in Oklahoma.

The result of the constant, ongoing ideological juggling process results in news about political violence becoming both *their* news (the deviant part) and *our* news (the ideologically correct part), although *they* are used for *our* purposes. This outcome becomes more or less necessary because news of political violence needs to match up to the expectations and understandings of the audience for whom the news is being written. News does not necessarily have to meet expectations for the *other* audience, those for whom the news items constitute the "their" component. As Nossek (2001) explains, the first stage of this ideological work introduces *localization*, where "relevance to national interests" is indicated. A second stage furthers this localization, as the news is *tailored* to a specific local audience and its immediate interests. Quickly, the news has shrunk to gain its "our" dimension, rather than being stretched to address the global nature of the incident. Through this journalistically ideological work, the news process shapes the selection of occurrences that become news. An even more intriguing outcome arises in *how* journalism constructs a selected occurrence, placing it into a specific casting where it is refined and reshaped from basic cultural raw materials of society (Berkowitz, 1997; Schudson, 2000).

An example of this ideological shaping appears in news about the actions of social movements—groups generally outside the ideological mainstream. These groups may be selected to become news, but the them/us dialectic quickly cements the casting of that news, simultaneously demonstrating deviance and ideological correctness. Here, part of the "us" becomes the "them," creating divisions that are political rather than geographical, or even cultural (Hall, 1982; Stein et al., 2003). As this ideological newswork unfolds, a social movement and its members receive their stigmatic baggage and the die is cast for their future. The same casting and labeling, of course, takes place when social movements and social actors reside outside the United States, or even when they cross into American borders to commit their mayhem (such as the perpetrators of the World Trade Center attacks).

Fundamentally, when covering news that threatens society and questions its values, the journalistic frame of reference centers on the nation state, shifting to a more factual telling that represents a normative, professional frame once the threat is lifted. This factuality—especially when used to tell the news of America doing something to ideologically marginalized groups and societies—simulates an aura of unquestionable ideological objec-

tivity that demonstrates the correctness of the action to the media audience.
As Nossek (2001) explained,

> . . . when an event is defined as "our" political violence, it is covered as
> a closed event. Conversely, if it is defined as "their" political violence, it
> is covered as an open event . . . the national position takes precedence
> over professional norms when an event is defined as "our" political vio-
> lence. . . .

One last point concerns the definition of "our" political violence. One
argument would suggest that the perpetrator of the violence would retain
ownership of that violence, regardless of how the news is presented. That is,
news of a terrorist attacker would be about the terrorist, not the attacked. A
counterargument would allocate ownership of the violence on the basis of
the media construction, considering whether an occurrence was depicted as
an act of political voyeurism happening elsewhere—or as something that
would actually have audience impact and sociopolitical significance to the
newspaper's audience. From the perspective of this chapter, the latter is most
important: not which political unit caused or received the violence, but
rather, whether the occurrence was perceived as directly relevant and how
that relevance was cast. Thus, although acts of terrorism and political violence are intended by their instigator to communicate a certain message, that
message may or may not get through to its audience (Tuman, 2003). What
shapes the outcome is the ideological correspondence between the instigator
and the media audience.

From this framework, these three questions follow:

RQ1: To what degree does news of political violence involving a
country outside the U.S. follow or depart from journalistic
conventions because of its ideological alignment?

RQ2: How do the kinds of actors appearing in news of political violence correspond to news coverage being cast as "ours" or
"theirs"?

RQ3: How does the location of the story influence the telling of the
news as "ours" or "theirs"?

METHOD

Nossek (2001) draws on the work of Cohen and Roeh (1992) to explain that
the compelling nature of news about terrorism or political violence comes
not only from its upheaval of everyday life, but through its intense degree of

spectacle. To reach this pinnacle, occurrences become journalistically approved as newsworthy, yet their treatment as news is not preordained by what has happened. To present political violence as balanced, factual, and neutral is considered an *open* construction—a variety of perspectives can be represented in a news item. When a news item becomes less balanced, more stylized and mythical, a greater emphasis on storytelling and moral (ideological) judgment appears and the coverage is labeled as *closed*. For closed news, the range of details and the people involved become constrained by its framing.

To make these general dimensions more tangible, this chapter draws on five elements of news content from a larger set of eleven outlined by Nossek (and Cohen & Roeh). The smaller set was chosen to allow a more efficient and focused analysis. These dimensions include:

- *Balance*, the degree to which multiple positions have been presented. Closed events are presented in a less balanced fashion.
- *Fact/Commentary*, considering the degree to which a story centers mainly on details or instead incorporates anecdotes and other storytelling devices. Closed events draw more on commentary rather than facts.
- *Historical References*, where the event is connected to a larger mythical legacy by highlighting connections to the past.
- *Information Sources*, where official spokespersons and ordinary people share roles in the journalistic storytelling. More open roles represent sources as the bearers of facts, whereas closed story roles relegate sources toward a more closed function that represents iconic actions of mythical characters.
- *Story Location*, which considers where the key story actors were located, and how story location shapes "ownership" of the story as ours or theirs.

To chose a realm of texts for the analysis, this chapter drew on *The New York Times*, not as a fallback text as with many studies, but because *The New York Times* serves as the newspaper most similar to the ones examined in other chapters of this book. For the United States, *The New York Times* represents something broader than other papers—a national versus regional or local readership—and also is the torch bearer of the American journalistic institution, the "newspaper of record" and torch bearer of journalistic professionalism (and professional ideology).

Because *The New York Times* coverage of the World Trade Center attack and the War on Iraq was so extensive, only one day was selected for each of the two events. In both cases, this was the first day of coverage, when the best opportunity existed for presenting either open or closed news, the days when the initial framing was cast. Coverage of the World Trade Center attack was especially extensive because of its impact on the newspaper's home town. To make the analysis more manageable, items were chosen from only the first section of the newspaper that were longer than 500 words. Opinion pieces and letters to the editor were excluded because of this chapter's emphasis on news.

In all, fifty-five news items were considered from the September 12, 2001 coverage. These items were located through a search of the Lexis-Nexis database using the term "world trade center." For the start of the War on Iraq, transcripts of official speeches were excluded, which left twelve news items for analysis. These items were located through a search that used the term "iraq." Both search terms were chosen to be broadly inclusive of relevant content given the one-day sampling period for each event.

TELLING "OUR" NEWS
AS "REALLY OUR NEWS"

Reporting on the World Trade Center attacks could be characterized as "really our news," not only because this was an attack on the United States, but also because it was an attack on *The New York Times'* home turf. News items stressed the heavy impact on American life, but equally as notable, the world of New York City residents was represented as everyday life turned upside-down. Clearly, some official news, some typically journalistic content mixed in with the day's coverage, but overall, the day's newspaper centered squarely on the city of New York and its residents. Further, the attackers were unknown and not clearly linked to another country, so there was little to say about them in news reports. Shaping the news this way became a necessary strategy for accomplishing culture work. Most simply, by drawing on a myriad of localized feature stories, the mega-magnitude of the attack could be signified. It was as if the newspaper and its journalists had taken on the role of official cultural guides for city residents (and *Times* readers, more broadly), suggesting how they should feel and highlighting which elements of the event should be seen as important. Just as notable, this was an event that could not be signified by the journalistic paradigm alone, requiring instead a stylized, mythical approach.

Considering the five specific analysis criteria (Balance, Fact/ Commentary, Historical Reference, Information Sources, Story Location) makes these observations sharper, illuminating their nuances. To address the criterion of *Balance* requires first to decide how sides of the issue should be considered and which actors would represent each side. The clearest way would be to pit Americans generally against the attackers. However, the attackers were all dead, their affiliation was not known, and there was no information to gain about them other than a smattering of second-hand reports from family members and airline officials who had received cell-phone calls and radio transmissions. A more manageable and meaningful method of defining sides, then, would be to look at American sources as different groups within one issue position, dividing residents of New York City (the hardcore "us") from other Americans, such as officials and residents in other parts of the country (still "us" but somewhat less so). People living outside the United States became the other side of the balance, but an anomaly arose when considering Americans of Middle East descent, because they appeared as both "us" and "them" at the same time.

Overall, the news balance was sharply tilted toward *our news*, with the strongest emphasis on the lives of New Yorkers rather than the nation as a whole. Within the coverage of city residents, the mayor often spoke, but at least as often, ordinary people appeared. A news item, "With City Transit Shut Down, New Yorkers Take to Eerily Empty Streets," (Kennedy, 2001) illustrates this by incorporating a subway conductor, a boat captain, a transit employee, and a produce stand owner, among others. The story painted a picture of an exodus of city dwellers:

> Tens of thousands of people streamed south across the Manhattan Bridge and the Brooklyn Bridge from Lower Manhattan, some stopping along the way to buy tennis shoes and bottled water, saying they were planning to walk as far as Bay Ridge or Staten Island.

The cast of characters continued to swell, with vignettes of Minnesotan dancers-to-be, bread truck drivers turned cabbies, office workers trudging home in newly bought flip-flops in lieu of high heels, and ferry passengers returning to their homes outside the city:

> As if any of the passengers needed a last reminder of the surreality they had just left behind in Manhattan, in several places in New Jersey last night officials were requiring people coming from the city to be fumigated as they stepped off the ferries . . . many people coming off the ferries were shoeless: workers were hosing down their feet and shoes. . . . One man said he got such a thorough dousing that he was wet down to his underwear.

Clearly, experts and local officials were also part of the "us" in the "our" side of this news—a New York architect who analyzed the Trade Center's structural design, private city contractors explaining how defense against the attack was not possible, Mayor Giuliani placing the area under curfew.

Sitting outside the inner circle were national officials who remained on the periphery of the story as they spoke of the large national threat.

Bringing a large contrast with the element of "us" was the "them" of people outside the United States who demonstrated their ideological deviance that separated them from the American victims while also reinforcing the deviance of the World Trade Center attack, as one news item showed. And although Arab leaders condemned the attack, they were depicted in other news items as quietly supporting it:

> Even without knowing who was behind this monstrous act, you could not shake off the televised images of crowds of Palestinians—not a handful of bloodthirsty extremists—chanting "God is great" and joyously handing out candy in celebration on the streets of Nablus in the West Bank. (Haberman, 2001)

Looking back at the question of balance, then, it stands out clearly that coverage was not balanced, and that two imbalances actually appeared. First was the imbalance between New York Americans and other Americans. Here, the story most closely concerned New York's Americans, whereas the news role of other Americans was to signify the magnitude of the occurrence that had befallen New Yorkers. National news media, for example, facilitated signification simply by mention of broadsweeping television coverage:

> By noon, all four major television networks had agreed to share video images. By midafternoon, almost all of AOL Time Warner's cable channels, like TBS and TNT, were carrying CNN. . . . Most of the networks used variations of the title adopted by CNN: America Under Attack. (Barringer & Fabrilant, 2001)

National leaders similarly signified the horror and scope of the attack through their assessments and pronouncements, such as Defense Secretary Donald H. Rumsfeld's assertion that "The United States government is functioning in the face of this terrible act" (Purdum & Toner, 2001). Moving farther away yet from the inner circle of city residents, world leaders with a degree of allegiance to the United States signified the magnitude of the occurrence through their comments:

> Giving expression to a sentiment voiced across the continent, the German chancellor, Gerhard Schroder, called the attacks "a declaration of war against the entire civilized world," and he spoke today with leaders of France, Russia and Britain about a coordinated European response. (Erlanger, 2001).

In all, balance clearly pointed toward a closed perspective of the story, one that created a sharp dividing line between the provincial "us" of New Yorkers and the broad "them" of other Americans and global citizens on the outside looking in.

Regarding the *Fact/Commentary* distinction, this coverage clearly leaned toward the commentary style of closed news, drawing on stories and vignettes rather than simply running through a series of facts and official responses. To do this, news items consisted chiefly of a series of stories about how city residents and workers were coping with adversity and the challenge of the day, such as a mother dashing down the street to pick up her school-aged daughter:

> "I went up Park Place; all I heard was 'go, go, go,'" she said. "People started running, and all I could think was I was not going to stop until I got my daughter." (Zernike & Hartocollis, 2001)

Clearly, these accounts were based on fact, but nonetheless the facts used were chosen from a wide array of possibilities, which were woven into a dramatic story. One such instance came from a news item about victims of the air crashes:

> One was a Washington figure known across the country from rough-and-tumble talk shows, who called her husband as the terrifying events unfolded in the sky.
>
> Another, a pilot whose plane plowed into the World Trade Center, was known for amiability in his placid Massachusetts community, where he was planning a picnic with his family this weekend.
>
> Last night, such fragments of lives interrupted began to frame the stories of the men and women who were on board the four planes at the center of yesterday's events. (Glaberson, 2001)

Looking through the mass of these fifty-five news items suggests that the news was clearly about "us," about our lives, told in a series of commentary-style news items honed to cement ownership of the attacks and their consequences.

Regarding the application of *Historical References*, the bombing of the World Trade Center in 1993 appeared occasionally as historical location of the new attack (Glanz, 2001), but it was not treated with much impact or importance. If mythification is accomplished by linking a current event to a monumental event of the past, then links to the previous small-scale Trade Center bombing were not adequate to signify the magnitude of the current attack. A much more dramatic historical reference was necessary instead, looking back toward the legendary Japanese attack on Pearl Harbor that brought America into World War II. An analysis piece drew out the comparison:

> This was Pearl Harbor redux without the face of an enemy. In today's more anomalous situation, Mr. Bush is likely to avail himself more fully than he has to date of the knowledge, experience and prestige of his secretary of state, retired Gen. Colin L. Powell. The president "needs Colin like he's never needed him before," an administration official said. (Apple, 2001)

At least a dozen news items did the same, as these examples show:

> For all the questions, what was clear was that the World Trade Center would take its place among the great calamities of American history, a day of infamy like Pearl Harbor, Oklahoma City, Lockerbie. (Schmemann, 2001)

> "The first thing I thought of was Pearl Harbor," said Hal Freeman, a security guard in a Los Angeles office building. "It's a wake-up call for the United States. It's something we've needed for a long time. Personally, I'd kill them all. Let God sort it out." (Harden, 2001)

This sense of history was also aimed toward comparisons with attacks on other countries. One striking example stands out, though, building an image of a globally terrorized society:

> An Israeli response to America's aptly dated wake-up call might well be, "Now you know." Regardless of whether the carnage is reliably traced to one of the jihad sects, it is true that the magnitude of the pain inflicted on America yesterday moves us into the very exclusive club of democracies for which terrorism is not peripheral, remote or episodic, but a horrible routine. (Keller, 2001)

In this day's news coverage, *Information Sources* represented a mix of officials and ordinary people, with ordinary people weighing in significantly as would be the case for more closed news that presents mythical narratives. Even officials brought more than facts to the news, with many offering commentary and opinion that enhanced the narrative drama. To a degree, the roles of these sources correspond to what has been presented so far in relation to balance, commentary, and historical reference. That is, the news items have woven a web of mythical narratives, so that sources naturally fall into storytelling roles. In fact, the examples offered in the discussion of balance and fact/commentary clearly back this assertion about sources.

In addition to the roles of New Yorkers, some other actors ultimately became involved in the storytelling, adding journalistic credence and signifying the event's magnitude and rarity. Elected federal officials made up one group that rendered the drama:

> "Senators, and House members, Democrats and Republicans, will stand shoulder to shoulder to fight this evil that is perpetrated on this nation," said House Speaker J. Dennis Hastert, Republican of Illinois. "We will stand together to make sure who perpetrated this evil deed will pay a price." (Mitchell & Seelye, 2001)

World leaders also became part of this signification function:

> Pope John Paul II also condemned the attacks in a message to Mr. Bush, calling them "an unspeakable horror." The Czech president, Vaclav Havel, said the attack was "a tremendous warning to civilization" that "challenges us to mobilize, supremely, our sense of responsibility for this world." (Erlanger, 2001)

Finally, considering *Story Location*, this element served as did the others to cement ownership of the World Trade Center attack as "really our news," with a very large proportion of the content taking place within New York City. These items referred not just to the attack itself, but to the myriad of little narratives depicting drastically changed lives of city residents and workers. These people lived in the city, they worked in the city (and often, did both), they grew up in the city (children and generations-old residents), and they helped the city function (including public officials and workers, such as the architects who helped build it). An occasional outsider did take a degree of ownership, such as Schroder's (and many other world leaders') pronouncement about the "civilized world," or President Bush's statement that broadened the attack to have broader implications:

> "These acts of mass murder were intended to frighten our nation into chaos and retreat, but they have failed," the president said in his first speech to the nation from the Oval Office. "Our country is strong. Terrorist acts can shake the foundation of our biggest buildings, but they cannot touch the foundation of America." (Bumiller & Sanger, 2001)

In all, though, a very large proportion of the locations placed ownership of the event squarely with the United States, and most often, with New York City itself.

Taken together, balance, fact/commentary, historical reference, information sources, and story location all coincided to cast news of the World Trade Center attacks clearly as "our news" the news of America, and even, "really our news" as the news of New York. "They" were barely involved in telling the story, and when they were, their role was to further support the news as "ours."

TELLING THEIR NEWS AS OUR NEWS

A superpower threatens, delivers ultimatums, sends its bombs, drives forward its troops. This depiction—far from what appeared in U.S. media at the start of the 2003 war on Iraq—suggests that news about this event should belong to the country where it took place, and even more so, to its people. It happened to *them*. But that was not the case in *The New York Times'* journalistic effort to cover the war with the Iraqi people standing on the sidelines. Once again, the event was localized for U.S. audiences, pointing toward American ownership of the occurrence.

This kind of news treatment allowed ideological maintenance through the American news media as the nation began to initiate political violence in Iraq. News coverage worked to demonstrate how this political violence was ideologically correct (and just) and how the initiator was not, in retrospect, the real initiator of the political violence.

Looking first at *Balance*, the positions largely reflected official American interests, although not as exclusively as might be expected. Much of this America-centered coverage focused on preparation, both domestically and abroad, including this outsider's view of "An Anticlimactic Strike":

> When explosions finally rang out in Baghdad, they seemed so mild that even an old warrior like Gen. Alexander M. Haig Jr. could not quite believe it was the first stage of the long-awaited war.
> "Iraqis are so goosey," General Haig drawled on Fox News, which, like other news channels, scrambled to interpret an image of the Baghdad skyline, "it might just be a flock of bats." (Stanley, 2003)

Thus, while discussing the war's opening *there*, calling Iraqis "goosey" implicitly makes a claim of American ownership of the situation, degrading

Iraqis in relation to American standards for "real" citizens. Taking this domestication of a foreign war one step further, another news item discussed preparation for security within the city. The story led off:

> Concerned that river crossings are among the likelier potential targets for terrorist attacks, the New York Police Department sharply increased its patrols at bridges and tunnels yesterday. The patrols, along with inspections of trucks in Manhattan, slowed traffic to a single-lane crawl on entrance ramps and avenues. (Rashbaum & Barron, 2003)

Even an account of President Bush's decision-making process personalized the event and worked to tilt the balance toward domestic ownership:

> As he sat behind his desk in the Oval Office just before he addressed the nation tonight at 10:15, President Bush picked up a copy of the speech in which he would tell the world that he had launched military strikes to topple Saddam Hussein. He gave a little shake of his fist, according to a person who saw the scene on a television monitor, turned to someone in the room and said, "Feels good." (Stevenson, 2003)

When *they* appear in the story, they often receive just a veiled reference, "the kingdom has hinted," "Western diplomats here say King Fahd's declaration . . . ", "the family of one well-placed official," "One man lingering in the dark outside the information ministry, watching high-ranking officials talking. . . ." Sometimes, though, *they* are named—especially Saddam Hussein—but are tied to counterideological assertions that are clearly downplayed, such as an except from one of Hussein's speeches "The little criminal Bush has committed a crime against humanity," or using outlandish sounding terms, "Zionist criminals," "The criminal little Bush," or "Junior Bush." Again, this news was quite imbalanced, allowing Iraqis to take part in the news narrative only when doing so would downplay their status and ownership of the news.

Occasionally, though, Iraqi citizens were cast into a role of impatient victim, with the story presented in a way that seemed invented rather than actually observed:

> . . . there was only one question that waiters, masons, vegetable sellers, physicians, government clerks and an endless roll call of other anxious Iraqis put to any foreigner:
> "America, what time?" they asked. "Bush, what time." (Burns, 2003)

Surprisingly, other countries were minimally involved in this story telling. Other Western nations were allowed little comment, and even America's allies were given only cameo appearances.

Fact/Commentary leaned somewhat toward the commentary end, but nonetheless news coverage contained a healthy smattering of factual information. One interesting effort at establishing the most important fact—that the war had begun—was accomplished by discussing reports of broadcast organizations, including NBC, MSNBC, Fox, and CNN:

> Tom Brokaw, who was on the air with a live edition of the NBC program "Dateline," was the first to announce reports of fire over Baghdad. He had Peter Arnett, on assignment in Baghdad for National Geographic Explorer, on the telephone. Mr. Arnett identified the sounds of sirens at 9:32. (Stanley, 2003)

Factual accounts further presented detailed information about military aircraft to be deployed, the number of troops located at Prince Sultan Air Base, the views of European leaders, and the type of bombs used in the initial strike. Yet, more of the story involved commentary, even "color commentary" similar to what would take place at a sporting event:

> With his four-minute address to the nation, delivered after he finished a quiet dinner with his wife, Laura, in the White House residence, Mr. Bush embarked on one of the country's most ambitious military ventures since Vietnam, and on a war his administration began planning over a year ago. (Sanger & Burns, 2003)

Indeed, if commentary draws deeply on anecdotes and other storytelling devices, much of the day's coverage could be called anecdote rich. Whether considering the lives of Iraqi citizens in their worries and fears, or stories of everyday New Yorkers who dreaded the possibility of reprisal, the story dwelled to a significant degree on these human dramas. Some anecdotes presented the cultural tales that spanned the emotions of both societies:

> Wednesday's passage into night was punctuated by desperate appeals for information that would help people decide when to leave their jobs, when to go to their basements, when to embrace their families and when to make their most impassioned appeals to a merciful God. (Burns, 2003)

Overall, by weaving these tales into the factual reports, news coverage worked to present some degree of facticity, but this was a facticity not overly concerned with the quantity of facts presented. In other words, the drama of the moment ruled the news as it closed the larger realm of fact and presented what fit best with the ownership of *their* story as *ours*. Some tales framing this presentation were especially vivid, clearly capturing story ownership:

> The neighbors who recounted the drills said that the wife of the party official had showed them how to sniff the air for the telltale scent of bananas and how to cut strips of gauze, moisten them, then hold them against eyes, nose, and mouth. (Burns, 2003)

The New York Times' coverage related to *Historical References* was surprisingly minimal, perhaps stemming from an effort to maintain continued ideological consistency in light of America's lack of military successes in the last decades of the twentieth century. One thread applying historical references compared the new war to the previous American-led Gulf War, seemingly to highlight the challenges that this effort would require and how it would face the Iraqi people. The most frequent historical comparison was to the 1991 war, calling the new war "a far riskier enterprise" (Sanger & Burns, 2003) and suggesting the challenges and the lessons learned by both sides, with one news item suggesting ". . . the invasion will be unmistakable and there will be no debates as to whether the war is truly under way." Another item cast the news as partly *theirs* (Burns, 2003) mentioning that 3,000 civilians had been killed in the 1991 bombing strikes:

> A deep-rooted fear was palpable, a fear of being obliterated in an Armageddon deployed by the world's greatest military power.
>
> While people here [in Iraq] are among the world's leading experts on the capabilities of America's "smart" weapons from their experiences in the 38-day air campaign that accompanied the war to oust Mr. Hussein from Kuwait in 1991 and from four days of similar attacks in 1998, they know, too, that the cleverest weapons and the best-trained pilots can make mistakes.

Together, these two examples begin to build a case for both American superiority and Iraqi fear, again supporting U.S. ideological justness in beginning the war and moving ownership of the event mainly to "us."

Other historical references spoke to America's ideological justness in pursuing the war, in one case suggesting Hussein's ideological deviance by mentioning "the totalitarian system of government he has built here on a model he took from Stalin" (Burns, 2003). Another piece reminded readers that Hussein has "attempted to assassinate Mr. Bush's father, and killed untold thousands of his opponents" (Sanger & Burns, 2003). At the same time, one news item refuted criticism from Germany's foreign minister that could have changed ideological ownership to *their news*. But journalists Sanger and Burns quickly presented White House spokesman Ari Fleischer's analogy to the Cuban missile crisis of 1962:

> . . . just as President Kennedy imposed a quarantine around Cuba—"an act of war," Mr. Fleischer said—to force it to remove nuclear missiles, Mr. Bush is acting to protect the United States from a threat that it would never see coming.

Finally, in probably the biggest—if somewhat ambiguous—historical reference, the same journalists likened war preparation to "one of the country's most ambitious military ventures since Vietnam." On the one hand, mention of the Vietnam conflict quickly brings back memories of a failed, large-scale military undertaking. On the other hand, this mention broadens ownership from just Bush and his advisers, expanding the news to the whole country and a time when the Vietnam war was forefront on the minds of the American public.

Looking toward *Information Sources*, coverage of the Iraq war's beginning rested most clearly with U.S. officials, especially top members of the Bush administration. This dimension clearly signified the war belonged to the country, if not necessarily to its people. Unlike coverage of the September 11 World Trade Center attacks, ordinary citizens rarely appeared in the news. This missing element holds true for rank-and-file military troops as well as for any effort to reflect views of the American people. One notable exception was a news item on page 21 of the first section of the newspaper, where New York City prepared to guard against terrorism (Rashbaum & Barron, 2003). In that unusual example, information sources included a police sergeant, a mayoral spokesman, and the police commissioner, mainly officials who moved event ownership briefly from national officials to local officials. A Gray Line tour guide and an appliance repairman both provided brief pieces of information, but their role as social actors was simply to confirm that the city's new security measures had created significant traffic.

More consequentially, a few voices were brought in for dissent, yet even those information sources appeared more as outside critics at the margins than as actors who had the power to shape ownership of the news. Thus, although these information sources played a part in the story, control of ideas—of ideology—did not significantly shift to their ownership through the information they provided. For example, a French Embassy spokeswoman criticized Fox News reports of possible French cooperation with Hussein's chemical weapon arsenal. Her speaking part was small, and her opinion was refuted quickly in the next paragraph with a response by a Fox News spokesperson clarifying that the "reporter" was only a contributor, not a staff person (Stanley, 2003). Similarly, when the German foreign minister declared, "Germany emphatically rejects the impending war," his impact was minimized by a quick turn to comments by Bush administration sources (Sanger & Burns, 2003).

When Iraqis spoke, journalists tended to take charge of shaping their ownership. One dissenting voice was Hussein himself, but his words tended to turn against him through fanatic-sounding phrases such as referring to the United States government as "Zionist criminals" or to the president as "Junior Bush" (Burns, 2003). When everyday Iraqi citizens appeared as information sources, their roles were reduced by a writing style that moved the journalist to the fore. Phrases such as "The neighbors who recounted the drills said that the wife of the party official . . ." (Burns, 2003) reduced their direct input by placing the journalist as observer, as did observations on the Saudi Royal family's stance, where quoted opposition was quickly countered by information that "Gen. Tommy R. Franks today visited the computer-crammed bunkers here that will serve as the command post . . ." (Smith, 2003). Likewise, "the kingdom has hinted" and "Western diplomats say" cut their clout on the news down to virtual hearsay.

In all, when official U.S. government sources spoke, their credibility gave them ownership of the news. Conversely, officials outside the U.S., although generally critical, had their impact on gaining ownership reduced through quick counter-replies and other reporting practices. Surprisingly, on "opening day" of the war, voices of American citizens were generally absent, so that domestic criticism (if present) did not surface.

Finally, in terms of *Story Location*, an interesting question surfaces in light of this dimension's definition. On one hand, the definition simply considers where key story actors are located. At the same time, though, the dimension links story location to ownership of a story. Examining this group of stories highlights how both ways are important to story ownership, because location clearly does not equate to ownership of news. In fact, although the news items analyzed in this section had four U.S. datelines and three Middle East datelines, the location was basically irrelevant for determining ownership.

Ownership did not appear related to story location or the location of actors, but instead about the ideology of the reporter, the media organization, and the audience. Thus, whether a dateline was domestic or foreign, the deciding factor in the *our news/their news* dialectic was in the way that the story was cast. Stories taking place outside the United States could just as easily be cast to support American policies as those stories based in Washington, D.C. In part, this was accomplished by marginalizing non-American actors through careful rebuttal from another source, and also by reducing the source credibility of the outsider by belittling their statements, as was done with the comments of Hussein regarding Bush.

Taking the five analytic dimensions together to examine the first day of the Iraq War suggests that selection of voices and their roles indeed cast a shape to the initial war coverage that facilitated ownership of the news as American. This outcome did not depend on the locations for the story nor the voices that would be heard. Dissenting voices—especially from abroad—were either absent or were juxtaposed against official messages in a way that simply furthered their surrender of news ownership. At the same time, it is important to mention that the American voices heard in this story were not broadly based, but instead participation was limited almost completely to powerful elites who added authority to the messages being passed along through the news. If the "really our news" designation fit the news of September 11, then this news nearly attained that degree of ownership as well, maintaining an aura of credible news while also building an ideologically secure case for the Bush administration's decision.

CONCLUSION

This chapter has connected ownership of news—of *our* news—with a society's dominant ideology. By analyzing two key moments in America's recent history, this chapter has shown how ownership of news in a situation of high importance such as terrorism or war tends to be cast in terms of American values, with little perspective lent to other positions. In both of these threatening situations, challenging American ideology would place media in an awkward position of appearing unpatriotic and unsupportive. Whether or not there were opposing viewpoints to the World Trade Center attack or the Iraq War, their counterideological positions would appear to cleave national unity, potentially turning the public against the news media.

These high-threat conditions quickly create an us-versus-them mentality among the citizenry that the media supports, if perhaps begrudgingly. Threats from the unseen *other* create potentially serious ideological consequences. Terrorism and political violence—both forms of communication—are localized not to represent the meaning behind the acts, but as simply the acts themselves. To the perpetrators of the World Trade Center attacks, their message was opposition to American policy in the Middle East; for the United States, the start of the War on Iraq represented a message that Hussein's regime was no longer to be tolerated. But those messages were both lost in the rhetoric of journalism, a journalism that focused on *what* was done, not *why*. The real messages of political violence did not get through, in part because media audiences do not want global confirmation about the fallacy of their government's policies. The World Trade Center attacks on a national symbol raised the likelihood that America's Middle East policies were not universally appreciated, so to remain ideologically true, coverage focused on the daily lives of those who were affected. Similarly, opposition of Bush's Iraq War could suggest that a democratic nation was not so terrifically democratic when it almost single-handedly decided to "adjust" the form and leadership of another country's government. Critical news was similarly adjusted to downplay the ideological counterpoint and regain ownership of this war news.

The five dimensions used for this analysis demonstrate how journalism selectively constructed news of an occurrence, localizing the story to the audience (and to national interests). Balance, fact/commentary, historical reference, information sources, and story location were all shrunk to clearly create an *our news* perspective each time. As part of that shrinking, groups (and their positions) outside the ideological mainstream got marginalized or ignored. The two cases addressed here have demonstrated how centering on the interests of nation state end up simulating an aura of ideological objectivity. Coverage of the event becomes "closed," so that ownership of the news unquestionably becomes "ours." These observations hold true beyond the cases presented here, informing how situations from Vietnam War protests to Desert Storm to the Murrah Building bombing all represent efforts to communicate political opposition yet are also journalistically managed to reflect ideological support. When oppositional messages appear in the news, they become ideologically deviant and support dominant ideology by their contrasts. This is not to say that these acts of political violence were legitimate in their means to an end, but rather to suggest that the intended message of the political violence gets lost behind the mass of mainstream journalistic interpretations.

Turning to this chapter's research questions, the first question asked how political violence stemming from outside the United States would adhere to or depart from journalistic conventions because of ideological alignment. One answer is to raise another question: What are journalistic conventions? If the term is meant to reflect the ideals of fairness, balance, and telling a well-rounded story—journalistic ideals—then the news of political violence would be departing from conventions. However, if the question were addressed another way—does this news depart from everyday working processes—then a reasonable answer would be to say that the story was still told the same way that everyday news is told, albeit with a greater degree of mythness and storytelling.

The second research question asked how social actors in this news might be used to sway the ours/theirs balance of coverage. What stood out in this analysis was how actors from mainstream America were valorized, whereas actors from the outside had their credibility and status downplayed. For example, New Yorkers were cast as mythical heroes on a quest to right the world after the World Trade Center was attacked. American leaders were portrayed in a similarly positive light as the war began in Iraq. As a counterpoint, terrorists, their organizations, and their messages were nearly gone from the World Trade Center story, and even Americans outside the New York core played little more than a supporting part in the story. Regarding the Iraq War, the arguments of dissenting European leaders were countered and minimized, and Iraqis and their leaders appeared as "goosey" simpleminded people, heading toward the mythical roles of savages and misguided tricksters whose actions bring about their own demise.

The third research question asked about story location and how it influenced ownership of news. An easy answer would argue that if it happened there, it was theirs, but if it happened here it would be ours. The analysis of these two cases, though, suggests that location does not carry a great deal of weight for story ownership. Instead, the ideas connected to that location seem to carry the weight of ownership. Any actor in any location can be cast in a number of ways, regardless of location. For example, an American military official could be located in the United States or in Iraq, but his perspective would reflect the same ideology regardless of location. In the same way, an official of another country's government could be downplayed, discredited, or contradicted in the United States just the same as in his or her home country.

In the big picture, as long as news remains an economic commodity and media organizations remain profit-seeking enterprises, news will continue to be ideological. To do otherwise would invite negative consequences on the bottom line. When *The New York Times* covered the World Trade Center attacks as an "everyman's" story, the paper ensured that readers would read it and advertisers would follow. Conversely, if *The New York Times* had chosen to present ideas counter to the Bush administration's sentiments as the country reached the brink of war in Iraq, readers would likely show resentment and stray toward the news of other media organizations with a more natural ideological perspective. When thinking about news ownership, this chapter clearly suggests that our ownership of our significant news will prevail by necessity.

Is all the news ours? When an occurrence presents a clear ideological threat, the answer is yes.

REFERENCES

Altschull, J. H. (1995). *Agents of power: The media and public policy* (4th ed.). White Plains, NY: Longman.

Apple, R. W. (2001, September 12). Awaiting the aftershocks. *The New York Times,* p. A1.

Barringer, F. & Fabrilant, G. (2001, September 12). As an attack unfolds, a struggle to provide vivid images to homes. *The New York Times,* p. A25.

Berkowitz, D. (1997). *Social meanings of news: A text-reader.* Thousand Oaks, CA: Sage.

Berkowitz, D. & TerKeurst, J. (1999). Community as interpretive community: Rethinking the journalist-source relationship. *Journal of Communication, 49,* 129-136.

Bumiller, E. & Sanger, D. (2001, September 12). A somber Bush says terrorism cannot prevail. *The New York Times,* p. A1.

Burns, J. (2003, March 20). Threats and responses: Iraq; Defiant response. *The New York Times,* p. A1.

Cohen, A. & Roeh, I. (1992). One of the bloodiest days: A comparative analysis of open and closed television news. *Journal of Communication, 42,* 42-55.

Erlanger, S. (2001, September 12). European nations stand with U.S., ready to respond. *The New York Times,* p. A23.

Gitlin, T. (1980). *The whole world is watching.* Berkeley: University of California Press.

Glaberson, W. (2001, September 12). Talk show figure and TV producer among lost passengers. *The New York Times,* p. A16.

Glanz, J. (2001, September 12). Towers believed to be safe proved vulnerable to an intense jet fuel fire, experts say. *The New York Times,* p. A3.

Golding, P. & Murdoch, G. (2000). Culture, communications and political economy. In J. Curran & M. Gurevitch (Eds.), *Mass media and society* (pp. 70-92). London: Arnold.

Greenberg, B. & Gantz, W. (Eds.). (1993). *Desert Storm and the mass media.* Cresskill, NJ: Hampton Press.

Haberman, C. (2001, September 12). When the unimaginable happens, and it's right outside your window. *The New York Times,* p. A10.

Hall, S. (1982). The rediscovery of "ideology": Return of the repressed in media studies. In M. Gurevitch, T. Bennett, J. Curran, & J. Woollacott (Eds.), *Culture, society, and the media* (pp. 56-90). Methuen: London.

Hallin, D. (2000). Commercialism and professionalism in the American news media. In J. Curran & M. Gurevitch (Eds.), *Mass media and society* (pp. 218-237). London: Arnold.

Harden, B. (2001, September 12). Physical and psychological paralysis of nation. *The New York Times,* p. A18.

Herman, E. & Chomsky, N. (1988). *Manufacturing consent: The political economy of the mass media.* New York: Pantheon.

Keller, B. (2001, September 12). Correspondent; America's emergency line: 9/11. *The New York Times,* p. A27.

Kennedy, R. (2001, September 12). With city transit shut down, New Yorkers take to eerily empty streets. *The New York Times,* p. A8.

Lichtenberg, J. (2000). In defence of objectivity revisited. In J. Curran & M. Gurevitch (Eds.), *Mass media and society* (pp. 238-254). London: Arnold.

Mitchell, A. & Seelye, K. Q. (2001, September 12). Horror knows no party as lawmakers huddle. *The New York Times,* p. A20.

Nossek, H. (2001, April). *Our news and their news: On the role of place in the definition of political violence and terrorism as news.* Paper presented at "What's News?" Symposium, Syracuse University, New York.

Purdum, T. S. & Toner, R. (2001, September 12). Driven underground, administration and congressional officials stay on the job. *The New York Times,* p. A5.

Rashbaum, W. K. & Barron, J. (2003, March 20). City fortifies entry points to guard against terrorism. *The New York Times,* p. A21.

Sanger, D. E. & Burns, J. F. (2003). Bush orders start of war on Iraq: Missles apparently miss Hussein. *The New York Times,* p. A1.

Schmemann, S. (2001, September 12). President vows to exact punishment for "evil." *The New York Times,* p. A1.

Schudson, M. (2000). The sociology of news production revisited (again). In J. Curran & M. Gurevitch (Eds.), *Mass media and society* (3rd ed., pp. 175-200). London: Arnold.

Smith, C. (2003). Reluctant Saudi Arabia prepares its quiet role in the U.S.-led war on Iraq. *The New York Times,* p. A1.

Stanley, A. (2003, March 20). After a lengthy buildup, an anticlimactic strike. *The New York Times,* p. A22.

Stein, S., Boyle, M., McCluskey, M., Devanathan, N., McLeod, D., Hillback, E., & Shevy, M. (2003, May). *Community influences on newspaper coverage of social and political protests.* Paper presented to the annual convention of the International Communication Association, San Diego, Calif.

Stevenson, R. W. (2003, March 20). Day of waiting and wondering with word from president. *The New York Times,* p. A1.

Tuman, J. (2003). *Communicating terror.* Thousand Oaks, CA: Sage.

Zernike, K. & Hartocollis, A. (2001, September 12). Parents converge to take students home, and officials seek to keep safe those who remain. *The New York Times,* p. A11.

Chapter 9

Round Up the Usual Suspects

Some Radical Implications of Indonesian and Euro-American Media Coverage of 'Terrorist' Attacks

Mark Hobart

The rule is: 10,000 deaths on another continent equal 1,000 deaths in another country equal 100 deaths in an outpost equal ten deaths in the centre of the capital equal one celebrity.

(van Ginneken 1998, pp. 23-24)

How, in a multicentered media world, do we set about a critical understanding of coverage of violence? Is it something that all right-thinking people anywhere instantly recognize and express concern over? Are those who fail to do so ipso facto barbarous, fanatic or depraved? When, and how, precisely does violence become "political"? And what representations of violence come to be published or broadcast? After all, several times more people are murdered annually in the United States than were killed on 9/11.[1] And, elsewhere, tens of millions die every year from preventable causes, inexpensive to remedy, such as dirty drinking water and lack of simple medicines. How is it that economic violence on such a scale is not considered political? So is what counts as political violence simply a matter of it being spectacular, perpetrated by someone we do not like, and happening to people like us? In what follows, I shall consider critically popular and professional assumptions about how violence is represented as political by considering some of the media coverage of two spectacular acts of political violence: the attacks on the twin trade towers in New York and the bomb blasts in Bali thirteen months later. Such an inquiry suggests that the mythology that media scholars identify at work in the media industry holds at least as true of their own analyses.

Some Western media professionals and media studies specialists might be surprised that I argue we now live in a multicentered media world. After all, does the whole world not depend on a handful of European and American satellite feeds and accept the unquestioned superiority of Western standards of news reporting, as exemplified for instance by the BBC? Considered from, say, India, China, or Indonesia, with thriving media industries such comfortable assumptions look less hegemonic than parochial and quaintly dated. Leaving aside the emergence of news agencies in many countries, such an account assumes a facile essentialism and determinism—for example, that video footage somehow predetermines not only how it will be presented by different channels and commented on, but how it will be appreciated by viewers. Coverage varies greatly. The world, as represented in Indonesian media for example, places Asia as central, with the Middle East important for its Islamic links. The status of America has become complicated. And these days, to the extent that Europe exists, like Latin America it is probably more for football than anything else.

Such diversity may be threatening to European and American media professionals and scholars not just because the loss of their taken-for-granted supremacy, but because it raises questions about what constitute the criteria for balanced and appropriate reporting.[2] If we let go of objectivity in reporting, the argument goes, then we have no standards by which to refute partisanship, bias, propaganda, and downright lies. The specter is relativism, often now with the added soubriquet of "postmodernist." As with other charges of relativism, the argument rests upon a false dichotomy. Either you accept absolute standards of objectivity (as enunciated by a Euro-American élite) or there is total dystopia when callow deceit claims the same status as shining truth. If only matters were so simple. Unfortunately, what counts as objective, as what is authentic, and what appropriate to talk about, varies historically and cross-culturally. As Fiske nicely put it, "Objectivity is the 'unauthored' voice of the bourgeoisie" (1987, p. 289).

As new bourgeoisies, different kinds of class, religious, and status groups around the world seek representation, it becomes hard to defend absolutist claims to an objectivity that seems suspiciously white Anglo-Saxon, be it the BBC, CNN, or even Fox News.

The alternative to imposing dubious and unacceptable Eurocentric standards is to rethink critically how we are to evaluate what is going on in a world of heterogeneous, labile audiences and broadcasters subject to diverse conflicting economic, political, and professional pressures and agendas. This is not loony relativism. It is pragmatism, in the strict sense of a philosophical critique of practice, including the practices of those claiming to be knowing subjects. It starts with the recognition that criteria for discussing good practice and ideas like objectivity change with industrial practices and involve an unending argument between media practitioners, commentators, and critical scholars that now embraces people right across the world. There is no unproblematic *terra firma* on which to stand. A critical understanding of media in the twenty-first century requires us to be firmly in between. In what follows, we shall see why adopting such a position is appropriate.

INDONESIAN COVERAGE
OF THE TRADE TOWERS ATTACK

The idiosyncrasies of different countries' broadcasting, not least news coverage, can create an uncomfortable, but revelatory, "media shock," not unlike the culture shock that anthropologists experience going to and from fieldwork. Returning each year from working on Indonesian television, switching on British television is mostly a rather unpleasant experience of insularity and parochialism. I find myself wondering, for instance, how could the BBC's supposedly "objective" news coverage seem even more selective, narrow, and biased than I remembered? How could anyone take it seriously? Although there were moments when Indonesian and British news coverage appeared to refer to roughly the same world from different angles, at others they appeared to occupy worlds that barely overlapped. If this is indeed so, such moments of radical difference raise serious problems of cultural translation.

As this is a first foray, my evidence is not systematically accrued, but is merely suggestive. It includes part coverage of two events. The first is some Indonesian television and print coverage of the attacks on the twin trade towers on 11 September 2001, together with Indonesian news producers' commentary on that coverage. The second is some British television and print coverage of the bombs in Bali of 12 October 2002 and a range of Indonesian print, television, and electronic sources. Such lopsided sources allow me at least to raise some questions about representing political violence.

Television in Indonesia is interesting, not least because of its key role in Suharto's New Order régime. The apparently extravagant Third World gesture—the launching of the first Palapa satellite in 1976 and placing a television set in every village in the archipelago[3]—was a brilliant stroke. It created a vast audience for re-imagining Indonesians no longer as Sukarno's revolutionary masses, but as the audience as nation, as citizens to be developed, so neatly defining the masses as in need of guidance and very childlike (Kitley, 2000, pp. 81-91). Television became so central to the New Order's self-artic- ulation as the agent of development that it is hard to imagine the régime's existence without it. So, after decades of tight control over the mass media, the shift to remarkably liberal policies after Suharto's resignation marked a significant change. Thousands of permits were granted for newspapers, mag- azines, and radio stations. There are now some twelve terrestrial television channels accessible in the most densely populated regions of Java, Bali, and the major cities elsewhere, and over 200 satellite channels are easily accessi- ble and affordable to the middle classes. And community radio and TV are proliferating exponentially. Media freedom has become at once a litmus test of, and a battlefield for, Indonesia's political future.

There are several notable aspects of television coverage of 11 September. Significantly for the country with the world's largest Muslim population, reporting on all channels studiously avoided suggesting that Islam had any- thing to do with the attacks on the World Trade Center. The perpetrators were described as Arab, and the invited talking heads, as Middle-Eastern experts. This is the more interesting in that the capital, Jakarta, had been the target for bombs. *Laskar Jihad* and several other militias were generally thought to be at work in the Moluccas, Sulawesi, and elsewhere.[4] The Trade Tower attacks were treated fairly matter-of-factly compared to European and American coverage. There were frequent comparisons to the United States' devastation of Nagasaki and Hiroshima; and extensive use of com- mentary from leading political figures around the world—many Asian— which framed the satellite feeds. Only three television stations actually broke schedules to cover the topic.

Why coverage should be relatively low-key is pertinent. Indonesia's colonial and postcolonial heritage has left several potential social divisions that interested parties can call upon, notably religion, ethnicity, region, class, gender, and age. The one much trumpeted among "ologists," foreign politi- cal commentators, and sometimes Indonesians themselves is the polarization between Islamic and nationalist political agendas. The coherence of both tends to be exaggerated. The long history and sheer diversity of Islam in Indonesia makes generalization impossible. I leave it to someone else to determine when religion serves as an idiom for other ways of organizing or dividing people, or vice versa. So the dark intrigues promoted by experts in that oxymoron "Western Intelligence" (as equally should Indonesian con- spiracy theories) should be treated as "representations-as." We need to inquire into their purposes. At the risk of generalizing, commentary on mil- itant Islam in the press and television is taken as a serious issue but not a major threat, especially compared to concern with how the United States is involved behind the scenes in Indonesian politics, not least in view of its now-demonstrated role in orchestrating the massacres of "communists" in the 1960s. Most secular liberal intellectuals I know are far more worried by certain elements of the armed forces than they are by Islamic terrorists.

THE MEDIA INDONESIA EDITORIAL

The themes of much coverage were summed up in an editorial, only hours after the attacks, in the daily newspaper, *Media Indonesia*, and broadcast on Metro TV, a station owned by the paper. The televised version was interesting because it revealed something of the complex relationship between image, text, and soundtrack. The images were unexceptional—snippets from the limited footage available at that time by satellite feed—interestingly, to the soundtrack of *Schindler's List*.

> **Media Indonesia Editorial 12 September 2002:**
> America and Terrorists
>
> The world is witnessing a great rivalry between two superpowers, the United States of America and terrorists. Last night the world saw the great power of the US collapse under the attack of those deemed to be terrorists.
>
> The World Trade Center, one of the biggest business and office centres in the world, and a symbol of American economic power, easily collapsed, struck down by aeroplanes. At almost the same moment the Pentagon, the symbol of American military might, shattered under the impact of another plane. In the meantime, a string of explosions hit the Congress Building and State Department. Almost all the symbols of American strength were destroyed because of the event. People were in fear; government offices closed, business centres shut down. The US president George Bush and his staff were evacuated from the White House. The world condemned. Last night the US was like Japan surrendering to the Allies in World War II, struck down by the bombs in Hiroshima and Nagasaki.
>
> But we do not want to establish who won and lost in this tragedy in New York and Washington. What we wish to show is that this tragedy is the climax of a never-ending arrogant rivalry. America and these terrorists are long time enemies that never see eye to eye. The United States, which claims to be the champion of democracy, was tempted to use force when dealing with those it considers terrorists. When someone, or a group of people, is accused of being terrorists by the United States, *that* equals a death sentence. Such verdicts unfortunately breed fanaticism, arrogance and a never-ending search for revenge on the part

of those called "terrorists." They—the United States and the terrorists—
are fighting because of they suffer from a kind of "split personality."
Both use the language of force, but in the name of peace and order.

We are deeply saddened for the hundreds, even thousands, buried under
the rubble of the World Trade Center. What is certain is that our sorrow
will become greater as, after not too long, as usual the US will retaliate
in its own way. Without question, yet again innocent people will be the
victims. Terrorism and Might both have a deadly arrogance. The US
may claim to be the mightiest in all matters to do with the military and
technology. Yet all that might succumbed at the hands of utterly single-
minded[5] people.

Therefore, for the sake of civilization, force in the name of—and for—
anything cannot be justified. The world cannot be given another spectacle of death by arrogant and unthinking people.

There were several interesting points in the editorial, reiterated in interviews with commentators. Not least was the juxtaposition of the United
States with terrorist networks as matched superpowers. The editorial treated the attack on the States as double. Its two greatest symbols of power—
military and economic—were destroyed (it was incorrect, though, about the
attacks on the State Department and Congress). More definitively though,
last night the world *saw* the great power of the United States collapse. Power
depends on being seen to be effective and invincible. The implicit presupposition, though, was that the media wield great power in being able to show
to the world how the mighty are fallen. And without the protection of force,
the invincible are shown to be frightened—with the President scurrying for
safety. As is common with editorials, the authorial position is exnominated.
The editorial speaks with general authority, bound neither by country, class,
religion nor any other specific interest.

The editorial moved to argue the causes of such destruction: arrogance,
arogansi (using the English-derived term four times to make the point
unambiguous). The consequence was equally unambiguously stated:
"Innocent people will be the victims yet again." But how did the United
States, the world's last superpower, and a terrorist network come to be comparable? Unlike most Euro-American sources I have seen, which were at
pains to hierarchize the attackers as members of small groups that were not
comparable to the majesty and legitimacy of a superpower, the editorial
compares the two forces. It is not just the scale of the damage, the nature of
the targets and mode of attack, or the degree of fear and response it generated in America, but the "rivalry," which stresses the inappropriateness of the
mutual motives behind the enmity. The editorial rested upon an interesting
presupposition. It is not technology, scale, global spread, or even sheer
damn-the-consequences determination that was responsible. The editorial

could hardly state it more clearly: "Terrorism and might both have a deadly arrogance," each feeding off the other.

The implicit countervailing theme, repeated in other commentaries and, significantly, in the *vox pops*, was that the attacks were *"tidak manusiawi."* They were inhuman, beyond recognition as human. Arrogance and humanity are the antithetical terms that underpin the editorial's analysis. By juxtaposition, however, the humanity of the United States in its policy of aggressive domination was called into question. The editorial ended by simply contrasting force and the inflicting of death with civilization, so neatly pre-empting arrogant claims to use violence in the name of civilization.

A striking feature of much Indonesian television and print coverage of 11 September, as of other world news is how they balance their own opinions with a recognition of hegemonic Euro-American narratives. (This is not to say, of course, that Indonesian media do not introduce their own forms of closure.) Writing about the role of gender in television reception, Mary Ellen Brown has argued that women have to learn a "double-voiced discourse" (1987), what Bakhtin termed "heteroglossia."[6] That is, they have to be familiar with the largely male-oriented articulations of much television exemplified by news but also relate what they watch to their own lives. Showalter designated this a feminine discourse, which partly escapes control and so constitutes a "wild zone" (1985). Without needing to essentialize a single discourse, the argument bears directly on the editorial above. Indonesians, here both viewers and producers, have to work with heteroglossia. They learn to appreciate the dominant discourse, here primarily American, beamed at them via satellite feeds into television stations, newspapers, and middle-class homes, while relating both what is going on and its discursive closure to their lives. They must buy "white news" not only of white goings-on, but also of their neighbors,' as part of the politics of cultural translation (cf. Asad, 1986). The image of the "wild zone" is apposite. The "surplus of meaning" (to use Laclau's phrase, 1990) that followed liberalization of censorship has led Indonesian conservatives to try to reintroduce censorship.[7]

MAKING THE WORLD SAFE
FOR DRUNKEN TOURISTS

A full analysis of news coverage of the bombs in Bali would require a monograph. I wish here just to consider briefly how British television news channels attributed responsibility for the attacks. Such a review raises issues of nomination and exnomination, the agentive nature of mythologizing, and, lastly, silencing.

The first day of news coverage is informative, because within hours a template, or chronotope, had been established that was largely common to all channels. I find Bakhtin's notion of chronotope (1981) very useful in understanding the conventions that determine how news events are portrayed. Particular assumptions about space, time, narrative, personhood, agency, and causation are distinctive of different genres; and are combined in ways that, through reiteration, give a sense of naturalness and self-evident truth to what are carefully constructed and inherently mediated accounts.

The first news I recorded was the BBC 24-hours news channel, which broke the story a few hours after the events on its program at 2 am on 13 October 2002. After the briefest of announcements that bombs had gone off in Bali, the voiceover proclaimed: "The Australian Foreign Minister believes it was a terrorist attack aimed at Westerners." Almost immediately the voiceover continued to footage of fires raging, "The US Embassy had recently issued warnings of possible attacks by Islamic militants linked to Al-Qaeda." The news item then introduced two themes that became standard later. The hospitals (and later "the Indonesian authorities") were overwhelmed, could not cope, and needed professional help from the Australians, British, and Americans — precisely the countries whose casualties were foregrounded. People from the rest of Europe and the world, let alone Indonesians, were effectively made to vanish.

The studio anchor then turned to Richard Galpin, the BBC's correspondent in Jakarta, to ask who did it:

Anchor: If it was in fact a coordinated terrorist attack, do we know who organized it?

Galpin: No. Not at all. Obviously it's far too early, but we've been speaking to the national police chief who, like us, is on his way to Bali, and he's saying that — he's described it as — an act of terror, but when asked who he thought was responsible, he said so far they don't know. They are still investigating. And of course no one has admitted responsibility.

This introduced two more themes. British television staff were determined immediately to identify the perpetrators, while the Indonesians kept stressing the need for thorough investigation and reliable evidence before making judgments, an antagonism that persists in new form. Finally, the prescience of the big Western powers (they had known attacks were coming) had been thwarted by foreigners' — here Indonesians' — incompetence, carelessness, or active connivance with the enemy.

By the time of the BBC's midday Sunday news and ITV's news at 1 pm, when it was possible to muster more accurate information and expert opinion, how much had changed? In fact, not only had little changed, but if anything the cautious questions and qualified replies were congealing into foregone certainties. Peter Sissons, as anchorman, asked their World Affairs Correspondent, James Robbins, what was going on. To yet more shots of fires, Robbins began with a toll of the destruction and carnage, aided by eyewitness accounts (footage that was repeated on several channels), then:

> Robbins: As the island of Bali and the whole of Indonesia tried to cope with the country's worst terrorist attack, suspicion falls immediately on radical Islamic groups, possibly working with Al-Qaeda members. Washington says it has compelling evidence they've linked up to plan attacks, although at this stage nothing about this massacre is certain. . . . Indonesia has the largest Muslim population in the world and the country has widely been regarded as the weak link in South East Asia's war on terrorism.

The singular mode of argument was clearer still in an opening statement by ITV's anchorman, Mark Austin.

> Austin: It is not clear who was responsible, but groups linked to Al-Qaeda are being blamed.

A sentence that starts as ostensibly open-minded and impartial is promptly contradicted by a subsequent clause, which exnominates the authority on which an unsubstantiated claim relies—"suspicion falls," classically by using the passive: "are being blamed." An argument that promptly blossomed as incontrovertible was built up of circumstantial evidence and ad hoc or unverified comments.

Set notionally within a discourse of reason and critical investigation, the news coverage ran the gamut of rhetoric devices. News people say among themselves that it is vital to capture and convey a complex situation in a neat image or phrase. The trope was already waiting. The TV anchor handed over to a titleless correspondent (Rob Smith), who was heard against yet more background of fire.

> Smith: For a time this paradise island was hell on earth. And many of the pictures are simply too horrific to show you.

Over the next days, this simple polarity provided the framework for virtually every story. The antithesis of political violence is not just peaceful, but apolitical, epitomized in innocent, idyllic, beautiful Bali and its innocent, beautiful, apolitical, and anonymized people, whose only desire is to make tourists happy.

The stern job of serious news reporting, however, is to investigate what lies behind. So Smith and then the London anchor repeat the same sleight of argument.

> Smith: It is still too early to say who planted the bombs, but the sheer scale and coordination involved would suggest a well-organized terrorist group. The fact that Westerners were so deliberately targeted has opened up the possibility that Al-Qaeda has struck again.

Back in the studio, Mark Austin continued.

> Austin: With the finger of blame pointing at extremist groups linked to Al-Qaeda, our international editor, Bill Neely, assesses the evidence and looks at what it could mean for the war on terrorism.

The background video switched to what looked like a (pretty peaceful) demonstration by women wearing scarves. What was visible on the placards they were carrying seemed to have as much to do with support of human rights as anything else.[8]

> Neely: No one is claiming responsibility, but Australia's support for the war against Al-Qaeda and the presence of many radical Islamic groups in Indonesia has fingers pointing towards Osama bin Laden and his supporters. . . . Many in Indonesia hate the West and want to see the world's most populous Muslim country become a fundamentalist Islamic state. It's the weakest link in the fight against bin Laden. Many experts have no doubt that Al-Qaeda is behind this bombing.

Whereas the media professionals like to emphasize the difference in styles between their coverage, their narratives and reasoning reiterate a single paradigm, as Channel 4 news at 19.00 demonstrated. After a brief résumé, the unnamed anchorman started promisingly, only to be contradicted by the reporter in the field, who reverted to type.

Anchor: The immediate assumption was that Al-Qaeda had carried
            out the bombings, but should we be so swift to jump to that
            conclusion? Here's Peter Morgan.

Morgan: It bears all the hallmarks of Al-Qaeda and its allies. The lat-
            est in a series of attacks linked to the terror network. Al-
            Qaeda is thought to have secret cells in over sixty countries.
            And Indonesia with 220 million people spread over 300
            islands is a perfect hiding place. Prime suspects for last
            night's terror attacks are the radical Islamic groups who want
            to turn Indonesia's secular republic into an Islamic state.

He then went on to list (inaccurately) the prime suspects, ending with
Jemaah Islamiyah, on which, conveniently, they had footage, as a Channel 4
reporter some time before had interviewed Abu Bakar Ba'asir, whom many
Western news sources were claiming to be its leader, despite his denials.[9] A
friend of mine in the seventies used to argue that the reason the food in all
Indian restaurants in London looked and tasted the same was that it all came
from one vast kitchen somewhere under the centre of the city. One could
perhaps be forgiven for thinking that all British news is concocted of canned
ingredients from one deeply buried soup kitchen. For "these stories are pre-
written, they 'write' the journalists, and their meanings are already in circulation" (Fiske 1987, p. 296).

(P)RE-TOLD TALES

The general starting point for coverage is that the "Third World" is unstable

> Third World countries are, for example, conventionally represented in
> western news as places of famines and natural disaster, of social revolu-
> tion, and of political corruption. These events are not seen as disrupting
> their social norms, but as confirming ours, confirming our dominant
> sense that western democracies provide the basics of life for everyone,
> are stable, and fairly and honestly governed. When deviations from these
> norms occur in our own countries they are represented as precisely that,
> deviations from the norm: in Third World countries, however, such
> occurrences are represented as their norms which differ markedly from
> ours. For the western mews media, the Third World is a place of natural
> and political disasters and not much else. (Fiske 1987, pp. 284-285)

The interesting question is in what circumstances "Third World" countries
find themselves reiterating such stereotypes in their own news.

The first problem that arose in news coverage was where—or to whom—did this tourist island with luxury hotels belong? There was inimitable footage of Australian tourists furious about "how could they do this to our Bali?" The shock was when Bali ceased for a moment to be the object of Western (and Asian) projections but became part of Indonesia and so the Third World, with its stereotypical volatility, instability, incompetence, and bureaucracy. And when such countries fail to conform—as when, at the time of writing, Indonesians conduct peaceful, largely fair, democratic elections that show support for radical Islam to be marginal—the solution is to declare them nonevents, not needing coverage. Silence is the default mode of news coverage.

Many other features of the reporting are boilerplate. We are invited to identify with relatives of the missing and with confused and frightened eyewitnesses, who are not too confused to forget to carry a handicam (or, like a fireman from Watford, make sure to be videoed on the way to help) and sell the footage. The chronotope demands heroes to domesticate the foreignness of foreign places. One Australian GP seems just to have gone along to the hospital to help if he could, only to be transmogrified in one news item into a savior by bringing white man's rationality and discipline to the incompetent natives.

Others are familiar themes but in a new form. A great deal of coverage was given to rugby clubs out on binges, that had lost members—a neatly overdetermined image. At once it underlined how wild out there really is, contrasted "fair" with unfair conflict, so sport with politics, as if the latter were wrong—the wrong way to deal with difference or at least to be kept away from decent folk, like the many other bombings of civilian targets in Indonesia. Sport aestheticizes and so depoliticizes.

Similarly "clawback" (how news media domesticate disruptive events) works neatly through the hierarchical imposition of "meaning" by studio anchors over field reporters and experts, without losing authenticity. The full passage from Fiske, cited above, reads:

> This authenticity guarantees the "truth" of the interpretation that this mediating involves and thus allows, paradoxically, that which has been interpreted to present itself as objective. Objectivity is the "unauthored" voice of the bourgeoisie. (Fiske, 1987, p. 289)

Within twelve hours, however, television and print journalists had found the trope that would condense the whole experience into two words: *Paradise Lost*. At a stroke, Islam, the transcendental agent of the outrage, had destroyed a Hindu-Buddhist heaven (on which see Adrian Vickers, 1989), so confirming the unity of all other religions in face of the aggressor. Quite why a Christian, indeed Miltonian, image should be imposed on the Balinese was never asked. Nor did anyone seem to notice that this brilliant encapsulation of the catastrophe reiterated a history of pre-interpretation of Bali that dates back over 400 years to the fantasies of a prelapsarian world fanned into life by Cornelis de Houtman's "discovery" of the island in 1597. On the evidence from themes repeatedly endlessly in subsequent days, some rather scary lineaments of the chronotope of political violence as imagined in British television news start to emerge.[10]

> Terrorism has revealed the underlying clash of civilizations, exemplified in political violence as a savagely destructive act against English-speaking people, carried out deliberately by fanatics, hell-bent on creating an anti-society or a dystopia (epitomized in the endless scenes of flames). It is political, in the sense of abnormal and against the natural order of things, which is people—or, rather, people rich enough to fly to Bali—being entitled to do whatever their wealth inclines them to. Such violence is made possible either because of a failure of proper government, because the general population is too lax, lethargic and incompetent to do anything about it, or because they harbour vicious feelings towards these normal English-speaking people, who only came to have a good time, notably parading half-naked and getting drunk—*Their only crime was to go on holiday.* (*The Daily Telegraph*, cited in Fox, n.d., p. 18)

Like the news broadcasts I have discussed, my summary contains a distinct element of caricature, one sadly borne out by a close scrutiny of news coverage. My general point is less tongue-in-cheek. Representations of political violence paint not just a dystopia, but a distinctly Christian dystopia with all the incongruities and plain lack of taste that come with imposing a contrary Utopia on a Hindu society. Perhaps to the surprise of some of its practitioners, British news enshrines a distinctly Christian worldview (quite how does that square with the BBC World Service's charter?). More seriously, even the brief extracts above make clear the extent to which news coverage—like some defences of the existence of Divinity—is teleological. In other words, the conclusion anticipates and determines the reasoning that will inevitably arrive at it. Opportunities and attempts to inquire into what might be happening are casually or ruthlessly swept aside, not followed up. Such moments of inquiry are, however, necessary. Like inoculations, they inject a little of something dangerous, something that the industrial processes of news production are only too familiar at dealing with. What British news lacks in any objectivity deriving from attempts at impartial critical inquiry, it more than makes up in objectivity as predestined certainty. Coincidentally, such predestined certainty is precisely what the broadcasters decry about those they label fanatics.

Over subsequent days' coverage there was little attempt to question the egregious logic by which Al-Qaeda or their acolytes had been proven guilty, still less to pay attention to Indonesian sources, which were pointing to all sorts of complexities. One significant change did occur, however. The images of a country full of fanatical Islamists gave way to what appeared to be clips from militants' training tapes accompanied by the increasingly standardized disavowal that most Indonesians had a reputation for moderation and tolerance. The conclusion correspondents and anchors usually drew was that, under the circumstances, the Indonesian authorities were responsible because of their incompetence and failure to do anything about the massive infiltration of their society by extremists, compounded by their blinkered (or downright collusive) refusal unconditionally to accept the verdict of the British reporters.

Why should we be surprised? After all,

> the idea of neutrality is certainly sympathetic, but it implies that one is really willing and able to put oneself in the shoes of all others. Very often, this is simply not feasible. Western media organizations active on a global scale will first of all cater to Western media audiences and their values. Rich clients such as the Japanese may be taken into account on occasion, but poorer clients from the Second and Third Worlds are obviously of marginal concern, particularly if their sensibilities clash with those of clients from the First World. (van Ginneken, 1998, p. 44)

The economics of news coverage encourages parachute and pack journalism (van Ginneken, 1998, pp. 135-137). If news is "the conventionalization of the real," the vital work of reasserting the vision of social and political equilibrium of a particular class or interest groups (aka "the bourgeoisie" in media studies) in the face of threats, then avoiding—not engaging with— cultural translation becomes an imperative. And newsrooms, that most functionally vital of culture industries, have perfected the art.

Does it matter? After all, even if some details were fuzzy, in the grand scheme of things did British television news not get it broadly right? Has Al-Qaeda not proven a major source of global violence? Following Goodman (1968), representations are acts: you always represent something *as* something else to someone on an occasion for a purpose. You cannot represent something as complex as Islam in Indonesia as it is, no more than you can something as shrouded in uncertainty and secrecy as the organization of political violence. As a pragmatist philosopher, Goodman's point was that representations have consequences. In all sorts of ways, ratings-chasing hyperbole about Al-Qaeda may well prove a self-fulfilling prophecy. Insofar as such representations transform what they purport to describe or reiterate prejudice, they themselves are part of the field of political violence.

WHODUNIT?

The determination of most non-Indonesian television and print coverage to pre-attribute responsibility stands in stark contrast to the concern in much of the Indonesian press. In part as a response to the international media's feeding frenzy, a key issue that emerged was the need to gather reliable evidence as to what had actually happened, who the perpetrators were and what lay behind the attacks.[11] Granted Indonesia's complex history of political violence and abuse of proper legal procedures, the questions were widely appreciated as forensic, not foregone. For example, the Balinese police officer placed in charge of the investigation, General I Madé Mangku Pastika, stated at the start that there were three separate questions: who had carried out the attack, who had supplied and funded it, and who had authorized it? It took the full weight of the world's media to ignore the point.

So what is at issue in this determination to find out whodunit? If the concern were really with establishing responsibility forensically and juridically, then the media were going about it in the worst possible way. Apart from the more obvious motives, the issue may be partly grammatical.[12] There are simple problems of consistently treating a network as a coherent subject of predication, which encourages its transformation into something more graspable, such as a unitary political agent. Theoretically, networks are rather awkward customers. This makes them at once both ideal and poor as subjects of media coverage. Being by definition uncentered, amorphous, and hard to pin down, they are perfect as objects of unfettered projection and association. In the absence of evidence, speculation becomes respectable. For the Bali bombings even chronomancy was pulled into play—it must be Al-Qaeda because it is so many days/weeks/months since X. By the same token, you cannot predicate the thinking, deciding, or acting of networks as you can a unitary subject. This does not stop reporters from doing so, of course.[13]

Another aspect to the identification of perpetrators is that naming and using the active mood about a chosen grammatical subject has the effect of making it appear as the agent that disrupts the natural order. The contrary process, which Barthes called exnomination, has the effect of masking agents.[14] In this instance exnomination did further work. For whatever reason—perhaps habit from New Order times or a fine sense of the political realities—the Indonesian mass media tended to be fairly circumspect in naming what, popularly, was mooted as a key suspect behind the violence; namely, those elements in the Indonesian armed forces thought to be loyal to the former President, Suharto.

I wish to raise just two issues. First, to what extent does this double exnomination ("The West" aka the bourgeoisie and parts of Indonesia's

army) enable an identification of interests? Put another way, how happy
would the Australians be if their government were involved in training and
funding precisely the people who turned out to have been behind the killing
of Australians in the Sari nightclub? Second, why should the agent many
Indonesians suspect as behind the attacks in Bali be so widely overlooked
even in the serious international and Indonesian press?

One of the few exceptions in the British press[15] was John Aglionby's
article in *The Guardian* on 16 October, in a piece which, as far as I know,
was never followed up, under the headline:

> The Secret Role of the Army in Sowing the Seeds of Religious Strife:
> Military Aid Was Key Element of Groups' Success

It contains the interesting paragraph:

> "If you scratch below the surface of any radical Islamic group in
> Indonesia you will find the hand of the military at work," said Sidney
> Jones, the head of the Jakarta office of the International Crisis Group.
> "And with many of them you don't really have to go beneath the sur-
> face."

One consequence of the news coverage of the Bali bombs was to
strengthen the repeated calls for Indonesia to get tough on terrorists, with
scant concern as to who exactly these terrorists were and what they were up
to. The implications could not be more serious to reform-minded
Indonesians concerned, after thirty-two years of quasi-military rule, to
bring about a modern democratic society governed by the rule of law. To
them, there was a real danger that "get tough on terrorism" would translate
as "strengthen the army and stop worrying about human rights, democratization, or systemic corruption." The media coverage of the bombings served
to maintain an illusion of order and a threat of disorder that, conveniently,
articulated with the political interests of the United States, but not of most
Indonesians.

MYTHMAKING

I would suggest, however, that there are other reasons for the extraordinary
speed with which closure occurred over responsibility for the bombings in
Bali. In order to understand these, it is useful to consider the television news
coverage as myth. By this I am not suggesting that the news is myth *tout*

court. Indeed myth in the popular sense is not myth. As anthropologists use the term, it is analytical, not substantive. It is used to distinguish as an object of critical examination those narratives that do not make sense according to conventional canons of scholarly rationality and require quite different styles of analysis. So Lévi-Strauss, for example, argued that mythological analysis is singularly important in revealing the paradigms that underlie all narratives. And Barthes drew upon this in his account of *Myth Today* (1973), in which he distinguished seven figures of contemporary bourgeois myth. Do they shed any light on news coverage of the Balinese and 9/11 bombings? The figures are:

1. *Inoculation*: "One immunizes the contents of the collective imagination by means of a small inoculation of acknowledged evil" (Barthes, 1973, p. 150). Whereas Indonesian coverage of the attacks in both New York and Bali were at pains to recognize failings and fault on all sides, the possibility that the governments or citizens of the United States, Europe, or Australia could have contributed in any way to the bombs in Bali was excluded from television coverage and emerged only in commentaries in print from a handful of critics. Instead reification, projection, and dichotomy were deployed. Radical Islam is a disease that it is too late to inoculate against, as it has broken out in Bali. So it is imperative for the rest of the world's health that the Indonesian government eradicate the cause, no matter what the cost. With a rigid dualism that, ironically, news broadcasters attributed to the Islamist "fanatics," evil could only lie "out there."

2. *Privation of history/culture*: "Myth deprives the object of which it speaks of all History" (1973, p. 151). Mass media coverage domesticates history and culture. Islam has no history, no culture. Bali was timeless, eternal and unchanging up to 12 October 2002.[16] It existed to serve up an "exotic festivity" for tourists. Its history and culture have become a world brand, a commodity that consumers have the absolute right to enjoy. That the behavior of many tourists in Kuta, the site of the main bombs, is offensive to many Balinese, as well as to devout Muslims, is scrupulously ignored. Indeed the island no longer belongs to the inhabitants or to Indonesia, as it is now "our Bali." And the reported setback to the economy becomes inseparable from the tourists' loss.

3. *Identification*:

   > The petit-bourgeois is a man unable to imagine the Other. If he comes face to face with him, he blinds himself, ignores and denies him, or else transforms him into himself . . . because the Other is a scandal which threatens his essence. (1973, p. 151)

From the moment reporting begins, the scene must be interpreted through the eyes of ordinary people like "us," now eternalized by videocams. So the bombings become the narrative of the married couples (who escaped, who died), the Watford fireman, the Melbourne GP, who are made to stand between us and the Indonesians, whose loss can only be acknowledged through a narrative of innocence tragically ended.

4. *Tautology*: "Tautology creates a dead, a motionless world" (1973, p. 153). The identification of the way the world should be with Euro-American bourgeois society and Christianity creaks and groans so badly that it is no surprise that the bombers have endlessly to be equated with Islam and as so self-evidently and essentially evil that there is no possibility of dialogue; no question of inquiring into the internal arguments within Islam between generations, traditions, countries; no point in asking the putative subjects what their concerns and objections are.

5. *Neither-norism*: "This mythological figure . . . consists in stating two opposites and balancing the one by the other so as to reject them both" (1973, p. 153). A frequently reiterated theme in news coverage was that Indonesia was desperately trapped between two appalling dangers. Either it would succumb to fundamentalism and become a new medieval Caliphate or the archipelago would disintegrate with unimaginable consequences. Faced with such grim alternatives, even at the cost of some human rights, infractions supporting firm military action against any possible suspects appears a welcome solution. News is, and presumably sometimes is intended to be, agentive. That is, its descriptions frame events so as to anticipate and imply the need for appropriate future action.

6. *Quantification of quality*: "By reducing any quality to quantity, myth economizes intelligence: it understands reality more cheaply" (1973, p. 153). Every broadcast in the first days started by listing the numbers of dead, injured, or missing foreigners. Even before the very limited repertoire of suitable adjectives to describe a singular event became overrepetitive, lists started to appear: of previous Al-Qaeda attacks, of extremist Muslim groups, of islands where they were active, or might be hiding. It did not take many months after the bombings for a new quantity to emerge. A major selling point became the drop in the cost of package tours to enjoy Bali's unique culture.

7. *The statement of fact*: This figure enshrines "universalism, the refusal of any explanation, an unalterable hierarchy of the world" (1973, p. 154). The trend was perhaps most blatant in the repeated trope of Paradise Lost. However, coverage depended on an endless

parading of facts—about Bali, about Islam, about Indonesia, about its government—that could only make sense to people who knew little or nothing about the country.

IS NEWS THE SAME EVERYWHERE?

How should we set about understanding the tight suturing of British television coverage of the bombings in Bali? And how does this differ from Indonesian coverage of the attacks in New York? Neither space nor my materials permit a definitive answer.

The obvious starting point is the economic determinants of coverage: for example the search for circulation or ratings, and the need to "cater to Western media audiences" (van Ginneken, 1998, p. 44). The former may offer an account of how many people are supposed to have read or watched and so indicate to producers the likely success of future coverage. The latter, in alluding to what "catering to" and "audiences" presuppose, threatens to open several cans of worms. Both may indicate something of how producers imagine the links between news content, audiences; and markets. Driven ultimately by industrialists' short-term concern with profit, such narratives are explanatorily primitive and leave most of the interesting questions unanswered. For a start, they tell us little of what people made of what they read or watched. Purporting to be stern, realistic, and masculine, such narratives inhabit a world of largely unfalsifiable generalities. They have to hover suitably detached from the actual daily practices of production, as these tell more confused stories of meeting deadlines, muddling through, and so on. And, in a beautiful demonstration of the quantification of quality, the myriad ways that readers and viewers engage, or fail to engage, with the news is magically converted into numerical ratings. Myth applies as much to the inner rationality of media industries as it does to how they imagine the world.

Can sociological approaches do better? For example, the dichotomizing of "us" and "them," the depiction of outsiders, the projection of evil are standard sociological fare. Certainly such explanations seem relevant. There are, however, problems. As Mary Douglas recognized over thirty years ago (1970), not all societies draw clear boundaries between themselves and others or treat outsiders as dangerous. And a part of the world famous for fuzzy categories and multiple overlapping taxonomies is South East Asia, exemplified perhaps above all by Javanese, the dominant ethnic group in Indonesia. Although it probably does not worry most of them too much, apart from the usual pre- and overinterpretative practices that are their trade, almost all American and European news correspondents also tend engage in a systematic taxonomic slippage when describing what is going on in Indonesia.

But what are the presuppositions behind Indonesian news coverage? Provisionally, I would suggest, for particular historical reasons there is currently an unusual degree of openness and uncertainty. Under Suharto, domestic news coverage especially was so tightly constrained that it often resembled theatrical tableaux.[17] The wide-ranging relaxation of censorship since 1998 and reaction against previous regimentation has left Indonesian reporters both fairly free and searching for new ways of thinking among the different various models now on offer.

More specifically, in reporting on 11 September, commentators deployed a range of rhetorical figures, but these had much to do with how to articulate, or how to avoid articulating, Islam and the military and other banned topics. The *Media Indonesia* editorial and the producers' comments suggest heteroglossia: that producers were working with different, often noncommensurate, frames of reference at the same time.

Some aspects of the Indonesian producers' presuppositions are worth noting. Human subjects are not unitary or stable. They have conflicting predispositions. For example, arrogance exemplifies itself in ignoring other people's interests in determined pursuit of your own, regardless of the consequences to others. Arrogance leads to violence and, *in extremis*, the ultimate violation of ceasing to be human, *manusiawi*, to the point of such benightedness that you become incapable of appreciating it.[18] Realizing benightedness has carried you away is a major theme in Indonesian television drama, film, and theater. What is involved in the repeated comparison of 11 September to the American detonation of atomic bombs over Japan in 1945? The excessive force the United States inflicted has brought inevitable retribution. There is an ineluctable link between action and reaction (in Indonesian Hindu-Buddhist terms, the law of *karma pala*).[19]

If the veracity of news is significantly a function of it instantiating viewers' expectations and prejudices, then Indonesia has its own tropes. The train of events of which 11 September was part had long been prefigured. Indonesians are familiar with giants of mind-boggling size and power throwing their weight around and trampling arrogantly upon the weak, secure in the belief of their invincibility. It is part of the paradigm of Javanese and Balinese shadow theater performances from the Mahabharata, Ramayana and other stories. And, however long these gargantuan *raksasa* may lord it over and terrify others diegetically, they are always brought low in the end, often by the very traits that gave them power. So were Indonesians watching on their screens a new episode of an ancient saga brought to them not by a puppeteer, but by CNN?

The image is as seductive and frequently invoked as it is problematic. The question is: whose image is it? Theater is popular as a totalizing trope for Indonesia (e.g., Geertz, 1980), not least since it removes agency from Indonesians onto something else. Ever since the Dutch, shadow theatre has been used as a portmanteau image that provides the key to the Javanese mind. And it has been seized upon as avidly by scholars in America as a synecdoche for Javanese culture (e.g., Anderson, 1965; Geertz, 1973) as by foreign correspondents and commentators (fictionally portrayed in *The Year of Living Dangerously*).

The problem is, as the distinguished Indonesian scholar Koentjaraningrat remarked, it is hard to generalize about the best part of a hundred million people who have barely been researched and few of whom, by most reckoning, have ever watched such theatre. After more than a century of such articulations, it does not mean, though, that Indonesians may not employ such tropes with one another.[20] Shadow theater however, was not usually invoked for its mythology, but for the useful image of the puppeteer who, unseen, manipulates the puppets from behind a screen. An example was the headline in *Republika* the day after the bombs. Referring to conflicting claims about who was responsible, it read: "America and Al-Qaida are accused of being masterminds (dalang) behind the bombings in Bali."[21]

Even were Indonesians obligingly to structure their imagery of political violence solely according to these grand epics, it would not help much. Interpretive freedom is paradigmatic. And on almost any exegesis, such violence cannot be reduced to a simple confrontation of good and evil, as in the British television coverage. For example, two common exegetical devices are *Bhinneka Tunggal Ika* and *Rwa Bhineda*. The former, which is also the Indonesian national motto, from the fourteenth century *kawi* poem "Sutasoma," is usually glossed "Unity in diversity." Another translation, however, goes: "Although in pieces, yet One." *Rwa Bhineda* is nigh impossible to translate. Crudely, "The two that are opposed" points to difference necessarily implying disjuncture and opposition, but equally complementarity and mutual dependence.[22] The philosophical nuances that Indonesians have grown up with get rather lost in hyperbolic reportage of irreconcilable difference, disintegration, and menace lurking throughout the archipelago. Parachute and pack journalism as a set of industrial practices is perfectly designed to prevent much possibility of cultural translation.

A problem with frequent-flyer journalists is that they have short memories. In 1965-1966 Indonesia was the site of an act of postwar violence on an almost unimaginable, and certainly unrecorded, scale. Something in the order of a million people were executed as the Indonesian army under Suharto, advised and directed by the United States, the United Kingdom and Australia, as it subsequently turned out, in retaliation for a supposed attempt at a communist coup. It is difficult to understand Indonesians' responses to events in the last years without appreciating the absolute ban on any discussion that did not conform to the régime's master narrative. In an elegant analysis of the New Order régime's success in staying in power, against assertions of the monolithic nature of power and its narratives,

Heryanto has argued that

> Even at the height of the New Order's authoritarianism, its fabric of
> power was far from being efficient and comprehensive. It was full of
> contradictions, anomalies, ironies and convivial misunderstanding.
> These did not necessarily make New Order authoritarianism less effec-
> tive. The contrary is more tenable. (1999, p. 148)

Heryanto nicely argued that people were obliged to deal with the dilemmas
they faced by adopting the practices of "hyperobedience," which could, of
course, turn out to be anything but. Several implications are germane. After
more than thirty years' subjection to judgments from on high, based on convenient, but changeable, master narratives, is it any surprise that sensible
Indonesians are cautious about attributing responsibility and wish to see
proper legal process instituted? A close examination of the practices of
attempting to institute myth, let alone subvert it, shows they take sinuous
paths. And how are foreign correspondents to understand answers to even
the simplest questions when hyperobedient "yeses" may mean "yes," "no,"
"maybe," "if you had any idea what is at issue, I might try to answer" or
many other possibilities? At this point many Western reporters retreat to the
nearest bar.

The point of this discussion is that there are at least two major problems
that both media correspondents and media scholars run into. The first is to
do with history and local practice. Practices of production and reception
anywhere in the world have particular histories. The export of Euro-
American conventions of news production should not blind scholars to the
fact that imported ideals rarely translate simply into practice. What is
remarkable for an ostensibly empirically oriented discipline is how rarely its
practitioners have engaged in the kind of detailed research into actual newsroom practices that would provide evidence for their sweeping assertions.
Audiences are more intractable. The problems of doing much more than
counting heads or expressed opinions is little excuse for wishing readers,
audiences, or viewers away. If media scholars boggle at the problems of
establishing what the subjects of mass media make of what is going on, they
attempt a total bypass at the fairly obvious point that readers and viewers do
not approach something as *tabula rasa*, but come with distinctive histories
of reading, viewing, and commenting on what they read. If media practitioners do not come off very well, media scholars scarcely fare better.

There is a second set of problems. The point of this chapter is that news
coverage may not be of the kind that, on the optimistic enlightenment scenario, can be addressed rationally by urging reporters and news channels to
be more balanced, better informed, and self-critical. If news reporting can
instructively be represented as mythologizing, then we are dealing with

opposed ways of imagining the world that are irreconcilable (which is what Lévi-Strauss was arguing with his distinction of bricolage and engineering, 1966). The idea that myth occurs where rationality has failed or is not yet applied (Sperber, 1975) fails to learn from *Rwa Bhineda* that opposition is at once constitutive and complementary. If we wish to change reporting practices, perhaps we should try to recognize at first what may be at issue. For all these reasons, news could never be the same everywhere.

My argument raises some awkward questions for media scholars. How are they positioned relative to what they talk about? Analyses of news rarely bother to indicate whose news practices are being discussed, it being taken for granted that Anglo-American news is the paradigm, from which others, if even recognized, are merely deviations. The rest of the world is so irrelevant as barely to be worth notice. What are the critical procedures they employ to avoid the mythological and ideological traps they accuse others of falling into? In a fine act of exnomination, we are rarely told. Barthes's modern mythology, on closer scrutiny, applies as much to media scholars as to media practitioners. More worrying, neither group seems to recognize or be much concerned that there is a difficulty. Were this not so, presumably the overriding priority would be careful, linguistically and culturally informed research of non-Western media. It would be a massive research program, but one, I would argue, that is vital to prevent globalization being a synonym for the continuation of cultural mistranslation by other means. Until something changes, sadly reporters and academics alike will continue to round up the usual suspects.

NOTES

1. For 2002, 16,110 people were murdered in the USA according to *Murder in the UK* (http://www.murderuk.com/misc/stats.htm). Of course the figure neatly obscures the problems of how you determine murder from all the other possibilities of sudden unexpected death.
2. I suspect this, in part, is behind the outrage expressed by many British and American print and television journalists at Al-Jazeera's coverage of the Iraq war of 2003. However many Al-Jazeera staff were trained at the BBC and are sensitive to the ethics of coverage.
3. Originally these were black and white sets, which received state television (TVRI) and were powered in remoter places by rechargeable car batteries.
4. I would like to express my thanks to my colleague, Richard Fox, who has specialized in coverage of violence in the media for his comments on the draft of this chapter. It was he who informed me at the time that *Laskar Jihad* had announced the temporary closure of its Web site on 12 October, apparently a few hours before the bombs in Bali.

5. The Indonesian is *nékat*. It suggests determination to do something quite regardless of the costs. "Unthinking" is one translation.
6. I prefer the Bakhtinian term with its recognition of the coexistence of distinct styles. Polyvocality suggests the existence of originary, authentic voices, with its "metaphysics of presence" (cf. Morson & Emerson, 1990, pp. 139-145).
7. Lack of space prevents me including detailed discussions my colleague Patsy Widakuswara had with senior news journalists from three television channels about their coverage of events.
8. Richard Fox found a beautiful photograph in an article entitled "Radical Islam Gains a Seductive New Voice," in *The New York Times*, 26 October 2003, section 4, page 1, showing several placard-bearing Indonesians. The caption presumably derive from one placard reads in English "Ugly and bad American. Go to hell!" However the others, all in Indonesian, explicitly eschew terrorism and any claims that Islam justifies it. Foreign languages presumably do not merit translation. The viability of much foreign news depends on not understanding the language.
9. An analysis of the role of "experts" would be fascinating. Several were briefly paraded. Most solemnly opined that this was indubitably the work of Al-Qaeda or associates. As many, like Morgan, also stressed the secrecy of these groups, how they could be so certain was quietly ignored. There were moments when a quite different scenario threatened to unfold, for example, on the Channel 4 program, when Dr Kirsten Schulze from the LSE raised strong grounds for questioning the role of Al-Qaeda and the pre-emptive judgment against Islamist militants. Citing the British Ambassador to Indonesia, she pointed out that extremist groups were small and deeply resented by the overwhelming majority of Indonesians, who were very moderate and tolerant. However the stereotype of Indonesians as extremist had captured the imagination of the media. That threatened to puncture the whole balloon, and the interview was terminated; just as one with the Indonesian Chargé d'affaires in London was cut off in midsentence when he questioned the wisdom of judging prior to evidence.
10. Although certain features seem on initial examination to be fairly common to other European and North American chronotopes, there are evidently also differences, which only a much more detailed analysis could address.
11. The picture was, of course, not uniform. For example, the broadsheet, *Republika*, associated with ICMI, the Association of Indonesian Muslim Intellectuals, included several articles that took the line that foreigners, notably the USA through the CIA, was involved. Others took quite different stances. Unfortunately I do not have sufficient Indonesian television from the time to draw a strict comparison. However British print news coverage, with a few exceptions, as it so often does, reiterated television coverage. So the comparison is not entirely vacuous.
12. This point is different from, but related to, the singular usage of English in news (e.g., Fowler, 1991). The issue of language use is not trivial. As Keith Waterhouse remarked "You cannot fight a war against an abstract noun." The issue, as Terry Jones noted in *The Observer* 23 February 2003, is "How do you know when you've won? When you've got it removed from the *Oxford English* Dictionary?"

For the Pentagon, the ineffability offers even more scope than the Cold War, as effectively they get to decide.

13. The chronotope of American, and increasingly European, media (here print, television, and film partly coalesce) works by a process of identification—hence the necessity for heroes and villains. So networks, even groups, are unsuitable subjects and must be transformed into person-functions. Osama bin Laden is a narrative necessity.

14. Fiske (1989, pp. 296-301) uses a story on Australian Channel Nine News to make the point about how reporting striking power workers in the active mood and management in the passive mood nominates the former and makes them seem unreasonable and exnominates the latter, so naturalizing their position. Fiske draws on Barthes's analysis of the bourgeoisie as a class that avoids being named.

> As a political fact, the bourgeoisie has some difficulty in acknowledging itself: there are no "bourgeois" parties in the Chamber. As an ideological fact, it completely disappears: the bourgeoisie has obliterated its name in passing from reality to representation, from economic man to mental man. It comes to an agreement with the facts, but does not compromise about values, it makes its status undergo a real *ex-nominating* operation: the bourgeoisie is defined as *the social class which does not want to be named*. (1973, p. 138, italics in the original).

By a process of condensation is this exnominated class Christian, so creating problems for the rest of the world's middle-class people?

15. To gain a sense of how far the British television and print media had painted themselves into a corner, there is a good overview of the available range of critical investigative journalism in Indonesia and internationally, see http://www.berubah.org/BaliBombing/Tragedy1.htm.

16. Amusingly, it is not just news coverage that seeks to eliminate history. So do the writings of a celebrated American scholar, Clifford Geertz, whose vision was not only of a place where nothing much changed over hundreds of years (1980, p. 134), but where the natives went to great lengths to deny temporality altogether (1966).

17. The history and changes of Indonesian television have been well documented by Philip Kitley (2000)

18. My favourite example from the argument over the proprieties and legality of engaging in war against Iraq in 2003 is the American self-righteous descriptions of the French as "Cheese-eating Surrender-Monkeys."

19. The complex ways that Hindu and Buddhist thinking have intertwined in Indonesia, and that both coexist with Islam in Java in particular, exemplifies the overlap of taxonomies in practice mentioned above.

20. Ruth McVey, for instance, offers a thoughtful analysis of why, at his tribunal, Sudisman, one of the leaders of the Indonesian Communist Party, should have invoked the feudal image of the Pandawa brothers to refer to the leadership (1986).

21. *Amerika dan Al-Qaida Dituduh Dalang Pemboman di Bali. Republika* 13 October 2002, accessed online on 13 October 2002.

22. Both expressions have been used hegemonically, but in changing ways, in post-Independence Indonesia, which raises interesting questions about what work they have been doing.

REFERENCES

Anderson, B.R. (1965). *Mythology and the tolerance of the Javanese.* Modern Indonesia Project, Monograph Series. Ithaca, NY: Cornell University Press.

Asad, T. (1986). The concept of cultural translation in British social anthropology. In J. Clifford & G. Marcus (Eds.), *Writing culture: The poetics and politics of ethnography* (pp. 141-164). London: University of California Press.

Bakhtin, M.M. (1981). Forms of time in the chronotope of the novel. In M. Holquist (Ed.), & C. Emerson & M. Holquist (Trans.), *The dialogic imagination: Four essays.* Austin: University of Texas Press.

Barthes, R. (1973). Myth today. In R. Barthes, *Mythologies.* St. Albans: Paladin.

Brown, M.E. (1987). The politics of soaps: Pleasure and feminine empowerment. *Australian Journal of Cultural Studies* ,4(2), 1-25.

Douglas, M. (1970). *Natural symbols: Explorations in cosmology.* London: Cresset.

Fiske, J. (1987). *Television culture.* London: Methuen.

Fowler, R. (1991). *Language in the news: Discourse and ideology in the press.* London: Routledge.

Fox, R. (n.d.). *Visions of terror: Critical remarks on mass mediated images of the 12 October bombings in Bali.* Unpublished essay.

Geertz, C. (1966). *Person, time and conduct in Bali: An essay in cultural analysis.* New Haven: Yale Southeast Asia Program, Cultural Report Series #14.

Geertz, C. (1973). Ethos, world view, and the analysis of sacred symbols. In C. Geertz, *The interpretation of cultures.* New York: Basic Books.

Geertz, C. (1980). *Negara: The theatre state in nineteenth-century Bali.* Princeton, NJ: Princeton University Press.

van Ginneken, J. (1998). *Understanding global news: A critical introduction.* London: Sage.

Goodman, N. (1968). *Languages of art.* Indianapolis: Bobbs-Merrill.

Heryanto, A. (1999). Where communism never dies: Violence, trauma and narration in the last cold war capitalist authoritarian state. *International Journal of Cultural Studies, 2*(2), 147-177.

Kitley, P. (2000). *Television, nation, and culture in Indonesia.* Athens: Ohio University Press.

Laclau, E. (1990). The impossibility of society. In E. Laclau, *New reflections on the revolution of our time.* London: Verso.

Lévi-Strauss, C. (1966). *The savage mind.* London: Weidenfeld & Nicholson.

McVey, R. (1986). The wayang controversy in Indonesian communism. In M. Hobart & R.H. Taylor (Eds.), *Context, meaning, and power in Southeast Asia.* Ithaca: Cornell University Southeast Asia Program.

Morson, G.S. & Emerson, C. (1990). *Mikhail Bakhtin: Creation of a prosaics.* Stanford, CA: Stanford University Press.

Showalter, E. (1985). Feminist criticism in the wilderness. In E. Showalter (Ed.), *The new feminist criticism: Essays on women, literature and theory.* New York: Pantheon.
Sperber, D. (1975). *Rethinking symbolism.* Cambridge: Cambridge University Press.
Vickers, A. (1989). *Bali: A paradise created.* Ringwood, Victoria: Penguin.

WEB SOURCES

http://www.berubah.org/BaliBombing/Tragedy1.htm—accessed on 16 April 2004.
http://www.murderuk.com/misc/stats.htm—accessed 14 April 2004

Chapter 10

Visions of Terror

On the Use of Images in the Mass-Mediated Representations of the Bali Bombing

Richard Fox*

When, days after September 11 2001, our gaze was transfixed by the images of the plane hitting one of the WTC towers, we were all forced to experience what the "compulsion to repeat" and *jouissance* beyond the pleasure principle are: we wanted to see it again and again; the same shots were repeated *ad nauseum*, and the uncanny satisfaction we got from it was *jouissance* at its purist.

—Slavoj Zizek, *Welcome to the Desert of the Real*
(2002, pp. 11-12)

---

*I would like to thank the editors of this volume, as well as Mark Hobart, David Morgan, and my wife, Judith, for reading and commenting on earlier drafts of this chapter. I also wish to acknowledge the constructive comments, questions, and discussion of the paper on which the chapter is based both at a recent conference at the University of Hawaii's East-West Center and at a special seminar at Gaja Mada University's Center for Cultural Studies (*Pusat Studi Kebudayaan*) in Yogyakarta, Indonesia. I, of course, accept full responsibility for any mistakes or shortcomings in my analysis.

On 23 April 2003, the op-ed page of *The New York Times* carried an ad from the National Resources Defense Council (NRDC)—a nongovernment "environmental action organization"—showing a pair of belching smokestacks silhouetted against a clear sky. The banner over the image read "We have enough to worry about without attacking our own land, water, and air" (see Figure 10.1).

In the ad's soft-edged porthole photo, the billowing smoke is frozen, blowing to one side, with the two smokestacks both backlit and flanked by a third and seemingly inactive chimney. In both perspective and form, the image is strikingly similar to photographs that were taken of the smoking Trade Towers just before their collapse on September 11, 2001. The following morning, such images were published on front pages around the country (Finkel, 2001), and "the towers were established very quickly as the predominant visual marker of the events of September 11" (Zelizer, 2002, p. 58). Zelizer went on to point out that 'Images of the towers appeared repeatedly over time, with the shot of the burning towers featured at year's end as *Newsweek*'s cover photo of its special double issue (*Newsweek,* 2001-2). And, on December 31, 2001, the image topped a special *New York Times* section entitled "The year in pictures" (Zelizer, 2002, pp. 58-59).

Through its use of this image, the ad from the NRDC seemed to suggest that, with the now seemingly ubiquitous threat of terrorism, "We have enough to worry about" without the added troubles that will result from environmental irresponsibility. Yet, as much as I agree with the general concerns of the NRDC, I must admit that my first reaction on seeing the ad was

FIGURE 10.1. From *The New York Times* op-ed page. April 23, 2003. Reprinted with the permission of the NRDC.

FIGURE 10.2. Front page of the *Boston Herald*, 12 September 2001. Reprinted with permission of the *Boston Herald*.

that it was exploitative, capitalizing both on popular fears of terrorism and on the memory of a national tragedy. It was, of course, not merely a *national* tragedy—as citizens of many countries died in the attack (to say nothing of those who have suffered as a result of the ensuing "war on terror"). But, if these first thoughts were admittedly trite (i.e., who cares! this was, after all, one of the more benign of many recent exploitations of 9/11), my next thought was—having been told that "We have enough to worry about"—*who are "we" anyhow?*

WHO ARE "WE"?

In her recent book on images of war, Susan Sontag (2003) suggested that "No we should be taken for granted when the subject is looking at other people's pain." Commenting on wartime photographs of the dead and injured, she asked "Who are the we at whom such shock-pictures are aimed?" Although the NRDC's image of the smoking towers is not exactly a "shock picture" of the sort Sontag was addressing, "we" were nevertheless explicitly invoked. So under what conditions might "we" be susceptible to critical analysis?

Generally speaking, "we" figured prominently in post–9/11 America. Initially, following the attacks, "we" were cast retrospectively as the collective patient of an action perpetrated by shadowy agents (or, perhaps more precisely, *instruments*) of "evil."[1] Subsequently, "we" emerged in both scholarly and popular discourse as the collective agent of "bearing witness" (Zelizer, 2002), "recovering from trauma" (Sreberny, 2002), and showing the resolve to get on with life.[2] As Edward Said remarked in November 2001, just two months after the attacks:

> There really is a feeling being manufactured by the media and the government that a collective "we" exists and that "we" all act and feel together, as witnessed by such perhaps unimportant surface phenomena as flag-flying and the use of the collective "we" by journalists in describing events all over the world in which the US is involved. We bombed, we said, we decided, we acted, we feel, we believe, etc., etc. Of course this has only marginally to do with the reality, which is far more complicated and far less reassuring. (Said, 2001, cited in Sreberny, 2002, p. 225)

For Said, this "reality" included—among other things—the silenced opposition from within "the collective" as "we" marched off to war. He went on to explain:

> There is plenty of unrecorded or unregistered scepticism, even outspoken dissent, but it seems hidden by overt patriotism. So, American unity is being projected with such force as to allow very little questioning of US policy, which in many ways is heading towards a series of unexpected events in Afghanistan and elsewhere, the meaning of which many people will not realise until too late. (Said, 2001)

Although much of what occurred subsequently was not—at least to many—entirely "unexpected," it is difficult to imagine a better example of disarticulation (Hobart, n.d.). Those of "us" who might have been skeptical of—or even outright opposed to—prevailing government policy were left little room to mount effective public opposition. In short, "we" do not dissent. When "we" eventually got around to invading Iraq, the antiwar demonstrations in various parts of the country—despite their record numbers—received scant coverage in mainstream American network and cable news. In line with the broader *with-us-or-against-us* swagger associated with "the war on terror," consent was cast dominantly in terms of "supporting our troops"—a responsibility none of "us" could abrogate in good conscience. So who, then, are "we"?

In the first instance, I would argue that "we" are the outcome of an articulation (Laclau & Mouffe, 1985)—a temporary suturing-over of the many antagonisms underpinning events that, as Said noted, were "far more complicated and far less reassuring."[3] But, more specifically, in the advertisement from the NRDC, I would suggest that "we" are Americans. As the blurb in the lower part of the ad explains, "The Bush administration is staging an all-out assault on our environment," and we must "help shore up our defenses at home." Through the ad's deployment of one of the administration's own rhetorical strategies, "we" surface as a collectivity under threat — under threat from that very administration. In calling for the protection of "our own land, water, and air," "we" emerge as responsible for "our own" natural resources. But, further, in juxtaposing the image of the smoking WTC/chimneys with this call to collective environmental responsibility, the ad also articulates "us" in a very particular state-ideological manner: its use of the first-person plural is parasitic on the "we" of "*we* will never forget," "united *we* stand" and the many other invocations of post–9/11 patriotic unity. In short, "We" are a nation under threat, in fear, and in need of "defenses at home."

This, however, is not an essay on American uses of 9/11. I began with the ad from the NRDC because it raises some rather important questions for critical media studies and, in particular, for the analysis of mass mediated images of terrorism and violence such as those linked to the coverage of the tragic bombings in Bali. If, for instance, the photograph of the smoking WTC/chimneys helped to articulate a particular kind of subject — in this case, an environmentally responsible (and implicitly patriotic) collectivity under threat — what kinds of subject do other images of terrorism articulate? The picture of backlit chimneys may reiterate a popular image of the smoking Towers, but how is one to account critically for such a reiteration? Using these questions as a point of departure, I shall examine in the following pages the use of photographs and other images in the coverage of the tragic bombings in Bali on 12 October 2002.

I have limited my analysis here to the first few days of coverage for two related reasons. First, there is the complexity of the coverage itself. Representations of the Bali bombing have been anything but uniform, both through time and across the different regional media. As Zelizer pointed out in her analysis of "Photography, Journalism and Trauma," photography was a central feature of commentary on 9/11 long after "the three- or four-day period of photographic documentation that has tended to characterize other traumatic events" (2002, p. 54). The Bali bombing also appears to have been an exception to this general tendency. So, in the first instance, this chapter is meant as a contribution to the analysis of how Euro-American and Indonesian media went about producing a coherent account of events in the aftermath of the Bali bombing. Second, there is the matter of what Jaap van Ginneken called the "primary definition" of a news story:

> [T]hree major world news agencies, the major American, British and French news-gathering organizations [Associated Press, Reuters and Agence France-Presse], have a quasi monopoly in providing prime def-

initions of breaking news in the world periphery. Even if they are not
actually the first on the spot, they are usually the first to inform the rest
of the world. (1998, p. 114; bracketed addition mine)

And, once the story is framed, "there is a certain resistance to change. The
Gestalt or configuration will tend to perpetuate itself" (1998, p. 113). So, I
am interested specifically in the question of how visual representation figured in the broader process of making sense of the bombing. How, for
example, did pictures and video footage figure in that initial process of "primary definition"? What regularities and disjunctures may be discerned in
this respect between Indonesian and broadly Euro-American media? And
how did their respective representations relate to broader configurations of
conflict, power, and violence? In the course of trying to answer these questions, I shall argue that critical approaches to media and visual representation may end up telling us more about the assumptions of their proponents
than they do about the events that they purport to explain.

ON THE IMPORTANCE OF BEING VISUAL

Show, don't tell.

—a journalistic adage

In the first newswire reports from Bali on the night of the bombings, it was
not altogether clear what had happened. It seemed that a bomb had exploded near the U.S. Consulate in Renon, and a much larger explosion in Kuta
was said to have destroyed several buildings, leaving numerous dead and
many more seriously injured. There was an earlier report of a bombing at
the Philippine Consulate in Manado, though it was uncertain whether it was
linked in any way to the blasts in Kuta (Hakim, 2002). Although photographs did not accompany these earliest reports, their representation of the
incident was not entirely nonvisual.[4]

Explosion in Kuta

The earliest news report of the Kuta bombing that I was able to find online
came from the *Tempo* News Room in Jakarta, and was posted at midnight
(Jakarta time)—approximately an hour and a half to two hours after the
blast:

Explosion in Kuta killed approximately 10 people

13 Oct 2002 00:00:35, Western Indonesian Time

TEMPO Interactive, Jakarta: A bomb exploded in front of the Sari Club, on Jalan Legian, Kuta, Bali, Saturday (12/10), around 11:10 Central Indonesian Time. As a result of the explosion, no less than 10 visitors to the Sari Club died and approximately forty others were injured.

Tonight ambulance workers went back and forth transporting the injured to Sanglah Hospital, Denpasar. Their number cannot be estimated with any certainty. In addition to those who died, tens of buildings in the vicinity were seriously damaged, among others the Paddy's Club building and the White Rose Hotel.

There was great commotion at the location of the incident. The electricity in the area was out and the tourists who were staying in the vicinity of the blast were milling about. A tourist from Australia was seen bawling because her child, who was 17 years old, had been in the Sari Club. Balinese Regional Police Chief, Brigadier General Budi Setiawan immediately led his agency to the location to handle the case.

—Jalil Hakim – *Tempo* News Room[5]

The report begins with what might be considered "the facts" of the incident as they were known at the time: a bomb exploded in front of the Sari Club on Jalan Legian in Kuta around 11:10 leaving no less than ten dead, forty injured, and tens of buildings destroyed. Although the number of victims was woefully underestimated and the precise time of the explosions may or may not have been given accurately, the report does indicate some aspects of the scene that followed the blasts: tourists milling about and ambulances going to and from the hospital—presumably in the dark as a result of the electricity having gone out. One gets from reading these details a sense of the commotion around the bombsite; but it is worth noting that, despite the apparent carnage, the tone of the reporting seems rather matter-of-fact.

So soon after the bombing, it would not be terribly surprising if there were little in the way of visual detail available to the journalists working the night shift in the *Tempo* News Room in Jakarta, which is roughly an hour and a half from Bali by plane. A photograph did not accompany the report, though in this connection it should also be noted that the *Tempo Interaktif* Web site tends to be rather sparing with the use of photos. (The lead page, for instance, did not display a photograph associated with the bombing until the 16th—i.e., four days later.) Nevertheless, this initial report was not entirely devoid of visual representation.

At a stretch, the reference to specific buildings that were destroyed might be interpreted as representing a particular scene. For someone who had visited this part of Kuta, it could be argued that the description represented a specific and visually distinguishable object. But that sort of "imagery" would also require a particular kind of reader—one who had either *been there* or, at the very least, had perhaps seen a photograph of the buildings. Of course there is no saying what sort of image it might or might not evoke for that reader; and, what is more, this approach would also require a critical account of (visual) memory, which is anything but unproblematic.[6]

Looking more closely at the text of the report, the tourists "milling about" and the bawling Australian woman were both introduced with the word *tampak*—to appear, be visible or obvious, in sight and so forth—and, in the latter case, the woman was explicitly said to have been "seen" (*terlihat*). Without wishing to overinterpret what comes down to the use of just two words in a rather short article, I think it is safe to say that visual representation was fairly limited in this first report. But was the sparing use of the visual merely a result of time constraints and insufficient information? How, for instance, did this report compare in this respect with subsequent Indonesian-language reports on the bombing? And what about the earliest reports in the Anglophone media?

On the Scene

The earliest English-language report that I found online was posted to *TheJakartaPost.com* at 12:54 AM, Jakarta time—that is, less than an hour after the report from the *Tempo* News Room, and possibly as little as two and half hours after the explosions.[7] The report was attributed to Reuters.

Three dead, 100 hurt in blasts on Indonesia's Bali

10/13/2002 12:54:26 AM

JAKARTA: At least three people were killed and some 100 injured, including foreigners, in a series of explosions on Indonesia's popular resort island of Bali, police and hospital officials said on Saturday.

One police officer who declined to be identified said the explosions had occurred simultaneously, one of them not far from the U.S. consulate on Bali. Police said there were two blasts.

"At this stage there are three dead. It could be up to 100 hurt," said the officer as quoted by Reuters.

An official at a local hospital also said at least 100 people had been hurt, including Americans and Australians.

Eyewitnesses spoke of chaos in the area near one of the explosions, at the Sari nightclub around the famous Kuta beach strip, as foreign tourists were reveling on a typical Saturday night. The southern Indonesian island is a particularly popular holiday destination for Australians.

One witness said windows on shops had been blown out up to 500 meters (yards) away.

One witness reported hearing at least three explosions on the island in Indonesia, the world's most populous Muslim nation.

"I saw one man, who looked Indonesian, whose head had been blown off," said the witness, a local photographer, Murdani Usman, speaking from the scene near a night club.—Reuters

Coming less than an hour after the report from the *Tempo* News Room, the details of the incident still seem to have been somewhat sketchy. There was a series of explosions—either two or possibly three blasts—that occurred on "Indonesia's popular resort island of Bali." Unlike the report from *Tempo*, there is no mention of a bomb—instead, the account simply referred to "explosions" and "blasts." However, in addition to reporting a lower body count (as presumably based on an earlier—or perhaps simply different—estimation), the incident was also contextualized in a specific manner—namely, through reference to Indonesia as "the world's most populous Muslim nation" and to Bali as a "particularly popular holiday destination for Australians" with its "famous Kuta strip." In at least one respect, I presume such difference in the mode of contextualization may be explained through reference to the kinds of readers imagined for each of the two reports. (e.g., readers of *Tempo* would probably be expected to know that Bali is in Indonesia.)

One minute "foreign tourists were reveling on a typical Saturday night," and the next there was "chaos." As with the report from *Tempo*, there were no photographs to accompany this report. Yet over half the text is devoted to "eyewitness" accounts. These "eyewitnesses" appear to be cited on more or less equal footing with other sources of information. For instance, the police reported "two blasts," and "One witness reported hearing at least three explosions." In other words, at this early stage in the coverage, these two accounts appear to be juxtaposed without either being attributed with discernible privilege.

But, before taking the analysis further, for reasons that will become apparent, I would like to consider a second English-language report that was posted to CNN.com roughly an hour and three quarters later—that is to say, at least four hours after the explosions.[8] Like the reports from both *Tempo* and Reuters/*Jakarta Post*, there were neither photographic nor other images to accompany the article.

Bali explosions: '12 dead'

Saturday, October 12, 2002 Posted: 3:39 PM EDT (1939 GMT)

JAKARTA, Indonesia (CNN) — At least twelve people have been killed and some 100 hurt, including American and Australian tourists, in a series of explosions on Indonesia's popular resort island of Bali, local media and hospital officials said.

The explosions came at Kuta Beach and Ubud on Saturday night. Bali is a popular holiday destination and particularly popular with Australians. Early reports say the explosion at Kuta Beach, which caused the greatest damage, was caused by a car bomb.

The Kuta Beach blast came at the Sari Club, a disco in the Kuta area of Bali. The other explosion occurred in downtown Denpasar, the capital of Bali, Lt. Col. Yatim Suyatno, a police spokesman, told The Associated Press.

One police officer who declined to be identified told Reuters that the explosions had occurred simultaneously, one of them not far from the U.S. consulate on Bali. Police said there were two blasts.

An official at a local hospital told Reuters that at least 100 people had been hurt, including Americans and Australians.

Eyewitnesses spoke of chaos in the area near one of the explosions at the Sari nightclub as foreign tourists were revelling on a typical Saturday night. One eyewitness said windows on shops had been blown out up to 500 metres away.

Another eyewitness reported hearing at least three explosions on the island in Indonesia, the world's most populous Moslem nation.

"I saw one man, who looked Indonesian, whose head had been blown off," a local photographer, Murdani Usman, told Reuters.

There had been warnings recently from the U.S. embassy in Jakarta of possible violence linked to extreme Muslim groups.

Some critics say Indonesia is the weakest link in the U.S.-led war on terror in Southeast Asia, partly because the government has concerns about cracking down on radical Muslim groups for fear of upsetting the vast moderate mainstream.

It was not clear whether the explosions in Bali were related to an earlier blast Saturday at a Philippine consulate on North Sulwesi Island that caused minor damage but no injuries.

An earlier blast Saturday on Indonesia's Sulawesi island broke three windows of the Philippine consulate in the city of Manado, said Suleman Munde, a security guard at the building, which was closed at the time of the explosion.

Police Lt. Col. Henjke Kuwara said the small explosive device had been planted at the fence of building.

There was no immediate claim of responsibility. Manado is a port city and a transit point to the southern Philippines, close to where the Islamic militant Abu Sayyaf group is active.

— CNN Producer Atika Shubert contributed to this report

The contributing CNN Producer, Atika Shubert, would later appear on CNN television news, reporting "live from Bali"; but this first report was filed from Jakarta. In examining the report, I would tentatively suggest that the prominence of "eyewitness" testimony is linked to a journalistic aesthetic of the visual ("show, don't tell"), as well as to a particular configuration of "on the scene" authority that is, in certain respects, not entirely unlike that of traditional ethnographic monographs. But, before pressing this line of inquiry further, I would first like to have a closer look at the report from CNN.

Comparing the syntax and diction from one paragraph to the next—for example, the repeated indefinite reference to "an earlier blast" in the third and fourth from the final paragraph—the article appears to have been put together rather quickly. Comparison with the report from Reuters also indicates that the CNN article incorporates—almost verbatim—practically the entire text of that earlier report.

A COMPARISON OF EXCERPTS FROM THE TWO ENGLISH-LANGUAGE REPORTS

Reuters (as posted to the *Jakarta Post* website) Posted 12:54, Jakarta Time (01:54 Bali Time; 17:54 GMT)	CNN.com Posted 15:39, US Eastern Daylight Time (03:39 Bali Time; 19:39 GMT)
(A) JAKARTA: At least three people were killed and some 100 injured, including foreigners, in a series of explosions on Indonesia's popular resort island of Bali, police and hospital officials said on Saturday.	JAKARTA, Indonesia (CNN)—At least twelve people have been killed and some 100 hurt, including American and Australian tourists, in a series of explosions on Indonesia's popular resort island of Bali, local media and hospital officials said.
(B) One police officer who declined to be identified said the explosions had occurred simultaneously, one of them not far from the U.S. consulate on Bali. Police said there were two blasts.	One police officer who declined to be identified told Reuters that the explosions had occurred simultaneously, one of them not far from the U.S. consulate on Bali. Police said there were two blasts.
(C) An official at a local hospital also said at least 100 people had been hurt, including Americans and Australians.	An official at a local hospital told Reuters that at least 100 people had been hurt, including Americans and Australians.
(D) Eyewitnesses spoke of chaos in the area near one of the explosions, at the Sari nightclub around the famous	Eyewitnesses spoke of chaos in the area near one of the explosions at the Sari nightclub as foreign tourists were

	Kuta beach strip, as foreign tourists were reveling on a typical Saturday night.	reveling on a typical Saturday night.
(E)	One witness said windows on shops had been blown out up to 500 meters (yards) away.	One eyewitness said windows on shops had been blown out up to 500 metres away.
(F)	One witness reported hearing at least three explosions on the island in Indonesia,the world's most populous Muslim nation.	Another eyewitness reported hearing at least three explosions on the island in Indonesia, the world's most populous Moslem nation.
(G)	"I saw one man, who looked Indonesian, whose head had been blown off," said the witness, a local photographer, Murdani Usman, speaking from the scene near a night club.	"I saw one man, who looked Indonesian, whose head had been blown off," a local photographer, Murdani Usman, told Reuters.

The same eyewitness accounts and contextual stock-phrases (e.g., Bali as "Indonesia's popular resort island of Bali," Indonesia as "the world's most populous Muslim nation") occur not only in both of these reports, but they are also found in numerous articles published in the days following the bombing. Permutations of the paragraph that I have labeled as (G) appeared, for instance, on the front page of the London editions of both *The Sunday Times* and *The Independent on Sunday*. Yet, despite being posted less than two hours after the Reuters report, the article from CNN is decidedly more complex. "The facts" of the incident remain fairly straightforward, if still a little sketchy. There were, as indicated in the title, "12 dead" as well as "some 100 hurt, including American and Australian tourists." There were either two or three blasts located in Kuta, Ubud, and downtown Denpasar "not far from the U.S. Consulate on Bali." Here it is worth noting that, in this earliest stage of the reporting, it was often less than clear how reference to places such as "downtown Denpasar" and "not far from the U.S. Consulate on Bali" were related. Although these two phrases occur in successive paragraphs (fourth and fifth) of the report from CNN, it is ambiguous whether the two sources cited were referring to the same place or not. It was unclear at this point whether the blasts were related to the bombing near the Philippine Consulate in Manado, North Sulawesi. (Later, it turned out to be a totally unrelated incident.) But "early reports" indicated that the destruction in Kuta was caused by a car bomb, blowing out windows "up to 500 meters away." And, perhaps most importantly—despite the seemingly innocent reference to Manado being "close to where the Islamic militant Abu Sayyaf group is active"—"There was no immediate claim of responsibility."

The initial article from Reuters went further than the *Tempo* report in trying to make sense of what had happened; and this report from CNN went further still in articulating the incident within the framework of a specific set of assumptions regarding Bali, Indonesia, Islam and "the US–led war on terror." As in the previous report, Bali, as the location of the bombing, was represented as 'Indonesia's popular resort island," where "foreign tourists were reveling on a typical Saturday night." Although located in Indonesia, which is "the world's most populous Moslem nation," Bali was implicitly cordoned off as a "popular holiday destination." This distinction between Bali and Indonesia proceeds from a complex of longstanding caricatures of Oriental otherness: Bali as exotic paradise (see, e.g., Vickers, 1989), and Indonesia as Islamic threat—which are, in many ways, two sides of the same coin. And this distinction would become more pronounced in the coverage in the days to come.

The implicit framing of the story in terms of "the US–led war on terror," and Indonesia as its "weakest link," was introduced through reference to the U.S. embassy's alleged warning to Indonesia "of possible violence linked to extreme Muslim groups"—a perhaps rather less than subtle "we told you so"—and this was followed by the then seemingly natural reproach of the perceived Indonesian reticence to "[crack] down on radical Muslim groups for fear of upsetting the vast moderate mainstream." I should note, at this juncture, that I am not taking issue with the idea of there being a "vast moderate mainstream" in Indonesia, nor even necessarily with its perceived role in determining either governmental intervention or its absence. Rather, I am tracing the outlines of an emerging interpretive framework and drawing attention to a series of discursive figures that would grow both in prominence and seeming naturalness in the days to come.

It may be noted that, in both the Reuters and CNN reports, almost every line is attributed to some source or another. (The CNN report even distances itself from the body count by placing it within inverted commas in the title: '12 dead.') In contrast to the report from *Tempo*, which cited no sources apart from a concluding by-line, the CNN report cited "local media and hospital officials," newswire reports from AP and Reuters, nonspecified "early reports,"' a local photographer, both named and anonymous police officers, a security guard and—perhaps most importantly—several "eyewitnesses." Although the Indonesian report from *Tempo* did refer to the bawling Australian woman as having been "seen," there was nothing even approaching the degree of visual detail presented in the reports from Jakarta Post/Reuters and CNN. So the question is whether the comparatively sparing use of visual imagery in the *Tempo* report was merely due to a dearth of information or, alternatively, whether this might indicate a more significant disjuncture between the Indonesian and broadly Euro-American coverage of the bombing.

I Witness

In addition to noting the approximate times and locations of the explosions, the mainstream Indonesian-language reports that were posted online over the next twenty-four hours seemed primarily concerned with the number of victims and their countries of origin, the physical destruction—buildings, cars, and so forth—and the ongoing effort to get medical attention for those who were injured in the blasts. The arrival of the Australian foreign minister, as well as of medical (and the possibility of investigative) assistance, was also a prominent theme.

Several articles were devoted almost entirely to the comments made by governmental officials and others of similar stature, from both Indonesia and abroad. The question of "terrorism" was also an important (though contentious) issue, with several Indonesian officials weighing in on the related questions of who was responsible and how to prevent such an attack from happening again. However, whereas the CNN report cast the bombing clearly within the framework of "the U.S.–led war on terror" and a perceived "resurgence" of al-Qaeda, the Indonesian media—at least at the outset—seemed to be more concerned with the impact the event would have on internal stability and the image of Indonesia in the eyes of the rest of the world.

In comparison with the initial report from the *Tempo* News Room, visual imagery was somewhat more pronounced in the Indonesian reports that were published the morning after the blasts (13 October). Eyewitnesses (*saksi mata*) were occasionally cited; though, more often than not, their comments were addressed to the physical damage in Kuta. Having described the destruction of the Sari Club, for instance, an article published in the Jakarta-based daily newspaper, *Kompas*, went on to note:

> Additionally, dozens of other buildings within a radius of ten to twenty meters sustained heavy damage. Meanwhile, shop windows as well as the windows in hotels and other places of entertainment that were within a radius of one kilometer were smashed. "I saw the windows in the Kuta Square shopping complex, smashed" said Dadi who was there in Kuta Square, approximately one kilometer from the bombsite.[9]

There were also descriptions of the "panic" (*kepanikan*) and commotion that followed the explosions as, for instance, in the opening lines of the lead article in Sunday morning's (13 October) edition of the *Jawa Pos*:

> There was extraordinary panic in Bali last night. Two bombs exploded almost simultaneously in Kuta and Renon, Denpasar, 20 kilometers away. The first explosion occurred near the United States Consulate in

> Renon, and was followed by a truly massive explosion in a club for for-
> eigners in the tourist center of Kuta.[10] (*Kompas*, 2002)

Nevertheless, "eyewitness" accounts in the Indonesian coverage were comparatively rare and, almost without exception, they notably did not include
explicit descriptions of bloodied victims, mutilated bodies, and the like.

By contrast, perhaps the most striking aspect of the early Anglophone
coverage of the bombing was the sense of horror and chaos articulated
through the eyewitness accounts of what might best be described as anecdotal gore—descriptions, for example, of dismembered bodies and other
images of carnage. It may be recalled that the reports from both Reuters and
CNN, for instance, reproduced three "eyewitness" accounts including that
of "a local photographer" who described seeing "one man, who looked
Indonesian, whose head had been blown off." This very anecdote would be
cited more or less verbatim among other places in front-page articles in *The
Sunday Times* and *The Telegraph on Sunday* in London, and similar
accounts could be found in many of the reports posted in the hours and days
following the bombing.

> Mr. Hawkins said he saw one man with his leg blown off and saw
> women and children screaming. (*Sydney Morning Herald*, 2002)
>
> Australian flight attendant Kylie Denae . . . saw bodies being flung out
> of the open-air club. Body parts and glass were splattered everywhere
> and she witnessed a man's leg being blown off right in front of her.
> (*Straits Times*, 2002)
>
> New Zealander Lonny McDowell, 25, was at Paddy's when the blast
> blew chairs and concrete through the bar. . . . He said he saw a man with
> no legs and another with a cable stuck through his stomach. (CNN,
> 2002b)

Very much as the earlier CNN article (2002a) reiterated verbatim the text
from Reuters/*Jakarta Post* (2002), each of these "eyewitness" accounts were
also reiterated in subsequent reports. In this connection, I would suggest
that, if *The Washington Post*'s Philip Graham could call journalism "the first
draft of history," then this kind of *breaking news* appears to be the product
of something like what R.G. Collingwood called the method of "scissors-
and-paste":

> The method by which it proceeds is first to decide what we want to
> know about, and then to go in search of statements about it, oral or
> written, purporting to be made by actors in the events concerned, or by
> eyewitnesses of them, or by persons repeating what actors or eyewit-

nesses have told them, or have told their informants, or those who informed their informants, and so on. (1946, p. 257)

As Collingwood put it, "history for the scissors-and-paste historian means repeating statements that other people have made before him" (1946, p. 274). That is to say, it is not "historical" in any serious sense of the word.

Here it is interesting to note that the eyewitnesses are often identified by name, occupation, and/or place of residence, whereas (often by default) the people/bodies they describe are—without exception, I believe—anonymous. But why all the blood and guts? Why does there appear to be such a preponderance of graphic detail in the Anglophone media when there seems to be so little in their Indonesian counterparts? Is this simply an extension of their more generally divergent uses of visual imagery? And, if so, how is the disjuncture to be explained?

Eye Present

I suggested earlier that the prominence of "eyewitnesses" and, later, "on the scene" reporting in Euro-American coverage of the bombing suggests a journalistic aesthetic of the visual ("show, don't tell"), as well as a particular configuration of "on the scene" authority that is, in certain respects, not entirely unlike that of traditional ethnographic tracts. In the editorial introduction to their now classic volume, on *Writing Culture*, Clifford and Marcus pointed out that "The predominant metaphors in anthropological research have been participant observation, data collection, and cultural description, all of which presuppose a standpoint outside—looking at, objectifying, or, somewhat closer, reading a given reality" (Crapanzano, 1986, p. 11). As several contributors to the volume argued, such visual tropes for ethnographic knowledge tend to give a rather misleading sense of the kinds of practices in which one engages when "in the field." In a related connection, Hobart noted that

> . . . the visual metaphor of knowing creates a world of relatively stable states. . . . When you see something in the field, you usually have to go and ask someone what it is that you have just seen. We ask questions. The problem is how to get from shifting, intensely situated polylogues and dialogues to the timeless monologues of the professionals. (1996, p. 15)

The problem is that ethnographic authority tends to rest on a contradiction between the immediacy (hence authenticity) of ethnographic detail and the distance (hence objectivity) associated with a visualist epistemology (Fabian, 1983, pp. 105ff).

Returning to the news media's deployment of "eyewitness" accounts, the personalized viewing subject and the anonymous object fit this traditional ethnographic mold rather nicely, and the affinity with ethnographic writing became more pronounced in subsequent coverage, when these eyewitness accounts—that is, often the *same* eyewitness accounts—shifted from their position as sources of information to their deployment in a more anecdotal fashion. As with Malinowski's description of arriving in the Trobriand Islands or the Geertzes' arrival on Bali, and so forth (see Pratt, 1986), CNN's reporting garners authenticity through various rituals of presence and vision: being "on the scene," citing "eyewitnesses," "live" coverage, and so on. But, as with traditional ethnographic writing, the pretense to *being there* is usually not what it appears. For, as van Ginneken noted, "Very often live coverage of an unexpected event is really live coverage of the *aftermath* of an unexpected event" (1998, p. 112).

Nevertheless, it is perhaps difficult to overstate the importance of presence—and the visual—in the broadly Western coverage of the bombing. As the CNN anchor asked Atika Shubert, the correspondent in Bali, on the night of the bombing: "Atika, you've been to the hospital, you've been to the scene, what can you tell us?" But, this association of representational authenticity with presence and vision is anything but fortuitous. Rather, it situates EurAm news media well within the more generally logocentric framework of Western thought. Unfortunately, the critical implications of logocentrism are understood perhaps somewhat less frequently than the term itself is actually used. Although in use, albeit in a more limited sense, earlier in the twentieth century (the OED cites uses back to the late 1930s), "logocentrism" is better known as the term Jacques Derrida deployed in his early work to characterize the broadly Western *metaphysics of presence*. The term was glossed with unusual clarity in the following translator's note to Derrida's *Dissemination*:

> "Logocentric"—that which is "centered" on the "Logos" (= speech, logic, reason, the Word of God)—is the term used by Derrida to characterize any signifying system governed by the notion of the self-presence of meaning; i.e. any system structured by a valorization of speech over writing, immediacy over distance, identity over difference, and (self-) presence over all forms of absence, ambiguity, simulation, substitution, or negativity. (Derrida, 1981, p. 4, *n.*1)

In this sense, the practices of mainstream EurAm news media are unambiguously logocentric. The question is how this emphasis on presence is linked—if at all—to the preponderance of graphic imagery and the more general framing of the Bali bombing in terms of "the war on terror."

A PHOTOGRAPHIC SUPPLEMENT?

Not everybody trusts paintings
but people believe photographs.

—Ansel Adams

I noted that eyewitnesses were at first cited as sources of information, but were subsequently redeployed in a more anecdotal capacity. In other words, as time passed, the eyewitness accounts came to provide a sense of a "scene" that was caused by forces that could be explained not by the eyewitnesses themselves, but instead by police, "experts," and government officials who gradually came center stage. Concurrent with this shift in authority was the growing prominence of photographs and other images.

Shock, Awe, and a Few Questions

On Thursday, October 17—that is, five days after the blast—*The New York Times* published a photographic survey of "Front-Page Headlines in Australian Newspapers after a Bombing Attack in Bali." From the small composite image that appeared in the *Times*, it is impossible to distinguish their respective dates of publication; but the headlines were large and clear enough to discern some general themes: TERRORISM STRIKES HOME (*The Sydney Morning Herald*), TERROR BLAST (*The Canberra Times*), TERROR HITS HOME (*The Australian*), VICTIMS OF WAR and THEIR ONLY CRIME WAS TO GO ON HOLIDAY (*The Daily Telegraph*), EVIL (*Herald Sun*), TERRORISM ON OUR DOORSTEP (*The Advertiser*).

The lead photographs depict scenes of conflagration, images of destruction that might best be described as "the day after" and a collage of portraits—presumably of the victims. Many of these same images would appear in several different publications. In *The New York Times'* composite alone, the photographs on the front pages of *The Australian, The Daily Telegraph,* and *The Advertiser* all appear to be taken from the same original, albeit cropped to varying degrees. As it happens, the British *Daily Telegraph* also ran this photo on the front page of the October 14th edition, under the headline "Al-Qa'eda Link to Club Bombing" (see Figure 10.4, p. 236).

More generally speaking, similar images (actually, often images taken from what appear to be the same photographs) appeared on other front pages in Britain and the United States. Although on the morning after the blast *The New York Times* did not carry a photograph associated with the bombing on the front page, a front-page story entitled "Bombing at an Indonesian Resort Leaves at Least 58 People Dead" was continued onto the sixth page, where it was accompanied by a black-and-white photo of a street strewn with debris and burning cars. What appears to be the same photo-graph of the burning cars appeared in color on the CNN Web site, among other places, and the use of this image was very much in line with the more general preponderance of scenes of destruction and conflagration that also dominated both British and American television coverage.

In addition to the "breaking news" updates and news segments on the bombing shown as part of regular programming, news magazine programs such as MSNBC's *Hardball with Chris Matthews* cast the bombing as their main story for discussion. While the "experts" were questioned on the prob-ability of al-Qaeda involvement in the bombing, the camera would fre-quently cut to prerecorded footage of cars and buildings ablaze, victims being shuttled to the hospital, and other images "from the scene." Often the same twenty-second clip would run over and over, on tape-loop, as the pun-dits speculated on the apparent "resurgence" of al-Qaeda. To a surprising degree, the same footage was used across all major United States network and cable news stations. More generally speaking, the replication of press photographs (and footage) is a well-documented aspect of the industry (see van Ginneken, 1998, p. 114); and, institutionally speaking, it can often be explained by the fact that a small number of photographic services tend to provide the images for the vast majority of mainstream news media produc-ers. But there is still the question: why *these* images?

Having examined the coverage of the bombing in both online and hard-copy print editions for several mainstream Indonesian-language publica-tions, there seems to be much less emphasis on—for lack of a better phrase—shock and awe. Whereas any number of horrific scenes may be found in the mainstream Anglophone press, similar images were few and far between in the mainstream Indonesian media. On the morning of the 13th, the *Jawa Pos* ran an article accompanied by a picture of flaming buildings, with people standing in the foreground—notably, not looking either injured or particu-larly panicked. A gallery of images at the *Kompas* Web site included a cou-ple of photographs of charred remains; and the *Bali Post* updated its lead page that same morning with three small pictures: two of buildings ablaze and one of a partially visible corpse covered by a straw mat. (The latter pho-tographs, though unattributed, appear elsewhere with attribution to AP and Reuters.) These exceptions aside, most of the photographs published in the Indonesian press seemed to depict the physical destruction—burnt-out buildings and so forth—as photographed "the morning after." This disjunc-ture between the Indonesian and broadly Western coverage was evident in the photo galleries posted the day after the bombing to the Web sites for *Kompas* and *The Sydney Morning Herald*, respectively. The *Kompas* gallery was dominated by images associated with the aftermath of the bombing; almost half the images in the latter displayed scenes of conflagration and what might best be described as terror-in-progress.

Some Provisional Labels

Before going on to address how this disjuncture played out, it is helpful to have a few provisional labels to characterize the different kinds of images that were used in the coverage. I felt there was adequate overlap between the Indonesian and broadly Euro-American materials to justify treating them together. However, suggesting that "the same pictures" were used by both, while accurate in one sense, is misleading in another. I would argue, ultimately, that the photographs cannot be analyzed (or even labeled) in isolation from the particular occasions of their deployment. In this sense, the labels are not *pre-analytic*, but rather they are the product of a first step in the analysis of use.

1. Horror and conflagration: Burning buildings and vehicles, as well as bloodied victims and others either looking on from a distance or, occasionally, picking their way through the rubble.
2. Rescue and hospital: Transport and treatment of victims, both on the night of the bombing and subsequently; many of these images might equally well be considered under "horror and conflagration"; also photos of people looking through lists of known and anonymous victims.
3. Damage and aftermath: Photographs taken the following morning, or afterward, including pictures of victims who survived the explosions, as well as those who did not. (The latter range from corpses that are more or less intact to piles of burned and only vaguely recognizable body parts.)

   A prominent subset of these photographs might more aptly be labeled pictures of "the morning after," as they depict from various perspectives (in among the rubble, from the air, etc.) the physical destruction of Kuta, including burnt-out buildings and the smoking remains of cars and other vehicles that were destroyed in the blast.
4. Security and investigation: Members of the police, security, and investigation teams from both Indonesia and abroad engaged in various kinds of activity.
5. Evacuation: Images either of planes on the runway (often probably taken at an earlier date) or of people waiting in queues or in the departure lounge preparing to leave Bali.
6. Homecoming: People in varying degrees of health arriving home —usually at the airport, and often appear to be met by friends or family.
7. Official intervention: Images of governmental officials, often labeled as taken from photos "on file" (i.e., not necessarily current).

8. Mourning: Images of people praying, lighting candles, attending vigils etc.
9. In memory of . . . : Pictures of victims, usually a portrait or some-times a picture of someone engaged in an activity cited as some-thing they loved to do (football, horseback riding, etc.); unlike victims photographed in "horror and conflagration," "rescue and hospital," and so forth the subjects are almost always named.
10. Maps: Maps indicating the location of Kuta in Bali, Bali in Indonesia, Indonesia in Southeast Asia, and so forth; often indi-cating sites of recent terrorist attacks or religion-related violence; also more elaborate maps with reconstructions of the events sur-rounding the bombing.
11. *The suspicious* at large: Not "suspects" proper (Amrozi, Imam Samudra, et al.), but photos of well-known "militants" such as Abu Bakar Ba'asyir and Ja'far Umar Thalib emerge in some of the earliest reporting; these pictures, like those of political leaders, are often taken from collections of photos taken at an earlier date and on file.
12. Composite images: These images generally bring together photo-graphs with maps and other images at the heading of an article or web page.

For subsequent coverage, I would also include (13) composite sketches (of the suspects), (14) suspects in custody, (15) diagrams of various processes associated with the bombing (building the bomb, detonation, etc.) and, finally, (16) photographs of the re-enactment. For the time being, I shall leave aside the images deployed in the coverage of the trials.

First, a question: how might these kinds of photographs be related to the events they represent? Are the images ideologically charged, like the smokestacks in the NRDC ad? One might argue that the series of provision-al labels that I have listed above parallel a natural progression from chaos, horror, and conflagration through the various processes (rescue, investiga-tion, etc.) that would eventually culminate in the restoration of order, the delivery of justice and so forth. The "restoration of order," however, has long been a set piece for cultural and media studies' analyses of how the news articulates an ideological version of prevailing social relations (see, e.g., Fiske 1987, pp. 281ff; Hartley, 1982, pp. 63ff). Jaap van Ginneken succinct-ly summarized the "overarching logic" of the news as "twofold; on the one hand a vivid evocation of new threats to convention, normality and order; on the other hand their labeling, categorization and neutralization" (1998, p. 188). Paralleling classical myths of cosmogony, segments on the evening news generally begin with chaos and end with the restoration of (white, male, and upper-middle-class) order.

As Fiske (1987, p. 281) pointed out, the news often ends with "something for the ladies." That is to say, once (masculine) order is restored, the world is safe for a little "human interest," perhaps demonstrating that life, indeed, can now go on. It is also worth noting that chaos tends to happen to Others (usually of the exotic variety). In the United States, the contrast between the shock-and-awe of the Bali bombing coverage and the almost clinical sterility of the images displayed in coverage of the "DC sniper" case lined up very nicely with cultural and media studies' accounts of the way in which the news articulates domestic order in opposition to the chaotic danger occurring somewhere "out there." Yet, despite these generic mechanisms, achieving closure is no easy task, as events in the world are not always amenable to the expectations and constraints of news production. According to Fiske, "The real is too multifaceted, too contradictory, to submit easily to the control of the news conventions. There is simply too much reality for it to be contained" (1987, p. 302).

Setting such invocations of "reality" aside for the moment, the use of photographs and other images were an important aspect of the push toward interpretive closure in coverage of the Bali bombings. Various degrees and kinds of pre-interpretation may be discerned in the composite images and maps published in the days and weeks following the blasts. The two come together nicely in a CNN montage of the notorious OBL looming behind a map of the Indonesian archipelago, flanked by smaller images of Hambali, Abu Bakar Ba'asyir; and others (see Figure 10.3).

FIGURE 10.3. "War Against Terror: Southeast Asia Front" CNN Web site, downloaded 13 Oct 2002.

Through simple juxtaposition, this image links Osama bin Laden with four now-infamous regional "militants"—and, together, they appear to be quite literally *behind* (recent events in) Indonesia. Deconstructing such an image may not be terribly difficult. But what about the pictures of burning buildings, bloodied victims, and the like? These are the images that seem to mark the most pronounced point of disjuncture between the Indonesian and broadly Euro-American visual coverage of the bombing. So, from a critical perspective, what can be said about these images? Like most of the people/bodies described by eyewitnesses, the victims depicted in these photographs are usually anonymous while the viewing subject is, in at least one sense, particular. But how are these photographs related to other aspects of the coverage? Are they anecdotal, like many of the eyewitness reports? Perhaps illustrative? Demonstrative? Or even evocative?

The Innocence of Smokestacks (and the Bloody Ground of the Visual)

In one of his earliest essays on photography, Roland Barthes set out to lay the groundwork for a structural analysis of "the photographic message." Offering a permutation of the default sender/receiver model of communication (i.e., following Shannon & Weaver; 1998 [1949]),[11] he suggested that

> the photograph is not simply a product or a channel but also an object endowed with a structural autonomy. Without in any way intending to divorce this object from its use, it is necessary to provide for a specific method prior to sociological analysis [i.e., of its transmission and eventual reception] and which can only be the immanent analysis of the unique structure that a photograph constitutes. (1977, p. 16; bracketed addition mine)

However, Barthes had already begun to shy away from this "structural autonomy" of the photograph on the very next page, noting that "even from the perspective of a purely immanent analysis, the structure of the photograph is not an isolated structure; it is in communication with at least one other structure, namely the text—title, caption or article—accompanying every press photograph" (1977, p. 16). He suggested that, with the rise to prominence of "the press photograph" as a mode of visual communication, the traditional relationship between image and text was inverted: "it is not the image which comes to elucidate or realize the text, but the latter which comes to sublimate, patheticize or rationalize the image" (1977 [1961], p. 25). In other words, "Formerly, the image illustrated the text (made it clearer); today, the text loads the image, burdening it with a culture, a moral, an imagination" (1977, p. 25).

Barthes may have been painting with a fairly broad brush, but as usual he was onto an important problem: namely, the critical-ontological implications of the relationship between text and image. I noted, at the outset, that the advertisement for the NRDC works on a mutually constitutive interplay between its text and photograph to articulate a particular kind of collective subject: one under threat, in fear—perhaps patriotic—and definitely in need of "defenses at home." In Barthes' terms, "the photographic message" is "loaded" through association with the call to collective environmental responsibility ("We have enough to worry about . . . "), while, simultaneously, the invocation of collective responsibility gains a very particular charge through its juxtaposition with the image of the burning WTC/chimneys. Neither text nor image could have done the job on its own. Rallying "us" to defend against a threat to "our" environment required both text and image. So, returning to the news media coverage of the Bali bombing, what is one to make of the interplay between the front-page photos depicting scenes of conflagration and the headlines that read "TERRORISM STRIKES HOME," "EVIL" and so on?

For Barthes, at least in this particular essay, the question was how to separate out the *denotative* "structural autonomy" of the photograph from its *connotative,* or "cultural," associations. Returning again briefly to the ad from the NRDC, the picture of smoking WTC/chimneys would have been comparatively inert prior to the events of 9/11. So, do pictures of bloodied victims have an "imminent" message? Or are the images themselves innocent (like smokestacks), relying instead on connotative association?

By the end of the essay, having addressed various modes of connotation (i.e., ways of imposing a "second meaning on the photographic message proper"), Barthes had more or less abandoned the possibility of pure denotation. He concluded, in short, that "connotation goes a long way" (1977, p. 30). However, he continued:

> Is this to say that a pure denotation, a this-side of language, is impossible? If such a denotation exists, it is perhaps not at the level of what ordinary languages calls the insignificant, the neutral, the objective, but on the contrary, at the level of absolutely traumatic images. (1977, p. 30)

Barthes suggested that, perhaps, if denotation was to be found anywhere, it was in photographs of "fires, shipwrecks, catastrophes, violent deaths, all captured 'from life as lived'"—it is "the photograph about which there is nothing to say" (1977, pp. 30-31). So might there have been such a photograph in the media coverage of the bombing; an image that, to use Barthes' phrase (1977, p. 18), "completely fills its substance and leaves no place for the development of a second-order message"? Recalling the journalistic rituals of presence—eyewitnesses, "on the scene" and "live" coverage and so forth—Barthes qualified his invocation of the traumatic rather tellingly:

> Truly traumatic photographs are rare, for in photography the trauma is wholly dependent on the certainty that the scene "really" happened: *the photographer has to be there* (the mythical definition of denotation). (1977, p. 30; significantly, the emphasis is in the original; cf. Hall, 1972, p. 84)

Insofar as they depict fires, violent deaths and so forth apparently "from life as lived," I believe that in one sense many of the images from the Bali bombing coverage (especially those I labeled "horror and conflagration") might qualify as truly traumatic. However, there remains the question of whether there is nothing to say about these images.

Imag(in)ing al-Qaeda

In the first instance, were the pictures *in themselves* adequate to the task of representation, there would have been no need for headlines—in fact, no need for articles at all, let alone captions. But the "photographic message" is notoriously unreliable, as Sontag recently noted:

> [A]ll photographs wait to be explained or falsified by their captions. During the fighting between Serbs and Croats at the beginning of the recent Balkan wars, the same photographs of children killed in the shelling of a village were passed around at both Serb and Croat propaganda briefings. Alter the caption, and the children's deaths could be used and reused. (2003, p. 10)

And, indeed, the morning after the bombing, the images in themselves were not adequate to the task of representing the bombing. The headlines almost seemed to shout: TERROR HITS HOME, VICTIMS OF WAR and so forth. (Perhaps as Barthes suggested, "today, the text loads the image.") But, if images are not adequate in themselves, is the converse also the case—that, were words adequate in themselves, there would be no need for pictures?

In the ad for the NRDC, I suggested that the "We" of "We have enough to worry about" was parasitic on the image of the smoking chimneys/WTC. In other words, the image supplemented the text. Without that image, the "We" would not have been the same. So what about the photographs and other images used in media coverage of the Bali bombing? Were they in some way supplemental? Or perhaps supplemented? Both, or neither? If we return to the photograph published on the front page of London edition of

The Daily Telegraph on the morning of the 14th, we see a bloodied and shirtless young man picking his way through the rubble with a woman of similar age, against the backdrop of a flaming car, and the whole scene is framed by the dark of night. It is, at least to my eye, a dramatic picture (Figure 10.4).

There is a wooden post in the foreground, broken off perhaps by the blast, with a cable of some sort attached, sagging and leading out of frame to the left. I mention this only in passing, as the picture is composed beautifully. As Reed Johnson (2002) recently noted in an opinion piece for the *LA Times*, "But war is also beautiful." The young man's face is dirty, and the two are depicted stepping cautiously as they clutch one another, with their eyes turned down toward the ground. (And, again, they are anonymous.) The headline simply reads "Al-Qa'eda Link to Club Bombing," and the caption beneath the picture explains: "Injured victims of the Bali terrorist attack stagger past burning cars on their way to safety after two nightclubs were destroyed on Saturday night. Al-Qa'eda is thought to be responsible."

Examining the overall layout, the caption seems to articulate the headline and image (see Hall, 1972, p. 53), bringing together the two dominant elements of the front page: "injured victims" and "al-Qa'eda." Recalling the

FIGURE 10.4. Headline: Al-Qa'eda Link to Club Bombing The Daily Telegraph (14 Oct. 2002). Reprinted with permission of *The Daily Telegraph* and Gamma

anonymity of the people/bodies described in eyewitness accounts, a similar observation may be made with respect to photographs of what I would call victimhood-in-progress. The images of victims who are still in the fray are rarely if ever named, nor are they often depicted looking into the camera. It seems that victims are usually only *personalized* after the fact—either as a specialized form of eyewitness or in memory. (Pictures *in memoriam*, for instance, were often portraits.) "Horror and conflagration," "rescue" and so forth appear as a backdrop for the viewing of anonymous victims by particular personalized subjects. But where does al-Qaeda fit in?

In representing the subjects of the photograph as "injured victims of the Bali terrorist attack," one might argue that—like Sontag's photograph of Serb/Croat children killed in the shelling—the *Daily Telegraph* caption pins down an otherwise unreliable photo. (They could be anyone, anywhere.) But, recalling the ad for the NRDC, is it possible that it is the image that is required to underwrite the caption? In other words, might the invocation of al-Qaeda be somehow parasitic on the image of anonymous "injured victims"? Perhaps significantly, although victims are discussed at some length in the article, there is only brief—and decidedly inconclusive—mention of al-Qaeda:

> No group claimed responsibility. But the attacks heightened concerns that the al-Qa'eda network had regrouped after the war in Afghanistan and was behind them.
> The killing of American troops in Kuwait and the Philippines this month and a suicide attack against a French oil tanker have indicated that the network has launched a global offensive against "crusader" targets, a code for those linked to America and its allies. (Spillius & Dutter, 2002)

As in this brief excerpt, the incidents in Kuwait, Yemen, and the Philippines were widely deployed in the Anglophone media as evidence of "a global offensive," thereby implicitly articulating the Bali bombing in terms of "the war on terror" through little more than simple juxtaposition.

As it happens, the article to which the headline most closely corresponds—a piece citing Jemaah Islamiyah (JI) and Laskar Jihad as possible suspects (headline: "Finger points to the men with al-Qa'eda links")—may be found back on the fourth page, above an aerial shot of "morning after" destruction in Kuta. The article suggests that the "prime suspects are from a hardline Indonesian Islamist group with links to al-Qa'eda." Yet the actual "links" that are cited in the article—previous accusations against JI, non-committal comments from a "terrorism expert" and so forth—are rather tenuous. But if the article is a little short on fact, it is also accompanied by a chronological survey entitled "The list of terror attacks."

The List of Terror Attacks

These are the suspected Islamic militant terrorist attacks since September 11:

Dec 22, 2001: Attempt by British Muslim Richard Reid to blow up American Airlines flight with shoe bomb.

Jan 22: Four Indian police killed in Calcutta when armed men open fire on US Centre.

Jan 23: American journalist Daniel Pearl kidnapped and later killed in Karachi.

March 17: Five killed in grenade attack on Protestant church in Islamabad.

April 11: Nineteen people killed by lorry bomb outside Tunisian synagogue.

May 8: Fourteen people killed in suicide car bomb attack on bus in Karachi.

June 14: Twelve Pakistanis killed in car bomb attack on US consulate, Karachi.

Aug 5: Six Pakistanis killed in armed attack on Christian church in Muree.

August 25: Two hurt in blast near UN flats in Kabul.

Oct 6: One crewman dies when small boat blows up French oil tanker off Yemen.

Oct 8: US marine killed when two gunmen open fire during exercise in Kuwait.

(*The Daily Telegraph*, 2003)

Although not on the list itself, the Bali bombing implicitly emerges from the juxtaposition as the latest of many "Islamic militant terrorist attacks since September 11." The implications of this representation are perhaps best approached through a comparison with a similar list published that same morning in the Semarang-based Indonesian daily paper, *Suara Merdeka*. The latter list—a "List of 2001-2002 BOMBINGS"—came at the end of an article entitled "Bomb goes off, Bali cries" (*Bomb meledak, Bali menangis*).

List of 2001-2002 bombings

31-07-01 18.30 Church of Bethel Tabernakel Kristus Alfa Omega, Gajahmada Street, 114-118, Jakarta.
23-08-01 10.30 Plaza Atrium Senen, Central Jakarta
12-10-01 13.00 Kentucky Fried Chicken (KFC) Makassar Shopping Complex.
01-01-02 Type K-75 grenade, Bulungan Jakarta 1 Killed.
18-01-02 A fishing bomb exploded in a guardhouse at the State Electricity Enterprise complex in Cawang, East Jakarta.

13-02-02 21.18 Ambon post-Malino. Outskirts of Desa Batumerah
21.23 - Mardika, Kecamatan Sirimau.
09-06-02 A minor bomb exploded in the parking lot of the Hotel
Jayakarta, Tamansari Jakarta, 3 seriously injured and 3 cars destroyed.
09-06-02 Two bombs were found in the parking lot of the Sarinah shopping center in Central Jakarta. The bomb was defused.
01-07-02 A large firecracker exploded in the Graha Cijantung shopping
center in Central Jakarta, 1 seriously injured, 6 injured lightly.
17-08-02 10.00 Bomb exploded at Blang Padang Field in Aceh prior to
the celebration of the Indonesian Republic's 57th year, 20 people were
injured.

(*Suara Merdeka*, 2002)

Interestingly, although they were published on the very same morning,
there is not a single incident that is common to the two lists. The *Daily
Telegraph* list includes various attacks (in numerous countries) that have
been widely covered in the Euro-American press in connection with "the
war on terror," whereas the *Suara Merdeka* list includes a string of bombings that occurred in Indonesia during 2001 and 2002 (and which, incidentally, received little if any attention in mainstream Euro-American media).
The *Suara Merdeka* article also refers to the attacks of 9/11, but the link is
made through the similarity in consequence—"lives needlessly cut short"—
and not through the suspected perpetrators.

Perhaps the point to be taken from this apparent disjuncture was that
the nature of the link between the Bali bombing and other recent high-pro-
file "terrorist attacks" was not only somewhat less than taken-for-granted in
much of Indonesia. But the entire edifice—"the global offensive" and even
al-Qaeda itself as a coherent organization and something for ordinary people to be afraid of—is critically unstable. In the immediate aftermath of the
bombing, there were isolated commentators in Europe and the United
States—John Pilger and Jeffery Winters come to mind—who explicitly
questioned the ease and rapidity with which the attack was made to make
sense within the prefigured framework of "the war on terror." And, at the
time these early news reports were published, there was no publicly available evidence whatsoever for a connection to al-Qaeda or even, to my
knowledge, to international terrorism more generally. (In this connection,
what happened subsequently is, strictly speaking, irrelevant.) What there
was, however, were pictures. Lots of them. Pictures of victims and conflagration. Pictures of flaming cars, burned-out buildings, and charred corpses.
An al-Qaeda affiliate/look-alike/whatever may have been behind the bombings. But there was absolutely no way to know one way or another at the
time these stories went to press.

Really?

In the first days after the bombing, Indonesian media displayed neither the preponderance of graphic images nor the strong articulation of al-Qaeda responsibility—two more or less ubiquitous aspects of the mainstream Euro-American coverage. With regard to the latter, I would like to propose that the initial articulation of the bombing in terms of "the war on terror" was perhaps more than a little parasitic on images of what I called "horror and conflagration." The speculations about al-Qaeda involvement were repeatedly set against the backdrop of flaming cars, burned-out buildings, and bloodied victims. If the former lacked substance, might the latter have filled the gap? Recalling the ad from the NRDC, perhaps the heavily charged photo was required precisely because "we" did not register without it. That is to say, the strong articulation of a collectivity under threat might in fact have been indicative of its absence. But, could a similar argument be made for the images of "horror and conflagration" in Bali?

It may be recalled that Barthes retained "the traumatic" as being the only object even possibly capable of effecting pure photographic denotation (cf. Sontag, 2003, p. 7). I believe this to be of interest not for what it says about photography, nor even about trauma, but rather for its indication of a very particular *desire* for the real. In the editorial introduction to their volume on *Journalism after September 11*, Zelizer and Allan noted that "If the coverage, especially the repetition of images showing the towers being hit was too much to handle for some viewers, for others it somehow authenticated their experience" (2002, p. 4). There is, I believe, an interesting relationship between this sense of authenticity, absence, and the compulsion to repeat. It was in a not entirely dissimilar connection (philosophically, at least), that Judith Butler commented on the relationship between performativity and materiality in the articulation of sexual difference:

> "Sex" is an ideal construct which is forcibly materialized through time. It is not a simple fact or static condition of a body, but a process whereby regulatory norms materialize "sex" and achieve this materialization through a forcible reiteration of those norms. That this reiteration is necessary is a sign that materialization is never quite complete, that bodies never quite comply with the norms by which their materialization is impelled. (1993, p. 2)

So what might absence and repetition have to do with the collapse of the twin towers and the images that were used to represent the bombing in Bali? In his reflections on 9/11, Zizek described a distinctly Western and late twentieth- to early twenty-first century hankering after unmediated reality (which, in the end, "culminates in the thrill of the Real as the ultimate 'effect'"). It is in this respect that I would argue that Barthes' retention of trauma was not indicative of anything essential about photography or even human suffering. Rather, I would suggest that it was perhaps symptomatic of something historical—something about images, presence, and violence in a particular period of Western history. Might this not be why, following 9/11, there was a sense that "we wanted to see it again and again"?

APPENDIX

The following is the original text for the earliest online report (Hakim, 2002) I was able to find on the Bali bombing.

Ledakan di Kuta Menewaskan Sekitar 10 Orang

13 Oct 2002 0:0:35 WIB

TEMPO Interaktif, Jakarta: Sebuah bom meledak di depan Sari Klub, Jl. Legian, Kuta, Bali, Sabtu (12/10), sekitar pukul 11.10 Wita. Akibat ledakan ini, tak kurang dari 10 orang pengunjung Sari Klub meninggal dan sekitar 40 lainnya luka-luka.

Hingga malam ini, petugas ambulans mondar mandir mengangkut korban yang luka-luka ke Rumah Sakit Sanglah, Denpasar. Jumlahnya, belum bisa diperkirakan secara pasti. Selain korban meninggal, puluhan bangunan yang berada di sekitar lokasi, rusak parah, beberapa di antaranya bangunan Padis Club dan Hotel White Rose.

Suasana di lokasi kejadian sangat hiruk pikuk. Sebab, listrik di sekitar lokasi padam dan para turis yang sedang berada di sekitar area ledakan tampak lalu lalang. Tampak seorang turis asal Australia terlihat meraung-raung karena anaknya, yang berumur 17 tahun, berada di Sari Club. Kapolda Bali Brigjen Pol. Budi Setiawan langsung memimpin aparatnya di lokasi untuk menangani kasus ini. (Jalil Hakim-*Tempo* News Room; *Tempo*, 2002)

NOTES

1. Here, I have used the term "patient" in the sense of "A person or thing that undergoes some action, or to whom or which something is done; that which receives impressions from external agents (J.), as correlative to agent, and distinguished from instrument; a recipient" (*Oxford English Dictionary*; see Hobart, 1990).

2. "The media" have frequently been invoked by scholars and other commentators as instrumental in the process of collective recovery from the "trauma" of 9/11. The implicit functionalism underpinning this way of imagining the post–9/11 American community is an adequately complex and important subject as to require a separate study.

3. In this connection, it is worth emphasizing the extent to which Laclau and Mouffe differ from Hall (e.g., 1996) in their account of articulatory practices (Hobart, n.d.). For Hall, "the social" precedes, in the strongest sense, the practices through which it is known (e.g., in Hall's account, language is ultimately superstructural, an epiphenomenon that obscures the "real" workings of social relations). This leaves the rather serious (and, to my knowledge, un-addressed) problem of how Hall and his acolytes are able to know "the social" extra-discursively—in other words, independently of any and all epistemological conditions (Fox, 2002, pp. 20-23).

4. My analysis is based on a unique archive of media materials that includes over 300 digital television recordings and some 45,000 articles, in both Indonesian and English, from sources in Australia, Indonesia, Singapore, the UK, and United States. Compiled on a systematic basis since the 12 October 2002, the collection is focused on the Bali bombing, but also includes a wide range of materials related more generally to representations of religion, violence, and "the war on terror." It is, to my knowledge, the most comprehensive archive of its kind.

5. The full Indonesian text is given in the Appendix.

6. On the complex genealogies for contemporary theories of memory, see Hacking (1998).

7. See appendix.

8. The posting time listed here is equivalent to Sunday, October 13, 2002; 02:39 AM Western Indonesian Time. I should note that I have also seen other posting times for the same article (e.g., 19:06 GMT), but they are all within about 40 minutes of one another.

9. The original text read as follows:
   Selain itu puluhan bangunan lainnya dalam radius 10 sampai 20-an meter rusak berat. Sedangkan kaca-kaca toko, hotel maupun tempat hiburan lainnya yang berada dalam radius satu kilometer, pecah. 'Saya melihat kaca-kaca di kompleks pertokoan Kuta Square, pecah,' tutur Dadi yang berada di Kuta Square, sekitar satu kilometer dari tempat ledakan (*Kompas* 2002).

10. The original text read as follows:
    Kepanikan luar biasa terjadi di Bali tadi malam. Dua bom meledak hampir bersamaan di Kuta dan Renon, Denpasar, yang berjarak 20 km. Ledakan pertama terjadi di dekat Konsulat Amerika Serikat di Renon, disusul kemudian ledakan sangat dahsyat di klub orang asing di sentra wisata Kuta (*Jawa Pos*, 2002).

11. Barthes began the essay as follows: "The press photograph is a message. Considered overall this message is formed by a source of emission, a channel of transmission and a point of reception" and so forth (1977 [1964], p. 15). Relying heavily on Barthes, Hall proposed a similar model of communication in his early essay on news photography (1972), which, incidentally, would later provide the basis for his oft-cited model of encoding/decoding (1980). The latter rode on a

series of presuppositions that—with minor (and philosophically inconsequential) alterations—has underpinned the vast majority of subsequent work in cultural and media studies.

REFERENCES*

Barthes, R. (1972). *Mythologies* (Selections) (A. Lavers, Trans.). New York: Hill and Wang.

Barthes, R. (1977). The photographic message. In *Image, music, text* (S. Heath, Trans.). New York: Hill and Wang. (Originally published as Le message photographique, in *Communications, 4,* 1964)

Butler, J. (1993). *Bodies that matter: On the discursive limits of "sex."* London & New York: Routledge.

CNN (2002a). Bali explosions: "12 dead." *CNN.com*. Posted 3:39 PM, Eastern Daylight Time. http://www.cnn.com/2002/WORLD/asiapcf/southeast/10/12/bali.explosions/

CNN (2002b). Bali bomb survivors recall night of horror. *CNN.com*. Posted 14 Oct 2002, 5:03 AM Eastern Daylight Time. http://www.cnn.com/2002/WORLD/asiapcf/southeast/10/13/bali.blast.survivors/index.html

Collingwood, R.G. (1946). *The idea of history.* Oxford: Clarendon Press.

Crapanzano, V. (1986). Hermes dilemma: The masking of subversion in ethnographic description. In J. Clifford & G.E. Marcus (Eds.), *Writing culture; The poetics and politics of ethnography.* London: University of California Press.

The Daily Telegraph (2003, October 14). The list of terror attacks.

Derrida, J. (1981). *Dissemination* (Translated, with an introduction and additional notes by B. Johnson). Chicago: University of Chicago Press.

Fabian, J. (1983). *Time and the other; How anthropology makes its object.* New York: Columbia University Press.

Finkel, K. (2001). Sept. 12 front pages left a lasting impression. In *Crisis journalism: A handbook for media response.* Reston, VA: American Press Institute. http://www.americanpressinstitute.org/crisis_report.pdf

Fiske, J. (1987). *Television culture.* London & New York: Routledge.

Fox, R. (2002). *From text to television: Mediating religion in contemporary Bali.* Unpublished doctoral dissertation, University of London (School of Oriental and African Studies).

van Ginneken, J. (1998). *Understanding global news; A critical introduction.* London, Thousand Oaks, & New Delhi: Sage.

Hacking, I. (1998). *Rewriting the soul: Multiple personality and the sciences of memory.* Princeton, NJ: Princeton University Press.

---

*I have listed news articles by author when one was listed, and otherwise by publication (e.g., Kompas, *Tempo*).

Hakim, J. (2002). Ledakan di Kuta menewaskan sekitar 10 orang. *Tempo Interaktif*. Posted 13 Oct. 2002, 0:0:35 Western Indonesian Time. Downloaded on 12 Oct 2002 (EST), from http://www.tempo.co.id/news/2002/10/12/1,1,25,id

Hall, S. (1972, Autumn). The determinations of newsphotographs. *Working Papers in Cultural Studies, 3*, 53-87.

Hall, S. (1980). Encoding/decoding. In S. Hall et al. (Eds.), *Culture, media, language; Working papers in cultural studies, 1972-1979*. [This article comprises an edited extract from Hall, S. (1973). Encoding and decoding in television discourse. CCCS Stencilled Paper no. 7.]

Hall, S. (1996). On postmodernism and articulation; An interview with Stuart Hall (edited by L. Grossberg). In D. Morley and K.H. Chen (Eds.), *Stuart Hall; Critical dialogues in cultural studies*. London & New York: Routledge.

Hartley, J. (1982). *Understanding news*. London & New York: Routledge.

Hobart, M. (n.d.) *The end of the world news: Television and a problem of articulation in Bali*. Unpublished paper.

Hobart, M. (1990). The patience of plants: A note on agency in Bali. *Review of Indonesian and Malaysian Affairs, 24*(2), 90-135.

Hobart, M. (1996). Ethnography as a practice, or the unimportance of penguins. *Europaea*, II(1), 3-36.

Jawa Pos (2002). Bom Dashsyat Guncang Bali. *Jawa Pos Online*, Posted 13 Oct 2002. http://www.jawapos.co.id/index.php?act=detail&id=331

Johnson, R. (2002, April 20). War in all its awful beauty. *Los Angeles Times,* p. E.1

Kompas (2002). Kuta, Denpasar, Manado diguncang ledakan bom. *Kompas*, Posted 13 Oct 2002. http://www.kompas.com/kompas-cetak/0210/13/utama/aaku01.htm

Laclau, E. & Mouffe, C. (1985). *Hegemony and socialist strategy; Towards a radical democratic politics*. London & New York: Verso.

Newsweek (2001-2) September 11, December 31 - January 7.

The Oxford English Dictionary (1994). CD-ROM. (2nd ed.). Oxford: Oxford University Press.

Pratt, M.L. (1986). Fieldwork in common places. In J. Clifford & G.E. Marcus (Eds.), *Writing culture; The poetics and politics of ethnography*. London: University of California Press.

Reuters (2002). Three dead, 100 hurt in blasts on Indonesia's Bali. *TheJakartaPost.com*. Posted 13 Oct 2002, 12:54:26 AM (Western Indonesian Time).

Said, E. (2001, November 15-21). Suicidal ignorance. *Al-Ahram Weekly Online,* issue 560. http://www.ahram.org.eg/weekly/2001/560/op2.htm

Shannon, C.E. & Weaver, W. (1998 [1949]). *The mathematical theory of communication*. Urbana & Chicago: University of Chicago Press.

Sontag, S. (2003). *Regarding the pain of others*. New York: Farrar, Straus and Giroux.

Spillius, A. & Dutter, B. (2002, October 14). al-Qaeda link to club bombing. *The Daily Telegraph*, p. 1.

Sreberny, A. (2002). Trauma talk: Reconfiguring the inside and outside. In B. Zelizer & S. Allen (Eds.), *Journalism after September 11*. London & New York: Routledge.

Straits Times. (2002). They were there. *Straits Times Interactive*. Posted 15 Oct 2002. http://straitstimes.asia1.com.sg/topstories/story/0,4386,149037,00.html?

Suara Merdeka (2002) Bom Meledak, Bali Menangis. *Suara Merdeka Cyber News.* Posted 14 Oct 2002. http://www.suaramerdeka.com/harian/0210/14/nas2.htm

Sydney Morning Herald (2002). British tourist saved by pillar. *SMH.com*. Posted 13 Oct 2002. http://www.smh.com.au/articles/2002/10/13/1034222669597.html

Vickers, A. (1989). *Bali; A paradise created*. Berkeley & Singapore: Periplus.

Zelizer, B. (2002). Photography, journalism, and trauma. In B. Zelizer & S. Allan (Eds.), *Journalism after September 11*. London & New York: Routledge.

Zelizer, B. & Allan S. (2002). Introduction: When trauma shapes the news. In B. Zelizer & S. Allen (Eds.), *Journalism after September 11*. London & New York: Routledge.

Zizek, S. (2002). *Welcome to the desert of the real! Five essays on September 11 and related dates*. London & New York: Verso.

Chapter 11

Disturbing the Banality of Journalism

Political Violence, Gujarat 2002, and the Indian News Media

Prasun Sonwalkar

Journalism is predicated on its power to main the status quo in a society. It nurtures and reinforces a power geometry that is inherently unfair—some versions of reality are routinely presented as *the* version of reality and the marginalization of the life situation of some sections of society in news columns is routinely presented as normal. Seib (2002, p. 2) terms such selectivity in the events and issues that the news media cover or ignore as "journalism of convenience." I have called this "banal journalism"—preferring some events and issues to others, limiting the range of perspectives offered, reflecting the priorities of the dominant power groupings in society (Sonwalkar, 2005). This is also true of events and issues of political violence—some are chosen by the media for sustained coverage but most are routinely ignored. The status quo is usually deeply entrenched and it is rare that the news media are able to disturb it.

This chapter presents one such example when the banality of the prevailing status quo was disturbed by the power of the news media. I focus on India, where the high coverage of the Kashmir conflict and the marginalization of other such conflicts elsewhere in the country is a fact of banal journalism (Sonwalkar, 2004). Here, the events and issues involving the Hindu and Muslim sections of Indian society (such as Kashmir) are privileged in the news discourse, whereas those involving minorities (tribes, lower castes, women) are routinely marginalized. But a recent example of political violence and its media coverage shows that citizens are not always powerless against the prevailing status quo; journalism, when practiced with rigorous attention to detail and fairness, can make a difference.

I focus on the coverage of the political violence in the western Indian state of Gujarat in the spring of 2002—it was widely seen as a pogrom against Muslims—and explore some of the ethical, political, and professional dilemmas faced by journalists covering such events. Even though the events and their coverage highlighted the divisions within the Indian news media, several examples of accurate and fair reporting ensured that authorities came to the rescue of the victims. This chapter details how the banality of Indian journalism was disturbed. Several journalists covering the events came under attack; there were attempts to "shoot the messenger," but in the final analysis, rigorous and fair journalism practiced by sections of the Indian news media saved the day.

Gujarat, the land of Mahatma Gandhi, has lately been in the news for the events of 2002, when politically mobilized mobs went on a rampage against Muslims and perpetrated some of the most gory acts of violence since India's independence in 1947. The nature of the news coverage made as much news as the acts of political violence.

My starting point is to propose that given the close relationship between the news media and political violence, Hansen's (2004, p. 19) notion of "politics as permanent performance" is useful to understand and unpack major contemporary events. Acts of political violence should be viewed as political performance enacted by state and nonstate actors. Such acts do not take place in a vacuum, but within political frameworks that privilege or marginalize the pursuit of certain ideologies, values, and beliefs. Violence is central to a democratic framework that sees the state having legal control over organized violence (police, army, security forces, and vigilantes of ruling parties). In Hansen's words, political performance "comprises the construction of images and spectacles, forms of speech, dress and public behaviour that promotes the identity of a movement or party, defines its members and promotes its cause or worldview" (2004, p. 23). This formulation is particularly useful in multicultural societies that witness constant tension between majorities and minorities, widely constituted as "insiders" and "outsiders," or as "us" and "them."

In such contexts, the macrodimensions of religion, community, language and ethnicity are played out at the micro level as politics of permanent performance. Most acts of political violence take place between unequal groups or actors, which places the news media in a piquant situation: both sides court journalists, but they may also be despised if their professional output does not fit within contending frames. It is not uncommon for dominant political actors to hail the news media when convenient and to heap flak on them when they do not toe the "party line." They are damned if they report and damned if they don't. It is also not uncommon for dominant political forces, including their supporters in the news media, to brand or stereotype journalists who may not be amenable to following their perspectives. In media and political circles in London or Delhi or elsewhere, the political inclination of most journalists is known. The problem arises when a journalist with no ostensible allegiance towards any party or ideology comes to be branded simply because his or her output does not fit into certain political frames.

The chapter is also informed by my experience of covering the activities of the Hindutva[1] forces, including several defining events, for *The Times of India* and other publications between 1988 and 1999. Some of the events I covered were based in Gujarat or had strong connections with the state. I have some experience of the damned-if-you-cover-damned-if-you-don't conundrum. The very act of reporting that the Hindutva forces were making waves through their grassroots political mobilization in Gujarat in 1990 invited opprobrium from some ideologically driven journalist colleagues and others. It betrayed the hope that by merely not reporting certain political events, somehow the growth of certain ideologies would be prevented. It also implied that the English-language press in India had overweening status in a country of 1 billion plus people, of whom barely a small but influential minority uses the English language.

When journalists face sustained criticism from political actors, many of them ask the question: are the news media responsible for political violence or do they merely report political violence? That the Hindutva forces went on to wield power in New Delhi in the late 1990s and become one of the poles of Indian politics, despite trenchant criticism in the English-language press over the years, suggests a disjuncture between the spaces that English language journalists inhabit and the vast non-English reality in India. As Smith (1980, p. 160) observed, "India is a country with an intellectual elite which is perhaps further alienated from its own masses than that of any other developing country." India's English-language press is closely implicated with the values of the political and social elites, most of them exposed to Western ideas of modernity. On the other hand, the non-English language press may more adequately reflect the life situation of the vast majority that is relatively unfamiliar with the English language and Western values.

This disjuncture within the Indian media was also evident during the coverage of Gujarat 2002—widely dubbed as India's first communal riot for the satellite television era. The events in Gujarat reflected and reinforced a politics that, since the late 1980s, had been enacted as "permanent performance" on a stage carefully nurtured by the pro-Hindutva forces. As Hansen (2004, p. 23) observed,

Democracy in India has produced a culture of politics that is incredibly fluid, situational and dynamic—where stable constituencies, alliances, equations and ideological principles are in constant flux and redefinition. In such a culture it is those who can create a collective mood, or the illusion of a collectivity driven by a mood—both highly ephemeral phenomena—that can set political agendas at least for some time . . . To perform this type of politics depends, therefore, on the ability to stage public performances, to use and employ a range of registers that can generate authority, and put the power of rumours, myth and other cultural registers to effective use.

Politics and political violence in India are framed against the shifting quicksands of religion, caste, community, language, gender, region, and individuals belonging to influential groups or families. Nandy (1970, p. 58) observed that "it is possible to interpret the political process in India as a continuing attempt to reconcile older categories of thought and social character to the demands of nation-building and political culture as a complex of continuities." Generating collective moods, particularly during elections, has been a key method of political mobilization. More often than not, such mobilization also involves violence—indeed, violence has been central to electoral politics in northern states such as Bihar and Uttar Pradesh.

But before setting out an overview of contemporary Hindutva-oriented politics, it is important to set out definitions of some key terms used in the discourse:

- *Sangh parivar*: This is the umbrella term used for various organizations owing allegiance to the Hindutva ideology. These organizations, such as the Vishwa Hindu Parishad (VHP; World Hindu Council) and the Bajrang Dal (an organization of young devotees of Lord Hanuman, considered a symbol of physical strength and power), have been formed by, and work under the close supervision of, the Rashtriya Swayamsevak Sangh (RSS), or the national volunteers association. "*Parivar*" is the Hindi word for family and "*sangh parivar*" refers to the family of organizations spawned by the RSS.
- *BJP*: Bharatiya Janata Party, which literally means Indian People's Party. It is the political front of the *sangh parivar* and strives to capture political power while aiming at reviving the Hindu social order and traditions in order to reinforce and distinctively establish the dominance of Hindus in India.
- *Kar sevaks*: This means people working on Hindu religious projects. The term has been widely used for the thousands of supporters who volunteer to help in the construction of a temple to the Hindu god, Lord Ram, at Ayodhya in north India. The *kar sevaks*

were accused of demolishing the Babri mosque at Ayodhya on 6
December 1992, which set off a rash of Hindu-Muslim clashes in
India.

HINDUTVA AND GUJARAT

Gujarat is better known as the birthplace of Gandhi, the apostle of peace.
But here, Hindu-Muslim clashes have been endemic—the state has the worst
record of Hindu-Muslim clashes in the country since India's independence
in 1947 (Varshney, 2002, pp. 97-98). Three Gujarat towns have been particularly prone to Hindu-Muslim clashes: Ahmedabad, Vadodara, and Godhra.
Since the early 1980s, the state has been one of the major areas where
Hindutva forces have focused their attention. Political adversaries of the
sangh parivar allege that such forces have treated Gujarat as a "Hindutva
laboratory" to conduct political, social, and cultural experiments in order to
replicate them in other parts of India.

As Shah (1998, p. 244) observed, "The Sangh Parivar has disseminated
Hindutva ideology in Gujarat over many decades. The party (BJP) and its
allies have built the organization brick by brick. It began to reap the benefits of these endeavours in the early 1990s and captured power in 1995."
When the BJP won an overwhelming majority in the Gujarat local elections
in December 2002, months after the pogrom against Muslims, there was
much speculation in the media that the BJP would adopt the "Gujarat for-
mula" to win power in other states in the country.

Over the years, Gujarat has been turned into a Hindutva powerhouse
that the BJP and the *sangh parivar* often tap into for human and material
resources for activities in other parts of India. Gujarat is one of India's most
prosperous states; people of the state are known for their business acumen
and spirit of enterprise. The factor of "long-distance nationalism" also plays
a role, with prosperous Gujaratis in Britain, the United States and elsewhere
generously contributing funds to organizations of the *sangh parivar*. It is
also a fact that in several cities in Gujarat, Hindus and Muslims are linked
together in trade relations, bound by economic compulsions and the
Gujarati language and culture. Hindutva supporters from Gujarat have been
in the forefront of the BJP's political mobilization. From the late 1980s
onwards, the BJP openly joined other organizations of the *sangh parivar*
such as the VHP and the Bajrang Dal to create a national mood for the construction of a temple in honor of Lord Ram at Ayodhya in north India, at
precisely the same spot where the Babri mosque stood.

Ayodhya has a prominent place in the myths and mists of Hinduism,
mainly in the ancient religious text, the *Ramayana*, as the birthplace of Lord

Ram. The *sangh parivar's* argument has been that a Ram temple had existed at the very spot on which the Mughal emperor Babur built the Babri mosque in the sixteenth century to humiliate the Hindus, and that the mosque needed to be replaced by a grand temple of Lord Ram. In the late 1980s, before the mosque was demolished, the *sangh parivar* unleashed a nationwide campaign to mobilize people in favor of the temple and effectively used the mosque as a symbol for a variety of (real and imaginary) grievances suffered by the Hindus. The campaign was described by the *sangh parivar*, not without foundation, as the largest popular phenomenon in India since the freedom movement (Rajagopal, 2001, p. 155). Hindutva elements argued that the Muslim community had been favored and appeased by the Congress party that had been in power most of the time in independent India. In Gujarat, as Chattarji (2004, p. 114) argued, there was a "mythic construction of wronged Hindu majorities now wreaking vengeance to reverse centuries of Muslim barbarism and atrocity, and the media is shocked at government complicity."

The mosque was demolished by *kar sevaks* in a frenzy on 6 December 1992. The issue has since remained on and off the political agenda even as the BJP and its allies, for the first time, went on to win political power in New Delhi under the moderate BJP leader, Atal Bihari Vajpayee (the BJP-led government had a brief tenure between May-June 1996 and was then in office between March 1998 and May 2004). During the Gujarat 2002 clashes, the BJP was in power in Gujarat as well as in New Delhi. Several of the BJP's allies in the government did not support the Ayodhya agenda, and the compulsions of power forced the Vajpayee government to tone down its Hindutva rhetoric and try to build a political consensus on constructing the temple in Ayodhya. However, this consensus was hard to reach, because most political parties in India are opposed to Hindutva-oriented politics. The issue continues to simmer in political discourse and tortuous legal proceedings, while the VHP continues its work to sculpt pillars and other material to be used when—and if—the construction of the temple is legally allowed to begin.

It was against this political and religious backdrop that the infamous events occurred in Gujarat in February-March 2002. It all began on 27 February when the Sabarmati Express train carrying *kar sevaks* was returning home from Ayodhya. They were returning from a political ceremony organized by the VHP as part of its campaign to construct the temple. At around 8 am, the train pulled out of the Godhra station in Gujarat on the last leg of what was to be dubbed as one of the most catastrophic rail journeys of post-Partition India (Varadarajan, 2002a, p. 3). As the train left the station, it was stoned by an angry mob and some 20 minutes later, one of the coaches was burned to cinders along with 58 passengers, many of them later identified as members of the *sangh parivar*. Why the mob gathered and attacked the train has been the subject of much speculation and mystery. Inquiries into the Godhra tragedy were yet to deliver their final conclusions in mid-2005. The identity of the mob was not immediately known, but local Hindutva leaders promptly declared that the attackers were Muslims and that the community needed to be taught a lesson. Retaliation for the Godhra tragedy was swift, with politically mobilized mobs launching fierce attacks on Muslims in several parts of the state. Narendra Modi, chief minister of the Gujarat government and a leading member of the *sangh parivar*, tried to justify the attacks on helpless Muslims in Newtonian terms: every action has an equal and opposite reaction.

From 27 February there was barbarous violence for over 40 days, as revenge against the killing of *kar sevaks* in Godhra. The federal government informed parliament in May 2005 that in all 254 Hindus and 790 Muslims had been killed in the post-Godhra disturbances. In addition 223 people were reported missing, 2,584 sustained injuries, 919 were rendered widows, and 606 children were orphaned. However, the unofficial figure of Muslims killed was over 2,000. As many as 200,000 people were displaced because homes had been burned or looted. Property belonging to Muslims worth millions of rupees was destroyed, and the police and the state administration controlled by the BJP were accused of passivity, if not complicity. Adverse coverage in the media of the Gujarat's government's role in handling the violence played a major role in the federal government intervening to bring the violence to an end. The federal government, even while being critical of the media coverage, belatedly acted and put pressure on the local government, particularly when India started getting a bad press in the international news media.

It is important to note that apart from the Hindu-Muslim violence accompanying the partition of undivided India into independent India and Pakistan in 1947, incidents of major political violence on such a mass scale have taken place in recent decades. The BJP and the Hindutva forces have not been the only ones practicing such politics. The Congress party, which was in power in New Delhi in 1984, resorted to similar principles and actions when Sikh guards assassinated Prime Minister Indira Gandhi. The incident led to targeted attacks against the Sikh community in New Delhi and other parts of north India as revenge for killing Indira Gandhi. Congress leaders and workers were allegedly armed with voters' lists to identify the location of Sikhs, who were attacked almost all over India, but mainly in the northern states. After the Babri mosque was demolished in 1992, Hindu and Muslim groups clashed in Mumbai and elsewhere, resulting in a large number of deaths across India.

During every such episode of mass killings, the role of the state has come in for much criticism. The state is seen as complicit in such acts of mass political violence. As Varshney observed, "(No) amount of critique since 1947 has yet brought about *durable changes* in the behaviour of the state on

Hindu-Muslim relations. Even if Narendra Modi, Gujarat's Chief Minister at the time of the communal violence . . . were to fall tomorrow, the bigger questions of Indian politics on Hindu-Muslims relations would remain" (2002, p. xi; emphasis in original). Over the years, despite several inquiries, most of the perpetrators of the gory events of 1984, 1992, and 2002 have remained unpunished.

If the political violence in Gujarat and its aftermath added yet another dubious chapter in India's record of handling Hindu-Muslim tensions, what was new in 2002 was the way in which the news media covered the events. For the first time, due to the proliferation of satellite television since the early 1990s, and the bold and independent coverage of Gujarat 2002, the news media emerged as prominent players in the political discourse. As Rajagopal (2001) observed, since the mid-1980s when Doordarshan, the state-owned television network, telecast serials based on the ancient religious texts of Ramayana and Mahabharata, television had reshaped the context in which Indian politics was "conceived, enacted and understood."

The next section examines the media coverage of Gujarat 2002 primarily through four lenses:

- The breakdown of long-held ethical norms in Indian journalism about not identifying victims and attackers by religion;
- The use of flak by the Hindutva forces to discipline the media;
- The pro-Hindutva bias of sections of the mass circulation Gujarati-language press; and,
- The dangers and problems faced by journalists while covering the Gujarat events.

In several respects, the coverage marked a significant departure from the way the Indian news media had approached Hindu-Muslim relations since 1947. It also highlighted the disjuncture between the English-language press and the influential sections of the Gujarati-language press.

India's First Television Riot

During the Gujarat 2002 events, for the first time in the history of covering Hindu-Muslim clashes, "violence was carried live" on television (Ninan, 2002) as television cameras brought home graphic images to viewers in Gujarat and elsewhere. There was no live coverage of the attacks against Sikhs in 1984 or of the 1992 Hindu-Muslim clashes in Mumbai and elsewhere; it was then the era of print, and television news reporting was years away. It was only in 1996, when STAR News, the first of the 24-hour news channels, was launched, that television news added a visual dimension to politics, political violence, and the public sphere in India.[2] In 2005, the television newscape had turned dense, with several 24-hour news channels broadcasting in different languages, drawing more people and regions into the public sphere and rejuvenating local networks of culture, politics and economy. The proliferation of satellite television also sparked off an intensely competitive brand of journalism. During the Gujarat events, there was a large presence of journalists and television crews in the streets, each trying to outdo the other, as politically mobilized mobs attacked Muslim men, women (including pregnant women), children and their property. Reporting the clashes, often live, made for riveting television, the likes of which the Indian audience had never seen.

The coverage by the print media, English and Gujarati-language, also made news when sections of the press (Gujarati-language dailies *Sandesh* and *Gujarat Samachar*) covered the events from a pro-Hindutva perspective while other sections (*The Times of India, Indian Express*) were severely critical of the attacks against Muslims. The burning of the train bogey and its inmates in Godhra occurred on 27 February and was reported extensively the next day. But news channels and newspaper editors devoted more time and space to the Union budget that was presented in the Indian parliament in New Delhi on 28 February. The budget's coverage pushed the Godhra incident to the margins, and it dropped further down the news agenda when large-scale retaliation against Muslims began in others parts of the state.

Ethics: Medium is the Message

Since the 1950s and 1960s, the Indian news media followed a set of guidelines formulated by the Press Council of India, a quasi-judicial watchdog organization, stipulating that the identity of victims or attackers should not be mentioned in news reports to prevent further escalation of communal violence. The guidelines were drawn up against the backdrop of India's partition and tense Hindu-Muslim relations that accompanied it. There was no television in those days and until the transistor revolution of the 1970s, even radio was confined to the affluent sections of society. When Gandhi was shot dead on 30 January 1948, the second sentence on state-owned All India Radio's news bulletin was that the killer was not a Muslim.[3] The editor of the bulletin wanted to nip all chances of rumors. The speedy announcement that Gandhi's assailant was not a Muslim prevented attacks against the millions of Muslims who had chosen not to migrate to the new (Islamic) state of Pakistan.

But the ban on naming communities in the news media never really worked. The identity of the victims and attackers was all too evident when news reports used euphemistic phrases such as "members of a particular community" or "members of the minority community" (meaning Muslims) or "members of the majority community" (meaning Hindus). For decades, both the privately owned press and the government-controlled electronic media adhered to the guidelines. Varadarajan (1999, pp. 160-229) argued that the convention of not identifying communities "works to increase the sense of suspicion and anxiety amongst ordinary citizens not just in riot-affected areas but also elsewhere in the country . . . people tend to assume that the victims are 'their own' while their attackers are 'the other.'"

But while covering Gujarat 2002, television journalists openly identified the attackers and victims in their voice-overs as the footage showed graphic images of violence. As Phillip (2002) observed:

> When the television camera focuses on a riotous mob or its victims, it leaves little to the imagination of the viewers. . . . The ban on naming the communities was a fit case for review, although with the advent of television it has become redundant. Questions also remain whether the guidelines are applicable to the electronic media. . . . (The) argument that the violence in Gujarat would have been worse if the media, particularly electronic, had not aroused public opinion against the killing spree through focused and sustained reporting cannot be dismissed out of hand.

Television coverage of the events made it impossible to adhere to the Press Council guidelines. Television correspondents such as Rajdeep Sardesai and Barkha Dutt of STAR News identified attackers and victims as "Hindus" and "Muslims." However, as Varadarajan (2002b, p. 275) pointed out, it was improper to use "Hindus" to describe for what was basically a politically mobilized mob: "The discourse of communal riots had no room to acknowledge that some Hindus brought together by political or economic motivation to attack Muslims at large cannot really be referred to as "the Hindus" or even as "some Hindus"' (2002, p. 275). Naming the attackers as "Hindus" also concealed the reality that the overwhelming majority of Indians who happen to be categorized as Hindus—practicing or nonpracticing—have been vociferous in their criticism of the attacks against Muslims.

Referring to the practice of not naming communities, Sardesai observed that "no one is quite sure who initiated this practice, but . . . it does seem a bit like obfuscation, and an attempt to inject a false blandness to the harsh and grim reality of a communal riot. If a shop of a Bohra Muslim has been attacked, should that be disguised by suggesting that a shop belonging to a member of a minority within the minority community was attacked?" (2002a). As Barkha Dutt stated: "Naming the community under siege in Gujarat was moot to the story. In fact it was *the* story, revealing as it did a prejudiced administrative and political system that was happy to just stand by and watch" (2002; emphasis in original). The press also abandoned its earlier restraint: "Newspapers were both sensational and fairly upfront about identifying the communities involved" (Ninan, 2002). Some newspapers published from other parts of India adhered to the guidelines, but many, including the English-language *The Asian Age*, named the Muslim victims.

L. K. Advani, deputy prime minister at the time and a leading figure in the Hindutva mobilization, used the U.S. media's coverage of the September 11 attacks to criticize the way the Gujarat events were being reported by the Indian media. He asked the media to draw lessons from the coverage of September 11, which displayed media sensitivity towards victims and their families, and suggested that "sometimes, speaking the truth may not be an act of responsibility" (*The Telegraph*, 2002). He was against the graphic coverage of the violence against the Muslims on the ground that it could inflame passions elsewhere. Advani, a former journalist, recalled the practice of not naming communities, and remarked, "But now all that has been flouted" (*ibid.*).

The open identification of communities involved during the Gujarat events sets a precedent for the reporting of Hindu-Muslim clashes in the future. However, such identification is unlikely to be adopted across the news media, mainly because of the deep-rooted convention of not naming the religion of those involved, and because of the criticism—or flak—that the coverage of Gujarat 2002 attracted. Also, the original motivation that led to the Press Council of India formulating the guidelines—to prevent further escalation of violence—remains valid.

Hindutva Flak: Disciplining the Media

Bold and independent coverage by the news media invites flak from leading political actors who are shown in a bad light. Criticizing the BJP and Hindutva forces severely for their role in the Gujarat events got STAR News and English-language newspapers such as *The Times of India* and the *Indian Express* a bad press. As journalists who covered the political activities of the Hindutva forces over the last two decades are well aware, one of methods of disciplining the media is physical violence. When the Babri mosque was being demolished on 6 December 1992, several journalists suffered injuries when they were attacked by *kar sevaks*; many had their cameras broken.

As Herman and Chomsky (1988, p. 26) observed, flak is often used by political elites to discipline the media:

> It (flak) may take the form of letters, telegrams, phone calls, petitions, lawsuits, and other modes of complaint, threat, and punitive action. It may be organized centrally or locally, or it may consist of the entirely independent actions of individuals. If flak is produced on a large scale, or by individuals or groups with substantial resources, it can be both

uncomfortable and costly to the media. . . . If certain kinds of fact, position, or program are thought likely to elicit flak, this prospect can be a
deterrent.

The BJP was in power in Gujarat and New Delhi during the clashes. After
the initial days of violence, when the coverage of the attacks against Muslims
started reflecting badly on the BJP governments, its leaders came down
heavily on journalists. A day after Prime Minister Vajpayee's televised
address to the nation on 3 March, regretting the "disgraceful" violence in
Gujarat, he told a group of concerned citizens that the news media were presenting "exaggerated" accounts of the situation (*The Times of India*, 2002a).
    The BJP and the Gujarat government singled out STAR News and
banned cable operators from showing it in the state. Soon, viewers in
Ahmedabad, the state capital and the scene of some of the worst violence,
were met with blank television screens. Other channels were also banned,
including two local channels in Surat, MY TV and Channel Surat. In Rajkot,
the police banned the publication of special supplements of three Gujarati
dailies. Cable operators received calls from local officials in Ahmedabad and
elsewhere to black out STAR News, Zee News, CNN, and Aaj Tak (*The
Times of India*, 2002b). Dossiers and "hitlists" on journalists were reportedly prepared while "those channels and newspapers who are critical of the
chief minister are not invited to his press conferences and denied the basic
right to information by the state apparatus" (Sardesai, 2004).
    The main complaint of the BJP and its allies was that the news media did
not criticize those responsible for the Godhra train tragedy in which kar
sevaks were the victims. This, however, was less than true, because every
channel and newspaper had covered the Godhra tragedy extensively, but fol-
low-ups on subsequent days were overtaken by the Union budget on 28
February and the retaliation unleashed on Muslims in Ahmedabad and other
parts of Gujarat. Another complaint was that the news media "inflamed
communal passions" by providing graphic television coverage of the events.
Journalists and others critical of the attacks against Muslims countered this
by saying that the level of violence would have been much worse if the news
media had not sounded the alarm through graphic coverage.
    The BJP and its allies also used the technique of branding to discipline
the media. Journalists who criticized the attacks on Muslims were dubbed as
the "Marxist-Mullah combine" and the "secular Taliban." A group of angry
Hindutva supporters told members of the Editors Guild of India who visited Gujarat to inquire into the media side of the events that news channels and
the English-language national press had defamed the Hindu community with
one-sided coverage: "They only listen to Muslims and ignore the Hindus,"
the team was told (Patel, Padgaonkar, & Verghese, 2002). Sardesai (2002a)
pointed out the predicament faced by journalists while covering the events:

(If) any reporter, whether print or television, sees large-scale violence being committed, is the journalist to ignore the hard reality and merely present the facts as seen through government binoculars? If the chief minister says that the situation is returning to normal even while reports are streaming in of continuing violence in several parts of the state, are not the lies to be exposed? And if the government insists that the army is out on the street when the fact is that the army has been kept on stand-by and is waiting for transport trucks, whose version is to be broadcast?

In India, the state has been the biggest source of news, and journalists routinely use information disseminated by officials. But, as Sardesai pointed out, the situation becomes unclear for journalists when the government, with its vast powers, is itself openly seen to be on the side of the mob. The government used its formidable powers to discipline the critical news media by a variety of methods: outright banning of news channels or publications; withholding access to information and advertisements; and severe criticism. Dominant political forces may also distribute largesse and heap praise on journalists and news outlets perceived to be favorable to their interests. Gujarat chief minister Modi applauded *Sandesh*, the Gujarati-language newspaper that had published several rumors and false reports with a pro-nounced anti-Muslim and pro-Hindutva bias. In a letter to the newspaper's editor, Modi wrote:

The newspapers of the state played a decisive role as a link between the people and the government. You have served the humanity in a big way. . . . It is the state government's primary duty to restore peace, security and communal harmony when violence takes place. . . . The timely measures taken by the government turned out to be effective and nor-malcy was returned within a short period. It is noteworthy that the newspapers of Gujarat gave their full support to the state government in undertaking this difficult task. I am happy to note that your newspa-per exercised restraint during the communal disturbances in the wake of the Godhra incident. I am grateful to you. (cited in Varadarajan, 2002b, p. 286)

Modi, who once took a course in New York on media management, is considered one of the most media-savvy politicians in India. However, he turned selective in providing access and information to journalists and refused to interact with journalists from the English-language press. The accreditation of local journalists critical of his politics was not renewed, and he made it difficult for journalists to access centers of information such as the legislative assembly. He refused to meet the press and also instruct-ed his ministers not to meet journalists unless he permitted them to do so.

Several local newspapers faced reduced advertising support from the government, while some had court cases slapped against them. A senior Gujarat police official told an Ahmedabad-based journalist of the *Indian Express*: "Darshan, you are blacklisted" (Desai, 2004, p. 228). Journalists of the English-language press were dubbed as members of the "secular Taliban."

Faced with the concerted campaign of criticism, Sardesai, one of the key targets of Hindutva forces for his coverage of Gujarat 2002, admitted: "The sheer viciousness of the campaign has pushed the media on the defensive.... The messenger has been shot again" (2002a).

Objectivity and Bias in the Press

The graphic coverage by television channels hit the headlines, but the nature of the press coverage also made news. The team of the Editors Guild of India met several editors, journalists, chief minister Modi, and others and concluded that the English-language national press and sections of the Gujarati media, barring notable offenders, played an exemplary role. The charge of the BJP and its allies that graphic coverage by the news media was a major aggravating factor in the situation, the team concluded, was "specious, self-serving and must be dismissed" (Patel et al., 2002). The team observed:

> (Our) finding is that the prompt and extensive portrayal by sections of the local press and national media of the untold horrors visited on innocent people in the wake of the Godhra carnage was a saving grace. The exposure of the supine if not complicit attitude of the State and manifest outpourings of communal hatred, stirred the conscience of the nation, compelled remedial action, howsoever defensively and belatedly.... However, the role of sections of the Gujarati media, especially the *Gujarat Samachar* and more notably *Sandesh*, was provocative, irresponsible and blatantly violative of all accepted norms of media ethics. This cannot be lightly passed over.

Being the largest selling dailies in the state, coverage by the *Gujarat Samachar* (Gujarat News, circulation 810,000) and *Sandesh* (Message, circulation 705,000) had considerable impact. The editors' team found several instances of distorted and false reporting in the two dailies, but the team also found that because of *Sandesh*'s pro-Hindutva stand, its circulation rose by 150,000 copies. A study of the *Sandesh* coverage found that when Muslims were at fault, names were mentioned and perpetrators clearly identified. But when Muslims were victims of murderers, arsonists, looters, and so forth, the attackers remained unnamed. The study concluded: "No sources were quoted for headlines, even when they were simply lifted from speeches by VHP leaders. Headlines were also misleading, and often followed up by reports that did not substantiate, and even negated the headlines completely. . . . The anti-minority stand was obvious in the slant in news reporting" (PUCL, 2002).

Sandesh used headlines to "provoke, communalize and terrorise people" (PUCL, 2002). On 28 February, the main headline read: "70 Hindus Burnt Alive in Godhra." Another report on the front page said: "Avenge Blood with Blood," which was actually a quote from a statement issued by a VHP leader, but the newspaper simply used the words as a headline. On 6 March, the headline was: "Hindus Beware: Haj Pilgrims return with a Deadly Conspiracy," when the fact was that hundreds of terrified Haj pilgrims had returned to Gujarat armed with police escort. The study found that most news reports of the post-Godhra violence in *Sandesh* began with the sentence: "In the continuing spiral of communal rioting that broke out as a reaction to the demonic/barbaric, etc. Godhra incident. . . ." The study observed: "The denunciatory adjectives used liberally to describe the Godhra incident were strikingly absent in reporting the subsequent genocide" (PUCL, 2002).

The study found that the *Gujarat Samachar* also played a role in heightening tensions. But unlike *Sandesh*, it did not devote all its space to "hawkish and inflammatory reportage in the first few weeks, and did carry reports highlighting communal harmony" (PUCL, 2002). *Gujarat Today*, a Gujarati-language daily started by Muslim liberals, was praised for its balanced and restrained reporting of the events.

> The paper was . . . temperate in its language and eschewed shrill and potentially provocative matter. It regularly carried items highlighting interdependence of communities and incidents of help and cooperation extending across community barriers. It investigated incidents and carried detailed information that did not appear in other newspapers. Overall, our analysis suggests that *Gujarat Today* played a responsible and positive role during the violence in the state, for which it deserves to be commended. (PUCL, 2002)

Gujarat Today's sober coverage stood out amid the dominant pro-Hindutva news discourse of the Gujarati-language press. The editors' team interviewed editors of several newspapers, including those of *Gujarat Samachar* and *Sandesh*. In its report, the team mentioned the example of a banner headline in *Sandesh* that the breasts of two Hindu women had been chopped off by mobs during the Godhra incident, a report that was subsequently proved to be false. The newspaper's editor told the team that the information was from the local police. But this was contradicted and the contradiction appeared in the rival *Gujarat Samachar*. The *Sandesh* editor told the team that it was the paper's policy "not to carry corrections and clarifications" (Patel et al., 2002). The Press Council of India subsequently censured both the newspapers "for the infraction of the norms of journalistic conduct" (Prerna, 2003).

The two English-language national newspapers, *The Times of India* and the *Indian Express*, publish editions from Gujarat. A clear divide was evident between the news content of these English-language newspapers and the two Gujarati-language newspapers. Whereas the former was trenchant in its criticism of chief minister Modi, the state government, and the Hindutva forces, the two Gujarati-language dailies espoused the cause of the Hindutva forces. Desai, an Ahmedabad-based correspondent on the *Indian Express*, wrote:

> Today, all the people who once used to look at me with respect question me and abuse me. They do this because I represented a publication whose medium is English and because I reported human misery in its right perspective. . . . A friend said: "All of you from the English language media have tarnished the image of Gujarat." . . . Today, the "common man" in Gujarat hates the English language media. The Gujarati language media hates the English language media. Even a section of the English language media hates the English language media. (Desai, 2004, p. 228)

Journalists' Experience of Covering Gujarat Violence

Journalists, particularly those critical of the Hindutva forces, had been subjected to much criticism, threats, violence and worse over the years. As noted earlier, journalists were attacked by kar sevaks while the Babri mosque was being demolished in Ayodhya. The story was repeated in Gujarat. During a peace meeting organized at Gandhi's Sabarmati Ashram in April 2002, when the level of violence had come down, nearly a dozen journalists were attacked by the police and Hindutva supporters. Sharma (2002) chronicled several such instances:

- Sonal Kellog, a woman reporter of *The Asian Age*, and a male reporter from a Surat-based newspaper, were pounced upon by the police when they went into the Ahmedabad inner city to interview women who had been attacked;
- Raju Chiniwala, a photographer for *Sandesh* in Surat, was caught by a mob. They poured kerosene and petrol on him and were about to set him on fire when a police van came on the scene;
- Bhargav Parikh, news coordinator for *Zee News*, was beaten up by a mob in Ahmedabad while the channel's cameraman, Tejas Gondalia, had his camera smashed and he was beaten up;

- Parish Joshi, photographer for the *Indian Express* in Rajkot, was pushed around by a mob, the roll in his camera removed and his camera smashed;
- Sudhir Vyas of *The Times of India* in Rajkot was beaten up by the police;
- Tanvir Siddiqui, senior reporter for the *Indian Express* and Javed Raja, senior photographer for the newspaper, could not go out to report because anti-Muslim mobs were roaming the streets.

Being a journalist in a conflict zone once lent a degree of immunity to the person. This is no longer the case. In fact, the presence of journalists with their still and television cameras now makes them visible and easy targets. Television journalists enjoy a high profile due to regular appearances on the screen. They are recognized on the streets and, depending on the timing and context, are greeted or derided. Sardesai and Dutt, prominent television journalists for STAR News, stood out for their bold and independent reporting.

They each recounted some of their experiences of covering Gujarat 2002. Sardesai wrote (2002b):

> Amidst the kaleidoscope of images that one has encountered during the Gujarat violence . . . one incident stands out. We had just finished interviewing the Gujarat chief minister at his residence in Gandhinagar shortly before midnight. As we were driving back to Ahmedabad, we were stopped by a mob of around 30 to 40 "trishul" (trident) and lathi (stick)-wielding youth. They asked us our names, our religious identity and wanted to inspect our cameras. We desperately tried to flash our press credentials, but before we could react, one youth climbed on the bonnet of out Tata Sumo and proceeded to smash our windscreen. Claiming that if any one of us belonged to the minority community we would be killed, our identities were closely inspected. Then, after the car's side window was also smashed, we were allowed to leave, but only after we had joined the chorus in chanting "Jai Shri Ram." ("Hail Lord Ram")

Dutt (2002) described the attack even more vividly:

> They came swooping down on us like vultures lunging at a carcass. There were at least 20 of them, faces remarkably indistinguishable. In fact, frenzied though these men may have been on your TV screens, they had an almost robotic, rehearsed air about them as they thrust their gleaming swords into our windshield and barked: "What's your religion?" There was only one answer to that. "Hindu," I said (aware that an articulation of my agnostic beliefs would guarantee the unspeakable),

privately cringing for my cameraperson Ajmal Jami. What would we do if he were asked to produce an identity card? For the rest of the journey we mentally made up false names for him, and avoided addressing him in public.

An educated man stopped our crew on the streets of Vadodara, and excitedly leapt out of his car. "You're doing a good job, madam," he said almost kindly, "but why don't you ask the Muslims of Gujarat to apologise for Godhra?" By this time my patience had run thin. "I agree, sir," I said, trying to sound calm, "but will all the Hindus of Gujarat also say sorry for the 600 Muslims who have been killed?"

"It's not the same," he declared, before stomping off.

Journalists negotiate a minefield of situations while covering conflict. Their own religious and cultural identities are often called into question— even if it is not to their liking. The culture of intolerance of dissent or the mere presence of reporters results in the messenger himself or herself becoming a target of attack.

CONCLUSION

The events of Gujarat 2002 acquire salience when viewed as part of Gujarat chief minister Modi's politics as permanent performance. It was widely dubbed as India's first riot for the satellite TV era, but it was less a riot than a pogrom. The attacks against Muslims were clinically one-sided, much as the 1984 attacks against the Sikhs had been. In the era of satellite television, the news media can help highlight the abuse of power and acts of state complicity in acts of political violence. Journalists face serious questions in such situations: How should they use information provided by the government? How credible is such information when journalists witness a different reality? And what implications do such contours of power geometry have for democracy, citizenship, and multiculturalism?

The coverage of Gujarat 2002 marked a departure in the way the Indian media approached communal clashes. It also highlighted the disjuncture in the news cultures of the English-language news media and the non-English variety. Windmiller (1954, pp. 313-315) observed that "India's English language press is the only national press and it is paramount in the world of Indian journalism," but it is also true that this was one of the many instances when the English-language press' disconnect with the wider Indian realities showed up. It will be incorrect to generalize that the entire English-language press is balanced and impartial, or that the entire non-English language press is biased and one-sided. There are instances of biased reporting in the former and instances of impartial reporting by the latter. But during events of such magnitude, such as the events after the mosque demolition in Ayodhya, influential sections of the non-English language press are known to have provided biased coverage while major sections of the English-language press made efforts to provide critical reporting by covering different versions.

In the era of media proliferation, the importance of the news media has increased, even going by the flak unleashed by dominant political groups. The proliferation of television channels and growing viewership, rising literacy, and the increasing circulation of newspapers indicates that barring notable exceptions of blatant bias, the Indian news media will continue to play the role of a watchdog in the world's largest democracy. Since the early 1990s, there are apprehensions that the news media will not be able to highlight the abuse of power or signify weaknesses in society due to the gnawing march of corporatization (Sonwalkar, 2002). But the bold and independent coverage of Gujarat 2002 provides ground for some hope because Indian journalism's ability to hold the state accountable, when power is abused, has not been obliterated by infotainment—yet.

NOTES

1. Hindutva stands for Hindu-ness but is widely used as a synonym for political Hinduism that seeks to win political power on the basis of India's Hindu majority. Hindutva supporters conflate "Hindu" with "Indian" and seek to build a *de facto* Hindu nation, if not a de jure theocratic state. In the Indian context, such politics is often referred to as "communalism," which refers to the organized politics of hostility and antagonism between members of religious communities—in this case, between Hindus and Muslims.
2. Launched in 1996, Rupert Murdoch's STAR News enjoyed much credibility as its news content was provided until March 2003, by NDTV, a respected Indian production house headed by Prannoy Roy, who had built a reputation on Indian television over a decade covering elections, budgets, and foreign events. After March 2003, the channel set up its own editorial infrastructure.
3. Gandhi was shot dead by Nathuram Godse, a Hindu.

REFERENCES

Chattarji, S. (2004). Media representations of the Kargil war and the Gujarat riots. *Sarai reader: Crisis/media.*

Desai, D. (2004). Massacres and the media: A field reporter looks back on Gujarat 2002. *Sarai reader: Crisis/media.*

Dutt, B. (2002, March 25). Covert riots and the media. *Outlook.*

Hansen, T.B. (2004). Politics as permanent performance: The production of political authority in the locality. In J. Zavos, A. Wyatt, & V. Hewitt (Eds.), *The politics of cultural mobilization in India*. Oxford: Oxford University Press.

Herman, E. & Chomsky, N. (1988). *Manufacturing consent: The political economy of the mass media*. New York: Pantheon.

Nandy, A. (1970). The culture of Indian politics: A stock taking. *Journal of Asian Studies*, *30*(1), 57-79.

Ninan, S. (2002, March 10) Media on the rampage. *The Hindu*.

Patel, A., Padgaonkar, D., & Verghese, B.G. (2002). *Rights and wrongs: Ordeal by fire in the killing fields of Gujarat*. Editors Guild Fact Finding Report; released on 3 May.

Phillip, A.J. (2002, March 13) It wasn't a conventional riot in Gujarat. *Indian Express*.

Prerna, R. (2003, July 1) Press Council slams Gujarati dailies for role in riots. www.rediff.com/news/2003/jul/01guj4.htm?zcc=rl

PUCL. (2002, May). *Violence in Vadodara: A report*. Submitted to the Editors Guild of India by the People's Union of Civil Liberties, Vadodara and Vadodara Shanti Abhiyan.

Rajagopal, A. (2001). *Politics after television: Hindu nationalism and the reshaping of the public in India*. Cambridge: Cambridge University Press.

Sardesai, R. (2002a, March 7). The media did not ransack shops, take lives, Mr Modi. *Indian Express*.

Sardesai, R. (2002b, June 10) When the mob rules. *NDTV.com*. www.ndtv.com/columns/showcolumns.asp?id=812.

Sardesai, R. (2004, January). Drawing the Ram-rekha. *Seminar*, p. 533.

Seib, P. (2002). *The global journalist: News and conscience in a world of conflict*. Oxford: Rowman & Littlefield.

Shah, G. (1998). The BJP's riddle in Gujarat: Caste, factionalism and Hindutva. In C. Jaffrelot & T.B.Hansen (Eds.), *The BJP and compulsions of politics in India*. Oxford: Oxford University Press.

Sharma, K. (2002, April 9). Gujarat and the freedom of the press. *The Hindu*.

Smith, A. (1980). *The geopolitics of information: How western culture dominates the world*. New York: Oxford University Press.

Sonwalkar, P. (2002). Murdochization of the Indian press: From by-line to bottom-line. *Media, Culture & Society*, *24*(6), 821-834.

Sonwalkar, P. (2004). Out of sight, out of mind? The non-reporting of small wars and insurgencies. In S. Allan & B. Zelizer (Eds.), *Reporting war: Journalism in wartime*. London: Routledge.

Sonwalkar, P. (2005). Banal journalism: The centrality of the "us-them" binary in news discourse. In S. Allan (Ed.), *Journalism: Critical issues*. Maidenhead and New York: Open University Press.

The Telegraph (2002, April 7). BJP builds Bush shield for Modi.

The Times of India (2002a, March 5). Media not playing a constructive role: PM.

The Times of India (2002b, March 2). Gag orders issued against TV news channels.

Varadarajan, S. (1999). The ink link: Communalism and the evasion of politics. In K. N. Panikker (Ed.), *The concerned Indian's guide to communalism*. New Delhi: Viking.

Varadarajan, S. (2002a). Chronicle of a tragedy foretold. In S. Varadarajan (Ed.), *Gujarat: The making of a tragedy*. New Delhi: Penguin.

Varadarajan, S. (2002b). The truth hurts. In S. Varadarajan (Ed.), *Gujarat: The making of a tragedy*. New Delhi: Penguin.

Varshney, A. (2002). *Ethnic conflict and civic life: Hindus and Muslims in India*. Oxford: Oxford University Press.

Windmiller, M. (1954, December). Linguistic regionalism in India. *Pacific Affairs, 27*(4), 291-318.

Chapter 12

Terrorism and the Media

Does the Weapon Matter to the Coverage?

Hillel Nossek[*]

INTRODUCTION

The relationship between the mass media and insurgent terrorism in western democracies has been fiercely debated and researched. September 11, 2001 raised important questions on this subject, and other terrorist threats, like the mailing of envelopes containing anthrax (September 23, 2001 to January 2002), and the discovery of a plot to assemble a "dirty bomb"—a bomb containing radioactive material (June 11, 2002 to June 15, 2002)—further highlighted these questions.

The reciprocal relationship between terrorism and the media is a complex one, and, among other things, it concerns the goals of terrorist organizations and the competition between the large number of rapidly proliferating media. This reciprocity is based on a central, traditional assumption that terrorism needs the exposure and publicity provided by the media in order to communicate its message and place political pressure on the state systems

[*]Thanks are due to my devoted research assistants Ronie Kolker for the data collection and analysis and Tally Gross for her help in updating the literature review.

they fight, pressure that terrorism tries to create by influencing the political agenda and government decisions (Laqueur, 1977; Norris, Kern, & Just, 2003).

Many studies have defined *terrorism* as a symbolic act aimed at influencing political behavior through the radical means of the threat of violence. This definition suggests a view that regards terrorism as an indirect, psychological propaganda strategy directed at a maximal target audience, with the principle aim of creating a climate of fear that disrupts the social order and causes governments to succumb to the terrorists (see Carruthers, 2000; Thornton, 1964, for examples). Crelinsten (1989) has similarly defined terrorism as a "special kind of communication" (p. 313), which combines coercion through violence and persuasion in the form of antigovernment propaganda delivered through terrorism. An act of terrorism allows its perpetrators to exploit the media to communicate with their own organization, a specific (enemy) target audience, and wider audiences, such as the international community.

Nacos (1994) added to this the argument that the media have the function of mediating among the terrorist organizations, their target audiences, and the decision makers (governments). She suggests a model describing acts of terrorism as a calculus of violence whose aim is simply to maximize the audiences exposed to the organization's political messages and goals, through which they can reach and influence decision makers using diverse tactics and strategies. The premise of this model is that terrorism is useless without the drama and "horror pictures" (a "good story") that it delivers to the media. Nacos argues, therefore, that, for example, in local terrorism (i.e., terrorism in the country attacked by the terrorist), what influences the decision makers are the immediate victims, in other words, the media's exposure of their vulnerability. In contrast, she argues that with international terrorism, the terrorist organizations reach far larger and more diversified audiences, achieve far greater exposure for their agenda, and affect far more decision-making factors. She also maintains that terrorist organizations are even more successful when targeting American organizations and individuals because this draws greater international media coverage (in contrast to an attack on a smaller or "weaker" country). She also writes that because of the nature of American politics, political representatives are very attentive to public feelings, so that any attack on the public will inevitably influence decision makers.

Another study, which investigated terrorism as a communication dialogue (Tuman, 2003), defined terrorism as a communication, in other words, a message—not simply murder and violence. This study is based on the encoding/decoding model (Hall, 1980), which described the rhetorical use and impact of symbols. The terrorist is the encoder and the government or public the decoder, and terrorism involves the bi-directional rhetorical communication of a reactive message from the government or public in response to the terrorist organization's message.

However, terrorist attacks are also often framed as acts of violence involving illegitimate, condemnable methods, whose goals are to gain media exposure by stirring political discontent. Whereas war has certain "rules of the game," and similar violence is regarded as legitimate, terrorism is viewed as a breach of those norms because it violates citizens, usually occurs in times of peace, is perpetrated by outlawed groups, and is described as a criminal act as opposed to legitimate warfare (Walzer, 1992).

The discussion of terrorism and the media in the research literature has focused on the illegitimacy of the perpetrators, their goals, their means of achieving their goals, and the type of victim they target (citizens, women, children, indiscriminate, not soldiers). The present chapter, however, seeks to examine a different dimension: the nature and legitimacy of the type of weapons used by terrorist organizations: what is in fact used in a terror attack—the threat of violence or the actual use of violence.

Differentiation between different types of weapons is not new to the discussion of warfare between armies from different countries. If we examine the Geneva Convention (1949), we find clear criteria for determining what constitutes a "permissible" weapon and what is "prohibited." Some weapons are recognized as "legitimate" (rifles, rockets, mines, etc.), whereas others are classed "illegitimate" (phosphorous bombs, chemical weapons etc.) and are mainly mentioned with reference to combatant armies. The discussion of what constitutes "legitimate" weaponry also notes variations in armament legitimacy. One example of this is unconventional weapons (biological, chemical, and radioactive). On the one hand, the international community bans the possession of such weapons while at the same time recognizes that some countries can own this type of weapon and report to the UN Monitoring Committee for Nuclear Armament. On the other hand, international sanctions have been imposed on some countries for possessing such weapons and failing to report them (Iran for example), and in other cases (Iraq) war has resulted.

The discussion is even more intense regarding terrorist organizations and unconventional weapons because these are illegal organizations, using illegal means to sow death and destruction. Moreover, it seems that in recent years, mostly after September 11, which led to the "war on terror," there has been increasing fear of a terrorist organization gaining control of unconventional weapons, in other words, weapons of mass destruction, and actually using them.

Moreover, beside the fear of terrorist organizations using unconventional weapons, there is anxiety that they will deploy other means, namely, objects not created as weapons originally, such as transportation: aircraft, buses, and so on. The term given to these is "non-weapons." These are contrasted with weapons originally designed and produced for combat purposes, to be used by a country's legitimate army to cause injury and death and protect its citizens against violent attack inside the country or defend them against attack from an enemy from outside.

The question is whether the mass media coverage of terrorist organizations and their activities differs depending on which kind of weapon is used by the terrorist organization. In other words, does the use or threatened use of unconventional weapons, or the use of instruments not originally created to kill and injure people, affect media coverage and produce an entirely different type of coverage to that observed when terrorists deploy conventional weapons? Moreover, if the coverage is indeed different, what are the implications in terms of the terrorist organization's use of the media to achieve their aims? How do different types of coverage affect government handling of terrorist threats and the use of non-weapons or weapons classed as unconventional weapons? How do the different types of coverage affect the audiences? And what are the implications of the above in terms of the media and media function when covering terrorist incidents involving non-weapons or unconventional weapons, compared with past coverage of acts where conventional weapons were used and when considering the possible future use of such weapons?

To determine whether media coverage changes when different types of weapons are used and whether the different types of coverage have a different effect depending on whether the weapon is conventional or unconventional, we first require an operational definition of *political terrorism* to help differentiate between different acts of violence. For this, I propose Wilkinson's (2000) empirical definition of terrorism: ". . . It (terrorism) is used to create and exploit a climate of fear among a wider target group than the immediate victims of the violence, and to publicize a cause . . ." (p. 12). This definition is very similar to the one I already used in a previous study, based on Wardlaw (1982) and the official CIA definition of political terrorism (Nossek, 1990).

Second, we need to define *conventional terrorism, unconventional terrorism* and the *uses of non-weapons for terrorism.*

1. Conventional terrorism ("old school" terrorism, Schwartz & Falk, 2003, p. 1) involves political violence with a physical threat using light weapons, hijacking, or suicide bombing to provoke a government response. The principle underlying this weapon is that it is legitimate to use a weapon that was designed to kill.
2. Unconventional terrorism ("postmodern or mega-terrorism," Littleton, 1995; Schwartz & Falk, 2003, p. 1), on the other hand, involves the use or threat of using nuclear, biological, or chemical weapons with the intention of causing mass destruction and max-

imizing the number of fatalities. Indeed, there is a significant relative advantage to unconventional terrorism because its very capacity to inflict horrendous damage and a colossal number of deaths allows it command of the local and international media and brings great attention-drawing power (Ganor, 1998; Schwartz & Falk, 2003).

3. A "non-weapon" is something not originally produced as a weapon, that is, not originally designed to cause death or destruction, but whose traditional use and functions are suddenly used in warfare. The non-weapon takes something out of its usual context and uses it in a new way, which transforms it into a weapon for killing nonmilitary individuals and destroying nonmilitary property. Thus, for example, prior to 9/11, civil aircrafts were not considered to be weapons, apart from cases of hijacking and hostage negotiations, in which the weapons are the instrument that the terrorists use to take control of an aircraft crew and passengers.

A non-weapon is used at a specific time for a specific purpose, after which, even though it was used as a weapon, it reverts to its original qualities and functions. Returning once more to the aircraft example, after 9/11, civil aircraft eventually resumed being perceived as a means of transport, not as weapons. In other words, the public fear of this weapon had passed. Aircraft returned to being seen and used as aircraft and ceased to be a cause of public anxiety, beyond the normal fears of hijacking associated with any form of transport. To prevent a recurrence of the use of a non-weapon as a tool for a terrorist attack, defensive security measures are taken by the state: aircraft security on land and in the air, security for sailing vessels, buses, and trains, and so on.

However, these definitions seem most relevant to strategic studies and approaches, and I would therefore like to suggest a definition that concerns the field of communication. It seems that the fundamental difference between conventional and unconventional terrorism relates to the characteristics of the threat. In the case of conventional weapons and non-weapons, the threat is immediate, the terror is an aftereffect, and the fears of similar threats may be managed and controlled by the potential victim. Life can resume and fears can be set aside — at least for a while — until the next attack.

In contrast, the threat and terror surrounding unconventional weapons, such as radioactive, biological, or chemical weapons, gives rise to ongoing, ubiquitous fear and a high sense of personal threat, a sense that "something could easily happen to me."

For a while, it seemed that American perceptions of terrorism changed after 9/11, and concern was growing over the threat from terrorism (The Pew Research Center for the People and the Press, 2001). Americans began to feel an ominous and pervasive sense that terrorism could strike anyone, anywhere. This became sufficiently grave that citizens were willing to forgo their constitutional rights (Norris, Kent, & Just, 2003) following increased terrorist alerts and heightened public fear (Hewit, 1992). In time, the threat perceived after 9/11 seemed to match the conventional terrorism frame, as the use of non-weapons (aircraft) seemed more like the use of conventional weapons than unconventional ones.

To understand how the type of weapon can affect the type of coverage and explore the impact of different types of coverage on the various actors (terrorists, government, public, and media), we must first examine some of the relevant theoretical approaches and empirical studies on this subject.

DIFFERENT APPROACHES TO STUDYING THE RECIPROCAL RELATIONS BETWEEN TERRORISM AND THE MEDIA

The literature on the relationship between the mass media and terrorism tries to answer this question and can broadly be divided into three main approaches: the Classical approach, the Critical approach, and the Functional-Professional approach. Theorists and researchers, journalists, governments, and politicians have used all three.

The *Classical approach* considers the media part of the problem and promotes media control. Proponents of this approach usually blame the media for encouraging terrorism and occasionally being at least one, if not *the,* source of terrorism (Laqueur, 1977). This approach conceives of the state and democracy as a value with rules and behavioral norms, whereas the actors who use acts of terror for political ends are perceived as striking against democracy and the state. Consequently, this approach sees the media as collaborating with those who attack the state using undemocratic means. The metaphor generally used to describe the relationship between terrorism and the media is "symbiosis" (Carruthers, 2000), meaning that the media benefit from the coverage of terrorist events no less than the terrorists.

According to the Classical approach, the media serve terrorism in three ways: by providing exposure, legitimizing the reasons for terrorism, and providing information regarding the tactics and strategies of different terrorist organizations, allowing terrorists all over the world to learn from each other.

The assumed effect of the spread of terrorism and terrorist tactics is often referred to as "contagion theory" (Dobkin, 1992), or the "contagion effect," as it conceives the media as a "loudspeaker" for terrorism and a fan for its flames by maximizing audiences and drawing attention to terrorist tactics and messages by offering a platform. This corresponds with the argument that if the media did not provide terrorists with a platform terrorism would decline because terrorists could not place their issue on the public agenda or legitimize their behavior (Dowling, 1986; Nacos, 2002).

This approach often castigates the media for being a partner in crime and considers media coverage of terrorism as a "reward" for terrorists. Often, the media is accused of providing "oxygen" for terrorists, because without it, the bulletins, posters, photographs, and other publicity would fail to reach large audiences and only reach limited audiences, who share the terrorists ideas (Carruthers, 2000; Jenkins, 1975). Moreover, the constant exposure for terrorist attacks sustains the threat on the "back burner," which serves terrorist interests (Alexander, 1979).

Jenkins (1988) argued even more radically that terrorism does not need the deaths of many at all, just a large audience, which only needs to witness one victim and destruction to be affected.

There is another side to this reciprocity however. Tuman (2003) suggested that terrorism-media symbiosis is reflected in the dependence and benefit that each gains from the other: where audiences are maximized and terrorist messages are communicated maximally both at the same time. Thus, like others before, Tuman argued that the media message has the power to grant terrorists legitimacy, though by the same token, the message can also reduce public sympathy toward their cause. Carruthers (2000) responded to this by arguing that it makes no difference to terrorists whether coverage is hostile or sympathetic, because the sole aim is exposure. Moreover, he contends, coverage cannot possibly be hostile, because terrorism undergoes a process of glorification via the media.

Nacos (2002) argued that the media covers terrorist attacks relating to conflict, while sensationalizing, dramatizing, and sowing fear in the public. Such framing not only allows terrorists to achieve their goals but also causes citizens to prematurely view terrorist attacks as "important" and a matter of public interest, and increases the amount of public exposure achieved by the terrorist organizations. Nacos also maintained that the "success" in gaining exposure for themselves, spreading the message of public terror, and communicating their political message encourages terrorists to continue their attacks.

Schlesinger (1981) summarized the Classical approach by defining the media as the willing victims of the terrorist organizations by virtue of their symbiotic connection and the mutual benefit that media coverage brings. According to this view, the main beneficiaries of media coverage of terrorism are the terrorists, but it is the media too that is willing to be "raped" by those responsible for the terrorist attacks.

In the same vein, Weimann (Weimann, 1992; Weimann & Winn, 1994) added that the media often bolsters the terrorists' image. This is evident in the rationalization of terrorist organizations, when newspaper reporters, commentators, and even the terrorists themselves in interviews portray terrorism as having "genuine" political, social, or cultural motives, and when this rationalization has the power to generate sympathy and identification for terrorist organizations. Weimann also argued that terrorists are described using many different labels, from murderers to freedom fighters, and that many of the labels encourage positive attitudes and interpretations. For example, the image of the terrorist as the underdog, the image of "the few against the many," and fighters willing to die for their cause who strive against powerful governments and armies.

The Critical approach tends to blame governments for using the media coverage of terrorist attacks to consolidate power. Media-amplified panic, it is argued, actually serves government aims. This approach maintains that the excessive coverage of terrorist attacks benefits mainly the government and/or the ruling elite. Most reports on terrorist attacks rely on information and commentary from official government sources, professional experts, and military personnel, with no confirmation of the report's reliability or veracity, and are couched in terms that encourage support for political figures and present the government's political agenda (Herman & Chomsky, 1988). Such coverage becomes more extreme and takes more space following attacks in locations preventing free media access, or where the only access is through military or political spokespersons as in the Falklands War (The Glasgow University Media Group, 1985), the Gulf War (Greenberg & Gantz, 1993), the war in Afghanistan, and the war in Iraq, or when a future terrorist attack threatens. Even newspapers that would like to criticize the government are afraid of being perceived as supporting terrorism and helping it gain media exposure and therefore "prefer" the government position to objective and critical reporting (Viera, 1991).

This critical-radical approach further argues that in western democracies the media are simply government-controlled devices, and this can be seen from the way western media accept government definitions of terrorism that see it as a threat to the peace of the state and public order and an irrational act and unjustifiable violence. These definitions imply that the government is only responding to terrorist attacks to defend its citizens. According to this approach, the terms "terror" and "terrorism" further government entrenchment and strengthen the government position by creating a climate of fear that facilitates government control over the public agenda (Chomsky & Herman, 1979). The approach criticizes the media for ignoring acts of violence by the state that seek to sow terror in the public mind so that people will obey and overlook government actions that violate their rights and weaken their ability to criticize government measures. In a study following September 11, which examined the media discourse on the subject of government policies in the "war on terror," Chomsky (2002) found that the media failed to question American operations in Afghanistan (use of smart bombs within civilian populations); in other words, there was no criticism as such of the government. The media acquired most of its information from official government sources (government officials) and coupled with this complete lack of criticism there was a loud call for meaningful "and strong" action against terrorism.

Thus, the media's behavior regarding terrorism, reflecting the public's fear and panic, simply strengthens the position and power of the government. According to this approach, the main, if not sole beneficiary of excessive media coverage of terrorist attacks are the government and government agencies involved in preventing and foiling terrorism.

The Functional-Professional approach tends to see matters more from the point of view of the media and academics studying the sociological aspect of the issues involved. For example, Kelly and Mitchel (1984) found that only terrorist attacks considered newsworthy received media coverage. They also claimed that the media covers terrorism superficially. This may be inferred from the lack of coverage of the reasons for terrorism and the fact that no substantial background is offered on the subject. Instead, there is a media preoccupation with the actual act of terrorism, its drama and sensation, and a complete lacuna regarding the important underlying issues. Moreover, the media disregard some terrorist attacks entirely because they do not supply the necessary drama and are, therefore, not deemed newsworthy.

According to a study of printed and electronic media, that analyzed what makes a terrorist attack "newsworthy" (Weimann & Brosius, 1991), the criteria for whether an attack "gets in" to a news report is the number of deaths, the type of attack, the identity of the perpetrators, and how much responsibility is ascribed to the actors (terrorists and government). In terms of the number of deaths, over the years the media has to all practical intent established a fatality threshold for drawing attention to attacks and "earning" the right to exposure.

These ways of covering events are a consequence of the media's role and the professional criteria applied to reporting and attack or the threat of attack by media professionals. Thus, in some cases, the media works to the benefit of terrorist organizations, but other times, it can completely ignore it (Crelinsten, 1989). Wardlaw (1982) claimed that often the media cannot ignore terrorist attacks as they are "prepackaged" for consumption; in other words, they are the kind of dramatic events that guarantee high ratings and are often targeted at peak viewing hours.

Thus, although terrorists endeavor to channel the media to their purposes, according to this approach, the media have different criteria so that terrorist organizations cannot "exploit" them. Accordingly, the real beneficiary of coverage is the public and not the terrorist or government because what matters to the newspapers and the media systems is their public responsibility toward their audiences and providing controlled information in a professional fashion, which prevents terrorists and government from inappropriately benefitting.

The Functional-Professional approach may provide a theoretical framework and further our investigation of the media and how it functions; it can help us gain theoretical and practical insights without ignoring the contribution of other approaches, particularly the Critical approach, to understanding the media's role in democracies, especially at times of crisis resulting from different kinds of political violence.

In this context we can examine the implications of media coverage of terrorism on the various "actors": the actual terrorists, the governments, the public, and the media.

The Terrorists

Terrorist organizations have several psychological goals that are served by media coverage: (a) emphasizing the power of the terrorist organization, (b) exposing the vulnerability of the authorities it is fighting, (c) boosting the morale of the organizations' supporters, (d) garnering sympathy and support, (5) emphasizing that violence is essential, and (e) sowing fear, whipping up anger, and so on (Gerrits, 1992). Essentially, terrorist organizations see media coverage as having two main uses:

1. Media coverage intensifies panic and helps terrorists to reach their political or social goals (Alexander, 1981; Laqueur, 1976). We should ask here whether terrorists who threaten to deploy weapons of mass destruction need the media *more* than terrorists who use conventional weapons.
2. Terrorists are usually denied access to the media because they are outlawed organizations or enemies of the state. In this sense, terrorist organizations are similar to any challengers to the regime who choose to wage unconventional war in order to gain back door entry to the media stage (Wolfsfeld, 1997).

Terrorist organizations have a range of communication strategies at their disposal: choosing the optimal time and place to attack in terms of publicity, issuing statements and communiqués, presenting their story without outside interference, maintaining constant contact with journalists and inviting interviews, claiming responsibility for attacks after they occur, and using symbols to convey messages, for example, by targeting a specific individual in order to illustrate the organization's goals (Gerrits, 1992). A good example of terrorist use of a location with symbolic significance was the attack on Israeli athletes at the 1972 Munich Olympics (Nossek, 1990).

Regarding unconventional weapons, many of the above strategies are unnecessary to gain access to the media, sow panic, and so on. The threat of unconventional weapons appears sufficient. Naturally, other factors such as a symbolic location or victim can enhance efficacy, although they are not always critical to achieving terrorist goals.

Governments and Decision Makers

There are a variety of patterns of control of the media's coverage of "traditional" terrorism (Hocking, 1992). For example, Carruthers (2000) identified two important models, the American and the British model, which differ chiefly with regard to the media restrictions on coverage for terrorist acts with conventional weapons. Media control would be no less relevant in cases involving the use of unconventional terrorism.

Regarding government anti-terrorist measures, these would involve media self-regulation in order to prevent valuable information from reaching the terrorists, while at the same time recommending a certain amount of coverage of the terrorists and their actions as a source of government intelligence (e.g., hostage situations).

We can assume that in the case of an unconventional terrorist attack or unconventional terrorist threat, the main media coverage would be based on reports and commentaries by government officials, and professional and military experts (Herman & Chomsky, 1988).

The Public

Naturally, when discussing the public, we first must identify which audience the terrorist wants to address. However, for the purposes of this discussion, the focus is on the audience of viewers and readers of the media covering the threat, in other words, the terrorists' target audience.

According to Hewit (1992), different factors affect media impact on the public's view of terrorism. It is possible to reduce the impact of media coverage if the audience knows more about the organization and its activities. This argument is consistent with Media Dependency Theory (Defleur & Ball-Rokeach, 1989), which maintains that the less direct experienced (geographical distance) and knowledge (cultural distance) an audience is regarding an event, the more important the media's role and the greater its influence. This assumption can also be applied to terrorism and its causes. We can therefore speculate that because of the uncertain implications of the threatened use of unconventional weapons and the sense that everyone is a potential victim, the panic generated will be far greater than the panic generated by the threat or even the actual use of conventional weapons. In the former case, the media's coverage of the terrorist threat is far more crucial than the act.

We can assume that in the case of conventional terrorism, the coverage would typically have a finite danger frame, in other words, the terrorist attack would have already happened, and be over, and therefore the probability of everyone being a potential victim is low; it is therefore presented as arbitrary/coincidental and minor, like a traffic accident. Conversely, we may suppose that in the case of an attack, or where unconventional terrorism is threatened, media coverage will be characterized by an infinite danger frame with a high probability of everyone being a potential victim.

Based on these definitions, the coverage of 9/11 fits into a "normal" conventional terrorist frame despite the huge number of victims and vast physical damage. Thus, the relationships between the "actors" has not changed.

I also suggest that regarding the threat to use unconventional weapons, the Classical approach will claim that the media covers terrorism for rating purposes, and we should prevent terrorists from gaining media exposure of their threats to use unconventional weapons because lack of coverage will diminish their attacks.

For their part, Critical approach proponents argue that the government wants the threat to gain extensive publicity, not because of its responsibility for preparing the public, but for its own interest in furthering its power over the citizens and sanctioning additional abuse of citizens and general human rights. According to this approach, the media should criticize government information and actions, otherwise it is not fulfilling its main role as the flag bearers of human rights and the control over abuse of power. This I claim is the paradox of this approach: if the media criticizes the government on professional matters, revealing the vulnerability of the country's public defense against the threat, then the terrorist organizations have "won" because the threat will be perceived as greater, thus aggravating the climate of public apprehension and alarm.

In contrast, according to the Functional-Professional approach, the media should inform the public responsibly about the reality of the threat while suspending its critical "watch dog" role.

The Media

According to the Classical approach, the media should deny coverage to the terrorists and down play their actions. However, in cases of the threat to use unconventional weapons, would the proponents of this approach still argue to deny media coverage to terrorists? Would that be prudent given that the terrorists might escalate their attacks to exact the desired coverage? What criteria do proponents of this approach believe the media should apply when deciding when and what to cover?

The Critical approach argues that the media is controlled by the government, or at least by the hegemonic elite, and that because they can exploit panic to their own advantage, the media will continue to cover both threats and attacks until the government, the elite, or the media system (but preferably all three) are changed.

Proponents of the Functional-Professional approach, as it is also known, and journalists all recommend that terrorists should be granted controlled access to the media to enable them to vent their anger. According to this view, the media's power to inform the public regarding terrorist groups and threats and monitor government actions is part of its duty of safeguarding the public interest.

The Functional-Professional approach also calls for media self-regulation and expects journalists and editors to demonstrate social responsibility (Nossek, 1985). According to this approach, because of the "novelty factor," the use of unconventional weapons receives far more coverage than the already much-covered terrorism to which the public and the media have grown accustomed. The newsworthiness of this newly emerged form of terrorism makes it more attractive to terrorist groups, which can be reduced by preparing the public well before anything happens, thus robbing it of its novelty.

RESEARCH ON SEPTEMBER 11 AND THE ANTHRAX SCARE

In the summary of the collection of research articles on September 11 edited by Greenberg (Greenberg, 2002), Greenberg and Hofschire (2002) indicated several issues emerging from the collection. The main issue was the role of television and interpersonal communication in creating a forum for public response and helping the public to cope with fears. As for the coverage of the event, the research found that it dealt mostly with what happened and did not analyze why it happened. The comparison of their findings with the literature review of previous events presented in an earlier section of this chapter shows very clearly, in my view, that the coverage and response to September 11 followed the same pattern as the coverage of previous terrorist attacks on the United States and other Western democracies.

Schudson (2002) suggested that when faced with a public threat, reporters exchange their objective professional norms for neighborly reassurance, seeking ways to express the feelings of society as a whole (and which journalists share as members of the public). This is accompanied by efforts to provide practical information on how to cope with the crisis. Furthermore, the press sets impartial professional values aside when national security is threatened or catastrophe strikes. September 11 was, in fact, a combination of a threat to the public, a threat to national security, and a catastrophe, and therefore, Schudson argues, the patriotic tenor of the coverage is understandable. Carey (2002), too, described the American TV networks' patriotic coverage of the tragedy, and their efforts to establish a forum for collective national grief. According to Dooley and Corman (2002), if we examine the coverage of the 9/11 attacks, we find a media discourse on the subject of fear and threat. Dooley and Corman applied CRA methodology to a qualitative content analysis of Reuter news items for the 66 days from September 11 to November 15, 2001.

Waisbord (2002) saw a link between patriotism as a functional tool for coping with the threat. He has maintained that patriotism provides both an analytical framework for understanding the threat and a way of coping with it. This is achieved by making the threat understandable and thus defensible.

With reference to the anthrax scare Waisbord claims that U.S. coverage expressed the idea that perceptions of the risk reflected society's perception of the social distribution of the risk (who is vulnerable and why), and responsibility for it (who is responsible), and denotes a conflict between ideologies of risk. According to Waisbord, the media serves as the link between the public and the risk and the objective and subjective perception of the risk. Waisbord concluded that the "nation under threat" narrative after September 11 was further reinforced by the coverage of the bioterrorism threat. He maintains that this illustrates the shortcomings of a patriotic press under circumstances of this nature, the chief drawback being an inability to present the risk with caution without spilling over into panic. Waisbord identifies two themes in the anthrax scare coverage: the first was the public health theme (the social distribution of the risk), the second was the identity of the group responsible for the attacks (responsibility for risk). Waisbord believes that as with conventional terrorism, bioterrorism only gained news value when it became reality.

In contrast to Waisbord, I would like to suggest that the threat of unconventional weapons is newsworthy in itself, and thus from the terrorist's standpoint, there is no need to implement the threat as it contains no added value.

With reference to the distinctions made between the different types of weapons in the introduction and the different conceptualizations of the reciprocity between terrorism and the media, the question arises, what are the similarities and differences in media coverage of terrorist attacks using the different types of weapons?

This chapter hypothesizes that terrorism using non-weapons will attract the same sort of coverage as attacks with conventional weapons; in other words, events that have high news value. This type and amount of coverage will depend on the location and duration of attack, the degree of innovation, the level of drama, and above all the number of victims, and will stress the rapid return to normality and army and government control of the situation. However, a different type of coverage will emerge for attacks using unconventional weapons, especially regarding the threat of such weapons. In this case, the coverage will last longer, the dramatization will relate to what could happen, and it will dwell on the potential risks rather than actual emergencies; it will also focus more on the need for action than the resumption of routine. This is true both when something has already happened—mailing substances defined as unconventional weapons—and when there is a future threat from such a weapon.

Given the predicted difference in coverage, the question as noted is what are the implications of the different characteristics of the coverage of terrorism using or threatening to use unconventional weapons, in terms of how terrorist organizations use the media to achieve their goals? What are the implications of the difference in coverage with reference to how the government uses the media to deal with terrorism using unconventional weapons? Third, what are the implications of the coverage of such acts of terrorism in terms of audience responses, and last, what are the implications for the media's handling of the coverage of terrorism?

METHODOLOGY

To answer this, *The New York Times* coverage of three events was analyzed—the 9/11 attack, the anthrax scare, and the dirty bomb. *The New York Times* coverage of the dirty bomb and anthrax and September 11 stories was chosen for analysis because *The New York Times* is a leader in its field and recognized for journalistic standards and quality and is a role model for professional journalism. With regard to how these stories may have been handled by the popular press, we can speculate that the popular press would have treated the same subject matter less "delicately" than *The New York Times*, which is recognized for its restraint.

The analysis investigates the *Times* portrayal of the four actors, whose behavior and media coverage shows whether the coverage of a terrorist threat involving unconventional weapons is the same or different than the coverage of a threat involving conventional weapons or the use of non-weapons for terrorist attack. In other words, we are trying to discover whether the threat of unconventional weapons changes the focus of media coverage to a focus on the threat of the attack as opposed to the actual attack aftermath. If this is so, and if the threat of unconventional weapons causes media coverage to concentrate on the implications of the threat, then essentially the terrorists have achieved their aims without actually using a weapon.

The chapter examines the sources of information, its presentation, and the main coverage emphasis. The sources are compared in terms of the tone and content of their statements and reveal whether *experts* provide accurate information or influence the public's fears; how *government* statements demonstrate confidence and control, or alarm or confusion; and how *public interviewees* are carefully chosen for statements minimizing the threat and stressing the need "to stay calm." Finally it is shown how *the media*, by doing their job and criticizing the government for an ineffectual response to the threat, may contribute to panic rather than helping calm fears.

The purpose of this analysis is to show whether the coverage of 9/11, in which "non-weapons" were used, showed the same patterns as the coverage of conventional terrorism, or whether unconventional terrorism coverage exhibits different patterns than conventional weapons and non-weapons as well.

To analyze the coverage of three terrorist attacks, a sample of the items published in *The New York Times* between September 23, 2001 and the end of January 2002 about the anthrax scare were selected, as well as all the items published about the dirty bomb between June 11, 2002 and June 15, 2002, the entire coverage. As for the 9/11 coverage, another sample of articles was used from *The New York Times*. These articles were published in the first two weeks following the attack on the Twin Towers (12/9/01-1/10/01).

All articles sampled were from *The New York Times* archive, which is accessible via the newspaper's Web site. Articles were randomly sampled from the news pages, editorials, and letters to the editor, based on order of appearance on the Web site (first articles of each day), on condition that they were at least 600 words long (except letters to the editor).

FINDINGS

Coverage of the Anthrax Scare by *The New York Times*

The anthrax scare received wide coverage over many weeks. A search of the archives on *The New York Times* Web site (www.nytimes.com) revealed over 800 articles, editorials, and letters to the editor on the subject of the anthrax scare, starting with the outbreak of the scare on September 23, 2001, and ending in January 2002. Over 400 articles appeared on the main news pages, mostly in October 2001. Other articles appeared in the health and science columns, local news columns, and others. A wide variety of reporters covered the story, including Tamar Lewin, a journalist who received an envelope with suspect powder herself.

The analysis focuses on articles from the news pages (a sample of 12 articles, mostly written in October, the month when the coverage peaked). Two editorial articles and several letters to the editor were also analyzed.

The analysis reveals three types of information sources:

Experts—physicians, scientists, and researchers from different universities and research institutes (e.g., the American Institute for Contamination Research). Such sources were the most commonly used. In most news items, several sources of this kind were quoted.

The public—many articles contained reactions from "the person in the street"—as witnesses (i.e., people who had encountered the phenomenon or belonged to an at-risk group), or simply interviewees reflecting the general mood, without any special reason for questioning them. This category also included representatives of the media. Media representatives are mentioned under the heading of "Public" because they are not quoted as media experts, but simply as individuals exposed to the threat (it will be recalled that envelopes with anthrax were sent to several media organizations, including *The New York Times*).

Government and senior officials—this refers to various government and FBI spokespersons and to reactions from the president and directors of government departments. Apart from one item quoting the text of a press conference by President Bush, these sources appeared in all other items along with other sources. Note that this category also contains experts in biology, science, and terrorism in official government positions. Such officials were placed in this category as they operate within the administration.

Portrayals of the actors. The public viewpoint in this case is very clearly illustrated by the following quote from an article on how the American public feels:

> . . . "Working in the tallest building in Denver is unsettling," said Chris Kirkland, a legal assistant." **It's like waiting for the other shoe to drop. I feel powerless." Most of the dozens of people interviewed today across the country said much the same.** . . . The nation seemed to be experiencing a collective sense of dread and foreboding. Juanita Guerrero, a property manager for a building in the Chicago Loop, said she had just come off the subway when she saw a capsule on the ground and immediately thought, "Anthrax." (Nieves, 10/13/01, *NY Times*, p. 7; **highlighting mine (H.N.)**

The media were presented as part of the public's response, which seems to indicate *The New York Times'* perspective and role perception. The media were not hesitant about criticizing the government and its response to the use of anthrax. We can see an example of this is an editorial article published in *The New York Times'* Sunday paper, September 23, 2001:

> America has never tried to protect itself from the inside out. The Bush team says this is a different kind of war. The country is hoping the Bush crew won't fall back on conventional thinking. . . . Mr. Bush promised, as his father once did, to draw a line in the sand. But how do you draw a line in a maze? (Dowd, 9/23/01, *NY Times*, p. 17)

In this quotation, the press seems to be doing its job, showing social responsibility, and taking pains to criticize the administration where needed. However, when we analyze the rest of the coverage we see that this is not so. In fact, the media (the newspaper) regards itself as an integral part of the story. With the criticism, we find expressions of anxieties and concerns written in the first person. The best example of this is an article in which the reporter describes what happened when she received an envelope containing suspicious looking powder, and how she felt:

> It looked like baby powder. A cloud of hospital white, sweet-smelling powder rose from the letter—dusting my face, sweater and hands. . . . An anthrax hoax, I thought. . . . **Yet now I was no longer covering a story. I was the story.** . . . What did matter was that this was a relatively inexpensive way to spread maximum terror without having to solve the technical challenges of spreading the disease widely. Whoever did this had spread panic with only a few anthrax spores, or perhaps only baby powder, and the price of a few stamps. (Miller, 10/14/01, *NY Times*, p. 4)

Here is another reaction from a reporter who received an anthrax envelope:

> **"It's like a lottery**, you pull out your numbers and some of them win and some of them lose," **said one writer for The Enquirer.** It could be me. It makes people less likely to go back in the building." (Canedy & Yardley, 10/14/01, *NY Times*, p. 3)

The government position was naturally different. As noted earlier, government officials stressed the ineffectuality of the threat before America's might. President Bush presented the situation as a trial period, as we see from this statement at his press conference:

> We are aggressively pursuing the agents of terror around the world. And we are aggressively strengthening our protections here at home. . . . Your

government is doing everything we can to recover from these attacks and to try to prevent others. We're acting to make planes and airports safer, rebuild New York and the Pentagon. . . . This is a time of testing—this time of testing has revealed the true character of the American people. We're angry at the evil that was done to us, yet patient and just in our response. (Following are excerpts from President Bush's news conference last night, as recorded by *The New York Times*, 10/12/01, p. 4)

Other government officials stressed that the main aim of the scare was to sow panic and voiced both direct and subtle criticism of the media's handling of the affair:

> **"There's a huge fear factor, but when we stop and think about it, the probability of getting exposed is pretty low,"** said Mr. Woods, who is also chairman of the environmental health committee of the American Society of Heating, Refrigerating and Air Conditioning Engineers, which sets standards for the field. (Glantz & Rosenbaum, 10/18/01, *NY Times*, p. 6)

Needless to say, the government received no backing from the *Times* coverage. The *Times* quoted several official sources who, as we saw, attempted to downplay the scale of the threat. There were also comments from official sources that, in fact, the anthrax scare was very limited. However, these were invariably accompanied by references to the threat.

In general, the analysis of The New York Times' coverage supports the assumption that the coverage stressed the threat before anything had happened. This is corroborated by the main story headline. All articles opened with the heading *A NATION CHALLENGED*, underneath which appeared headings such as *"THE DISEASE," "THE PLAGUE," "THE THREAT"* or *"THE FEAR,"* and so on. We find, in fact, that the message concerning the threat contained the following elements:

1. A lack of information and difficulties in identifying the powder

> Articles, experts and reports kept repeating that this was a new type of threat. The lack of information about the use of anthrax as a biological weapon accentuated the sense of menace. Examples appear in numerous articles:

> > Inhalation anthrax, the form of the disease that killed Robert Stevens, a photography editor in South Florida is so rare that very few doctors have ever seen it. . . . **Because there are so few cases of human anthrax,**

and because it would be unethical to deliberately expose people to the
bacteria in tests, little is known about treating people exposed to it.
(Yardley & Canedy, 10/12/01, *NY Times*, p. 9)

**The inability of scientists to answer these questions points up how
little experience they have with the illness.** . . . "If you're investigating
a serial killer, it's very hard to know the pattern of that serial killer after
one or two murders," said Dr. Osterholm, of the University of
Minnesota. (Broad, Engelberg, Miller, & Stolberg, 10/31/01, *NY Times*,
p. 1)

**"We are not going to have a bomb fly out of the sky and land on
somebody so that we can say, 'Look, there's a bomb, and we are all
dying of anthrax,'"** said Asha M. George, who studies biological warfare for the Nunn-Turner Initiative, a nonprofit foundation in
Washington. (Stolberg, 9/30/01, *NY Times*, p. 1)

2. Emphasis on the lack of practical solutions

Various articles discussed alternative solutions. Reports on the prophy-
lactic use of antibiotics and other resources such as gas masks also pointed out their lack of efficacy, presenting anthrax as a threat that cannot be
fought properly. This type of reporting naturally exacerbates public
apprehension regarding the threat.

This vaccine is now given to military personnel, but its effectiveness
against inhaled anthrax has been questioned. (Yardley & Canedy,
10/12/01, *NY Times*, p. 9)

Many New Yorkers—and to a lesser extent, people across the country—are stocking up on Cipro, an antibiotic that they believe can be
used to treat anthrax. . . . **Many doctors and public-health officials say
there is no cause to stock up on Cipro. They point out that neither
Cipro nor any other antibiotic works on botulism, smallpox or
other possible weapons of bio-terrorism.** (Lewin, 9/27/01, *NY Times*,
p. 8)

3. Criticism of the lack of readiness to handle the threat

The newspaper published articles criticizing the government and its
arrangements for dealing with the crisis and highlighted the helplessness
of the agencies supposed to handle such emergencies. Numerous articles
stressed these failings.

> The United States is inadequately prepared to confront bio-terrorist attacks, according to a broad range of health experts and officials. The nation must develop new vaccines and treatments they say. . . . Doctors are poorly trained to recognize symptoms of infection with possible biological weapons, like plague and anthrax, which can resemble the flu. Many of the nation's hospitals lack necessary equipment. . . . In a report issued last week, the General Accounting Office said the government's bio-terrorism planning was so disjointed that the agencies involved could not even agree on which biological agents posed the biggest threat. (Stolberg, 9/30/01, *NY Times*, p. 1)

The actual media companies were also portrayed as ill-prepared for such threats, relating to this on an organization level, and their capacity (or incapacity) to protect their employees:

> Had the Times planned for such an emergency, I would have been isolated from my colleagues and the potentially deadly letter. But like most organizations, we had not conducted drills for a biological or chemical attack. (Stolberg, 10/14/01, *NY Times*, p. 1)

4. Other threatening scenarios

A significant amount of coverage concerned the possibility of future threats. Several articles dwelt in length on the question of biological weapons in general, the possibility of contaminated reservoirs, and so on. The reason for stressing such scenarios was that the current crisis carried implications beyond the immediate story, and the anthrax scare bespoke a new era, or more precisely, a new and different menace.

> Cities and states are reassessing the safety of their drinking water, probing for weaknesses and shoring up defenses in what experts consider the unlikely event of a terrorist attack on water supplies. (Winter & Broad, 10/26/01, *NY Times*, p. 7)

To sum up, the findings revealed that in the case of the anthrax coverage, the media, in this case *The New York Times*, chose to focus on the actual threat and the novelty involved, namely, the unorthodox (unconventional) weapon. All of the points emphasized in the coverage served this end and drove the message home. The criticism of those agencies responsible only stressed and reinforced this message, as if to say, not only is this a totally new kind of threat, but the people who are meant to deal with it are actually powerless.

Coverage of the "Dirty Bomb" Scare
by *The New York Times*

The dirty bomb case study examines a threat that never materialized. The arrest of an American citizen on suspicion of intent and attempt to construct a dirty bomb, a bomb containing radioactive materials, attracted relatively wide coverage, although just for a short time—June 11, 2002 to June 15, 2002. During this period, 18 articles, 4 editorial articles, and 10 letters to the editor were published regarding the dirty bomb. Most of the articles appeared on the main news pages of the "National Desk" column. The headline read **"TRACES OF TERROR"** and was accompanied by headings referring to panic, the bomb, government action, and the ongoing investigation.

Analysis of the coverage revealed three categories of information sources:

> *Senior government representatives and other representatives of the authorities*—the American President, government department directors, senior administration officials, the FBI.
>
> *The public*—this category was divided into two sub-categories: (a) people who shed light on the case, that is, witnesses—neighbors, people acquainted with the suspect as a child, and others, and (b) the general public, whose reactions were quoted to reflect the public mood—for example, a waitress at a local diner.
>
> *Professionals with relevant information*—lawyers involved in the case and experts.

Unlike the anthrax scare, in which the most common sources were non-government experts, in the case of the dirty bomb, the most common sources of information were senior government officials and other representatives of the authorities. Note that with the dirty bomb, details of the threat only became public with an official government press release. This was the main difference between the dirty bomb and the anthrax scare. Whereas in the anthrax case, the threat became public when the envelopes were mailed, giving the government no actual control over the story's publication, the dirty bomb case was completely different. The suspect was arrested before the incident was publicized, and without an official press release, neither the media nor the public would have been any wiser. Thus, with the dirty bomb there was clearly great dependence on official sources for information. Note too that the high profile of the sources did not automatically affect how the threat was presented in the media. In the dirty bomb case, the government position was described clearly, although criticism was also voiced in the coverage. Statements from official sources were criticized, and criticism of official methods counterbalanced official pride at successfully intercepting an attack. As a rule, *The New York Times* criticism showed a responsible media stance: exposing flaws and questioning government measures.

Here are some examples:

> "The dirty bomb is something that is so easy to execute, I could go so far as to say I believe that one person who has done their homework, acting alone today, could do significant damage, certainly more psychological than real," Dr. Anderson said. . . . Others disagreed that it would be easy, citing practical difficulties. (Wald, 6/11/02, *NY Times*, p. 18)

Another example appeared in an article published on June 11, 2002:

> James R. Schlesinger, **the former Secretary of Defense who also served as Director of Central Intelligence during the Nixon administration,** said the prospect that Mr. Padilla was likely to build a dirty bomb was "**not realistic.**"
>
> **But in the new age of terror,** the notion is back of a non-nuclear radiological weapon, one that uses the poisonous **effects of radiation to spread panic and disrupt the economy.** (Tyler, 6/11/02, *NY Times*, p. 1)

The article in which the above appeared also described the public reaction to the case, namely one of great anxiety, which effectively added further support to the qualms voiced by the media.

> Dolly Frock, owner and head waitress at the Idle Hour here, serves up a heap of philosophy as she takes orders for burgers "all the way" from her lunchtime crowd. (Tyler, 6/11/02, *NY Times*, p. 1)
>
> "**The way the world's going today, we don't know what's going to happen,**" she said, slinging a plate of fries . . . "It could be germ warfare. Or they could put something in the water. If you dwell on it, you'd go crazy." . . . Although residents here have lived with nuclear weapons, the arrival of Mr. Padilla **adds an element of uncertainty.** . . . "Those of us in small towns in the South didn't feel as threatened," Mr. Hendrick said. "But now we have to think about it." (Seelye, 6/12/02, *NY Times*, p. 26)

The New York Times coverage of the story revealed several important foci:

1. The political focus

The quoted sources in the editorial articles and the language used all raise questions regarding the government's motive for publicizing the case. For example, an editorial article on June 11, 2002 said:

> For the president, **the drama of the dirty-bomb threat and its successful interdiction also sent a clear warning to those Congressional leaders who are preparing to focus a long political season on how the nation's intelligence-gathering system broke down during Mr. Bush's watch.** (Tyler, 6/11/02, *NY Times*, p. 18)

> Some Democrats and civil liberties advocates **have questioned whether the disclosure was timed to help counter criticism that the authorities,** especially those at the Federal Bureau of Investigation, had mishandled signals that might have uncovered the Sept. 11 plot. (Lewis, 6/12/02, *NY Times*, p. 24)

2. The legal process and the legal steps taken

The New York Times particularly focused on the unusual nature of the arrest and the transfer of the suspect, an American citizen considered a security threat, to a military jail. The paper also queried U.S. readiness and defense capabilities in the face of such bombs. A report on June 11, 2002 wondered:

> There are about two million radiation sources in this country, in the hands of 21,000 licensees, used for purposes that include irradiating cancer patients and checking the thickness of asphalt, according to the Nuclear Regulatory Commission. **There were 107 reports of lost or stolen sources in the six months ending March 31, commission** data show. In recent years the annual rate of reports has been about 375. (Wald, 6/11/02, *NY Times*, p. 18)

An editorial of June 12, 2002 was unequivocal:

> **The government's position is unacceptable.** (Editorial desk, 6/12/02, *NY Times*, p. 28)

3. The threat

The New York Times gave a detailed analysis of the threat of this type of bomb. Besides reporting on the small number of potential victims that it could claim, experts, as well as the language of the report, stressed that the threat, that is, the psychological and economic effect of such a bomb, was real. For example:

> **The psychological damage, though, could be** tremendous, they say, especially with a public confused about the difference between a nuclear bomb, . . . and a radiological weapon. (Wald, 6/11/02, *NY Times*, p. 18)

> A nuclear physicist, Arjun Makhijani, president of the Institute for Energy and Environmental Research, said radioactive materials **for a dirty bomb would be** "difficult to handle, and difficult to disperse radiologically" but could cause "terrible economic damage." . . . The impact would be nothing like a crude nuclear weapon that might kill tens of thousands or hundreds of thousands of people. **But the radioactive material dispersed by the blast could contaminate a large swath of a city, force residents to evacuate, and cost billions of dollars to clean up and additional billions in disrupted economic activity.** (Editorial desk, 6/11/02, *NY Times*, p. 28)

Generally, the first two categories of the coverage focus—the political focus and the focus on the legal process and government measures—reveal a critical stance by the paper. *The New York Times* criticizes government motives for publicizing the incident as purely political and questions government statements. Criticism of the government's handling of the case reinforces the criticism of its motives.

The probing discussion of the political moves, legal process, and legal measures adds to magnitude of the threat, whereas criticism of government actions and motives stresses its certainty: "if the administration is not handling the threat properly, how safe can we be?"

The discussion of the threat focused on two points:

1. *The arrest of an American citizen identified a new situation,* namely the possibility of an American citizen working for a dangerous foe (not spying, but plotting a real attack!). The danger is also from enemies within—not just from the outside.
2. *The dirty bomb—an unconventional weapon*—the threatened use of a radioactive substance against the United States.

> Dirty bombs are not mass killers, they are weapons designed to inspire panic and cause disruption. . . . What makes dirty bombs one of the more worrisome threats is that they would be relatively easy to make from materials that are widely available. (Editorial desk, 6/11/02, *NY Times*, p. 28)

To sum up, in the coverage of the dirty bomb story, *The New York Times* presents the bomb as a new and unknown threat, which although lacking large-scale implications, could not be predicted with any accuracy. The stress on this new class of threat came with a lot of criticism for the administration.

Items on these two stories stress that the affairs are a new departure in terrorism; in one case, the first time an American had been involved in such things, and in the second, an entirely new type of bomb with an unclear potential for harm. In both cases, the message conveyed was that the American people were confronting a new departure, or more precisely—a new menace.

Despite the similarities between the dirty bomb and anthrax stories, both of which concern a terrorist threat from unconventional weapons, they are in fact intrinsically different. With the anthrax envelopes, the envelopes were mailed before the coverage started, in other words, there actually was an attack, which made the danger extremely real. With the dirty bomb, however, the story only came to light and was covered after the attack had been foiled, although the threat was not entirely prevented. However, despite this important difference, the two stories were reported quite similarly. Clearly, if we examine the common elements between the two stories, we will be able to draw a number of inferences regarding the use of unconventional terrorism for propaganda ends and the media's response.

New York Times Coverage of September 11

To reach any conclusions from the analysis of the two incidents, we must compare the findings for unconventional terrorism cases with those of conventional terrorism cases. This is achieved by comparing the summary of the analysis of the coverage of the two terrorist events using unconventional weapons with that of the coverage of 9/11 in *The New York Times*.

A sample of items published in the two week after 9/11 was analyzed including stories, editorials, and letters to the editor. A search in *The New York Times* archives produced 954 items, 21 of which were chosen randomly for the analysis. The findings and comparison are presented in Table 12.1.

Analysis of the comparisons in Table 12.1 for the different actors clearly shows that whereas the coverage of September 11 followed the well-researched pattern of conventional terrorist attacks even though a non-weapon was used, the anthrax and dirty bomb scares show a different pattern for each actor and in the general frame of the coverage. The story sources in the conventional attack were considerably more diversified, especially those involving the public and security forces. The story emphasis also diverged. With 9/11, the emphasis was on calming and assuring the public

TABLE 12.1. Comparison of the Coverage of the Anthrax Envelope and Dirty Bomb Incidents with the Coverage of September 11 in The *New York Times*

	COVERAGE OF THE "DIRTY BOMB" AND THE ANTHRAX SCARE	COVERAGE OF SEPTEMBER 11
INFORMATION SOURCES	Government and senior officials The public Experts	Government and other officials (Intelligence, Senators, FBI, etc.) Experts Witnesses to the incident. NY citizens (parents, children, etc.) Firefighters, doctors, policemen, etc.—rescue forces
MAIN EMPHASIS	Both stories chiefly emphasized the threat. The Dirty Bomb incident mainly emphasized the political context.	Description of the incident and the severity of the disaster. The investigation conducted and U.S. government reactions. Safety concerns and rescue effort. Victims of the tragedy Previous attacks on the U.S.A. (Pearl Harbor, Oklahoma City)
THE GOVERNMENT	Greater emphasis on the threat than on dealing with the threat— intensifies threat and exposes the authorities' helplessness.	Coverage of government actions is watchful and calm. Emphasis on factual coverage in earlier reports and about rescue efforts and the official investigation.
THE MEDIA	Focus on the actual threat and the new factor	Helps to restore calm by reporting on the resumption of routine. Emphasis on grief and loss but also on the strength of the city and its citizens.
THE PUBLIC	Emphasis on fear	Emphasis on the grief and the loss, but also on the strength of the city and its people.

that the government was in control; the coverage also focused on symbols of integration and the fortitude of the city of New York and the American people. There was almost no criticism. Like other media, *The New York Times* took a patriotic stance. Not so with the two acts involving unconventional weapons. Here, the sources were limited, and there was strong criticism of the government for its inadequate response.

As for the other actors, the terrorists, the media and the public, the comparisons reveal a different pattern of coverage. There is no information on the organizations behind the unconventional weapons and their demand, while, in the 9/11 attack we knew quite early who was responsible and what were his aims. This makes the threat of the two unconventional terrorist attacks much more intense than the one with a known enemy that can be fought. As for the government, with September 11, the government voices expressed a relief and desire for revenge, while in the other two cases, the government exacerbated panic by intensifying people's fears. *The New York Times* coverage of September 11 was uncritical of the government and mainly covered the return to routine. In the other two cases, the paper emphasized the threat and the potential dangers threatened by the new weapons. The representation of the public's voices in the coverage of 9/11 focuses on the grief and strength of the city dwellers and their resumption of routine.

DISCUSSION AND CONCLUSION

The discussion follows the framework suggested in the introduction and literature review. We show how the three theoretical perspectives—the Classical, the Critical and the Functional-Professional—explain the findings with reference to all four actors: terrorists, government, media and public. Our main conclusion is that media coverage of terrorist acts involving unconventional weapons differs from the coverage of terrorism with conventional weapons and non-weapons, and that the different coverage effects the interrelations between all the actors and the media. The findings show that in the case of non-weapons, that is in 9/11, the coverage conforms to the known pattern for conventional terrorist attacks rather than creating a new pattern of relations. However, whereas with terrorism involving conventional weapons or non-weapons, the actual act of terrorism opens the channels of communication for the terrorists, the government, and the public, if the threat involves unconventional weapons, it is the threat and the uncertainty regarding the potential damage that opens the channels for the actors. The content of the information flow in the conventional act seeks to downplay fear and terror, whereas in the case of the unconventional threat, the coverage content amplifies fear and terror.

Terrorism is an action or threat to perpetrate an act, a description applicable to both the anthrax envelopes and the dirty bomb. In both the anthrax and dirty bomb stories, *The New York Times* focused more on the actual threat and less on the specific action. This supports Ganor's (1998) suggestion that the power of the unconventional weapon lies in its threat, thus obviating the need to use it. With the dirty bomb, the attack was foiled, whereas in the anthrax case, the threat was partially actualized, and we saw how the coverage focused on the implications of the attacks, future scenarios, and the fears provoked by the threats.

According to the Classical Approach, the terrorists and the media benefit most from the media coverage of conventional terrorism, and the government and public are its victims. Though empirical research has shown that this view is overly simplistic, and that the terrorists and the media are not usually the beneficiaries, and the government and public not generally the losers, in the case of unconventional weapons, the Classical approach may, in fact, provide some accurate predictions: indeed, terrorists are rewarded with coverage without even using their weapons—they just threaten to use them. The media does play an active role in spreading fear (unlike conventional terrorism when it is generally passive); the government does aggravate the country's fears by trying to do its job, and the media, by criticizing the government, plays a critical role in assisting terrorism to intensify public fears. The public, for its part, which at times of conventional terrorism is reassured by the media, when faced with unconventional weapons becomes more uncertain and confused by the coverage than encouraged and emboldened.

According to the Classical Approach, there is no need for terrorists to change their weapons. Whatever they use—conventional weapons, non-weapons, or unconventional weapons—the media is the terrorist's best friend and terrorism is the "hottest" media story. Whatever happens, the media tries to maximize the story for their own use and, therefore, the government and the public should take pains to restrain the media to prevent it assisting terror. The premise of this approach is that in the first place, the media should not provide terrorists with a platform regardless of the level of threat to the public, because no matter what, if it covers terrorism less or if it ceases to cover it at all, the level of terrorism will gradually dwindle until it disappears altogether (Dowling, 1986). Moreover, and in line with the arguments of Tuman (2003), Weimann (1992), and Carruthers (2000), it is immaterial what kind of weapons terrorists use as the very exposure, regardless of the nature of the message (antagonistic or supportive), leads to glorification, legitimization, and rationalization of terrorist organization activities.

In contrast, the Critical Approach contends that the sole beneficiary of extensive media coverage of terrorist attack is the government. The media amplifies the public's fears and the threat and suspends its professional and critical norms when covering terrorist acts. In the name of the war on terror, it enables the government to rally the nation around the flag and curtail civil rights unrestricted by criticism. Although this critique was very applicable in the case of 9/11, it does not explain the coverage of unconventional terrorism. Although the government did utilize public fear, the rally around the flag never took place, and the media, at least *The New York Times*, did criticize the government. By playing their watchdog role, the media aggravated public panic by showing the lack of government readiness and challenging government assurances of nothing to fear from anthrax or the dirty bomb. The public's responses reported in the newspaper accentuated the panic, whereas the public's voices in the conventional case were calming and assuring.

As for the third approach—Functional-Professional—in the case of conventional terrorism it could be argued that the sole beneficiary of the coverage was the public. Regarding unconventional terrorism, it seems paradoxically that by adhering to its professional norms and playing the watchdog role, the media actively contributes to spreading fear and uncertainty and is directly targeted by the terrorists. The media not only covers the facts, but is highly speculative. Paradoxically, one could argue that by doing its job, the media benefits the terrorists and the government, but does not necessarily serve the public good.

Paradoxically, too, even when the media adhere to professional criteria and address the details/facts, they nevertheless help to expose government failures and inadequacies, which as we saw, intensifies public anxiety and furthers terrorists' aims of spreading panic and undermining the social order (Carruthers, 2000; Thornton, 1964). On the other hand, if the media functioned as the Classical Approach would like and worked for the good of the country and democracy by not reporting terror attacks or threats, it would play into the government's hands, fail in its guard-dog duty, possibly cause the spread of unfounded rumors, increase public fears and anxieties, ultimately cause mass panic, and still serve the terrorists' interests.

In the anthrax and dirty bomb cases, the main message was the threat. This was most obvious in the anthrax case, although it is also evident with the dirty bomb. Other points of focus were also linked to the threat (e.g., criticism of the administration). However, whereas the media coverage of conventional terrorist attacks usually provides details of the attack, with the anthrax envelopes *The New York Times* discussed the attack implications, not the details. The fact that the number of potential victims in an unconventional terrorist attack is an unknown quantity makes it hard to predict the impact with any accuracy and relays a message of helplessness before the threat. With both the anthrax and the dirty bomb, criticism of the government response and discussions of the government's position served to reinforce this message.

Regarding these two terrorist events, we find that the media did not conform to the basic hypothesis of the Critical approach (Herman & Chomsky, 1988). It criticized the government and exposed its weakness, and paradoxically benefitted the terrorists by massively reporting and intensifying the threat, which simply fomented panic. This served the terrorist interests of publicizing a political message, which earlier research on the effect of conventional terrorism (Norris, Kern, & Just, 2003) has identified as a prime objective.

This study's findings support the findings of other researchers (Dooley & Corman, 2002; Waisbord, 2002). Its findings show that with the anthrax mailing and the dirty bomb (unconventional terrorism), respectively a partially successful attack and a foiled attack, *The New York Times* coverage was about future threats and implications rather than real damage. This not only showed a change in the public and media attitude toward terrorist attacks, but a change in how terrorists might see their ability to communicate their political message. Whereas, once they harnessed the power of the media and adapted themselves to its requirements (Norris, Kent, & Just, 2003; Wardlaw, 1982), now they see the strength that lies in the terrorist threat (Schwartz & Falk, 2003), and no longer need the act of terrorism itself.

The New York Times treatment of the stories intensified the impact of terrorist act and threat, by aggravating the fear and confusion. This intensification even occurred in the case of the dirty bomb, where nothing happened.

The analysis of media coverage of the threat to use unconventional weapons by terrorist organizations shows that by threatening to use unconventional weapons these organizations can achieve their propaganda aims without actually using the weapon. It seems that the kind of weapon terrorist organizations have in their arsenal does matter. By threatening to use biological/chemical/nuclear weapons, the organizations use a new communication tactics: "propaganda by threats." Conversely, the use of conventional weapons or non-weapons (as in the WTC attack) for terrorism (car bombs, placing bombs in public places, suicide bombers, etc.) represents "propaganda by deeds" (Carruthers, 2000; Crelinsten, 1989; Thornton, 1964).

As discussed in the theoretical review, the aim of terrorism is to sow maximum public panic. Our findings indicate that it is possible to generate significant public fear without actually implementing an act of terrorism (or by carrying out a limited act of terrorism). We have also seen how the terrorist's goal of provoking public panic in the target country is well served by the threat of unconventional weapons, and that the portrayal of the government by the media as helpless before such terror also helps to magnify this message.

As it has for the use of conventional weapons and non-weapons, the Functional-Professional approach also provides a theoretical frame to explain the kind of coverage found in cases involving unconventional weapons. The media's conduct may be explained in terms of story newsworthiness and estimated functional value of the subject matter to the public. When conventional weapons or non-weapon are involved, the media focuses on the event and the need to calm the public, whereas if an unconventional weapon is used or threatened, the media focuses on what will happen in the future and on information it thinks will help the public reach decisions.

The paradox in the Functional-Professional approach that I wish to discuss, is that the threat of unconventional weapons produces the type of coverage identified by the other two approaches. According to the Classical Approach, the type of coverage given helps terrorists to achieve their media goals of generating fear, anxiety, and panic, which as the above mentioned empirical studies point out, are not generated by the coverage of conventional terrorist attacks. Their findings also show that when the media adopt the Professional-Normative approach in their coverage of unconventional terrorist attacks, the Critical approach is also corroborated. This is because the media's coverage promotes public support for government measures to prevent similar events in future, because the media has no other authoritative and reassuring source of information besides the government.

It seems, therefore, that when unconventional weapons are used, if the media wishes to avoid the pitfalls of coverage according to conventional norms they should adopt special "unconventional" norms for such events that would enable them to continue fulfilling their professional functions and demonstrate social responsibility.

REFERENCES

Alexander, Y. (1979). Terrorism, the media and police. In R. Kupperman & D. Trent (Eds.), *Terrorism, threat, reality, response* (pp. 331-348). Stanford: Hoover University Press.

Alexander, Y. (1981). The media and terrorism. In D. Carlton & C. Schaerf (Eds.), *Contemporary terror* (pp. 51-56). London: McMillan Press.

Broad, J., Engelberg, S., Miller, J., & Stolberg, S. G. (2001, October 31). Excruciating lessons in the ways of a disease. *New York Times*, p. 1.

Carey, J. W. (2002). American journalism on, before, and after September 11. In B. Zelizer & S. Allan (Eds.), *Journalism after September 11* (pp. 71-90). London & New York: Routledge.

Canedy, D. & Yardley, J. (2001, October 14). 5 more at Florida office test positive for anthrax. *New York Times*, p. 3.

Carruthers, S. L. (2000). *The media at war*. New York: St. Martin's Press.

Chomsky, N. (2002). *9/11*. New York: Seven Stories Press

Chomsky, N. & Herman, E. (1979). *After the cataclysm: The political economy of human rights* (Vol. 2). Nottingham: Spokesman Books.

Crelinsten, R. D. (1989). Terrorism and the media: Problems, solution and counter-problems. *Political Communication and Persuasion, 6,* 311-339.

Defleur, M. L. & Ball-Rokeach, S. (1989). *Theories of mass communication.* New York: Routledge.

Dobkin, B. (1992). *Tales of terror: Television news and the construction of the terrorist threat.* Westport, CT: Praeger.

Dooley, K. J. & Corman, S. R. (2002). The dynamics of electronic media coverage. In B. S. Greenberg (Ed.), *Communication and terrorism: Public and media responses to 9/11* (pp. 121-136). Cresskill, NJ: Hampton Press.

Dowd, M. (2001, September 23). Liberties: Autumn of fears. *New York Times,* p. 17.

Dowling, H. L. (1986). Terrorism and the media: A rhetorical genre. *Journal of Communication, 36*(1), 12-24.

Editorial Desk. (2002, June 11). After a 'dirty bomb' explodes. *New York Times,* p. 28.

Editorial Desk. (2002, June 12). Dirty bomb and civil rights. *New York Times,* p. 28.

Ganor, B. (1998). *Nonconventional terrorism: Chemical, nuclear, biological.* Retrieved February, 21, 2005, from International Policy Institute for Counter-Terrorism. http://www.ict.org.il/

Gerrits, R. (1992). Terrorists' perspective: Memoirs. In D.L. Paletz & A. P. Schmid (Eds.), *Terrorism and the media* (pp. 29-61). London: Sage.

Glasgow University Media Group. (1985). *News about war and peace.* Milton Keynes & Philadelphia: Open University Press.

Glanz, J. & Rosenbaum, D. E. (2001, October 18). Experts say spores won't spread in ventilation system. *New York Times,* p. 6.

Greenberg, B. S. (Ed.). (2002). *Communication and terrorism: Public and media responses to 9/11.* Cresskill, NJ: Hampton Press.

Greenberg B. S. & Hofschire L. (2002). Summary and discussion. In B.S. Greenberg (Ed.), *Communication and terrorism: Public and media responses to 9/11* (pp. 317-332). Cresskill, NJ: Hampton Press.

Greenberg B. S. & Gantz, W. (Eds.). (1993). *Desert Storm and the mass media.* Cresskill, NJ: Hampton Press.

Hall, S. (1980). Encoding/decoding. In S. Hall, D. Hobson, A. Lowe & P. Willis (Eds.), *Culture, media, language* (pp. 128-138). London: Hutchinson.

Herman, E. & Chomsky, N. (1988). *Manufacturing consent: The political economy of the mass media.* New York: Pantheon.

Hewit, C. (1992). Public's perspectives. In D.L. Paletz & A. P. Schmid (Eds.), *Terrorism and the media* (pp. 170-207). London: Sage.

Hocking, J. J. (1992). Governments' perspectives. In D.L. Paletz & A.P. Schmid (Eds.), *Terrorism and the media* (pp. 86-104). London: Sage.

Jenkins, B. (1975). *International terrorism: A new mode of conflict.* Los Angeles, CA: Crescent Publications.

Jenkins, B. (1988). Future trends in international terrorism. In R. Slater & M. Stohl (Eds.), *Current perspectives on international terrorism.* London: McMillan.

Kelly, M. J. & Mitchell, H. T. (1984). Transnational terrorism and the western elite press. *Political Communication and Persuasion, 1*(3), 269-296.

Laqueur, W. (1976). The futility of terrorism. *Harper's,* 102-106.

Laqueur, W. (1977). *Terrorism.* London: Weidenfeld and Nicolson.

Lewin, J. (2001, September 27). Anthrax scare prompts run on an antibiotic. *New York Times*, p. 8.

Lewis, N. A. (2002, June 12). Questions of timing arise with new information. *New York Times*, p. 24.

Littleton, M. J. (1995). *Information age terrorism: Toward cyber-terrorism*. Retrieved March 3, 2005 from http://www.fas.org/irp/threat/cyber/docs/ npgs/terror.htm #TOC

Miller, J. (2001, October 14). Fear hits newsroom in a cloud of powder. *New York Times*, p. 4.

Nacos, B. L. (1994). *Terrorism & the media*. New York: Columbia University Press.

Nacos, B. L. (2002). *Mass-mediated terrorism: The central role of the media in terrorism and counterterrorism*. Lanham, MD: Rowman & Littlefield.

Nieves, E. (10/13/01). The nerves of a nation stretch from coast to coast. *New York Times*, p. 7.

Norris, P., Kern, M., & Just, M. (2003). Introduction: Understanding crisis coverage. In P. Norris, M. Kern, & M. Just (Eds.), *Framing terrorism: The news media, the government and the public* (pp. 3-23). New York, London: Routledge.

Nossek, H. (1985). The impact of mass media on terrorists, supporters, and the public at large. In A. Merari (Ed.), *On terrorism and combating terrorism* (pp. 87-94). Fredrick, MD: University Publications of America.

Nossek, H. (1990). *Terrorism and the media*. Doctoral dissertation, Hebrew University, Jerusalem.

Schlesinger, P. (1981). Terrorism, the media and the liberal-democratic state: A critique of the orthodoxy. *Social Research*, Spring, 74-99.

Schudson, M. (2002). What's unusual about covering politics as usual. In B. Zelizer, & S. Allan (Eds.), *Journalism after September 11* (pp. 36-47). London & New York: Routledge.

Schwartz, Y. & Falk, O. (2003). *Chemical biological radiological nuclear terrorism*. Retrieved February, 21, 2005, from International Policy Institute for Counter-Terrorism http://www.ict.org.il/

Seeleye, K. Q. (2002, June 12). Man in brig puts a face on 9/11 in low country. *New York Times*, p. 26.

Stolberg, S. G. (2001, September 30). Some experts say U.S. is vulnerable to germ attack. *New York Times*, p. 1.

Stolberg, S. G. (2001, October 14). Anthrax threats points to limits in health systems. *New York Times*, p. 1.

The Pew Research for the People and the Press (2001, October). *How worried are you that there will soon be another terrorist attack in the United States?* Retrieved March 1, 2005, from www.people-press.org

Thornton, P. T. (1964). Terror as a weapon of political agitation. In H. Eckstein (Ed.), *Internal war* (pp. 73-84). New York: Free Press

Tuman, J. (2003). *Communication terror: The rhetorical dimensions of terrorism*. Thousand Oaks, CA: Sage.

Tyler, P. E. (2002, June 11). A message in an arrest. *New York Times*, p. 1.

Viera, J. D. (1991). Terrorism at the BBC: The IRA at the British television. In A. O. Alali & K. K. Eke (Eds.), *Media coverage of terrorism: Methods of diffusion* (pp. 73-85). Newbury Park, CA: Sage.

Waisbord, S. (2002). Journalism, risk, and patriotism. In B. Zelizer & S. Allan (Eds.), *Journalism after September 11* (pp. 201-219). London & New York: Routledge.

Wald, M. L. (2002, June 11). Fear itself is the main threat of a dirty bomb, experts say. *New York Times*, p. 18.

Walzer, M. (1992). *Just and unjust wars: A moral argument with historical illustrations*. New York: Basic books.

Wardlaw, G. (1982). *Political terrorism*. Cambridge: Cambridge University Press.

Weimann, G. (1992). Modern terrorism, the media and public opinion. In S. Rothman (Ed.), *The mass media* (pp. 103-119). New York: Professors World Peace Academy

Weimann, G. & Brosius, H. B. (1991). The newsworthiness of international terrorism. *Communication Research*, *18*(3), 333-354.

Weimann, G. & Winn, C. (1994) *The theater of terror: Mass media and international terrorism*. New York & London: Longman.

Winter, G. & Broad, W. J. (2001, September 26). Added security for dams, reservoirs and aqueducts. *New York Times*, p. 7.

Wilkinson, P. (2000). *Terrorism versus democracy: The liberal state response*. Portland, OR: Frank Cass Publishers.

Wolfsfeld, G. (1997). *Constructing news about war and peace*. Tel-Aviv: Tel-Aviv University, The Tami Steinmetz Center for Peace Research.

Yardley, J. & Canedy, D. (2001, October 12). Anxiety grows in South Florida as mystery of anthrax cases lingers. *New York Times*, p. 9.

PART IV

RECENT WARS,
CURRENT CRIES

Chapter 13

"They" Shocked, "We" Saw

Psychological Operations in Operation Iraqi Freedom, 2003[1]

Philip M. Taylor

During the spring 2003 conflict in Iraq that has already been dubbed the second Gulf War,[2] the conduct of psychological operations (or PSYOPS[3]) enjoyed an unusually high profile. As a weapon of war, what was previously termed combat propaganda or psychological warfare had in fact been deployed during every major conflict fought by Western powers since 1914, usually in the form of the airborne distribution of leaflets and, subsequently, via broadcast radio and television messages. The British pioneered its use in the First World War (Sanders & Taylor, 1982) although by the end of the Second the Americans had become its primary proponents, with the dropping of billions of leaflets by dedicated bomber squadrons over Germany and Japan (Laurie, 1996). Even in the much shorter and more limited military operations since then that have not been wars of national survival, these "paper bullets" have still been considered potent weapons. Twenty nine million leaflets, for example, were dropped in the first Gulf War of 1991, Operation Desert Storm, which lasted six weeks. In the two-month Kosovo conflict of 1999 (Operation Allied Force), the figure was an astonishing 103 million. In Afghanistan, from October 2001 to March 2002 (Operation Enduring Freedom), it was 80 million (Taylor, 2003). In the build-up to and during the three-week war in Iraq, March-April 2003 (Operation Iraqi Freedom), it was approaching 50 million.

Often dismissed by military historians as a sideshow, having little impact on the conduct of military operations or on the outcome of conflicts, these "munitions of the mind"[4] have nonetheless become an increasingly central aspect of American involvement in contemporary war fighting. Other NATO countries, including Britain, Germany[5] and Poland are also developing their PSYOPS capability—and not just for conflict. The sheer variety of military interventions since the end of the Cold War, from peace-keeping to nation-building (although it is rarely called that) has seen PSY-OPS evolve into increasingly sophisticated forms of communicating with the people caught up in what are highly dangerous situations. When one practitioner announced that "our motto is electrons, not bullets" (Morrow, 1993, p. 4), one could be forgiven for believing that communicating with the enemy had almost become a more acceptable alternative to destroying him. A more dispassionate enquiry by the Defence Science Task Force Board in 2000 asserted that, "in the future, bombs and missiles will still determine who militarily wins or loses a conflict at tactical level. PSYOP, though, will help determine how long a conflict lasts and the impact of a military strug-gle on long-term U.S. strategic interests" (Defense Science Task Force Board, 2000).

WHITE AND BLACK PSYOPS

One lesser-known aspect of the origins of communications studies as an aca-demic social science discipline is that much of the government-sponsored research in the United States during the 1950s was to determine the effec-tiveness of psychological warfare techniques (Simpson, 1994). Scholars such as Daniel Katz, Wilbur Schramm and Daniel Lerner all benefited from this Cold War climate in which communications research flourished (Glander, 2000). From the late 1950s onwards, attention focused more on the mass media, especially television, and its impact upon audiences, and the study of psychological warfare diminished or became more of an interest to histori-ans. Perhaps social scientists were attempting to distance themselves from an activity that erroneously had already come to be associated, in the mind of the public, at least, with "dirty tricks" and even "brainwashing." However, psychological warfare was in fact a form of propaganda directed largely at foreign rather than domestic audiences, usually at a clearly identified enemy or a potential enemy. In the climate of the Cold War and the threat of mutu-ally assured destruction through nuclear confrontation, psychological war-fare was thus regarded both in Washington and Moscow as an alternative weapon in the global competition for hearts and minds in what was essentially an ideological struggle between the West and communism. Indeed, for almost forty-five years, what had traditionally been a tactical weapon for use on battlefields or in low intensity conflicts became a weapon of wider strategic significance, used both overtly and covertly, and permeated every aspect of East-West relations from the Space Race to the Olympic Games. If the so-called "war" against terrorism is the latest conflict between a set of ideas (which some term as a "clash of civilizations") we are likely to see this weapon deployed strategically once again, especially in a prolonged conflict. But, for the moment, first in Afghanistan and now in Iraq, its tactical and operational deployment has been a marked feature of these new regional struggles for hearts and minds.

Before going on to examine this, we first need to distinguish between overt (or "white") PSYOPS and covert (or "black") activity. Overt PSYOPS refers to messages emanating from a clearly identifiable source, which in the American military context usually means it comes from the 4th Psychological Operations Group (4POG) based at Fort Bragg, North Carolina. Much less is known about the covert variety, which is usually conducted by the secret intelligence services and their agencies (e.g., the CIA, DIA, SIS) and which deliberately misleads as to its origins. Black PSYOPS usually takes the form of broadcasting from stations that disguise their true origins and purport to be run by someone other than the true source. Radio Tikrit, which began life in January 2003 as an apparently pro-Saddam station to attract audiences and then changed its tune, fell into this category (Grace, 2002). In the past, due to their covert nature, black propaganda operations are known to have deviated from official policy and to have been far more "economical with the truth" than their white counterparts, whose success is dependent upon credibility and therefore adheres largely to factual statements or what might be termed "credible truths." This does not mean the whole truth is told; it simply means that white PSYOPS do not lie deliberately, whereas black PSYOPS, born of a lie, tends to fall into the realm of political or military deception activities.

A Tale of Two Conflicts

The media of PSYOPS have become ever more sophisticated as new communications technologies become available courtesy of the ongoing communications revolution. Leaflets, posters, and radio broadcasts may seem rather old-fashioned in the age of the internet, but they remain important media, especially in foreign environments that are not sophisticated in terms of their communications infrastructures. With each new conflict, new communications technologies come to be deployed for the first time, and the 2003

Gulf War was no different. It was even reported that some PSYOPS communiqués were being sent to Iraqi commanders in the form of e-mails or SMS text messages on their mobile phones (Rosen, 2003). The internet was barely available in the Iraq of 2003, and it was really the Kosovo conflict of four years earlier that can justifiably be termed the first internet war: www.1 (Taylor, 2004). But whichever new medium is added to this arsenal of weapons of mass communication, the military objective behind overt PSYOPS on a battlefield has essentially remained the same: to persuade the enemy soldier to desert, defect, or surrender, thereby reducing his number and easing the path to victory. The purpose of covert PSYOPS is to foster insurrection and/or internal disruption.

It is probably too early to evaluate fully the effectiveness of the 2003 PSYOP campaign. But we do know that thousands of Iraqi soldiers surrendered, deserted, or "melted away" from the battlefield as coalition forces raced to Baghdad to secure their military objectives. An estimated 8,000 Iraqi soldiers from the Iraqi 51st Infantry Division surrendered and were taken prisoners of war within the first week (Geoghegan, 2003), suggesting some degree of success, although this has to be measured against the 69,000 who surrendered in 1991. In Iraqi Freedom, however, a major PSYOP theme was for Iraqi soldiers to stay at home or simply melt away from the rapidly advancing coalition forces, but it is unlikely that the success of this theme will ever be able to be measured accurately in terms of the sheer number of soldiers who complied with this message.

One aspect of the comparison between the PSYOPS campaigns in Desert Storm and Iraqi Freedom is striking. In 2003, while some observers were surprised at the lack of Iraqi military resistance to an "invasion" of their homeland, others were equally puzzled as to why the Iraqi people did not rise up against the hated regime of Saddam Hussein until relatively late in the day, and then only in isolated pockets. Given that a peoples' uprising was one of the primary aims of the 2003 PSYOP campaign, the record here is somewhat mixed. The failure to provoke a widespread civilian uprising to assist "regime change" was linked to memories of the 1991 conflict, when black PSYOP stations deviated from the official policy line that the war was only about the liberation of Kuwait and urged the Iraqi population to rise up against Saddam (Taylor, 1992). When the Shias and Kurds did just that, they were left to their own devices by that first coalition and were subsequently brutally suppressed. The problem in 1991 was that regime change was not an objective of Desert Storm; it was supposed to be simply about the liberation of Kuwait. The deviation of covert PSYOPS from stated coalition policy on that occasion would come back to haunt the second "coalition of the willing" in its later battle for control of Iraqi hearts and minds to "liberate" the Iraqi people from Saddam's regime. In other words, the success of the black campaign in 1991 severely jeopardized the white campaign of 2003, despite a reassuring handbill produced by the British PSYOPS team that "this time we won't abandon you."[6]

AN INTEGRATED CAMPAIGN

This chapter examines the 2003 tactical and operational PSYOP campaign, but it also needs to address some wider implications at the strategic level. This was because we witnessed, for the first time, the application of new military doctrines relating to Effects Based Operations and Rapid Deployment Operations—termed "shock and awe" in popular parlance. It is the "awe" element which interests us here because it suggests a co-ordinated use of force or military power alongside a highly visible use of that force through the global media in order to achieve the desired effect; namely to achieve rapid regime change with the minimum loss of casualties—on both sides.

There was plenty of evidence of this from the lips of American political leaders, especially President George W. Bush and Secretary of Defence Donald Rumsfeld, who frequently gave speeches to the world's media containing direct messages for the Iraqi people. In his first wartime news conference of the war, for example, Rumsfeld made a direct appeal to the Iraqi troops: "Do not follow orders to destroy dams or flood villages. Do not follow orders to destroy your country's oil. . . . See those orders for what they are—the last desperate gasp of a dying regime." Later in the first week, he repeated the exercise: "I urge the Iraqi people being threatened in the cities to try to remember the faces and the names of the death squad enforcers. Their time will come, and we will need your help and your testimony" (Department of Defense, 2003). And towards the end of the war, Bush was making PSYOPS videos for direct transmission (in Arabic) with the message:

> The nightmare that Saddam Hussein has brought to your nation will soon be over. You are a good and gifted people—the heirs of a great civilization that contributes to all humanity. You deserve better than tyranny and corruption and torture chambers. You deserve to live as free people. And I assure every citizen of Iraq: your nation will soon be free. (White House, 2003)

Between these two statements, there were numerous examples of an unprecedented degree of co-ordination of strategic and tactical PSYOPS from Washington right down to the tactical theater of operations, prompting the conclusion that Operation Iraqi Freedom was one gigantic psychological operation or, more precisely in military doctrine, an Information War.

Information Warfare

In terms of its communication elements, Operation Iraqi Freedom also borrowed heavily from much of the recent thinking about new and emerging military doctrines, especially that of Information Warfare (IW), which in turn has evolved into Information Operations (IO). This doctrine embraces the notion of information as a central weapon in the waging of contemporary warfare. The Pentagon's somewhat bland definition is "actions taken to affect adversary information and information systems while defending one's own information and information systems" (Joint Doctrine for Information Operations, 1996). Although this appears to focus on communications technologies, human factors also play a significant role. The doctrine can essentially be broken down into two interlocking components; namely Computer Network Operations (CNO) and Perception Management, the new euphemism for propaganda. The former tends towards the technical side of military electronic systems and satellites that have come increasingly to dominate the eyes and ears of waging modern warfare as a result of the "Revolution in Military Affairs." So, whereas in the past, the waging of industrialized warfare involved, for example, the often indiscriminate bombing of factories, shipyards, and their surrounding urban areas, information warfare prioritizes precision-guided attacks against command and control capabilities, including power stations, radio masts, telephone exchanges, television transmitters, and any other leadership targets that might produce a dramatic effect. This included the attempted "decapitation strike" against the Iraqi leadership on the opening night of the war, but its more dramatic manifestation came on the second night, when television cameras broadcast devastating—but surgically precise—coalition bombing of the city of Baghdad. By taking command and control of the flow of information in the conflict area, the idea was to deafen, dumb, and blind in one eye the enemy's command and control capabilities while leaving the other eye open for him and the wider world to see that his cause is futile. "The goal of information warfare is to win without ever firing a shot," said one Central Command spokesman rather optimistically, although he then modified this by adding: "If action does begin, information warfare is used to make the conflict as short as possible" (Shanker & Schmitt, 2003).

Much of this thinking originally derived from the first Gulf War of 1991, when the American-led coalition was able to disrupt much of Iraq's electronic defences on the opening nights of the war. On the Perception Management side, the coalition's ability to present a desired view of the conflict to the wider world through the mass media—the so-called "video game war"—was felt to have provided a template for management of the media. This desired view was of a clean, near bloodless war fought with high-tech weaponry causing minimal civilian damage (Taylor, 1992, ch. 4). But "media war" was only one part of the thinking. Another essential ingredient was Psychological Operations, defined by the United States as "planned operations to convey selected information and indicators to foreign audiences to influence their emotions, motives, objective reasoning and ultimately the behavior of foreign governments, organisations, groups and individuals" (Doctrine for Joint Psychological Operations, 1996). PSYOPS were deployed to great effect in the Gulf War of 1991, as evidenced by the huge numbers of Iraqi deserters, defectors, or surrenders, earning for it a renewed reputation as a "combat force multiplier" through the dissemination of millions of leaflets and the broadcast of hours of programming from ground and airborne transmitters—all of which were felt to have shaped the information space on the battlefield in the Kuwaiti theater of operations. The success of this campaign was tempered somewhat by the experience of Kosovo in 1999 when, despite a massive PSYOP campaign, this failed to crack the morale of the Yugoslav army or indeed of the Serb people. It was an ominous foresight of some of the things to come in the Gulf War of 2003.

TACTICAL PSYOPS IN IRAQ

The psychological preparation of the battlefield began months before the actual fighting. The first leaflets were dropped on 28 November 2002, with one simply stating that "Coalition Air Power Can Strike at Will. Any Time. Any Place."[7] Of course, the coalition had enjoyed air superiority over Iraq since 1991, demonstrated during the air strikes of 1998 during Operation Desert Fox, especially in the no fly zones imposed on northern and southern Iraq. But there were clearly some worries about anti-aircraft fire, and two other leaflets depicted in cartoon form the consequences of what would happen if coalition aircraft were fired upon or if military fibre optic cables were repaired ("repairing them places your lives at risk"). The first reminder that this was to be a war against the Saddam regime rather than the Iraqi people came on the obverse of the latter: "Military fiber optic cable are tools used by Saddam and his regime to suppress the Iraqi people." The same three leaflets were dropped in their millions again on 2 December. Two weeks later, a new leaflet product was dropped depicting a cartoon image of a radio tower with the words "Information Radio" and the frequencies on which these coalition transmissions could be heard. This was a clue that "Commando Solo" had been or was about to be deployed. This is a converted Hercules EC 130E aircraft operated by the 193rd Special Operations Wing of the Pennsylvanian National Guard that had been deployed on previous operations in the Gulf (then known as "Volant Solo"), Haiti, Kosovo and Afghanistan. This is one of the heaviest—and therefore most vulnerable—aircraft in the American air force, and capable of broadcasting radio and television messages on multifre-quencies; the United States possesses six in all. It is not yet known how many of these were deployed to the region, but it must have been at least two, given that by the end of March 2003 it was broadcasting 24 hours a day—another indication of confidence in air superiority.

The first target audience for "Information Radio," which began trans-missions on 12 December, was the Iraqi army. One of the earliest broadcasts went as follows:

> Soldiers of Iraq. Since the beginning of time, there has been no profes-sion more honorable than that of a soldier. Soldiers are decorated with awards and medals that show their achievements and mark their skills. The uniform of a soldier is an article that demands respect, and loyalty. Soldiers are the defenders of their people, and the protectors of women and children. A soldier is willing to sacrifice himself for his country and their way of life. Soldiers sacrifice their own personal freedoms to pro-tect others.
>
> Saddam has tarnished this legacy. Saddam spews forth political rhetoric along with a false sense of national pride to deceive these men to serve his own unlawful purposes. Saddam does not wish the soldiers of Iraq to have the honor and dignity that their profession warrants. Saddam seeks only to exploit these brave men. Saddam uses the soldiers of Iraq not as protectors of the peace, but rather as his own personal body-guards. Do not let Saddam tarnish the reputation of soldiers any longer. Saddam uses the military to persecute those who don't agree with his unjust agenda. Make the decision.[8]

Before long, the Iraqi civilian population was added to the target audience list. In the previous Gulf War, Saddam had been branded "a new Hitler" by coalition propaganda. This time, he was likened to Stalin: "the world has paid a higher price for not stopping men like Stalin when they had the chance. Many millions of people have lost their lives needlessly under these oppres-sive regimes and in wars started by these leaders. The loss of life and the need-less suffering could have been minimized had action been taken sooner. History has shown that appeasement of brutal domineering regimes only brings greater tragedy. Saddam too has a lust for power, and the world will stand up and put an end to the terror he imposes on others, before he destroys Iraq and crushes the hopes of its proud people."[9] It is worth noting that the appeasement argument was also being used as a prewar propaganda theme (albeit a somewhat spurious one) in the wider world, especially in Britain and the United States, in the build-up to hostilities. As Iraqi television was placing enormous emphasis on the divisions within the international community over the weapons inspectors being given more time, over whether a follow-up UN resolution to 1441 was required, and on the antiwar marches taking place throughout the world, Command Solo began to broadcast a mixture of factual programming relaying presidential speeches in full, with further appeals reminding the Iraqi people about the evils of Saddam's regime. "The world community [sic] . . . asks for your support" in removing Saddam from power not least because "every night, children go to sleep hungry in Iraq" while Saddam lives in lavish palaces, drives around in expensive cars and builds expensive monuments for his personal glorification.[10]

When the "shock and awe" bombing of Baghdad began on the night of 20-21 March 2003, Radio Baghdad appeared to have been jammed as words from Commando Solo announced over its frequencies that "the facilities of the Iraqi regime have started to be hit. . . . This is the day we have been waiting for. . . . The attack on Iraq has begun" (Grace, 2003). But Baghdad radio was back on the air several hours later and, surprisingly given the nature of IW thinking, Iraqi television continued to transmit for several weeks into the war. Why greater effort was not made to take out the indigenous media must, for the moment, remain open to speculation, especially as these were primary targets during the previous conflict (Taylor, 1992). Perhaps it was because the coalition wished the Iraqi leadership and people to witness the "awesome" precision of the coalition's bombing. But when two marketplaces in Baghdad were damaged during the first week of the war, the wisdom of allowing them to carry on broadcasting was brought into question. The Iraqi Information Minister, Mohammed al-Sahhaf, who appeared daily before the world's media (and who became known as "Comical Ali" when he refused to stare defeat in the face), proclaimed a barbaric bombing campaign directed at innocent women and children. It took a week for the coalition to undertake its BDA (Bomb Damage Assessment) before suggesting that the markets had been damaged by Iraqi anti-aircraft fire coming back to ground. By allowing Iraqi television to continue, including periodic but highly controversial appearances of Saddam himself, the coalition had effectively put itself in the business of Broadcasting Damage Assessment.

Meanwhile, American ground forces were racing towards Baghdad in a lightening strike. Leaflets were dropped telling Iraqi soldiers not to use their weapons of mass destruction and, as the army approached the Rumaila oil fields, telling the oil workers not to self-destruct Iraq's future wealth. According to Major General Renuart, Director of Operations at Central Command based in Dohar, when the southern oil fields were secured virtually intact, the troops found that many well heads were wired for explosion, but that the workers had told them: "We read your leaflets. We heard your broadcasts. We understand that keeping the oil infrastructure was important for our future" (Eason, 2003; Renuart, 2003). Interestingly, the northern and western fronts received comparatively little media coverage because those campaigns were fought largely by Special Operations forces whose policy is not to take journalists along with them. Some reporters, such as the BBC's John Simpson, were in northern Iraq attempting to cover the progress of the Kurdish forces as they seized the oil fields in that part of the country, but the coverage was patchy by comparison to the southern campaign where hundreds of reporters were "embedded" with the troops.

Commando Solo is purely a broadcast platform; it does not drop leaflets. That is done by other aircraft and by the M129 leaflet bomb, which explodes at around 4,000 feet and scatters the leaflets to the ground. One of the most important elements of the PSYOP campaign was to instruct Iraqi soldiers on how to surrender. Almost 70,000 surrendered in 1991 and similar figures were expected this time. According to some reports, however, the decision of the overall commander, General Franks, to start the ground offensive a day earlier than planned disrupted the surrender plan. Some leaflets had been dropped before the war, showing surface to surface missile crews how to surrender by walking away from their equipment, leaving their rifles behind; "abandon your weapons systems. Whether manned or unmanned, these weapons will be destroyed." Others carried the appeal: "Do not risk your life. And the lives of your comrades! Leave now and GO HOME. Watch your children learn, grow and prosper." However, according to Lieutenant Colonel George Smith, because of the decision to start early, it was only on that day that leaflets were printed giving specific instructions on how to capitulate—by turning the turrets of their tanks and artillery around, placing their vehicles in a square, staying at least 1,000 feet away from their weapons and hoisting white flags. "We weren't able to get the message out. If they got the message, it was probably right before ground forces were upon them." (Atkinson, Baker, & Ricks, 2003). The early surrender of an Iraqi division that would presumably encourage others to do the same was not replicated. Instead, Iraqi soldiers deserted their uniforms and returned home, leaving Ba'athist fanatics and Republican Guardsmen to do the fighting, including suicide bombings and other extremist acts. An unnamed Special Operations officer was also quoted as saying: "The end result was the Fedayeen was effective because the unconventional warfare effort did not have time to identify them and neutralize them." He added that the Fedayeen's attacks signalled to Iraqis in the early days that their government might fight and survive: "that small illusion of hope greatly impacted the psy-op campaign," he said (Atkinson, Baker, & Ricks, 2003).

As the Americans moved north, the British besieged the city of Basra and took the port of Umm Qsar. Neither rose up as expected. One local who was interviewed said that "the Iraqi citizen does not accept dishonour, therefore we do not accept any invasion on our land by any force no matter how powerful" (El-Awady, 2003). Clearly the strategic propaganda theme about the war being one of liberation of the Iraqi people[11] was proving unconvincing in the region, especially as Arab TV stations and other media were labelling the attack as an invasion and gave prominence to images of civilian damage (Khouri, 2003). PSYOPS leaflets warned locals not to "help the Iraqi military and regime leadership to escape. . . . If you observe defectors report it to the Coalition forces." As coalition forces surrounded towns, this gave rise to an increased emphasis on face-to-face communications, and a good deal was made in the media of the differences between the British forces, who replaced their helmets with less intimidating berets, and the full metal jacketed approach of the Americans (who had suffered casualties caused by an early suicide bombing outside Nassiriyah and were thus more sensitive to protection issues with the local populace). At Central Command, a spokesman pointed out:

> We do continue our efforts in communicating with the Iraqi population, as well as military forces, delivering leaflets by hand and by air, and our broadcasts over the airways. At this point, we've distributed more than a million leaflets yesterday alone, and have reached more than 43 million leaflets overall. And our broadcast messages are adjusting to account for the changes in circumstances as we find them. The good news is we are quickly moving beyond the one-way communications of broadcasts and interacting directly with the population every day. (Renuart, 2003)

Much of this was being done by mobile PSYOPS teams in Humvees mounted with loudspeakers, encouraging 20 Fedayeen fighters in Nasiriyah to surrender, among other small victories (Bebow, 2003). Black PSYOPS stations had also been busy trying to foster insurrection with little or no success. In addition to Radio Tikrit, interested groups were monitoring stations with such titles as the "Voice of Iraqi Liberation" (Grace, 2003). As further Iraqi towns and cities fell comparatively quickly from the end of the second week onwards, Washington was clearly becoming alarmed at the levels of Arab anti-Americanism on such stations as Al-Jazeera and announced the setting up of its own satellite television station, the Middle Eastern Television Network (METN) (Satloff, 2003).

As coalition forces surrounded Baghdad with its five million people, the critical point of the war was approaching. However, the Saddam regime collapsed with surprising speed and the city fell to American forces without the long-feared "downtown warfare" previously predicted by some pundits. By 10 April, METN became "Towards Freedom TV" (Hahwa al-Hurrieh) whose first broadcast—relayed by Commando Solo onto the former Iraqi TV terrestrial frequencies—included messages to the Baghdad population from President Bush and Prime Minister Blair, recorded two days earlier at the Hillsborough Castle summit in Northern Ireland (Waugh, 2003). This was the first time Commando Solo's television transmission capabilities were utilized fully; it had previously been largely a flying radio station. Its programming attempted to reassure Iraqis that coalition forces were "friends and liberators, not your conquerors." Back on the ground, much media attention was being given to the looting that was taking place. In the streets of Baghdad, PSYOPS teams distributed leaflets urging Iraqi citizens to stay at home: "Please avoid leaving your homes during the night hours after evening prayers and before the call to morning prayers. During this time, terrorist forces associated with the former regime of Saddam Hussein, as well as various criminal elements, are known to move through the area and engage in hostile acts" (Reuters, 2003). Other messages included instructions on how to approach military checkpoints (slowly and without appearing to be carrying a weapon) and appeals to medical and other civic personnel to return to work.

In the same week, coalition forces also began producing a newspaper, *The Times*, for southern Iraq (Coughlin, no date). A British-organized white PSYOP station, Two Rivers Radio (Radio Nahrain) was also set up around this time servicing the region around Basra. Thus began the transition from Combat PSYOPS to what is termed Consolidation PSYOPS, although the cessation of hostilities requires more of a civil affairs—or public relations— function. It is no coincidence that the American special forces command that deals with PSYOPS is also responsible for civil affairs, and it was this element of the "hearts and minds" campaign in-country that now came to the fore as the humanitarian mission to rebuild Iraq became an essential strand of the propaganda war. Leaflets were produced urging the looting that took place to stop, and the now infamous pack of cards was issued identifying the names and faces of America's "Most Wanted" list of fifty-five members of the regime. The ace of spades was Saddam himself and, although his personal destiny remained a mystery, his statues were pulled down and his murals defaced in full view of the world's media. Regime change had been achieved, law and order were gradually restored and the first steps were made towards convincing the Arab world and Iraqi people that this had indeed been a war of liberation from tyranny and not an exercise in neocolonialism. This did not stop the American forces from losing almost half as many men as had been killed in the war-fighting phase in the two months following President Bush's formal announcement of victory aboard the *USS Abraham Lincoln*. In a sense, the propaganda war that really mattered was only just beginning (Taylor, 2002).

THE STRATEGIC INFORMATION WAR

The very fact that such consolidation propaganda efforts were required was an indication of the degree of hostility that existed towards the "Anglo-American invasion," not just within Iraq or the Arab world, but globally.

The war may have commanded high levels of support in the United States, but throughout Europe, opposition levels were 70 percent or higher. Even in Britain, support levels rose from 37 percent to only 56 percent once the troops went into action—quite a jump, but far lower than any previous British military involvement since the 1956 Suez crisis. Even by the end of the war it stood at a mere 60 percent. The media in any given country, not surprisingly, reflected broadly the position of their governments, except in Spain and Italy where the media were highly critical of their government's support for the war effort. The British media therefore reflected a deeply divided country. The failure to secure a follow-up UN resolution to 1441, the non-use of weapons of mass destruction by the Iraqi forces, and indeed the difficulty of finding them even after military victory had been achieved, a "war for oil," an exercise in American imperialism—all such allegations were deeply felt around the world and received considerable publicity in the world's media, suggesting a serious failure by Washington of strategic Perception Management outside of the United States itself. As one White House official put it: "many of the Middle Eastern people have been fed a steady diet of anti-American propaganda," which helped to explain why "why not everyone shares our assessment" of why the war was necessary (Becker, 2003). There may, of course, have been other reasons, not least disquiet about the Bush doctrine and its principles of pre-emptive war and regime change against an identified "axis of evil" that might or might not one day supply weapons of mass destruction to terrorist groups such as al-Qaeda.

A week into the conflict, on March 28th, Rumsfeld had told a press conference:

> The outcome of this conflict is not in doubt. The regime will be removed. But for our coalition of free people, we believe it is important not just to win, but to win justly. The power of our coalition derives not simply from the vast overwhelming force at our disposal, but from the manner in which we employ that force. The Iraqi people will see how we employ our force and know that we are coming not to occupy their country, not to oppress them, but to liberate their country. (Department of Defense, 2003)

Note the emphasis on "coalition" in order to head off charges that this was, as many opponents maintained, a war of "American imperialism." The "coalition of the willing" in fact consisted of only four military contributors (the United States, the United Kingdom, Australia, and Poland) and a collection of states providing less visible support. Unlike 1991, no Arab forces were involved. So when television images were aired of an American flag being raised in Umm Qsar or over the head of a toppled statue of Saddam in

Baghdad, they tended to reinforce anti-American sentiment—hence Washington's irritation with Arab satellite television stations such as Al Jazeera, which focused on the Iraqi and wider Arab perspective, including images of military and civilian casualties that were not aired in the United States.

But the fact remained that Iraqi towns and cities had been targeted with largely precision-guided weaponry, which hit their targets with accuracy unprecedented in military history, and, compared to previous conflicts, the war was won with comparative ease and relatively low civilian casualties. That said, this did not prevent the global media from reporting when things did go wrong. Collateral damage, pictures of injured children in hospitals, looting, friendly-fire accidents—all secured prominence in media outlets that had opposed the "unjust war" from the outset, and detracted from the fact that, as Rumsfeld said, the American and British forces had tried to conduct the war in a manner which was supposed to reflect well on their "humanitarian" intervention to liberate Iraq from the Saddam regime. This was supposed to have been plain for all to see from the television images taken by the embedded journalists who, on their return, testified to how little military censorship they had experienced in producing probably the most vivid images of front-line combat ever seen. But such reports merely added to the "fog of war," because the demands of the 24/7 news cycle required journalists to feed their news-guzzling organizations with an endless stream of "on-the-spot" news "as it happened," often leaving the wider picture very much out of focus. Less of a fog and more like a snowstorm of information, the images would appear to have merely confirmed pre-existing attitudes of watching audiences about the rights and wrongs of the conflict.

CONCLUSIONS

These, by necessity, must be preliminary. Even so, the snowstorm of information about the war in Iraq does enable modern scholars to utilize their analytical training in a manner that would be the envy of their forebears. "Fools rush in where scholars fear to tread" may be an apposite corrective to this attitude, but we witness historical events courtesy of the mass media coverage of conflicts such as Operation Iraqi Freedom. It may well be that time will dismiss the reports from the embedded journalists as regurgitating the military line, but there were plenty of unembedded reporters providing their own ant's eye view of the war. And despite a media emphasis on the southern front, their preoccupation with bad news, and overconcentration on human interest stories at the expense of issues (on "Private Jessica" or "Chemical Ali" or "Comical Ali" or Ali Abbas, the 12-year-old Iraqi boy who lost both his arms and fifteen relatives) (Jones, 2003), none of these aspects of the war coverage should have come as any surprise to media scholars.

What is clear is that this conflict was as much a psychological operation as it was a demonstration of military might. The battle for hearts and minds was not just confined to the Iraqi people, but it was also directed at world opinion. Time will indeed tell if both the tactical and strategic campaigns had the desired effect. We do know that the Iraqi people did not rise up against Saddam on any significant scale, although the tactical PSYOP campaign would appear to have been successful persuading many Iraqi soldiers not to fight. After the fighting was over, however, resentment and impatience was evident in the attitude of many Iraqis towards the American "occupiers." Strategic levels of skepticism about the war's justification increased, even in the United States itself, as the so-called "smoking gun" of weapons of mass destruction failed to fire. "So where are they, Mr Blair?" demanded *The Independent on Sunday* a week after the fighting was all but over (20 April 2003). As for doctrinal developments, we have seen how the American government of George W. Bush no longer distinguishes between a press conference and a military PSYOP campaign. That indeed may be sea change in the development of Information Operations thinking, because the war was seen in Washington as being as much a struggle for moral high ground in the global information space as it was to secure command and control of the battlefield. Nor was it confined to the prewar and wartime environments. The real psychological struggle began after the fighting was over—on issues such as the "justness" of the war, on its legality, on its necessity in the first place, on the slow pace of Iraqi reconstruction. But many of these issues missed the point that for the power elite in Washington, the 2003 war in Iraq was not really a "war" in its own right. It was the second *battle* of the "war" against terrorism (with Afghanistan being the first). The hunt for Saddam Hussein may have subsumed this issue temporarily and raised all sorts of doubts about the wisdom of pre-emptive strikes against other nation states, rogue or otherwise. But these issues are bound to resurface, and they will continue to shock and awe.

NOTES

1. The research for this chapter was undertaken as part of the ESRC funded project on the Domestic Management of Terrorism led by King's College, London, in 2002–03.
2. Unfortunately because, in the Middle East, the Iran-Iraq war is regarded as the "First" Gulf War. The 2003 conflict should therefore, strictly speaking, be known as the *third* Gulf War, and hence this error merely serves to confirm within the region itself the lack of Western media understanding of the Arab world.

3. The U.S. tends to use PSYOP as an acronym, whereas in Europe the "s" tends to be added.
4. The phrase is Lord Beaverbrook's, Britain's first Minister of Information in 1918, and one that I used for my general history of propaganda, *Munitions of the Mind: A History of Propaganda from the Ancient World to the Present Era* (Manchester University Press, 3rd edition, 2003).
5. In Germany, the preferred term for PSYOP is Operational Information and, until recently, the British preferred Information Support.
6. British PSYOPS was produced by the 15th UK Psychological Operations Group, based at Chicksands. Its capability is tiny when compared to that of the Americans. Some of the British products, and most of the American, are available online in an extensive factual survey by Herbert A. Friedman entitled "Operation Iraqi Freedom" at www.psywarrior.com/OpnIraqiFreedom.html.
7. These and all leaflets subsequently discussed, were available on the Web site of Central Command. See http://www.centcom.mil/galleries/leaflets.
8. Transcripts of some of the broadcasts were also placed on Central Command's Web site. See http://www.centcom.mil/CENTCOMNews/Misc/RadioScripts. htm
9. *Ibid.*
10. *Ibid*
11. Although many analysts suggested that this theme was a last minute justification for the war, in fact President Bush had told American forces in early January 2003 that "You'll be fighting not to conquer anybody but to liberate people." See Andrew Buncombe and David Usborne, "US steps up propaganda war with call on Iraqi troops to turn against Saddam," *The Independent*, 3 January 2003.

REFERENCES

Atkinson, R., Baker, P., & Ricks, T. (2003, April 13). Confused start, decisive end. *The Washington Post*, p. A01.

Bebow, J. (2003, April 8) Humvee-mounted speakers blast Baghdad with artillery noise, appeals to surrender. *USA Today*.

Becker, E. (2003, April 5). The American portrayal of a war of liberation is faltering across the Arab world. *The New York Times*.

Coughlin, K. (n.d.). Success for hearts and minds hard to gauge. www.newhouse-news.com/archive/coughlin041403.html.

Defense Science Board Task Force on the Creation and Dissemination of All Forms of Information in Support of Psychological Operations (PSYOP) in Time of Military Conflict. (2000, May). Washington, DC: Office of the Under Secretary of Defense For Acquisition, Technology and Logistics.

Department of Defense news briefing, 28 March 2003. http://www.defenselink. mil/news/Mar2003/t03282003_t0328sd.html

Doctrine for Joint Psychological Operations. (1996). Joint Publication 3-53. Available as a pdf file at www.dtic.mil/doctrine/jel/new_pubs/jp3_53.pdf

Eason, G. (2003, April 16). Weapons that won the war. BBC Online. http://news.bbc.co.uk/1/hi/world/middle_east/2950403.stm

El-Awady, A. (2003, March 19). Psychological war: The war before the battle. IslamOnline. www.islam-online.net/English/Science/2003/03article07.shtml.

Geoghegan, T. (2003, April 15). New human rights fears in Iraq. BBC Web site. http://news.bbc.co.uk/1/hi/world/middle_east/2950089.stm

Glander, T. (2000). *Origins of mass communications research during the American cold war* Mahwah, NJ: Erlbaum.

Grace, N. (2002, March 31). New psyop frequencies suggest the emergence of the northern front. http://www.clandestineradio.com/intel/iraq.htm.

Grace, N. (2003, March 20). Iraqi state radio replaced with U.S. psyop broadcast. http://www.clandestineradio.com/dossier/iraq2003/2003_0320.htm.

Jones, S. (2003, April 19). Does he understand why war took place? The Iraqi boy cast as the human face of war. *The Guardian.*

Joint Doctrine for Information Operations (1996). J-P 3-13, available at www.dtic.mil/doctrine/jel/new_pubs/jp3_13.pdf.

Khouri, R. G. (2003, April 4). The war Americans don't see. *The New York Times.*

Laurie, C. D. (1996). *Propaganda warriors: America's crusade against Nazi Germany.* Lawrence: University of Kansas Press.

Morrow, Capt. J. M. (1993, February). Never seen, always heard. *Airman*, p. 4.

Renuart, Major General V. (2003, April 10). Director of Operations, CENTCOM Operation Iraqi Freedom. Briefing. http://www.centcom.mil/CENTCOM News/Transcripts/20030410.htm

Reuters. (2003, April 15). US urges Baghdad citizens to stay home at night. http://asia.reuters.com/newsArticle.jhtml?type=focusIraqNews&storyID=256 7044

Rosen, J. (2003, March 21). Rumsfeld sends clear message: In a new psychological warfare technique, Iraqi enemy troops hear directly from the top. *The Sacramento Bee.* Available on-line at http://www.sacbee.com/content/politics/ story/6314150p-7267543c.html.

Sanders, M. L. & Taylor, P. M. (1982). *British propaganda during the first world war.* Macmillan

Satloff, R. (2003, April 4). Wrong answer to Al Jazeera. *The Washington Post*, p. A21.

Shanker T. & Schmitt, E. (2003, February 24). Firing leaflets and electrons, US wages information war. *The New York Times.*

Simpson, C. (1994). *The science of coercion: Communications research and psychological warfare, 1945-60.* New York: Wiedenfeld & Nicolson.

Taylor, P. M. (1992). *War and the media: Propaganda and persuasion in the Gulf War.* Manchester: Manchester University Press.

Taylor, P. M. (2000). The world wide web goes to war. In D. Gauntlett (Ed.), *Web.studies: Rewiring media studies for the digital age* (pp. 194-201). London: Arnold

Taylor, P. M. (2002). Information warfare and information intervention. In M. E. Price & M. Thompson (Eds.), *Forging peace: Intervention, human rights and the management of media space* (pp. 313-328). Edinburgh: Edinburgh University Press.

Taylor, P. M. (2003). "We know where you are": Psychological operations media during enduring freedom. In D. K. Thussu & D. Freedman (Eds.), *War and the media: Reporting conflict 24/7.* Thousand Oaks, CA: Sage.

Waugh, P. (2003, April 13). Iraq's new TV station. *The Independent.*

White House. (2003). President's message to the Iraqi people, transcript released by the White House on 10 April 2003. http://www.whitehouse.gov/news/releases/2003/04/20030410-2.html.

Chapter 14

Framing Gender
in Afghanistan and Iraq

Unveiling the Gaze of Empire

Rashmi Luthra

The deployment of the gender card by U.S. news as part of the process of legitimizing the U.S. invasion of Afghanistan has been documented by several scholars (Abu-Lughod, 2002; Cooke, 2002; Franks, 2003; Thobani, 2002b). Building on the existing scholarship on gendered aspects of U.S. coverage of the war in Afghanistan, this chapter introduces a comparative perspective by doing a close textual analysis of U.S. news coverage of the gendered aspects of the war in Iraq. What emerges are very different patterns of coverage, with gender being relatively absent in U.S. coverage of the war in Iraq. By contrast to the coverage of the Afghani context, gender is not used explicitly to bolster the case for war. The article uncovers the differing patterns in terms of gender and some of the possible reasons for these differing patterns. By doing so, the article is able to identify the ideological work the U.S. news does in support of U.S. global hegemony, but also the limits within which particular elements such as gender can be deployed for ideological purposes.[1]

When the U.S. news picked up the story of the Taliban's atrocities against women in Afghanistan, they had already been occurring for five years (Cooke, 2002; Franks, 2003). They made it through the news sieve and were made central to the U.S. news frame just preceding and during the U.S.

bombing of Afghanistan. The news frame of the oppression of Afghan women at the hands of the Taliban served to legitimize the U.S. invasion and provide rationalizations for U.S. foreign policy once the troops went in. An invading force was vested with heroism through the trope of the once oppressed and veiled Afghan woman. Selective appropriation enabled the construction of a frame in which the United States became the liberating agent unveiling the Afghan woman. In the characteristic manner of U.S. news, the partially unveiled Afghan woman remained voiceless and thereby amenable to an imperial gaze. To have allowed her to speak would have risked the piercing of the ideological news frame.

By comparison, in the coverage of the U.S. invasion of Iraq the figure of the woman is nearly absent. The Iraqi woman is not as amenable to incorporation within the dominant news frames; her status is more ambivalent and therefore partially resistant to straightforward appropriation. The response of the press is to use news frames that are more serviceable in this instance and more consonant with a generally Orientalist leaning (Said, 1979).[2] Rather than deal with the complexities of gender in the Iraqi context, the press remains mostly silent on the gender question. Comparing news coverage in the two contexts allows us to see the ideological work the press does as it incorporates or excludes particular facets from the news frame. The relative absence of the gender frame in the Iraqi context makes visible the ideologies at play in both contexts. The comparison suggests that the figure of the Muslim woman is admissible only if she can be assimilated within dominant ideologies and subjected to an imperial gaze.

INVOKING THE AFGHAN WOMAN AS VICTIM

The figure of the Afghan woman was conveniently and easily assimilated into the news frame just preceding and immediately following the U.S. invasion of Afghanistan because it dovetailed almost seamlessly with the U.S. foreign policy agenda, prevailing ideologies vilifying Islamic fundamentalism, and particular strands of U.S. liberal feminism. The imagery associated with the victimization of Afghan women by the Taliban gained potency because of its continuities with already established and currently prevailing news constructs relating to Islamic fundamentalism and the victimization of postcolonial and especially Muslim women by religion and/or culture (Narayan, 1997; Parmeswaran, 1996). These news constructs depict postcolonial women as a monolithic entity oppressed by traditional patriarchal cultures and religions. In addition, these constructions often rob postcolonial women of agency, emphasizing their victimization rather than their resistance. This construction feeds into the notion that postcolonial women need to be saved by external forces such as a colonial power or occupying force. In a similar vein, the story of Afghan women's subjugation by the Taliban provided the basis for vesting American occupation forces with heroism. Having established women's seclusion in the form of the burqa-clad woman as the apotheosis and most visible symbol of the Taliban's oppressive regime, U.S. troops could be represented as "Lifting the Veil" (the title of the *Time* cover in the December 2001 issue) of the Afghan woman, and thereby representing the mirror opposite of the Taliban, lifting all that oppresses the Afghan woman. The image of the oppressed Afghani woman functioned to bolster the legitimacy of U.S. action. It was able to do so through processes of abstraction and equivalence (Goldman, 1994), or the mechanisms by which particular concepts, themes, or ideas are extricated from historically embedded chains of meaning and thereby made available for association with other concepts, themes, or ideas in sometimes very different contexts.[3] These processes allowed the selective appropriation of particular elements and facets of the "facts on the ground", and selective use of histories and stories told by U.S. feminists and Afghan women's groups.

The deployment of the figure of the Afghan woman in service of U.S. foreign policy was also made possible by the historical juncture. The attacks of September 11 created a context within which the telescoping of gender crimes by an Islamic fundamentalist group made perfect sense. In addition, the erosion of Afghani civil society and with it the space for the elaboration of women's rights through three decades of war in Afghanistan provided fertile ground for the free appropriation of choice elements of the story of Afghan women by the U.S. press, with no possibility of a frontal challenge to the news frames created as a result. The truth of the Taliban's atrocities against women could then stand alone as the ultimate truth of the situation to the neglect of all other truths that would provide a more contextual reading of the history of Afghan women and of the U.S. occupation.

The selective appropriation of information and images gathered by Afghan women's groups, particularly RAWA (the Revolutionary Association of the Women of Afghanistan), demonstrates the process of abstraction and equivalence at work in U.S. news. RAWA, along with a number of Afghan women's groups, were at the forefront of resistance to the Taliban and their Islamist predecessors such as the Northern Alliance. RAWA had developed a sophisticated analysis of the causes behind the rise of Islamist tendencies in Afghanistan, including the role of the United States in supporting and arming the Mujahedeen as part of the Cold War struggle against the occupation of Aghanistan by the U.S.S.R. Their warnings before September 11 that U.S. support for the Taliban and other Islamist groups would backfire went unheeded (Thobani, 2002a). After September 11, however, RAWA's depictions of Afghan women's suffering at the hands of the Taliban, including the documentary "Beneath the Veil" aired repeatedly by CNN and made available on its Web site, were used to justify the U.S. invasion of Afghanistan. These depictions were made to stand alone, abstracted from the larger critique of both U.S. policy and Islamic fundamentalism offered by RAWA. No mention was made of the terrible atrocities against women committed by the Northern Alliance before the Taliban came to power, and of the initial support of the United States for the Taliban and a number of Islamist groups sharing the gender ideology of the Taliban. The complex and varied causes of women's oppression in Afghanistan, including their continuing poverty, malnutrition, and ill health, were reduced to a one-dimensional portraiture of the abject victimization of women under the Taliban regime (Abu-Lughod, 2002). The veil, and more specifically the burqa, was deployed as a key image in the construction of this one-dimensional portrait, thereby flattening the complex history and multidimensional and contextually specific meanings of the veil itself (Abu-Loghod, 2002). Divested of history and context, the veil has been successfully used in the West to signify the oppression of women, a signification upon which the news coverage built. Both the image of the veil and the images of the oppression of women by the Taliban were abstracted from their historical and sociopolitical context and equated with the barbarity of the Taliban, and by extension, Islam.

The bracketing of the oppression of Afghan women at the hands of the Taliban is done both spatially and temporally. Spatially, it is acheived by excluding contradictory elements of the situation under the Taliban, such as the reduction in rates of rape and abduction of women under the Taliban and the presence of increased security, despite the severe restrictions on mobility, education, and employment (Franks, 2003; Hirschkind & Mahmood, 2002). Temporally, the representation of the Taliban as the distillation of evil and the just target of U.S. wrath is accomplished by erasing the history of U.S. involvement in the empowerment of the extreme Islamist groups including the Taliban, the oppression of women at the hands of the Northern Alliance before the Taliban came to power, and the continued oppression of women after the overthrow of the Taliban, especially the absence of actual security that would enable women's mobility. Although the *Time* article celebrating the "Lifting [of] The Veil" by U.S. forces does broach the question by asking "How much better will their lives be now?," the question is never answered because the gender question drops off the news radar soon after the U.S. invasion is accomplished.

The construction of Muslim woman as abject victim has been a seductive one for Western feminists as well. The Feminist Majority Foundation utilized this imagery to garner support for its campaign against "Gender Apartheid" in Afghanistan. In doing so, they participated in the logic of "saving Afghan women" from Muslim men, a logic that in the short term helped to legitimize the bombing of Afghanistan, and in the long term serves to reproduce the equation of Islam with fundamentalism and barbarism

(Kolhatkar, 2002; Moallem, 2001). RAWA's rhetoric has been selectively appropriated by the Feminist Majority Foundation, the Bush administration (particularly Laura Bush's radio address on Afghan women), and U.S. news, amplifying the wrongs of the Taliban against women and eclipsing the critique of U.S. imperialism and its fostering of an environment within which the most conservative strains of Islam could flourish. In addition, while RAWA's rhetoric has been conveniently appropriated, even the Feminist Majority Foundation has been relatively silent on the question of the continued oppression of women after the overthrow of the Taliban and the exclusion of groups like RAWA from the formal political process (Kolhatkar, 2002). While RAWA's rhetoric has been deployed, RAWA's agency has not been adequately acknowledged. As Kolhatkar points out, the Feminist Majority Foundation chose to use the squares of mesh cloth standing in for the burqa as a symbol for their campaign, imploring women in the U.S. to "Wear a symbol of remembrance for Afghan women," whereas it would have been a much more potent expression of solidarity to use a pin with a hand folded into a fist as a symbol, enlisting women to "Celebrate the Resistance of Afghan women" (Kolhatkar, 2002). Although the intention may have been otherwise, in this instance the Foundation became complicit in and even instrumental to the process of selectively appropriating the rhetoric of postcolonial feminist organizations for imperialist ends (Hirschkind & Mahmood, 2002).

The divesting of postcolonial women's agency and the selective invocation of postcolonial women's suffering is an established trope within U.S. news discourse (Fair, 1996; Jansen, 1996; Luthra, 2003; Valdivia, 200), which in turn follows an entrenched pattern of "colonial feminism" practiced by the British and the French, among others (Ahmed, 1992). The British campaigned against sati (widow immolation) and child marriage as a way of justifying their rule in South Asia, and focused on the veil as a sign of oppression of Egyptian women (Ahmed, 1992; Spivak, 1988). The French obsessed on the veil in the Algerian context as a way of legitimizing their rule (Lazreg, 1994). The invocation of women's suffering by U.S. news was particularly potent in the Afghan context because of its direct use in the legitimation of the U.S. invasion and its confluence at this juncture with the construct of Islamic fundamentalism.

THE RELATIVE ABSENCE OF THE GENDER FRAME IN THE COVERAGE OF IRAQ

By contrast with U.S. news coverage of Afghanistan, the coverage of Iraq is relatively silent on the question of gender, and the oppression of women does not become a central news frame as it does in the Afghan context. When gendered oppression does enter the news discourse, it is equated not with Islamic fundamentalism but with the general brutality of Saddam Hussein's regime. The trope of Muslim women being rescued from Muslim men by white men is not invoked in the coverage of Iraq as it is in the coverage of Afghanistan. The relative absence of the gender frame in the Iraqi context makes visible the ideologies at play in both contexts. The comparison suggests that the figure of the Muslim woman is admissible only if she can be assimilated within dominant ideologies and subjected to the Orientalist gaze. The very conditions within the Afghan context that made it possible to abstract violence against women from its historical context and magnify it, such as the obvious and outwardly visible restrictions on women's mobility, education, and employment as dictated by religiously based law; the absence of separation between religion and state; and the erosion of a space for the elaboration of a discourse of women's rights were absent from the Iraqi context. Iraqi women's own vocality and their contradictory situation under the Baathist Hussein regime made it harder for either U.S. feminist discourse, U.S. administration discourse, or U.S. news discourse to appropriate aspects of their rhetoric and invoke it in the service of prevailing ideologies as well as in service of the U.S. invasion. In addition, there was no direct instigating factor such as the attacks on September 11 to provide fertile ground for the acceptance of hyperbolic images and easily conjured associations between women's oppression and a number of disparate elements. Whereas the suturing of hatred of America, Al-Qaeda, the Taliban, Islamic fundamentalism, and oppression of women into a singular image went unchallenged in the context of the invasion of Afghanistan, coming as it did on the heels of September 11, such facile and unwarranted associations would have been more open to scrutiny and less easily swallowed in the absence of an Iraqi connection to September 11 (notwithstanding Bush's attempts to make such a connection).

A few stories written after the invasion was underway did attempt to connect women's suffering to Hussein's tenure and to conjure an image of the United States as saving Iraqi women, but they were too few to constitute a significant mental map. A story in *Newsweek* focused on the imprisonment and torture of an Iraqi woman by Hussein's secret police. The story ends with a paraphrase of the woman saying that as far as she's concerned the coalition "did the right thing." (Nordland, 2003). In this way, the story works to legitimize the invasion. Another story in the *The New York Times* starts with "Emboldened by the fall of Saddam Hussein, Iraqi women are pushing for political freedoms many of them have never enjoyed. But as they do, a rising tide of religious zeal threatens even the small victories they have won" (Banerjee, 2004). Throughout the story one gets the impression that the United States is doing what it can to advance women's rights in Iraq, and that a rising Islamic fundamentalism is getting in the way of progress. Once again, selective articulation works to invest the United States with heroism and to obfuscate the complex causes of the rise of Islamism in Iraq since the 1990s, and especially at the current juncture. From other news articles and from interviews of Iraqi women activists in the feminist press it becomes apparent that Iraqi women did indeed have substantial rights in the 1970s and 1980s, and that the decline in their status and the rise in conservative versions of Islam was partly caused by the economic hardships resulting from the Persian Gulf War and economic sanctions imposed by the United States (Bahran, 2003; Collier, 2003).

Other articles work to invest heroism in the United States through circuitous routes. Two of these eulogize Fern Holland, a U.S. aid worker who set up a number of women's centers in Iraq, and who was slain by gunmen in March 2004 (Rubin, 2004; *San Antonio Express-News*, 2004). The representation of her is very much in keeping with the "white Lady Bountiful" image of the benevolent, selfless white woman administering to the masses of both internal and external colonies (Meiners, 2002). Another article creates a portrait of the Iraqi woman Iman Sabeeh, former Olympic athlete and now a Ph.D. in biomechanics. The story gives sketches of her defiance of Saddam's son Uday Hussein and the suffering of athletes under the Hussein regime. The closing note is that with the Husseins toppled by the U.S. government, Sabeeh can finally represent Iraq at the Olympic games. The U.S. comes across as her hero (Brennan, 2004). Yet another story paints a picture of Iraqi women as incapable of fighting for their rights, as having internalized Islamic tenets that oppress them. Describing a women's conference in postwar Iraq held by Iraqi women to press their demands, Faramarzi says, "even the most educated and liberal women dare not break taboos and question some of the more strict Islamic laws that render women half of men" (Faramarzi, 2004). This suggests that Iraqi women need U.S. help in formulating their demands.

Overall, very few news articles in the U.S print media preceding and leading up to the U.S. invasion in March 2003 address gender at all, and those that do reveal the contradictions of the situation in terms of gender. An article in the *San Francisco Chronicle* in January 2003, for example, is titled "1991 war cost Iraqi women rights," making it clear from the outset that the causes of the erosion of Iraqi women's rights are complex, and that the United States is directly implicated in the erosion of rights as a result of their invasion of Iraq in 1991, the ensuing sanctions, and the subsequent invasion in 2003 (Collier, 2003). In this and the few other articles on Iraqi women preceding the U.S. invasion in 2003, it becomes clear that Iraqi women are not suffering from "death by culture" (Narayan, 1997, p. 85) in any straightforward sense. Rather, the causes of their suffering appear more linked to war and economic sanctions, leading to the economic degradation of the country, which has in turn encouraged a conservative turn that erodes women's rights (Bahran, 2003; Collier, 2003; Malik, 2003). This leads the feminist publication *Herizons* to headline a story "Chauvinism no ground for war," implicitly making a comparison with Afghanistan where chauvinism *did* become ground for war within U.S. feminist rhetoric and then was deployed by the mainstream media to "manufacture consent" for the war (Herman & Chomsky, 1988; Malik, 2003; Thobani, 2002b). As the *Herizons* story explains, the otherwise dictatorial Baathist regime of Saddam Hussein put into place a number of measures for the educational and occupational advancement of women and for the advancement of women in the legal sphere, aiming to create gender parity in voting, divorces, taxes, and land ownership (Malik, 2003). To allow for a discussion of gender in the Iraqi context would have gone against the grain of an absolute demonization of Saddam Hussein, a demonization that had been entrenched in U.S. news frames since the time of the Persian Gulf War in 1991 (Morley & Robins, 1995). Although sexual violence was committed against women as part and parcel of the victimization of the people under Saddam Hussein, this victimization did not have an overriding or specifically gendered character, nor did it stem from Islam or interpretations of Islam (Moody & Mantilla, 2003). Hussein's regime was socialist rather than Islamist in its overall orientation, and his reforms benefiting women were in keeping with this general ideological framework (Bahran, 2003; Ismael, 2004). Hussein self-consciously positioned himself and Iraq as secular in opposition to the region's religious fundamentalists (Bahran, 2003). Therefore, even particular facets of women's suffering during Hussein's reign could not be causally linked to Islam without considerably stretching the truth. Although the U.S. news found plenty of symbolic ammunition to demonize Saddam Hussein, the wholesale oppression of women qua women was not available as a convenient trope in this context. Moreover, the confluence of women's oppression and Islamic fundamentalism that fit so well with prevailing U.S. ideologies in the Afghan context was entirely absent as a readily accessible connection in the Iraqi context.

Other contradictions regarding the U.S. role can be glimpsed from the news coverage. For example, one article in the *The San Francisco Chronicle* and another in *The Buffalo News* quotes Iraqi women activists as saying the Coalition Provisional Authority is not doing what it should to ensure adequate participation of Iraqi women in the process of crafting the constitution and forming the new government (Collier, 2003; Khalil, 2004). We hear Safia al-Souhail, an activist and leader of the Central Iraqi Beni-Tamim tribe, saying, "They're [the U.S.] forcing a lot of changes on this society. . . . Suddenly, women's rights are the red line?" referring to the reluctance of U.S. officials to impose a quota for female representation in the new government (Khalil, 2004). There has been enough evidence to show that women in Iraq are at risk of losing the rights they have had since the 1960s to prompt three U.S. women legislators to write a letter to George Bush, with forty-one members of Congress signing on, to urge the Administration to do what it can to ensure that legal protections that women have enjoyed in Iraq for decades are not erased by the Iraqi Governing Council (Ismael, 2004; Lobe, 2004; States News Service, 2004). Even though there are very few reports addressing the possibility of the erosion of Iraqi women's rights in the new government, their very presence puts a dent in the construction of the United States as the savior of Iraqi women. The unveiling metaphor is also unavailable in the Iraqi context because the veil has only been an issue from the late 1990s as a result of a rising conservatism for which the United States is at least as culpable as the Hussein regime (Banerjee, 2004).

The absence of veiling as an issue, as well as the generally mixed picture in terms of women's rights under the Hussein regime, is the reason we do not see the equivalent of the *Time* cover image and title "Lifting the Veil" that appeared after the invasion of Afghanistan. That image, displaying the face of the Afghani woman lit up in angelic fashion, exuding beneficence and passivity, was accompanied by a story that begins, "In the streets of Kabul, you can see something these days that has not been glimpsed there for almost five years—women's faces" (Lacayo, 2001, p. 36). Later in the story, the writers ask us beckoningly, "What are Afghan women really like beneath the burka?" (p. 38). The colonial obsessions with the veil, incorporating fantasies of intimacy, and the tendency to deploy spectacular practices affecting women in the process of defining the colonial Self in contrast to the other, have been well documented (Abu-Lughod, 2002; Alloula, 1986; Narayan, 1997). In the age of U.S. imperialism it is altogether too tempting to deploy this imagery in the current context. However, it was not available in the Iraqi context, and therefore the Iraqi woman is entirely absent from the cover of *Time* magazine. The women displayed instead are a U.S. woman soldier featuring the cover story "When Mom Goes to War" in the March 24, 2003 issue, and Jessica Lynch as cover girl accompanying the story "The Real Story of Jessica Lynch" in the November 17, 2003 issue.

CREATING CONTINUITIES AND DISCONTINUITIES AS IDEOLOGICAL WORK

The comparison between coverage of Afghanistan and Iraq makes visible some of ideological work that goes into the construction of news frames consonant with U.S. foreign policy. This construction involves the selective appropriation of information from a variety of sources, and the articulation of these abstracted bits of information with prevailing notions in the United

States regarding the definition of civilization and place of gender within it. The resulting construction reproduces the chasmic divides between "us and them," the civilized West and the uncivilized rest. Anything that would seriously disrupt the separation, particularly between Western and Islamic civilization, or create continuities between the two, is not allowable in current news frames. Gender is a particularly useful trope in this context when available because it serves as a convenient dividing marker between the West and Islam, between civilization and the absence of it. In general the ideological work of the press involves, among other mechanisms, making visible certain continuities and ignoring others from potentially infinite connections that can be made.

Among the continuities which the news coverage attempts is that of the oppression of Muslim women by Muslim men and by Islam. The *Time* December 2001 issue featuring "Lifting the Veil" on the cover page also includes a story on "The Women of Islam." The subtitle explains, "The Taliban perfected subjugation. But nowhere in the Muslim world are women treated as equals" (Beyer, 2001, p. 50). The story goes on to show the varied ways in which women's rights are restricted in several Islamic countries, ranging from Malaysia to Saudi Arabia. It would have been equally plausible to have emphasized the discontinuity between different Islamic countries in terms of various facets of equality, with great variance in political participation, education, literacy, and so forth. For example, Mernissi (2001) notes that in many Muslim countries women have aggressively infiltrated university faculties and male-dominated professional fields such as engineering, with Egypt outstripping France or Canada in terms of the proportion of university faculty who are women and Turkey and Syria far outpacing the United Kingdom or the Netherlands in terms of the percentage of female students enrolled in engineering courses.

The article in *Newsweek* suggests that where Muslim women are freest, this has been achieved by "overthrowing Islamic precepts in favor of secular rule" (Beyer, 2001, p. 52). Once again, it would have been equally plausible to show variance rather than continuity in this regard, showing how women have fought for their rights in varied contexts and in varied ways within Islamic countries, varying from the insistence on a secular state, as is the case with RAWA in Afghanistan, to a struggle over the interpretation of Islam, as is the case in the Iranian context. Even in specific countries such as Afghanistan, there is variance between women's groups as to whether they should work toward secularism or within the Islamic framework (Abu-Lughod, 2002). By flattening out these differences, it becomes possible to create a continuity of "women oppressed by Islam" that fits well with the prevailing Western ideologies, which are themselves part of the legacy of Orientalism from the colonial past. This continuity fits in with another one reproduced by the news, that of Islamic fundamentalism. In this continuity, the barbarism and lack of civilization of Islamic fundamentalism is evidenced by phenomena as varied as the call to jihad, the primitive forms of punishment accorded to people in Islamic countries, the lack of separation between religion and state, and the oppression of women. Once again, continuity is created where diversity among Islamic countries would be an equally plausible construct.

On the other hand, there are possible continuities that are repressed because they would pierce the ideological veil so carefully drawn over the public's eyes. One such possible continuity is the presence of women's oppression in the West and the Islamic world. For example, Franks (2003) analyzes the affinities that bind the United States with the Taliban, especially with regard to gender. She points to the high degree of sexual violence and the lucrative sex industry as two features binding U.S. society with Afghani society under the Taliban. She notes that the same rules of violent subjugation of women exist in both the United States and Taliban-controlled Afghanistan; the difference is that in the United States these rules are unwritten and in Afghanistan the Taliban codified them, writing them into law. In addition, the Taliban justified their control of women on the basis of "respect," hiding the sexual aspect of subjugation, whereas in the United States women are "compelled to formulate their identities as ever-available sexual beings under the guise of 'sexual liberation'" (Franks, 2003, p. 12). In both societies, Franks goes on to explain, the fantasy of women prevails over the reality of women; the two functions allowed in this fantasy are the mother or the whore, and in both women are subjugated. Franks says that this inadmissible continuity is one of the reasons the United States ignored the Taliban's treatment of women until it became convenient to do so for its own purposes, and why it again dropped the subject soon after the invasion.

Mernissi, in *Scherezade Goes West* (2001), contemplates the continuities between the West and East from a different angle. She says, "Framing youth as beauty and condemning maturity is the weapon used against women in the West just as limiting assess to public space is the weapon used in the East. The objective remains identical in both cultures: to make women feel unwelcome, inadequate, and ugly" (Mernissi, 2001, p. 216). She considers this use of time by Western men to control women as in some ways more insidious and more dangerous than the use of space by the Muslim man to establish male domination. Another possible continuity emerges from Mernissi's discussion. She sees extreme cases of violence against women such as in Afghanistan as constituting a reaction to the emergence of women in the Islamic world as a significant civic force pushing for change. When seen in this way, parallels immediately arise between the Islamic situation and the backlash against feminism experienced in the United States (Faludi, 1992). The point I'm making here is that there are quite plausible continuities between the United States and Afghanistan, the West and Islam, that are not admissible within the current ideological nexus, and that are repressed in favor of discontinuities such as the civilized United States with liberated women versus uncivilized Islam that oppresses its women.

Another repressed continuity is that of American imperialism, which deploys the gender card to legitimize its own ends, only to neglect gender issues once its military ends are accomplished. In addition, the United States has deliberately funded and made alliances with a number of countries that were in gross violation of women's rights. Through both direct military intervention and the arming of extremist groups within a number of countries for geopolitical ends, the U.S. has played a direct role in creating a situation inimical to women's rights. These connections are never made in the news coverage. Both in Afghanistan and Iraq, the United States has had a direct role to play in creating an environment that has encouraged the rise of extremist strains of Islam, which has in turn led to the curtailment of women's rights. In both countries, the United States has neglected to assure that women's rights are safeguarded in the new government, that women participate fully in the formation of the new government, and that security is established on the streets to allow for greater mobility for women (Franks, 2003; Kolhatkar, 2002; Osborn & Dalton, 2003). The fact that the gender card has been employed for narrow political purposes is clear when one realizes that the United States has supported regimes that have trampled on women's rights, such as Saudi Arabia during the Persian Gulf war, and Pakistan during the Zia ul Haq regime and in the present (Franks, 2003).

By selectively appropriating elements from women's movement rhetoric and by suturing certain elements together while repressing other connections, the U.S. press in this instance can be seen to reproduce prevailing Western ideologies regarding Islam and its relationship to gender. It can also be seen to help legitimize U.S. foreign policy. The role of the U.S. press as a handmaiden of U.S. foreign policy has been well documented (Herman & Chomsky, 1988; Kellner, 1992). The role of the press in extending prevailing ideologies that divide "us" from "them", the civilized West from the uncivilized East, has also been well documented. Narayan (1997) points out that "colonial encounters seem to instigate a process of defining 'the Self in *contrast* to the other' on the part of both colonizer and colonized, and practices affecting women commonly seem to become central elements in this project" (p. 66). Franks (2003) talks about how the West becomes "transfixed by the suffering of the other and by the idea of its own heroic status" (p. 146), which in turn justifies intervention. She suggests a deep collective psychic investment in maintaining the separation between "us" and "them", especially with regard to gender. To breach this divide would force Western societies to examine seriously their own "obscene underside", including the ways in which women are erased within their own borders (p. 135). Focusing on the surprising affinities between West and East, West and Islam, or between the United States and Afghanistan under the Taliban would risk "exposing a fissure within its perception of itself, the traumatic antagonism within its own cultural identity" (p. 151). Moallem (2001) points to the same psychic investment when she asks, "can it be that Islamic fundamentalism is the noxious reservoir of an unresolved past and an unexamined present in the West?" (p. 299).

Just as this examination of U.S. press coverage has shown the conservative role of the press in reproducing dominant ideologies and legitimizing the U.S. imperialism, it has also given glimmers of another possibility. The contradictions that appeared in both the mainstream and feminist press could become the basis of unraveling the ideological consensus that currently exists on the chasmic divide between the West and the rest, on the passivity and lack of agency of postcolonial women, and a host of other debilitating paradigms that act as a retrogressive pull on Western societies. Given the right conditions, the image of the angelic and oppressed Afghani woman could yet be replaced by the equally cogent and perhaps more telling image of the Afghani woman with her fists high in the air, marching to change her destiny.

NOTES

1. Although for analysis of U.S. coverage of the war in Afghanistan I rely primarily on existing scholarship, I do include some primary analysis of some of the most salient coverage such as the cover and articles in the December 2001 issue of *Time* magazine. For the textual analysis of U.S. coverage of the war in Iraq, I looked for all articles that had anything to do with women and Iraq from January 2003 to March 2004 through a Lexis Nexus search. I discarded all non–U.S. news articles.
2. Interpreting Said, Ganguly (1992) defines Orientalism as "the discursive apparatus by means of which the Orient is actively produced, fixed, and objectified by Western imagery and imaginations" (p. 73).
3. Goldman uses the terms abstraction and equivalence in relation to advertising, but the same processes can be seen at work in the news. These processes allow for the atomization and selective appropriation of particular concepts and ideas to create associations that serve particular commercial or political purposes.

REFERENCES

Abu-Lughod, L. (2002). Do Muslim women really need saving? Anthropological reflections on cultural relativism and its others. *American Anthropologist, 104(3)*, 783-790.

Ahmed, L. (1992). *Women and gender in Islam.* New Haven, CT: Yale University Press.

Alloula, M. (1986). *The colonial harem.* Minneapolis: University of Minnesota Press.

Bahran, Y. (2003). Iraq: The status of women now and in future. *WIN News, 29(1),* 63.

Banerjee, N. (2004, February 26). The struggle for Iraq: Equal rights. *The New York Times,* Section A, p. 13.

Beyer, L. (2001, December 3). The women of Islam. *Time, 158(24),* 50-59.

Brennan, C. (2004, April 22). Wait nearly over for Iraqi woman. *USA Today,* p. 2C.

Collier, R. (2003, January 25). 1991 war cost Iraqi women rights. *San Francisco Chronicle,* p. A1.

Cooke, M. (2002). Saving brown women. *Signs, 28(1),* 468-470.

Fair, J.E. (1996). The body politic, the bodies of women, and the politics of famine in U.S. television coverage of famine in the horn of Africa. *Journalism and Mass Communication Monographs, 158.*

Faludi, S. (1992). *Backlash: The undeclared war against American women.* New York: Knopf.

Faramarzi, S. (2004, February 24). Women trying to improve their lot in Iraq. *Associated Press Online.*

Franks, M.A. (2003). Obscene undersides: Women and evil between the Taliban and the United States. *Hypatia, 18(1),* 135-156.

Ganguly, K. (1992). Accounting for others: Feminism and representation. In L. Rakow (Ed.), *Women making meaning: New feminist directions in communication* (pp. 60-79). New York: Routledge.

Goldman, R. (1992). *Reading ads socially.* New York: Routledge.

Herman, E. & Chomsky, N. (1988). *Manufacturing consent: The political economy of the mass media.* New York: Pantheon Books.

Hirschkind, C., & Mahmood, S. (2002). Feminism, the Taliban, and politics of counter-insurgency. *Anthropological Quarterly, 75(2),* 339-354.

Ismael, S.T. (2004). Dismantling the Iraqi social fabric: From dictatorship through sanctions to occupation. *Journal of Comparative Family Studies, 35(2),* 333-349.

Jansen, S.C. (1996). Beaches without bases: The gender order. In G. Gerbner, H. Mowlana, & H.I. Schiller (Eds.), *Invisible crises: What conglomerate control of media means for America and the world* (pp.131-144). Boulder: CO: Westview Press.

Kellner, D. (1992). *The Persian Gulf TV war.* Boulder: Westview Press.

Khalil, A. (2004, February 22). What Iraqi women want. *The Buffalo News,* p. F1.

Kolhatkar, S. (2002, March 31). "Saving" Afghan women. *Women in Action, 1.*

Lacayo, R. (2001, Decmber 3). About face: An inside look at how women fared under Taliban oppression and what the future holds for them now. *Time, 158(24),* 34-49.

Lazreg, M. (1994). *The eloquence of silence: Algerian women in question.* New York: Routledge.

Lobe, J. (2004, February 3). U.S. lawmakers say council's plan curbs women's rights. *IPS-Inter Press Service.*

Luthra, R. (2003). Recovering women's voice: Communicative empowerment of women of the south. *Communication Yearbook, 27,* 45-66.

Malik, L. (2003, March). Chauvinism no ground for war. *Herizons, 16(4)*, 48.

Meiners, E. (2002). Contradictions at the Cook County jail: Snapshots on the complexities of volunteering for social change. In S. Jackson & A. Russo (Eds.), *Talking back and acting out: Women negotiating the media across cultures* (pp. 136-150). New York: Peter Lang.

Mernissi, F. (2001). *Scherezade goes west: Different cultures, different harems.* New York: Washington Square Press.

Moallem, M. (2001). Whose fundamentalism? *Meridians, 2(2)*, 298-301.

Moody, M., & Mantilla, K. (2003). After the war: Women in Iraq. *Off Our Backs, 33(7/8)*, 8.

Morley, D. & Robins, K. (1995). *Spaces of identity: Global media, electronic landscapes and cultural boundaries.* New York: Routledge.

Narayan, U. (1997). *Dislocating cultures: Identities, traditions, and third world feminism.* New York: Routledge.

Nordland, R. (2003, April 12). Iraqi metamorphoses. *Newsweek Web Exclusive.*

Osborne, C., & Dalton, M. (2003). Iraq: Streets of Baghdad still a war zone for city's women. *Off Our Backs, 33(9/10)*, 5.

Parmeswaran, R. (1996). Coverage of "bride burning" in the *Dallas Observer*: A cultural analysis of the "other". *Frontiers, 16 (2/3)*, 69-100.

Rubin, A.J. (2004, March 16). American put her life on the line for Iraqi women. *Los Angeles Times*, Part A, p. 1.

Said, E.W. (1979). *Orientalism.* London: Vintage Books.

San Antonio Express-News. (2004, April 23). Iraqi women need the coalition's help. *San Antonio Express-News*, p. 10B.

Spivak, G.C. (1988). Can the subaltern speak? In C. Nelson & L. Grossberg (Eds.), *Marxism and the interpretation of culture* (pp. 271-313). Urbana: University of Illinois Press.

States News Service. (2004, February 2). Members of Congress send letter to president asking U.S. to avert looming women's rights crisis in Iraq. *States News Service.*

Thobani, S. (2002a). Women's resistance conference—Excerpts from speech. *Meridians: Feminism, Race, Transnationalism, 2(2)*, 283-288.

Thobani, S. (2002b). War frenzy. *Meridians: Feminism, Race, Transnationalism, 2(2)*, 289-297.

Valdivia, A. (2000). *A Latina in the land of Hollywood and other essays on media culture.* Tucson: The University of Arizona Press.

Chapter 15

The Power of Myths

The War on Terror and Military Might

Justin Lewis

This chapter will argue that one of the most important political consequences of the "war on terror" is that it plays a key role in sustaining a political climate in which substantial public resources are allocated to military purposes. In so doing, I will make the following points.

First, in the post–Cold War era, current levels of military spending in Britain and, in particular, the United States, are far in excess of plausible defence needs. Indeed, the risks of military invasion are now so low that the rationale for military spending no longer has anything to do with defence. Although this is, on one level, acknowledged by governments, the fact that military spending remains high means that, in effect, the official modus operandi for military spending has undergone a radical shift, from the ability to deter invasion to the capacity to invade. This has occurred without any serious public debate and without clear evidence of public support.

Second, this is made possible partly by the failure of progressive political leaders to highlight the issue and by the failure of the news media to provide any serious analysis of the comparative levels of military spending and the shifting rationale that sustains it. But it has also been facilitated by the coverage given to the "war on terror," which is excessive and bears little relation to the actual risks posed by international terrorism. Indeed, analysis of the coverage given to the issue against the actual incidence of terrorist attacks—even as defined by the U.S. government—shows that media coverage is more a response to political rhetoric about terrorism than any serious analysis of the actual threat.

Third, media coverage and public debate is also marked by a failure to interrogate the myth that military spending can be used to fight terrorism. This myth has been sustained by the use of the U.S. and British forces to attack nation states in the name of the "war on terror," even while there is little evidence to suggest that such a strategy is effective. The "war on terror" is thereby allowed to provide political cover for a new neo-imperialist approach to military expenditure.

FROM DEFENCE TO ATTACK: THE SHIFTING RATIONALE FOR MILITARY SPENDING

The U.S.–based Center for Defense Information (CDI) produces data on military spending around the world. In isolation, the numbers themselves are hard to comprehend. Unless you're very rich indeed, it is difficult to conceive of figures like 5 billion, 50 billion or 500 billion dollars. Most people are likely to put all three in the same mental category: they're all well out of reach, on a scale that belongs to the world of governments and large corporations. So if we are told that our government spends so many billions on "defence"–as we occasionally are in Britain—the numbers by themselves are, for most people, fairly meaningless.

What makes the CDI data compelling is that it is comparative, allowing us to see how countries like Britain and the United States compare with the rest of the world. Indeed, it is only in comparative terms that military spending makes sense: one of the central rationales behind military spending, after all, is to spend as much as (or more) than the countries you might be at war with. It was just such comparisons that provided the calculus of the Cold War, as the U.S. and Soviet blocs both argued that parity was a necessary precondition for security—a process in which data collection became deeply politicized, with subterfuge on both sides. The irony was, of course, that both sides, for different reasons, saw it in their interests to exaggerate Soviet military strength.

All this changed when the Cold War ended, when comparisons of military strength suddenly became irrelevant to mainstream discourse about levels of spending. Comparative information (easily available from groups like the CDI) rarely makes its way into public discussion or debate. Indeed, when military spending is discussed, it is usually in the context of cutbacks and shortfalls rather than excess. Rarely do we see the central question of what such spending is for addressed, or any discussion of how it might be justified in relation to a specific military threat (Lewis, 2001).

In 2003, the United States spent $399 billion on its military. If you include related spending like foreign military aid and military space projects, the figure goes up to over $500 billion. This figure has little to do with the U.S. role in peacekeeping operations, which, while often newsworthy, accounted for a tiny proportion of overall spending ($1 billion in 2002). But it is only when we look at comparisons between the United States and the rest of the world that these figures begin to tell the story of the extent of U.S. military dominance.

Taking the first, smaller, figure, we find that not only is the U.S. spending at over six times the level of the second biggest military spender (Russia), the United States outspends the *next twenty biggest* military powers in the world, most of whom are allies, put together. Moreover, the United States' global allies consistently outspend countries the United States regards as hostile. So, for example, South Korea spends significantly more than North Korea, and Israel and Saudi Arabia easily outspend other countries in the Middle East. In other words, at *one fifth* of its present level, the United States would still be the world's foremost military power in, from its perspective, a relatively secure world, in which its regional allies are at a clear advantage to its enemies.

In 2003, the countries regarded by the U.S. State department as potential adversaries, even when combined, do not add up to a threatening military force. In 2003, Cuba, Iran, Iraq, Libya, North Korea, Syria, and Sudan *put together* were outspent by the United States alone by a factor of 33 to 1. Britain, meanwhile, as the United States' most prominent ally, may not be the most populous country in Western Europe but it has the largest military budget, significantly outspending France, Germany, Spain, and Italy.

These figures prompt a question rarely posed by politicians or journalists. Why does the United States—and to a lesser extent, Britain—devote so much public expenditure to defence? Why does Britain require more military expenditure than, say, France or Germany? Fifty years ago, the idea that a country like Britain needed to defend itself against possible invasion by a foreign power was made deeply plausible by recent history. Even if many doubted it, the Cold War kept such a prospect alive. But in the post–Cold War era, with an expanded European Union, the prospect has receded to such an extent that it would be difficult to imagine who would have either the will or the capacity to attempt such a thing. Indeed, the British government now ranks the risk of a military invasion as "zero."

In other words, military spending in the United States and Britain has little to do with the defense of its territory. If we look at U.S. foreign policy, for example, we can see how elite support for huge levels of military spending is not sustained by the threat of invasion but by neo-imperialist ideas about "full spectrum dominance," as well as by powerful bureaucratic, business, and political vested interests (Hellinger & Judd, 1991). In Britain, too, military spending has become entwined, once more, with notions of empire as its forces have been dispatched to defend not its borders but its "interests," whether in Kuwait, Kosovo, Afghanistan, or Iraq.

How far this actually represents a shift in foreign policy is a matter of debate. What *is* clear is that, in the last two decades, those who argued that the end of the Cold War allowed us to enjoy a "peace dividend" (transferring resources from defense to more pressing or tangible needs in transport, health, education, environmental protection, or poverty reduction), have, most notably in the United States but also in Britain, been outmaneuvered. Put bluntly, the logic of military spending has, without any serious public debate, shifted from defence to attack; or, to use rather gentler foreign policy parlance, from deterrence to a capacity for intervention.

Not only has this sea change occurred without public discussion, but the continuance of high levels of military spending has, at best, only tepid levels of public support. Public opinion in both countries on military spending and foreign policy tends to be idealistic, multilateralist, and anti-imperialist (Lewis, 2001). It is guided neither by strategic ambitions nor by the realpolitik of support for the defence industry (the United States and Britain are the world's largest military exporters). Surveys in the United States have, for some time, shown that public spending on areas like health and education are consistently more popular than military spending. Thus, although support in the United States for increased spending in areas like health and education regularly reaches levels between 60 and 80 percent, support for increasing military spending generally hovers around 20 to 25 percent (Page & Shapiro, 1992). More recently, a survey by the Program on International Policy Attitudes (PIPA) published in April 2004 found that support for increasing military spending was down to only 16 percent, while 41 percent were in favor of cutbacks. The survey also found that most Americans preferred arms control and multilateral agreements, rather than the threat of military force, as a way to combat the proliferation of weapons of mass destruction (http://www.pipa.org/whatsnew/html/new_4_15_04.html#1).

Similarly, Britain's position as Western Europe's biggest military spender is held without any clear enthusiasm from the British public who, when it comes to public expenditure, also tend to favor areas like health and education. A Guardian/ICM poll conducted in November 2002, for example, found 48 percent in favor of cutting military spending, with only 38 percent against. In effect, both countries maintain high levels of military spending for purposes other than defence without a clear, popular mandate for doing so.

In *Constructing Public Opinion* (Lewis, 2001), I argued that the political viability of high levels of military spending rested on three conditions.

The first condition is people's tendency to underestimate significantly the size of the military budget, especially in comparison to other areas of public spending or in an international context. The second condition is the ability of elites to exploit public support for a moral, principled foreign policy—based on support for democracy, human rights, and international law—by focusing on those instances where U.S. or British foreign policy might be presented in these terms (while playing down the many instances where it could not). The third, and perhaps most crucial, condition depends on the presence of a credible global military threat.

All these conditions rely upon patterns of media coverage to sustain them. The comparative size of military spending is rarely discussed in news coverage, except when the issue is generally raised in response to hawkish claims about the poverty of the armed forces. This happened, for example, on July 1, 2001, when the criticisms made by a parliamentary committee in Britain for what it saw as *shortfalls* in military spending were widely reported. Furthermore, in both Britain and the United States, military interventions are consistently associated in media discourse with democracy and human rights (despite both governments' questionable foreign policy record on these principles).

The collapse of the Soviet Union in 1989 appeared, however, to remove the last of these conditions. It was, with almost indecent haste, swiftly replaced by a discourse about "dangerous regimes," one in which Saddam Hussein featured prominently, supported by a cast that included Manuel Noriega and Slobodan Milosevic. For all its fragility (given the size of the threat), this discourse was sustained throughout the 1990s. It was perhaps best expressed by President George Bush during his election campaign when he said (at Iowa Western Community College on Jan. 21, 2000) that "When I was coming up, it was a dangerous world, and you knew exactly who they were. . . . It was us versus them, and it was clear who them was. Today, we are not so sure who the they are, but we know they're there." Although this statement was ridiculed in some quarters, the idea that the United States needed to be well armed in a potentially dangerous and unstable world, where the threat is vague rather than specific, was the defining logic for military spending increases endorsed by his predecessor, President Clinton, during his second term.

And yet the political purchase of the "dangerous regimes" discourse is inevitably diminished by the distance of the threat. So, for example, the senior George Bush's dramatic drop in approval ratings between the 1991 Gulf War and the 1992 presidential election revealed the flimsiness of the patriotic fervor that greeted the liberation of Kuwait. The U.S. victory quickly subsided into a feeling that the United States should sort out its problems at home rather than abroad—hence the success, in the 1992 election, of the Clinton campaign's credo that "It's the economy, stupid."

The idea that "the world changed" on September 11, 2001, has become something of a cliché and, I will argue, it was also a self-fulfilling prophecy. The emotive power of the tragic events of September 11, 2001, has been used with merciless frequency to win arguments or divert attention from else-where (Maxwell, 2002). It made the "terrorist threat" cruelly tangible and gave the war on terrorism an urgency and relevance it did not have before. Unlike the discourse about "dangerous dictators," the "war on terrorism" is analogous to the Cold War in the sense that the threat to the United States or Britain is seen as direct and invasive.

In short, there can be little doubt that the "war on terrorism" has been extraordinarily useful to those political, corporate, and military elites who are committed to maintaining high levels of military spending (Lewis, Maxwell, & Miller, 2002). If the appalling events of September 11, 2001, made this possible, it is hard to dispute Robert Entman's point that since then the Bush Administration, along with the Blair government in Britain, has done its best to construct the "war on terrorism" as the new foreign policy doctrine to replace anti-communism (Entman, 2004). They have been facili-tated in this endeavor by a significant shift in news values *since* the September 11 attacks. Although terrorism has always been newsworthy, it has never occupied the degree of sustained news prominence it currently receives. What we need to ask, however, is whether such prominence is justified.

THE THREAT OF TERRORISM

It is no surprise to find that international terrorism has received more cov-erage since September 11, 2001, than hitherto. So, for example, Table 15.1 shows that in a sample of British newspapers (the *Times* and the *Financial Times*, the *Guardian*, the *Mail*, and the *Mirror*) the phrase "international ter-rorism" occurred significantly more often in stories after September 2001. Between 1997 and 2000, the phrase was used, on average, 76 times per year, whereas from 2002 to 2004, the rate increased dramatically to 397 per year (over five times the previous rate).

Table 15.1 also suggests that the shift in news values after autumn 2001 was more than a temporary response to a major news event. Although we might have expected the coverage to diminish with time, the prominence of the term in press coverage appears to have strengthened rather than faded.

The significant increase in coverage given to international terrorism is, according to conventional wisdom, a response to an increase in the threat— one epitomized by the attacks on the twin towers and the Pentagon in 2001, and, to a lesser extent, subsequent attacks in Bali, Madrid, and London. Although these attacks were, of course, devastating to those affected, and all

TABLE 15.1. Number of Mentions of "International Terrorism" Since 1997 (includes Sunday editions of the *Times, Mail*, and *Mirror*).

	TIMES/FT	GUARDIAN	MAIL	MIRROR	TOTAL
1997	45	17	8	3	73
1998	59	26	18	9	112
1999	35	10	9	2	56
2000	48	8	4	3	63
2001	353	74	69	67	563
2002	234	91	44	53	422
2003	247	58	57	53	415
2004	198	58	42	55	353
2005	147	96	22	28	293

received intense news coverage, it is not at all clear that they were, in fact, indicative of a significant increase in the threat from international terrorism. The U.S. Government's own figures (revised to allow consistency of annual comparisons on 22 June 2004) indicate that, with occasional blips (notably 1991, 1995, 1999-2001), there is a general pattern of *decline* in international terrorist attacks since 1987. According to these figures, there were *three times* as many international terrorist attacks per year during the period 1985-88 as during the period 2002-03 (U.S. Department of State, Patterns of Global Terrorism, 2004). Interestingly, on April 7, 2005, less than one month before it was to issue its 2004 mandated annual report on global terrorism, the Department of State decided to stop publishing its reports on "Patterns of Global Terrorism." Its more recent reports do not include statistical data on significant international terrorist incidents.

This suggests, first of all, that media coverage of international terrorism is seriously out of kilter with the threat it poses. Indeed, if we look at the number of international terrorist incidents per year (according to the U.S. government data) and compare them with the number of mentions of "international terrorism" in a sample of the British press (the *Times, Sunday Times, Financial Times*, and the *Guardian*), we see remarkably little connection between the two. So, for example, Table 15.2 indicates that international terrorism became highly newsworthy in 1986 (receiving more mentions than any of the last twenty years except 2001). This was a year in which Libya became the bete noir of international terrorism, and when President Reagan ordered the bombing of Tripoli. But although the U.S. data show an increase in the number of terrorist attacks in the following year, news coverage actually drops significantly. Similarly, the increase in incidents in 1999 and 2000 are not matched by the coverage, which shows decreasing news media interest in the issue during these years.

TABLE 15.2. Number of Mentions of "International Terrorism" in the *Times*,
FT and *Guardian* since 1985 Compared with the Total Number
of Terrorist Attacks

	TIMES/FT	GUARDIAN	TOTAL MENTIONS	NO. OF INCIDENTS
1985	76	33	109	635
1986	237	101	338	612
1987	56	16	72	665
1988	44	30	74	605
1989	70	18	88	375
1990	32	20	52	437
1991	40	21	61	565
1992	24	19	43	363
1993	29	14	43	431
1994	36	17	53	322
1995	42	22	64	440
1996	62	28	90	296
1997	45	17	62	304
1998	59	26	85	274
1999	35	10	45	395
2000	48	8	56	426
2001	353	74	427	355
2002	234	91	325	205
2003	247	58	305	208

These figures do not, of course, take into account the scale, location or drama of the incidents. However, the biggest international terrorist incidents to occur on UK soil in the last 20 years were the Lockerbie/Pan Am plane bombing in late December 1998 and the attacks in London on 7 July 2005. While both received significant coverage as news events, neither event appears to have had a major impact in the *overall* coverage of international terrorism. In the case of Lockerbie, we see only a modest increase in coverage in 1988-89, while the year of the 2005 London bombings saw less coverage of international terrorism than any year since 2000.

Moreover, if we use a different criterion and look at the number of casualties from these incidents in the six years between 1998 and 2003, we find that the peak year was *not* 2001—despite the 4,465 casualties on September 11, accounting for 77 percent of annual casualties that year—but 1998. Yet the high number of casualties in 1998 did not prompt a significant increase in media coverage of international terrorism. The fact that 80 percent of the casualties that year were in Africa might partly explain (though not necessarily excuse) the lack of political and media interest; and yet there were also a comparatively high number of casualties (405) that year in Western Europe.

A similar lack of synchronicity between international terrorism and media coverage in the United States (where there have been no victims of *international* terrorism since 2001), has led Norris, Kern, and Just to argue that "what changed, and changed decisively with 9/11, were American perceptions of the threat of world terrorism rather than the actual reality" (Norris, Kern, & Just, 2003, p. 4). In other words, media coverage has not been driven by the incidence or scale of terrorist activity. In both Britain and the United States, the scale and imminence of the current threat would appear to have been overstated—especially when weighed against other risks to human life (such as climate change) or against other periods when more terrorist incidents took place.

Agenda-setting analysis has consistently shown that although the prominence of an issue in media coverage does not necessarily reflect actual risks or trends, it is *the coverage* that influences public levels of concern (e.g., Iyengar & Kinder, 1987; McCombs, Danielian, & Wanta, 1995). So, for example, if crime rates are falling while media coverage of crime is increasing, most people are likely to assume crime rates are going up. It is, therefore, not unusual for a story to become prominent without sustained or systematic evidence to support it. Media coverage will often fluctuate on the basis of news conventions and practices rather than because of coherent, measured responses to the wider world.

We should not be surprised, in this context, if the media coverage of terrorism is a poor indicator of actual levels of risk. It is also fairly predictable that the media's pre-occupation with terrorism should spill over into public perceptions. Hence, for example, an ICM poll for BBC Radio Five Live in February 2003 indicated that 80 percent of those surveyed thought that a major terrorist attack in the United Kingdom was "fairly likely," "very likely" or "certain" in the year to come. The fact that no such attack occurred is indicative of the discrepancy between media coverage and the actual level of risk.

Similarly, ICM/Retail Week polls measuring changes in consumer behavior as a result of terrorism indicate that around one in four people claim to have changed their behavior as result of the fear of terrorism. Public transport was easily the main area of concern, with respondents in the South East most likely to have changed their behavior and those in the North, Scotland, and Wales least likely to have done so.

In January 2004 the British government's chief scientific advisor, Sir David King, caused a stir when he wrote an article in *Science* in which he suggested that climate change was a far greater threat to the world than international terrorism. In terms of a data-driven risk analysis, King's assessment was unremarkable. In media terms, however, it was highly controversial, because it took place in a context in which the news coverage of the terrorist threat far outweighed coverage of the risks of climate change. As a consequence, polls have shown terrorism to be high on the public's list of concerns, whereas climate change hardly registers.

It hardly needs saying that the perception that there has been a high risk of terrorism since September 11, 2001 has had fundamental consequences, leading to tougher security measures, stricter immigration controls, and a doctrine of pre-emptive military action.

But although these aspects have received a degree of public scrutiny, one of its most profound—and less discussed—effects has been to provide the political conditions for the continuing allocation of significant public resources to military spending. Even though there is still little public support for increasing military spending, the prominence of the terrorist threat makes the political climate favorable to a new, costly, and interventionist foreign policy.

Two important questions are raised by these observations. First, what drives the excessive media coverage of international terrorism, and second, how is a nonmilitary threat used to justify spending on costly items like tanks, missiles, and aircraft carriers?

The answer to the first of these questions is, at least in part, fairly straightforward. Research has repeatedly shown that the news media tend to allow political elites to define the news agenda (see, e.g., Brookes, Lewis, & Wahl-Jorgensen, 2003; Gans, 1979; Tuchman, 1978), especially where there is a bipartisan consensus (Zaller, 1992), such as there is for the "war against terrorism." So, although the incidence of international terrorism may be decreasing, *the political rhetoric about terrorism has increased significantly.* The increase in news coverage is thus in response to words rather than deeds. News frameworks, once established, are powerful determinants of what is newsworthy and what is not (Kitzinger, 2000). The "threat of terrorism," having been established as a major story, is easily sustained by a series of reports of threats, arrests, assessment of risks, and attacks around the world.

SLEDGEHAMMERS AND MOSQUITOES: THE LINKING OF TERRORISM WITH MILITARY SPENDING

The link between terrorism and military preparedness is, in many ways, bizarre. The whole modus operandi of terrorist action is that it *bypasses* military barriers, operating in civic spaces rather than on battlefields. Even if nothing is done to address the conditions that increase the ability of terrorist groups to recruit, the only viable defences against terrorist activities are good intelligence, forms of policing, and well-equipped emergency services. The bulk of military spending, by contrast, is on weapons systems and on armed forces designed, equipped, and trained for conventional warfare, and thus largely irrelevant to the prevention of terrorism. The use of military force to counter terrorism is, in this sense, not even a case of using a sledgehammer to crack a nut, but like wielding a sledgehammer to swat a mosquito—both disproportionate and ineffective.

It is in this context that that the lazy bundling together of terrorism with national security and national defence feeds a neo-imperialist agenda for maintaining a powerful military for use in global forms of intervention. This is facilitated by a well-rehearsed discourse about "terrorist" or "rogue" states, one that is central to sustaining the terrorism/military link. If terrorism can be seen as fuelled by nation states, it provides a logic for a *military* solution to the problem of terrorism and, in turn, the rationale for high levels of military spending.

This has been part of U.S. State Department doctrine for some time (well before September 2001) with the branding of countries like Iraq, North Korea, Libya, Cuba, and Iran as "terrorist states." What has changed since September 11, 2001 is the ability of this discourse to engage public opinion, making terrorism highly newsworthy and a key area of public concern. The stakes here are high and involve a range of powerful vested interests. If the problem of terrorism can be linked to the need to take *military* action, it provides a rationale for military spending every bit as powerful as, though considerably less coherent than, the Cold War.

The shifting motives for the 2003 war on Iraq have been discussed elsewhere (Brookes et al., 2004; Lewis & Brookes, 2004; Tumber & Palmer, 2004), but whereas the connection between Iraq and international terrorism was, at best, opaque, the specter of the terrorist threat was constantly invoked by those making the prowar case. Although this sometimes involved specific—and unsupportable—claims about links between Saddam Hussein and Al-Qaeda (notably by members of the U.S. administration), the linking of the two was often vague and imprecise. At its most direct, the threat of Iraq's weapons of mass destruction was magnified by the possibility of such weapons ending up in the hands of terrorists, but often prowar rhetoric would simply invoke Saddam Hussein and the war on terrorism in the same breath. Like most contemporary advertising, this is a discourse of juxtaposition in which a connection is merely implied rather than stated.

This linkage, I would suggest, has seeped its way into media coverage and the public understanding of the issue. It is notable, in this respect, that the opinion pollsters MORI, in their regular ranking of issues the British public regard as important, lump "terrorism" in with "defence." What seems like a simple matter of convenience in coding categories is, in fact, an implicit acceptance of the logic that terrorism is a military matter rather than, say, an issue of crime or security.

On a cruder level, the success of this rhetorical strategy was illustrated by Kull's research into public beliefs and support for the war in Iraq (Kull, 2003). The study established that for large sections of the public, support in the United States for a war against Iraq was clearly connected to the discourse of antiterrorism. The assumptions that Saddam Hussein had connections to the September 11 attacks or to Al-Qaeda were not only widely held but also directly linked to support for the war in Iraq. Those people who accepted these links, in other words, were more likely—reasonably enough—to support the war. As Kull observes, there is no evidence to support a link between Saddam Hussein and Al-Qaeda, nor with the attack on the Twin Towers. On the contrary, the Iraqi regime was notably antagonistic towards this kind of fundamentalist politics.

What Kull's research highlights is the rhetorical power of a discourse linking nation states with the terrorist threat. Despite a palpable lack of evidence, this discourse made significant inroads onto public consciousness. And although the specificity of the Iraq/Al-Qaeda link has been discredited, a more general link between the war on terrorism and military action remains. This general link, for all its flimsiness, provides the political cover needed for maintaining military budgets at close to their Cold War levels. This, along with the interventionist foreign policy it makes possible, is perhaps the most significant political implication of the war on terrorism

The "fog of war" is often used as a metaphor to explain the mistakes, misunderstandings and misinformation that invariably surround the coverage of military conflicts. The fog that lingers around the "war on terrorism," on the other hand, is both more subtle and more profound. This is the foggiest of wars, bolstered by the claims of governments based on secret intelligence, but one that has provided cover for a major shift in foreign policy away from the principle of defence. And it is foggy thinking, based on a series of easy assumptions and associations, that has helped foster an acceptance of the link between the terrorist threat and the need for a well-funded military.

All this has been enabled by media coverage in which the threat of terrorism is constantly highlighted and the link between terrorism and military action repeated and largely unquestioned. Journalists have a key role to play here. If citizens or governments are to tackle terrorism seriously and rationally, we need to bring a sense of proportion to the discussion and to evaluate the risks of this threat in relation to other threats. We also need to interrogate the idea that the best way to swat a mosquito is by wielding a sledgehammer.

REFERENCES

Brookes, R. et al. (2004). *Too close for comfort: The role of embedded reporters during the 2003 Iraq war.* Cardiff: Cardiff School of Journalism, Media and Cultural Studies.

Entman, R. (2004). *Projections of power: Framing news, public opinion and U.S. foreign policy.* Chicago: University of Chicago Press.

Gans, H. (1979). *Deciding what's news.* New York: Vintage.

Hellinger, D. & Judd, D. (1991). *The democratic façade.* Pacific Grove, CA: Brooks Grove.

Iyengar, S. & Kinder, D. (1987). *News that matters.* Chicago: University of Chicago Press.

Kitzinger, J. (2000). Media templates: Patterns of association and the (re)construction of meaning over time. *Media, Culture and Society, 22*(1), 61-84.

Kull, S. (2003). *Misperceptions, the media and the Iraq war, program on international policy attitudes.* College Park: University of Maryland.

Lewis, J. (2001). *Constructing public opinion: How elites do what they like and why we seem to go along with it.* New York: Columbia University Press.

Lewis, J. (2004). Television, public opinion and the war in Iraq: The case of Britain. *International Journal of Public Opinion Research, 16*(3), 295-310.

Lewis, J. & Brookes, R. (2003). Reporting the war on British television. In D. Miller (Ed.), *Tell me lies.* London: Pluto.

Lewis, J. & Brookes, R. (2004). How British television news represented the case for the war in Iraq. In S. Allan & B. Zelizer (Eds.), *Reporting war: Journalism in wartime.* London and New York: Routledge.

Lewis, J., Maxwell, R., & Miller, T. (2002). 9–11. *Television and New Media, 3*(2), 125-131.

Maxwell, R. (2002). Honor among patriots? *Television and New Media, 3*(2), 239-248.

McCombs, M., Danielian, L., & Wanta, W. (1995). Issues in the news and the public agenda. In C. Salmon & T. Glasser (Eds.), *Public opinion and the communication of consent.* New York: Guilford.

Norris, P., Kern, M., & Just, M. (Eds.). (2003). *Framing terrorism: The news media, the government and the public.* New York: Routledge.

Page, B. & Shapiro, R. (1992). *The rational public.* Chicago: University of Chicago Press.

Threadgold, T. & Mosdell, N. (2004). Embedded reporting: Lessons learned. *Defence Management Journal, 25*, 12-16.

Tumber, H. & Palmer, J. (2004). *Media at war: The Iraq crisis.* London: Sage.

Tuchman, G. (1978). *Making news,* New York: Free Press.

U.S. Department of State (2004). *Patterns of global terrorism 2003.* http://www.state.gov/s/ct/rls/pgtrpt/2003/33771.htm

Zaller, J. R. (1992). *The nature and origins of mass opinion.* Cambridge: Cambridge University Press.

Chapter 16

The Pornographic Barbarism of the Self-Reflecting Sign

Paul Taylor*

> *Fundamentally, such violence is not so much an event as the explosive form assumed by an absence of events. Or rather the implosive form: and what implodes here is the political void . . . the silence of history which has been repressed at the level of individual psychology, and the indifference and silence of everyone. We are dealing, therefore, not with irrational episodes in the life of our society, but instead with something that is completely in accord with that society's accelerating plunge into the void.* (Baudrillard, 1993, p. 76 [emphasis in original])

Despite the heated debates and huge mass public demonstrations about the rights and wrongs of the second Gulf War (GW2) in 2003, the biggest shifts in the British and American publics' perception of the conflict occurred through a series of vivid, defining images at various crucial stages. Thus, what proved to be undue optimism was at its peak during the fall of Baghdad and the Ozymandias-like toppling of Saddam Hussein's statue, complete

*I would like to thank Salman Sayid of the University of Leeds, John Roberts at the University of Brunel, and Michael Higgins at the University of Sunderland for their helpful comments during the writing of this piece.

with a forewarning of the cultural misunderstandings to come when a U.S. soldier momentarily draped the Stars and Stripes around the statue's face. Further grounds for Western triumphalism were provided with the images of a disorientated and disheveled Saddam shortly after his capture on December 13, 2003, with the bathos of his last underground hiding-place that contrasted markedly with the pictures of abandoned palaces. In early May 2004, the flip side of this ability of images to dictate the political climate became apparent when President Bush and Prime Minister Blair came under sustained pressure because photographs of prisoner abuse in Baghdad's Abu Ghraib jail appeared in the world's media.

In political terms there are two key aspects to the furor. One is the unequal relationship between the effect the pictures had compared to the words of previously unheeded imageless reports. *Amnesty International*, for example, had reported months earlier, in February 2004, allegations of torture and serious human rights violations without any impact. The second is, specifically in relationship to a focus on political violence, why did these images make so much more of an impact compared to the large number of previously witnessed scenes of more conventional military violence and its civilian victims?

The thesis offered here as an answer to this question is that, even if only for a short while and for reasons perhaps still not adequately articulated or fully recognized, the Pornographic nature of the Abu Ghraib photographs spoke to a strong sense of unease in the public. Despite politicians' protestations about a few bad apples spoiling the barrel, the Western public had an intuitive sense that the photographs represented something deeper about the society that sent out such troops. It is this "something" this chapter seeks to explore.

Perhaps the most iconic and evocative of all the abuse photographs was that of an Iraqi man being subjected to the faked threat of electrocution. The prisoner is perched atop a box in a makeshift shroud, covered with a hood reminiscent of the Klu-Klux-Klan and pretend electrodes attached to his hands. The image is particularly evocative for Christian viewers. It resonates with connotations of the crucifixion and the representation of Christ the Redeemer with welcoming hands outstretched at his side. This chapter explores the profound implications such a poignant tableau has for our conceptualization of political violence and what it says about the nature of a society that could create the image of an abused, Christ-like figure standing on a box. For those who remain relatively impervious to any unusual level of moral disquiet over the Abu Ghraib pictures, the chapter also raises a pragmatic political issue for consideration. This is the extent to which there is a link between the social processes that constructed the prisoner abuse scandal and the wider political environment of the international coalition's "War against Terror."

The chapter concludes by arguing that a keen understanding of the West's unhealthy relationship to the mediated image may lie behind the malevolent orchestration of such heavily mediated events as the 9/11 tragedy. Marshall McLuhan (1995 [1964]) offers the myth of Narcissus as a defining metaphor for the West's problematic relationship to the screen. Influenced by McLuhan and his contemporary theoretical heir, Jean Baudrillard, this chapter implies that the failure of military intelligence which led to 9/11 is at least partially due to a myopic perspective upon our own culture. Dealing with international terrorism might be a lot easier if we stopped waging very real and bloody war on an abstract noun (terror) and instead sought to emulate the malevolently keen media savvy of such figures as Osama bin Laden. Although it is obvious the West desperately needs to develop a more sophisticated and less reified understanding of the Islamic Other, this would actually be much easier if we were more sensitive to the processes of meaning-construction within our own heavily mediated culture. This culture is increasingly pornographic in a manner both reflected in the Abu Ghraib photographs but also perhaps somewhat obscured by the misleadingly exceptional status claimed for them by our politicians.

THE SELF-REFLECTING SIGN

From the mutation and conflation of confessional culture and mediated "real life" had emerged the broader trend of the barbarism of the self-reflecting sign. (Bracewell, 2002a, p. 72)

Bracewell (2002a) refers to the "self-reflecting sign" as a defining feature of the contemporary mediascape. Note it is not the *self-reflexive sign*, which would involve a sense of reflection upon an image's substantive meaning. Rather, this chapter uses the conventional concept of pornography and Baudrillard's concept of *the obscene* to explore how the self-reflecting sign refers to the image that has no meaning beyond its own tautological facticity. We shall see how literal Pornography—henceforth referred to with a capital "P"—acts as a trope for the dominant social values of self-reflecting signs and their axiomatic visual excess—pornography with a small "p." We examine the present-day manifestations of this extenuated *social porn*, evident across a spectrum of confessional, confrontational, and violent media formats. Social porn has profound political consequences. Just as the obsessively repetitive attention paid by the media to the terrible images of the 9/11 tragedy occluded more substantive considerations of the event's significance, so too do debates about the Abu Ghraib images threaten to obscure the deep social causes and consequences of the symptoms they reflect.

The images of abuse caused widespread shock in the West (interestingly, in the Arab world, instead of shock, the pictures tended to be met with
a mixture of anger and a resigned sense of déjà vu [see Raban, 2004]). There
may also, however, be an element of denial in the Western response. Thus,
even some U.S. Senators and Congressmen/women highly critical of
Donald Rumsfeld during his evidence to both Houses, for example, took
the opportunity to emphasize how this behavior was not representative of
U.S. forces in general (see, e.g., Senator Joseph Lieberman's comments
[Washington Post, 2004]). Similarly, speaking to the media while standing
alongside King Abdullah II of Jordan in the White house garden on May 6,
2004, President Bush said, "sorry for the humiliation suffered by the Iraqi
prisoners," but then went on to say he was "as equally sorry that people
seeing these pictures didn't understand the true nature and heart of
America" (Sontag, 2004, p. 3). Although these assertions may be true, they
still distract from a key element of the disgust the images produced, which
is the central focus of this chapter: their pornographic rather than
Pornographic nature.

In Britain, the distraction from the deeper significance of the Abu
Ghraib photographs came in the form of a debate over whether similar pictures of British troops abusing Iraqi prisoners elsewhere were fake or not. In
May 2004, Piers Morgan, the editor of the U.K.'s Daily Mirror tabloid newspaper, was sacked when the photographs he printed were proved to be false.
It is interesting to note that when doubts were raised as to their veracity, at
least some debate took place as to whether they were still accurate representations of actual events not originally photographed. In this particular
instance, although the issue of authenticity dominated proceedings, possibly
fake pictures nevertheless did allow more substantive discussion about actual abuse that had taken place. The debate over The Daily Mirror pictures
provided an interesting example of Bracewell's assessment of the contemporary status of the image where: "'authenticity' is the hallmark of truth, and
hence the gauge of social value . . . there is now the sense that authenticity
itself can be sculpted to suggest veracity as an image, in which truth remains
ambiguous'" (Bracewell, 2002a, p. 66 [emphasis mine]). Although the fact
remains that both the U.S. and British images of prisoner abuse had a dis-
proportionately powerful political impact, the pictures also illustrate the
ambivalent political power of images.

Normally the postmodern concept of the hyperreal (typically in
Baudrillard and Eco's work [e.g., 1983 and 1986 respectively] the paradoxical notion of a mediated phenomenon that is more real than the real itself)
has negative connotations. Baudrillard argues that the hyperreal often dis-
tracts attention from the real issues. For example, in Simulations (1983) he
suggests that the public investigation that followed the Watergate scandal
merely hid the innate corruptness of U.S. politics, and Disneyland's main

purpose is to disguise the fact that American society at large is really modelled on a Disney-like ethos of commodified fantasia. In the particular instance of the British photographs, however, fake pictures provoked a valuable self-examination of the coalition's practices and values. This chapter argues that unfortunately, more often, the process tends to be reversed: *real images often produce inauthentic discourse*. Images determine politics largely irrespective of their truth or objective significance.

REDEFINING VIOLENCE

> *But why should we hear about body bags, and deaths, and how many, what day it's gonna happen, and how many this or what do you suppose? Or, I mean, it's, it's not relevant. So why should I waste my beautiful mind on something like that? And watch him suffer.*
>
> —Barbara Bush on Good Morning America, March 18, 2003

Notwithstanding his mother's reluctance to confront the full implications of the war in Iraq, the President's concern about the effect of the pictures upon people's perception of the United States is an indication of the need to broaden our understanding of the concept of political violence and the media's role in its portrayal. Political violence can be reinterpreted by concentrating upon the connotations that lie beyond its primary definition of the exertion of physical force. In addition to great physical harm suffered by the prisoners, (1) the word violence also denotes the following:

2. powerful, untamed, or devastating force.
3. great strength of feeling, as in language, etc.
4. an unjust, unwarranted, or unlawful display of force, esp. such as tends to overawe or intimidate
5. **do violence to (a)** to inflict harm upon; damage or violate: *they did violence to the prisoners.* **(b)** to distort or twist the sense or intention of: *the reporters did violence to my speech* (*Collins Softback English Dictionary*, 1992)

Contra President Bush, this chapter argues that the true nature and heart of America *is* in fact revealed by those photographs, and the media does violence to the fundamental nature of our political discourse. The Abu Ghraib images effected a response that mere words had failed to unblock: "It was the photographs that made all this real to President Bush and his associates. Up to then, there had been only words which are a lot easier to cover up in our age of infinite digital self-reproduction and self-dissemination."

(Sontag, 2004, p. 5). The violence Western reporters do to our political speech occurs with such covering-up examples being the now widespread preference for the term "abuse" rather than "torture" and the prevailing use of the euphemistic term "contractors" to describe in postwar Iraq what were previously conventionally referred to as mercenaries.

We will see in the following sections that definitions 2, 3 and 4 are all directly relevant to the media's images from Iraq. However, I will predominantly focus upon definition 5 and use the term violence to explore the harm done to the body politic by a societal excess of images of which the Abu Ghraib pictures are but a particularly offensive and malign example. The impact of the prison photographs brings together all the different definitions of violence. Their effects on public opinion were untamed and produced a great strength of feeling (definitions 2 and 3) and the activities they record-ed involved an unjust and intimidating display of force (definition 4). Definition 5, however, encapsulates the wider social harm of the image.

"THEY DID VIOLENCE TO THE PRISONERS"— THE p/PORNOGRAPHIC SOCIETY AND RITUAL HUMILIATION

- *Porno is far bigger than rock music and far bigger than Hollywood.*
- *Americans spend more on strip clubs than they spend on theatre, opera, ballet, jazz and classical concerts combined.*
- *In 1975 the total retail value of all the hard-core porno in America was estimated at $5-10 million. Last year Americans spent $8 billion on mediated sex.* (Amis, 2001, unpaginated)

The Abu Ghraib photographs are Pornographic because of their explicit sexual content but they are also pornographic in a more attenuated and abstract manner. The pornographic nature of the abuse was part of *a ritual humiliation* of the Iraqi prisoners. Such ritual abuse is but an extreme exam-ple of a ubiquitous, voyeuristic esthetic that now pervades wider Western society. It is increasingly Pornographic in the obvious literal and quantita-tive sense that Pornography is much more socially acceptable and widely available. In addition, more qualitatively, according to Amis, Porn, "is much, much dirtier than it used to be, but Gonzo porno is gonzo: way out there. The new element is violence" (Amis, 2001, unpaginated). *Gonzo* refers to wild, eccentric, or bizarre behavior and was first used to describe the almost ethnographic, drug-fuelled, direct experience journalism of the American reporter Hunter S. Thompson, who rose to prominence with *Hells Angels* (1966), a vivid account of his travels with the infamous motorcycling gang.

In more recent years *gonzo* is a label applied to a genre of Pornography. The advent of increasingly sophisticated hand-held cameras has added a new amateur look (and indeed amateur involvement) to the more glossy Hollywood-influenced esthetic that previously dominated the U.S. Porn industry. The Abu Ghraib pictures can be read in the light of this recent evolution in both Porn and its mirroring in the wider trend of social porn. More than this, the permeation of the gonzo esthetic is much evident in the Reality-TV formats that have evolved to produce increasingly extreme forms of ritualized humiliation. The retrospectively benign formats of such shows *as Candid Camera* (a 1970s U.S. and British TV show that caught unsuspecting members of the public on camera in foolish situations) have been replaced by a new harsher range of program.

In the hubris-generating/puncturing celebrity-obsessed genre, we have recently witnessed the conspicuous consumption/defecation of *MTV Cribs* and *Celebrity Detox*. *Cribs* is an MTV series that takes the viewer into the homes of various celebrities for an unabashed celebration of their conspicuous consumption. *Celebrity Detox* was a May 2003 program in which British B-list celebrities were filmed at a heath spa in Thailand undergoing a rigorous program of enemas. Another example of new gonzo TV would be the MTV program *JackAss*, which involves a group of U.S. friends performing dangerous physical stunts, involving either violence, nudity, bodily excretions, or, at times, all three. A much darker, but at first glance, semantically related format to both *JackAss* and *Celebrity Detox* is the recent best-selling gonzo-violence video *Bumfights*. This is an U.S.–produced underground video that has recently gained mainstream notoriety for showing homeless people bare-knuckle fighting in return for food, money, and alcohol (*Ghetto Brawls* is a similar product). In May 2004, British Channel 5 (colloquially known in the United Kingdom as "Channel Filth") used a "documentary" entitled *Bumfights: A Video Too Far* as a vehicle for showing footage from the video.

This rather sociological thesis that a general cultural climate is the underlying cause of the Abu Ghraib symptoms has recently received support from an unusual source. Rush Limbaugh, the U.S. right-wing radio shock-jock, claimed that too much was being made of the Abu Ghraib pictures. He claimed obtusely that they were very similar to the hazing ritual common in U.S. fraternities: "This is no different than what happens at the Skull and Bones initiation and we're going to ruin people's lives over it, and we're going to hamper our military effort, and then we are going to really hammer them because they had a good time" (cited in Sontag, 2004, p. 4). We can now examine in more detail the exact nature of that "good time" by exploring the roots of social porn.

THE PORNOGRAPHIC ZEITGEIST

. . . I have seen in the windows the pale blue glow of at least one television in every home. And I am told that many family meals are eaten in front of that screen as well. And perhaps this explains the face of Americans, the eyes that never appear satisfied, at peace with their work, or the day God has given them; these people have the eyes of very small children who are forever looking for their next source of distraction, entertainment, or a sweet taste in their mouth. (Andre Dubus III, 2001, p. 124)

. . . we need tits and arse because they have got to be available to us; to be pawed, fucked, wanked over. Because we're men? No. Because we're consumers. Because those are things we like, things we intrinsically feel or have been conned into believing will give us value, release satisfaction. We value them so we need to at least have the illusion of their availability. For tits and arse read coke, crisps, speedboats, cars, houses, computers, designer labels, replica shirts. That's why advertising and pornography are similar; they sell the illusion of availability and the non-consequence of consumption. (Welsh, 2002, p. 450)

. . . we were just that bit too old to buy into the rumble of a world described by advertising and products. . . . That was the world where everything had turned into an idea of itself, where life no longer had an inner life. . . . It's a process which just seems to have built up, like an accumulation of fat around the heart's weary muscle. (Bracewell, 2002b, pp. 8-9)

I have argued elsewhere (Taylor, 1998, 2001) for the importance of fiction as a useful resource with which to understand the social zeitgeist better. The effect of the Abu Ghraib pictures has been so shocking because, whether explicitly acknowledged or not, they evoke in the viewer recognition of a disturbing Western cultural trend that is only belatedly and involuntarily being faced. The symptoms have been previously acknowledged within contemporary zeitgeist-capturing novels such as those quoted above. The first quotation is particularly apposite to our purposes, given that it presents a Middle Eastern perspective on U.S. culture. In *The House of Sand and Fog*, through the voice of an exiled Iranian army officer, Andre Dubus (2001) highlights the childlike dependence upon distraction and entertainment that he perceives to be deep at the heart of U.S. culture. The second quotation is taken from Irvine Welsh's *Porno* (2002), a novel he wrote in response to the growth of gonzo-style, DIY porn he had observed in Britain. Given the sexual element to the events at Abu Ghraib, the key point to be taken from Welsh is the link between Porn and the essential values of a consumer society. Welsh's claim that commodities provide "things we intrinsically feel or have been conned into believing will give us value, release satisfaction" resonates closely with Rush Limbaugh's exculpatory rationale for the abuse: "You know, these people are being fired at every day. I'm talking about people having a good time, these people. You ever heard of emotional release?" (cited in Sontag 2004, p. 4). The third quotation, from Bracewell's *Perfect Tense* (2002b), gives an office worker's account of metropolitan ennui, and his expression of "the insistence of image over substance" provides a fictional variation of Baudrillard and Eco's concept of the hyperreal.[1] Bracewell's phrase, "the rumble of a world described by advertising and products" speaks directly to how the U.S. Government's explicit couching of America's overseas image functions in terms of a consumer brand.

BRANDING OR BRANDED?

> . . . there is a fundamental flaw in the American view of "perception management" on an international stage. . . . It emanates from a Harvard MBA type of mentality that if you get the marketing right, anything will sell. One of the case studies on that MBA programme was . . . Charlotte Beers, formerly of Madison Avenue (she once led J Walter Thompson Worldwide and Ogilvy & Mather), and until last year under secretary of state for public affairs and public diplomacy. Colin Powell is famously on record as saying "Well, guess what? She got me to buy Uncle Ben's rice, and so there's nothing wrong with getting somebody who knows how to sell something." Well, Uncle Sam isn't Uncle Ben and you can't sell something to people who have no water to boil it with. But now they do have oil on which to pour yet another troublesome example that Uncle Sam might not be who Uncle Sam says he is. Uncle Sam is looking more and more like the Ugly American . . . the soldiers who were photographed in these "trophy" pictures are of a different breed of Americans. **They are the Jerry Springer elements of American society,** and they are not pretty. . . . Seeing is believing, whether it's on the Jerry Springer show or in this week's newspapers. (Taylor, 2004, unpaginated [emphasis mine])

There is a certain morbid symmetry in the fact that, in addition to the literal imprisonment they depict, the controversy caused by the Abu Ghraib pictures reflect how U.S. society is confined by its excessive reliance upon the image. The visceral disgust they caused can, however, be seen as the flip side of the image-driven boosterism that is an intrinsic part of America's self-presentation. Its political use of images is violent in the sense of the above definitions 2-4, and a failure to adequately understand the negative consequences of this is at the core of the United States' poor "image" within international public opinion. Ironically, this image is so poor because of its desire to micromanage excessively the process of image-creation (definition 4). The concept of ideology is doubtless for some a quaint relic of Marxist theory and media effects are notoriously difficult to irrefutably "prove" to the satisfaction of all. Perhaps a fresh perspective upon both, however, can be gained by looking at the intimate relationship the concept of ideology has with the production of images and how the single most important contemporary ideology is an image-driven discourse of which Jerry Springer is but the (il)logical conclusion.

Mitchell (1986) emphasizes the iconic basis of ideology, arguing that the concept is etymologically grounded "in the notion of mental entities or 'ideas'" that provide the materials of thought. Insofar as these ideas are understood as images—as pictorial, graphic signs imprinted or projected on the medium of consciousness—then ideology . . . is really an iconology, a theory of imagery," (Mitchell 1986, p. 164). For Burke, ideology is thus related not to truthful images, "but of falsely reductive images that could only lead to political tyranny" (p. 167). For Coleridge, "... Any 'idea ' worthy of the name . . . is distinguished precisely by its inability to be rendered in pictorial or material form: it is a 'living educt' of the imagination, a 'power' that can be rendered only by the translucence of a symbolic form, never by a 'mere' image" (p. 167). An idiosyncratically expressed preference for the cultural richness of the symbolic over the essential emptiness of the overloaded, hyperrealistic, and technologically mediated images forms the basis of Jean Baudrillard's theory of the ideology of media images and is explored through his concept of the *obscene*.

THE OBSCENE IMAGE

> . . . this is the enterprise of our entire culture, whose natural condition is obscene: a culture of monstration, of demonstration, of productive monstrosity. (Baudrillard, 1990a, p. 35)

> . . . this viral contamination of things by images, which are the fatal characteristics of our culture. (Baudrillard, 1988, p. 36)

Perhaps protected from a wider readership due to his provocative style and rococo rhetoric, Jean Baudrillard has compared the West's relationship to images in terms of obscenity. In the light of events in Iraq, frequent accusations that his work is willfully abstruse perhaps need to be reconsidered. Baudrillard takes the notion of the *obscene* literally. An etymological analysis of the word gives us "ob"—a prefix meaning hindering—and "scene"—from the Latin and Greek words for "stage." Ignoring its conventional connotation of depravity, his rereading of the term *obscene* gives us the notion that Western media-dominated society is *ob-scene* because its proliferation of images has imploded the traditional, symbolically coded distance between the image and viewer that is implied with a stage. Baudrillard's writing contains the repeated theme that in the West we suffer from a viruslike proliferation of immediate images that replace the distance needed for either considered reflection or a developed sensitivity to the ambiguities of cultural meanings.

Baudrillard's analysis illuminates the present mediascape. For example, he argues: ". . . we shouldn't underestimate the power of the obscene, its power to exterminate all ambiguity and all seduction and deliver to us the definitive fascination of bodies without faces, faces without eyes, and eyes that don't look" (Baudrillard, 1990b, p. 60). This has chilling pertinence to the dehumanized images of Iraqi prisoners in which their faces are hooded, deliberately pixelated, or only appear as minor details within a broader tableau (e.g., the naked man cowering in front of snarling guard dogs). Originally used in a different context, Baudrillard also provides an unwittingly prescient description of the furor over the *Daily Mirror* pictures' authenticity: ". . . we don't look for definition or richness of imagination in these images; we look for the giddiness of their superficiality, for the artifice of detail, the intimacy of their technique. What we truly desire is their technical artificiality, and nothing more" (Baudrillard, 1988, p. 44).

Beyond the manifest obscenity of the Pornography of the Abu Ghraib photographs, Baudrillard's broader theoretical point relates to how their *staging* paradoxically relies upon the actual absence of a *stage*. A surfeit of images is presented to us so that: "Obscenity takes on all the semblances of modernity. We are used to seeing it, first of all, in the perpetration of sex, but it extends to everything that can be perpetrated in the visible—it becomes the perpetration of the visible itself" (Baudrillard, 1990b, p. 58). In a form of semiotic potlatch, images become their own justification for the decontextualized consumption-for-its-own sake of such formats as *MTV Cribs* and *Bumfights*. Everything becomes a potential image for the voyeuristic gaze, and less and less is ruled out on grounds of taste or any other consideration. The pornography of the image lies here in its explicitness. Nothing is left to the imagination and all is revealed to the passive viewer. An apparently overwhelming sexual will-to-reveal that Welsh identified in the rise of gonzo porn may at least partially explain the sexual aspect of the Abu Ghraib pictures. As Sontag recently argued, increasingly: "An erotic life is for more and more people what can be captured on video. To live is to be photographed, to have a record of one's life, oblivious or claiming to be oblivious to the camera's non-stop attentions. . . . Ours is a society in which secrets of private life that, formerly, you would have given nearly anything to conceal, you now clamour to get on a television show to reveal" (2004, pp. 3-4).

MEDIA TAUTOLOGY: REALITY TV AND THE
DEMOCRATISATION OF CELEBRITY

> *Today this critical energy of the stage . . . is in the process of being swept
> away. All that theatrical energy goes into the denial of the scenic illusion
> and into anti-theater in all its various forms . . . illusion is proscribed; the
> scission between stage and audience is abolished; theater goes down into
> the street and everydayness. . . . This is no longer the famous Aristotelian
> catharsis of the passions. . . . Illusion is no longer valid here: it is truth
> which bursts into free expression. We are all actors and spectators; there
> is no more stage: the stage is everywhere; no more rules: everyone plays
> out his own drama, improvising on his own fantasies. The obscene form
> of anti-theater, present everywhere.* (Baudrillard, 1990, p. 63)

In the *Ecstasy of Communication* (1988), among other works, Baudrillard
develops the theme of modern communication's tendency towards uncontrollable circulation (definition 2). The roots of this uncontrollable circulation can be found in Sontag's (1979 [1977]) earlier examination of photography's defining status as the groundbreaking technology of the image
where she asserts that: "Photographs document sequences of consumption
carried on outside the view of family, friends, neighbors" (Sontag, 1979, p.
9). This resonates with Welsh's previously cited linking of pornography
with consumerism, and is poignantly prescient in terms of the distress
caused to the families of such U.S. soldiers as the Porn-star sounding
Lynndie England. The lack of values with which to judge the appropriate-
ness of the image is for Sontag an intrinsic part of the conceptually reductive nature of the technology. She argues that: "there is an aggression
implicit in every use of the camera" and that it is responsible for "an ever
increasing spread of that mentality which looks at the world as a set of
potential photographs" (p. 7).

Specifically in the light of Abu Ghraib, Sontag points out that, although
"trophy" pictures have been taken in many previous military and social conflicts, these particular photographs:

> . . . reflect a shift in the use of pictures—less objects to be saved than
> evanescent messages to be disseminated, circulated . . . now the soldiers
> themselves are all photographers— recording their war, their fun, their
> observations of what they find picturesque, their atrocities—and swap-
> ping images among themselves, and emailing them around the globe . . .
> since the pictures were meant to be circulated and seen by many people,
> it was all fun. And this idea of fun is, alas, more and more—contrary to
> what Mr Bush is telling the world—part of the "true nature and heart of
> America." (Sontag, 2004, p. 3)

Again, the link between fiction and reality is instructive here. In Italo Calvino's short story about the increasingly obsessive mentality of a photographer in Trieste entitled "The Adventure of a Photographer (1983), for example, he portrays the tautological self-generating tendencies of the need to photograph. The person who feels the urge to photograph is, he argues:

> . . . already close to the view of the person who thinks that everything that is not photographed is lost, as if it had never existed, and that therefore in order really to live you must photograph as much as you can, you must either live in the most photographable way possible or else consider photographable every moment of your life. The first course leads to stupidity; the second, to madness. (Calvino 1983, p. 43)

Calvino compares Trieste's photographers to game hunters, describing in a relatively benign form the innately agressive and violent nature of the photographic act identified by Sontag: "When Spring comes, the city's inhabitants, by the hundreds of thousands, go out on Sundays with a leather case over their shoulder. And they photograph one another. They come back happy as hunters with bulging game-bags . . . " (Calvino, 1983, p. 40). Particularly apposite to the case of the Iraqi photographs, Oliver Wendell Holmes predicted that: "every conceivable object of Nature and Art will soon scale off its surface for us. Men will hunt all curious, beautiful, grand objects, as they hunt for cattle in South America, for their *skins*, and leave the carcasses as of little worth" (cited in Gamson, 1994, p. 20 [emphasis in original]).

Although they would seem unlikely bedfellows, Baudrillard's notion of the ecstasy of communication was implicitly acknowledged by Donald Rumsfeld who complained that it was much harder nowadays to control the information sent back home by soldiers serving overseas. Unlike conventional letters in which the censors can black out the offending parts, Rumsfeld bemoans the fact that U.S. soldiers were "running around with digital cameras and taking these unbelievable photographs and then passing them off, against the law, to the media, to our surprise" (cited in Sontag, 2004, p. 5). With U.S. troops thus acting like an extremely malevolent form of Trieste's Sunday promenaders, Calvino's story gives an imaginative account of photographic excesses whereas Rumsfeld's complaint provides a more practical illustration of its dynamics. Sontag's, Calvino's and Wendell Holmes' descriptions are all seen combined in the aggressive, acquisitive, trophy-seeking behavior of the Abu Ghraib photographers that so dramatically undermined the Coalition's attempts to brand itself as *Occupation-Lite*.

THE GEOPOLITICAL CONSEQUENCES:
THE POST–9/11 WAR OF IMAGES

*Of all nations in the world, the United States was built in nobody's image. It was the land of the unexpected, of unbounded hope, of ideals, of quest for an unknown perfection. It is all the more unfitting that we should offer ourselves in images. **And all the more fitting that the images which we make wittingly or unwittingly to sell America to the world should come back to haunt and curse us.*** (Boorstin, 1992 [1961], pp. 245-246 [emphasis mine])

I have focused in this piece upon the Abu Ghraib pictures, but their significance can be broadened out and linked with the tragic events of 9/11. Daniel Boorstin feared that America's overreliance upon images would come back to haunt it. With the events of September 11, 2001, Osama bin Laden confirmed Boorstin's foresight in a terrible fashion with an attack deliberately designed to be consumed as a media event. Writing a full forty years before 9/11, Boorstin feared the displacement of ideals by images. His fears have been realized to the extent that the emotional charge of the 9/11 images has been skillfully manipulated for the non sequitur of the "War on Terror." Writing at the height of the Cold War, Boorstin focused upon Communism, but his words are now painfully relevant to the gulf that exists not only as a geographical area to which troops are periodically dispatched, but also and more significantly as an ever-widening gap between Western and Islamic sensitivities:

> Accustomed to live in a world of pseudo-events, celebrities, dissolving forms, and shadowy but overshadowing images, we mistake our shadows for ourselves. To us they seem more real than the reality. . . . Our technique seems direct only because in our daily lives the pseudo-event always seems destined to dominate the natural facts. We no longer even recognise that our technique is indirect, that we have committed ourselves to managing shadows. We can live in our world of illusions. Although we find it hard to imagine, other peoples still live in the world of dreams. We live in a world of our making. Can we conjure others to live there too? We love the image, and believe it. But will they? (Boorstin, 1961, p. 249)

The images of prisoner abuse reflect the West's narcissistic obsession with the screen, and it is this unhealthy obsession which increasingly fuels Said's concept of neo-Orientalism (Said, 2003 [1978]). A keen awareness of this process arguably marks the malevolent acuity of Bin Laden. He is the latest in a string of key Islamic hate-figures that previously included the

Ayatollah Khomeni and who all have in common being bracketed within a discourse of evil (see "Whatever Happened to Evil?" in Baudrillard, 1993, for a full discussion of this theme). Bin Laden fulfills the role portrayed in Baudrillard's work of the Manichean demiurge who creates the evil illusions against which God and goodness avail themselves. The biggest danger for the West, however, is that Bin Laden and others play this role self-consciously. They know which buttons to press in order to produce effects that go right to the core of the West's own deeply embedded social pornography of which Abu Ghraib was but a particularly shocking example. An implicit notion from this chapter is therefore that the media's role in the facilitation of America's increasingly myopic separation from the Islamic Other has been incorporated into the terrorist game plan.

In his *Contributions to Analytical Psychology* (1928), Jung argued that an individual's psychology could be profoundly, albeit unwittingly, influenced by an underpinning dependency of the wider society (cited in McLuhan, 1995 [1964], p. 21). He used the example of the average Roman citizen who was inevitably infected by a general social atmosphere permeated by slavery and claimed that the individual is powerless to resist such an influence. Innis (2003 [1951]) and McLuhan (1985, [1964]) used a similar argument to describe the cultural impact of media technologies through history. This chapter suggests that social pornography now permeates media discourse in the West, and the *Jerry Springer* nature of the Iraqi pictures implies the validity of Jung's analysis. The social pornography of the image is a fertile resource from which Bin Laden and others base their media-savvy strategies. Social pornography facilitates the post –9/11 knee-jerk and unfocused political responses and provides Bin Laden with opportunities to further exacerbate the situation with such politically pornographic events as the tragically iconic 9/11 attack.

The true malevolent ingenuity of Bin Laden's outrage thus resides in his knowing incorporation of the West's inability to look beyond its own biased and distorted social porn. His malevolent success has been heightened by the repetitive nature and simply overwhelming presence of 9/11 images and their displacement of more considered debate. For example, Osama Bin Laden's image is now readily familiar to all but a tiny proportion of Western populations, but a similarly small number are likely to be aware of the more substantive issues lying behind the image. There is, for example, no significant public discussion of the historical parallels and links that can be made between his acts and the Royal House of Saud's uneasy yet perennially intertwined relationship with the Ikhwan bedouin fighters and the Wahabi fundamentalist strand of Islam. The United States was traumatized yet fundamentally unenlightened by the shocking yet constantly repeated images of the twin towers being hit. Unaccompanied by significant efforts to understand, mere repetition of the images reflected the fundamentally distorted perspective of a society increasingly incapable of thinking outside the self-referential media realm alluded to throughout this chapter.

Despite the very real effects experienced by those New Yorkers in the immediate vicinity and aftermath, the rest of the United States experienced the WTC attack Hollywood-style. The pictures of destruction were already disturbingly familiar to a public regularly exposed to the Hollywood imagination of disaster films. Soon after the tragedy U.S. intelligence services consulted Hollywood figures to brainstorm scenarios for possible future terrorist attacks, and the release of several movies was postponed because of their perceived similarity to actual events. The media's post–9/11 coverage consisted of an excessive, pornographic dose of the act of destruction and then a matching pornographic exploration of the personal suffering by the victims' families. The emergency workers of Ground Zero quickly became emotive icons and fodder for daytime TV. Hollywood's image-driven influence was much in evidence in the post–September 11 political response as Ronald Reagan's *Star Wars*–sounding Cold War "Empire of Evil" was quickly revised to the "Axis of Evil" and discussed in colloquial terms borrowed liberally from the Western film genre. In terms of Calvino's (1983) previously cited characterization of the photographic impulse, the madness of Bin Laden's designed-for-TV terrorist act was quickly matched by the stupidity of the media's mediated response.

CONCLUSION: GULF WAR 2 AS THE REVENGE OF THE IMAGE

The same law holds for evil as pornography. The shock of photographed atrocities wears off with repeated viewings, just as the surprise and bemusement felt the first time one sees a pornographic movie wear off after one sees a few more. (Sontag, 179 [1977], p. 20)

Have you seen the cicadas? These insects wake up every 17 years. These cicadas are brazen. Just today they made some cockroaches line up in a pyramid. (David Letterman on *The Late Show* May 26, 2004)

A key element of Pornography is the short-lived nature of the viewer's attention span. Its nature is such that once consumed there is an almost immediate demand for fresh images. The same tendency is evident in social pornography in which political discourse requires fresh images and the impact of the old ones fades rapidly. This perhaps at least partially explains the insensitivity of David Letterman, the most successful late-night talk show host on U.S. television, and his above "joke." It was made less than a month after the Abu Ghraib pictures first appeared in the U.S. press and when delivered produced a large amount of laughter in the New York theater audience to whom Letterman presents his show each weeknight.

Zizek (2002) delineates two major post–September 11 options open to America: "it can either further fortify its sphere from which it watches world tragedies via a TV screen or it can finally risk stepping through the fantasmatic screen that separates it from the Outside World, accepting its arrival in the Real World" (Zizek, 2002, p. 49). The Letterman incident suggests that Zizek's second option is unlikely to be taken up by America in the near future, and the complex reasons for this is a major theme of Baudrillard's work, and something we have only been able to touch upon here. What I have tried to show, however, is the deep-rooted nature of the West's unhealthy relationship to the image and the way in which this has repeatedly prevented the West from stepping through that fantasmatic screen and engaging meaningfully with the Muslim Other. This is a failure that has typified the post–9/11 political response, from its immediate aftermath right up to recent events in Iraq.

The apparently benign concept of *branding* the United States like any other commodity image is in fact a stark indication of how The Land of the Free is in fact imprisoned whether it is thought of in terms of Narcissus's pond surface or Zizek's screen. In keeping with Jung's above insight, social pornography reveals the darker, slavish element of the term *brand*. In order to provide the video's publicity shot, Rufus Hannah and Donnie Brennan, two of the homeless protagonists from *Bumfights*, were paid $200, while drunk, to have the show's logo tattooed in ink on the former's knuckles and the latter's forehead (see Doward & Deen, 2004, p. 11). Sometimes a brand connotes more than we would wish.

NOTE

1. Bracewell's approach is further developed in his later nonfictional analysis of British culture in the 1990s (2002a) as indicated by the book's subtitle, *When Surface Was Depth*, and a chapter heading, "The Barbarism of the Self-Reflecting Sign," that I have adapted for this piece.

REFERENCES

Amis, M. (2001, March 17). A rough trade. *The Guardian Online* (unpaginated). Available at: http://books.guardian.co.uk/departments/politicsphilosophyand-society/story/0,6000,458058,00.html. Checked June 11, 2004.

Baudrillard, J. (1983). *Simulations*. New York: Semiotext(e).

Baudrillard, J. (1988). *The ecstasy of communication*. New York: Semiotext(e).

Baudrillard, J. (1990a). *Seduction*. Montreal: New World Perspectives.

Baudrillard, J. (1990b). *Fatal strategies*. New York: Semiotext(e).

Baudrillard, J. (1993). *The transparency of evil*. New York: Semiotext(e).

Boorstin, D. (1992 [1961]). *The image: A guide to pseudo-events in America*. New York: Vintage.

Bracewell, M. (2002a). *The nineties: When surface was depth*. London: Flamingo.

Bracewell, M. (2002b). *Perfect tense*. London: Vintage.

Calvino, I. (1983). The adventure of a photographer. In I. Calvino, *Difficult loves*. London: Picador.

Collins softback English dictionary (1993). London: HarperCollins.

Doward, J. & Deen, S. (2004, May 16) Outrage as TV plans to screen brawling tramps. *The Observer*, p. 11.

Dubus, A. (2001). *House of sand and fog*. London: Vintage.

Gamson, J. (1994). *Claims to fame: Celebrity in contemporary America*. Berkeley: University of California Press.

Innis, H. (2003 [1951]). *The bias of communication*. Toronto: University of Toronto Press.

McLuhan, M. (1995 [1964]). *Understanding media*. London: Routledge.

Mitchell, W. J. T. (1987). *Iconology: Image, text, ideology*. Chicago: University of Chicago Press.

Raban, J. (2004, May 13). Emasculating Arabia. *The Guardian*, Section G2, p. 6.

Said, E. (2003 [1978]). *Orientalism*. London: Penguin.

Sontag, S. (1979 [1977]). *On photography*. London: Penguin.

Sontag, S. (2004, May 23). What have we done? *The Guardian*, Section G2, pp. 3-5.

Taylor, Paul (1998). Hackers: Cyberpunks or microserfs? *Information, Communication & Society*, *1*(4), 401-419.

Taylor, Paul (2001). Informational intimacy and futuristic flu: Love and confusion in the matrix. *Information, Communication & Society*, *4*(1), 74-94.

Taylor, Phil. (2004, May 20-26) Image and reality. *Al-Ahram Weekly*, 691 (unpaginated). Available at: http://weekly.ahram.org.eg/2004/691/re9.htm—checked May 25th, 2004.

Thompson, H. S. (1996 [1966]). *Hell's angels*. New York: Ballantine Books.

Washington Post. (2004). Rumsfeld testifies before Senate Armed Services Committee. (unpaginated). Available at: http://Articles/Rumsfeld Testifies Before Senate Armed Services Committee (washingtonpost_com).htm—checked May 25th, 2004.

Welsh, I. (2002). *Porno*. London: Jonathan Cape.

Zizek, S. (2002). *Welcome to the desert of the real*. London: Verso.

About the Authors

Stuart Allan is reader in the School of Cultural Studies, University of the West of England, Bristol. He is the author of *News Culture* (Open University Press, 1999; second edition, 2004) and *Media, Risk and Science* (Open University Press, 2002). His edited collections include *Journalism After September 11* (with B. Zelizer, Routledge, 2002), *Reporting War: Journalism in Wartime* (with B. Zelizer, Routledge, 2004), and *Journalism: Critical Issues* (Open University Press, 2005).

Dan Berkowitz is professor of Journalism and Mass Communication at the University of Iowa where he teaches public relations, research methods, sociology of news, and computer-assisted reporting. His research interests center on the sociology of news, including local television news; media and community; news sources; and news, myth, and terrorism. He has published in *Journal of Broadcasting & Electronic Media, Journal of Communication, Journal of Public Relations Research, Journalism: Theory, Practice and Criticism, Journalism and Mass Communication Quarterly, Ecquid Novi, International Journal of Public Opinion Research*, and *Public Relations Review*. He is the editor of *Social Meanings of News* (Sage, 1997).

Yaeli Bloch-Elkon is a senior instructor in the Department of Political Studies, Public Communications Program, at Bar-Ilan University, Israel. At present, she is conducting postdoctoral research as a Visiting Scholar at Columbia University, New York. She specializes in the interaction between mass media, public opinion, and foreign policy. Her PhD dissertation, on which the present chapter is based, received the Israel Political Science Association's 2004 Outstanding Dissertation Award.

Richard Fox is visiting assistant professor in the Religion Department at Williams College and Deputy Director of the Balinese and Javanese Research Archive. His current teaching and research focus on issues pertaining to religion and mass media in South and Southeast Asia, with a special emphasis on Indonesia. He has published articles on theoretical issues in religious studies and Old Javanese philology, as well as on religion, culture, and performance in contemporary Bali. He is currently working on a manuscript comparing representations of religion-related violence in Southeast Asian and Euro-American mass media.

Mark Hobart is convenor of the Media & Film Studies Program at SOAS, University of London. An anthropologist with over eight years field research in Indonesia, he has a longstanding interest in philosophical issues in the human sciences. His teaching has ranged from regional ethnography, semiotics, and theory in the human sciences to South East Asian cinema, media, and cultural studies theory. His recent book, *After Culture,* is downloadable at http://www.criticalia.org. Mark Hobart has been active in developing media and cultural studies in Indonesia, and the Balinese government recently awarded him the *Dharma Kusuma* for his contribution to Indonesian cultural scholarship.

Teresa La Porte is professor of International Communication in the School of Communication at the University of Navarre, Spain. She also holds the Dean position. Most of her research is related to analysis of international news in the media. In this field, her published work includes *Mediated Terrorism in Comparative Perspective, Le sommet á Nice, Entre la globalisation et la diversité, Foreign News in Spain: Reporting One's Own Image of the World,* and *Media Effect on International Controversies.* She has been Research Scholar at the London School of Economics, the Center for International Affairs at Harvard University (as a NATO Fellow) and the Graduate School of Political Management at George Washington University. She is the author of the book, *The European Policy of Franco's Regime: 1957-1963.*

Sam Lehman-Wilzig is professor and chairman of the Department of Political Studies and in charge of the Public Communications Program at Bar-Ilan University. He is editor-in-chief of *Patuakh*, Israel's academic journal for media, politics and society. He served as chairman of the Israel Political Science Association (1997-99). His research specialties include new media as well as political communication.

Rashmi Luthra is associate professor of communication at the University of Michigan-Dearborn. Her research interests include gender and postcolonial discourse; postcolonial feminist pedagogies in communication; and women's cultural production in the South Asian diaspora. Recent publications include "Recovering Women's Voice: Communicative Empowerment of Women of the South" in *Communication Yearbook;* "Negotiating the Minefield: Practicing Transformative Pedagogy as a Teacher of Color in a Classroom Climate of Suspicion" in *Women Faculty of Color in the White Classroom*; and "The Women's Movement and the Press in India: The Construction of Female Foeticide as a Social Issue" in *Women's Studies in Communication.*

Hillel Nossek is the academic director of the Teaching and Research Authority of the College of Management Academic Studies, Tel-Aviv, Israel, and professor at the School of Media Studies of the College. He was the head of Journalism and Broadcast Communication Studies (1996-2003) of the school, and the chair of the Israel Communication Association (1998-2002). He is currently the co-head (with F. Krotz of Germany) of the Psychology and Public Opinion Section of IAMCR.

Peter Putnis is professor of Communication Studies at the University of Canberra, Australia. He is currently chair of the History Section of the International Association for Media and Communication Research and is a past president of the Australian and New Zealand Communication Association. He is the author (with R. Petelin) of *Professional Communication: Principles and Applications* (Prentice Hall, 1999). The focus of his research is international communication history, especially the political economy of international news production in the 19th and early 20th centuries.

Prasun Sonwalkar is senior lecturer in Journalism Studies at the School of Cultural Studies, University of the West of England, Bristol. He worked over two decades as a journalist on *The Times of India, Business Standard, Zee News,* and *Indo-Asian News Service.* He recently contributed chapters to *Media, Violence and Terrorism* (with A. Sreberny, Unesco, 2003);

Reporting War: Journalism in Wartime (Routledge, 2004); *International News in the 21st Century* (John Libbey, 2004); *Issues and Challenges in Asian Journalism* (Times Press, 2005); *Journalism: Critical Issues* (Open University Press, 2005); and articles to *Media, Cultural & Society, Gazette, Modern Asian Studies, Contemporary South Asia,* and *Communicator.*

Annabelle Sreberny holds the first chair in Global Media and Communication at SOAS, University of London, and she is a vice-president of IAMCR with a remit for publications. Her most recent book, co-edited with Chris Paterson, is *International News in the 21st Century* (John Libbey, 2004).

Paul A. Taylor is a senior lecturer in communications theory at the Institute for Communication Studies, University of Leeds. He is the author of *Hackers: Crime in the Digital Sublime* (Routledge, 1999), joint author of *Hacktivists: Rebels with a Cause?* (Routledge, 2004), and *Digital Matters: The Theory and Culture of the Matrix* (Routledge, in press). In addition to digital culture his main research and teaching interests center upon critical theories of mass culture.

Philip M. Taylor is professor of International Communications at the Institute of Communications Studies, University of Leeds. He is an expert in the area of information warfare and military-media relations. His books include *Munitions of the Mind: A History of Propaganda from the Ancient World to the Present Day* (Manchester University Press, 2003), and *British Propaganda in the Twentieth Century: Selling Democracy* (Edinburgh University Press, 1999).

Howard Tumber is professor of Sociology at City University, London. Recent publications include *Media at War: The Iraq Crisis* (with Jerry Palmer; Sage, 2004); *Political Scandals and Media Across Democracies, Volumes 1&2* (with S. Waisbord; American Behavioral Scientist, 2004); *Media Power, Policies and Professionals* (Routledge, 2000); and *News: A Reader* (Oxford University Press, 1999). He is a founder and co-editor of *Journalism: Theory, Practice and Criticism.*

Author Index

A

Abramson, P., 133, *138*
Abu-Lughod,L., 325, 328, 333, *337*
Adoni, H., 11, *17*, 43, 46, *62*, *63*
Ahmed, L., 329, *338*
Alcalay, G., 156, *157*
Aldrich, R., 145, *157*
Alexander, Y., 275, 278, *300*
Allan, S., 121, *141*, 240, *245*
Alloula, M., 333, *338*
Altschull, J.H., 162, *180*
Alvira, R., 101, *116*
Amis, M., 360, *371*
Anderson, B., 66, *78*
Anderson, B.R., 203, *208*
Antonucci, J.A., 83, *96*
Antonucci, M.K., 83, *96*
Appadurai, A., 65, *78*
Apple, R.W., 170, *181*
Arant, M. D., 43, *62*
Arno, A., 24, 25, *36*, 121, *137*
Asad, T., 189, *208*
Atkinson, R., 316, *322*

B

Bahran, Y., 331, 332, *338*
Baker, P., 316, *322*
Bakhtin, M.M, 189, 190, *208*
Ball-Rokeach, S., 279, *301*

Ballotti, J., 12, *18*, 46, *63*
Banerjee, N., 330, 333, *338*
Bantz, C., 11, *17*, 46, *62*
Baranek, P.M., 146, *157*
Barnhurst, K.G., 9, *17*
Barringer, F., 168, *181*
Barron, J., 173, 176, *182*
Barthes, R., 197, 199, 205, 207, *208*, 233, 233(n1) 234, 235, 240, 241, *243*
Bartter, M.A., 83, *96*
Baudrillard, J., 355, 357, 358, 363, 364, 365, 366, 367, 369, *371*, *372*
Baumann, Z., 77, *78*
Beaudoin, C., 122, *137*
Bebow, J., 317, *322*
Becker, E., 319, *322*
Bennett, L.W., 33, *36*
Bennett, S. E., 122, *137*
Berkowitz, D., 12, *17*, 46, 60, *62*, *63*, 162, 163, *181*
Beyer, L., 334, *338*
Billig, M., 65, 66, *78*
Bird, E., 12, *17*
Bird, E.S., 123, *137*
Bird, K., 83, *96*
Blackman, L., 70, *78*
Bloch, Y., 122, *137*
Boltanski, L., 68, *78*
Boorstin, D., 368, *372*

Botes, J., 34, 35, *36*
Bourk, M., 146, 147, 148, *157*
Boyd-Barrett, O., 26, *36*
Boyer, P., 83, 84, 90, 94, *96*
Boyle, M., 163, *182*
Bracewell, M., 357, 358, 362, 363,
    363(*n*1), *372*
Brecher, M., 124, 127, *137*
Brennan, C., 331, *338*
Britton, R.L., 123, 125, 132, *138*
Broad, J., 288, 289, *300, 303*
Brody, R. A., 123, *137*
Brookes, R., 350, 351, *353*
Brosius, H.B., 4, 9, *19*, 46, 64, 277, *303*
Brown, M.E., 189, *208*
Brown, R., 122, *137*
Bumiller, E., 171, 174, 175, 176, 177,
    181
Burchett, W., 87, 89, *96*
Burns, J.F., 173, 174, 175, 176, 177, *181*,
    182
Butler, J., 240, *243*

C

Cairncross, F., 68, *78*
Caliendo, S.M., 10, *17*, 43, *62*
Callaghan, K., 122, *137*
Calvino, I., 367, *372*
Canedy, D., 286, 288, *300, 303*
Canel, M.J., 99, 106, *117*
Carey, J.W., 282, *300*
Carruthers, S.L., 8, *17*, 27, 28, *36*, 49,
    62, 270, 274, 275, 279, 297, 298, 299,
    300
Center of Research of Social Reality,
    103, *157*
Chan, B.L., 146, *157*
Chang, T., 11, *17*, 43, 44, *62*
Chanter, A., 153, *157*
Chapman, P., 122, *139*
Chattarji, S., 252, *265*
Chiu, D., 121, *141*
Chomsky, N., 8, *17*, 26, *37*, 45, *63*, 163,
    181, 257, *266*, 276, 277, 279, 298,
    300, 301, 332, 336, *338*
Clutterbuck, R., 97, *117*
CNN, 225, *243*

Cohen, A.A., 6, 11, *17*, 44, 46, 52, *62*,
    63, 164, *181*
Cohen, S., 68, *78*
Cohen, Y., 33, *36*
Cole, R.R., 43, 44, *64*
Collier, R., 331, 332, *338*
Collingwood, R.G., 225, 226, *243*
Committee for the Compilation of
    Materials, 93, *96*
Cooke, M., 325, *338*
Corman, S.R., 282, 299, *301*
Coser, L.A., 24, *37*
Coughlin,K., 318, *322*
Crapanzano, V., 226, *243*
Crelinsten, R.D., 270, 277, 299, *301*
Crenshaw, M., 30, *37*
Curran, J., 43, 61, *62*

D

Daalder, I.H., 125, *137*
Dahlgren, P., 123, *137*
Dalton, M., 336, *339*
D'Angelo, P., 122, *137*
Danielian, L., 349, *353*
Darbenne, W.R., 12, *17*
Darnton, R., 12, *17*
Davidson, W.P., 25, 33, *37*
De Graaf, J., 8, *19*
de Tarde, G., 119, *140*
Dearing, J.W., 123, *140*
Deen, S., 371, *372*
Defense Science Board Task Force, 308,
    322
Defleur, M.L., 279, *301*
Delgado Ruiz, M., 100, *117*
Derrida, J., 227, *243*
Desai, D., 260, 262, *265*
Desmond, R.W., 85(*n*2), *96*
Devanathan, N., 163, *182*
Diezhandino, P., 100, *117*
Dobkin, B., 274, *301*
Doctrine for Joint Psychological
    Operations, 313, *322*
Dooley, K. J., 282, 299, *301*
Douglas, M., 201, *208*
Doward, J., *371, 372*
Dowd, M., 286, *301*
Dowling, H.L., 275, 297, *301*

Draznin, J., 9, *18*
Dubus, A., 362, *372*
Durham, F.D., 122, *137*
Dutt, B., 256, 263, *265*
Dutter, B., 237, *244*

E

Eason, G., 315, *323*
Editorial Desk, 292, 293, *301*
Eilders, C., 122, *137*
El-Awady, A., 316, *323*
Eldred, N.A., 125, *139*
Eley, G., 35, *37*
Elliott, P.R., 29, 30, 31, *38*
Emerson, C., 189(*n*6), *208*
Engelberg, S., 288, 289, *300*
Entman, R.M., 10, *17*, 33, *37*, 45, 52, *62*,
    98, *117*, 121, 122, *138*, *141*, 144, *157*,
    346, *353*
Epstein, N., 126, *140*
Ericson, R.V., 146, *157*
Erlanger, S., 168, 171, *181*
Everts, P., 123, *138*

F

Fabian, J., 226, *243*
Fabrilant, G., 168, *181*
Fair, J.E., 329, *338*
Falk, O., 272, 273, 299, *302*
Faludi, S., 335, *338*
Faramarzi, S., 331, *338*
Feis, H., 91, *96*
Fenby, J., 43, 60, *62*, 143, *157*
Finkel, K., 212, *243*
Fiske, J., 193, 194, 197(*n*14), *208*, 231,
    232, *243*
Flickinger, R.S., 122, *137*
Forman, M.B.G., 125, *137*
Fowler, R., 197(*n*12), *208*
Fox, R., 184, 195, 205, 206, *208*,
    214(*n*3), *243*
Foyle, D.C., 123, *137*
Franks, M.A., 325, 328, 335, 336, *338*
Fukiyama, F., 26, *37*

G

Gaddy, G.D., 43, *64*
Galtung, J., 5, *17*, 26, *37*, 59, *62*
Gamson, J., 367, *372*

Gamson, W. A., 122, *138*
Ganguly, K., 326(*n*2), *338*
Ganor, B., 273, 296, *301*
Gans, H.J., 43, *62*, 350, *353*
Gantz, W., 163, *181*, 276, *301*
Gavrilos, D., 46, *63*
Geertz, C., 202, 203, 199(*n*16), *208*
Geoghegan, T., 310, *323*
Gerbner, G., 98, *117*
Gerrits, R., 278, *301*
Gibney, M.P., 10, *17*. 43, *62*
Giddens, A., 13, *17*, 26, *37*, 65, 78, 97,
    117
Gilboa, E., 33, *37*
Gitlin, T., 8, *17*, 43, 45(*n*2), *62*, 122, *138*,
    163, *181*
Glaberson, W., 169, *181*
Glander, T., 308, *323*
Glanz, J., 169, *181*, 287, *301*
Glasgow University Media Group, 8,
    17, 61, *62*, 276, *301*
Glasser, T.L., 98, *117*
Golan, G., 43, *62*
Golding, P., 163, *181*
Goldman, R., 327, *337*, *338*
Gonzenbach, W. J., 43, *62*
Goodman, N., 196, *208*
Grace, N., 309, 315, 317, *323*
Gramsci, A., 26, *37*
Gray, H.C., 27, 28, *37*
Greenberg, B.S., 163, *181*, 276, 281, *301*
Grosswiler, P., 126, 131, *138*
Grundmamn, R., 10, *17*, 45, *62*
Gurevitch, M., 6, 7, *17*, *18*, 44, *62*, 144,
    145, *158*

H

Haberman, C., 168, *181*
Habermas, J., 24, 26, *37*
Hacking, I., 218(*n*6), *243*
Hakim, J., 216, 217, 241, *244*
Hall, S., 162, 163, *181*, 235, 236,
    214(*n*3), 233(*n*11), *244*, 270, *301*
Halleck, D., 83, *96*
Hallin, D.C., 8, *18*, 32, 33, *37*, 45(*n*2),
    62, 162, *181*
Hammond, P., 94, *96*
Hansen, T.B., 249, *266*

Harcup, T., 5, *18*, 44(*n*1), *62*
Harden, B., 170, *181*
Harre, R., 65, *78*
Hartley, J., 66, *78*, 231, *244*
Hartocollis, A., 169, *182*
Harville, B., 12, *18*, 46, *63*
Hass, R.N., 125, *138*
Hellinger, D., 344, *353*
Herman, E.S., 8, *17*, 26, 30, *37*, 45, *63*,
    163, *181*, 257, *266*, 276, 279, 298,
    300, *301*, 332, 336, *338*
Hersey, J., 84, 90, 91, 92, 93, 94, *96*
Heryanto, A., 204, *208*
Herzog, H., 122, *138*
Hewit, C., 274, 279, *301*
Hillback, E., 163, *182*
Hirschkind, C., 328, 329, *338*
Hobart, M., 211, 213(*n*1), 214(*n*3), 214,
    226, 241, 242, *244*
Hobsbaum, E., 65, *78*
Hocking, J.J., 279, *301*
Hofschire, L., 281, *301*
Hogan, M.J., 94, *96*
Holbrooke, R., 125, *138*
Holsti, O.R., 121, *138*
Hutchins, R.M., 120(*n*1), *138*

I

Inglehart, R., 133, *138*
Innis, H., 369, *372*
Ismael, S.T., 332, 333, *338*
Iyengar, S., 113, *117*, 122, *138*, 349, *353*

J

Jacobs, L.R., 123, *140*
Jansen, S.C., 329, *338*
Jawa Pos, 224, 225(*n*1), 229, *244*
Jenkins, B., 30, *37*, 275, *301*
Jentleson, B. W., 123, 125, 132, *138*
Johansson, F., 44, *64*
Johnson, O.V., 6, *19*, 45, *64*
Johnson, R., 236, *244*
Joint Doctrine for Information
    Operations, 312, *323*
Jones, A.S., 122, *140*
Jones, S., 321, *323*
Judd, D., 344, *353*
Just, M., 4, 8, *18*, 270, 274, 275, 285,
    287, 290, 293, 297, 299, *302*, 349, *353*

K

Kaid, L.L., 12, *18*, 46, *63*
Kamen, J., 28, *37*
Kanner, M.D., 125, *138*
Karim, K.H., 122, *138*
Katz, E., 2, *18*
Keller, B., 170, *181*
Kellner, D., 8, *18*, 336, *338*
Kelly, M. J., 4, 9, *18*, 46, *63*, 277, *301*
Kennedy, R., 167, 176, *181*
Kern, M., 4, *18*, 270, 274, 275, 285, 287,
    290, 293, 297, 299, *302*, 349, *353*
Khalil, A., 332, *338*
Khouri, R.G., 317, *323*
Kinder, D., 349, *353*
Kingstone, S., 8, *18*
Kitley, P., 186, 202(*n*17), *208*
Kitzinger, J., 350, *353*
Klein, M., 67, *78*
Kolhatkar, S., 329, 336, *338*
Kompas, 224(*n*9), 225, *244*
Kull, S., 352, *353*
Kupperman, R., 28, *37*
Kuypers, J.A., 122, *139*

L

Lacayo, R., 333, *338*
Laclau, E., 189, *208*, 214, *244*
Laqueur, W., 29, *37*, 270, 274, 278, *301*
Laurence, W.L., 87(*n*3), *96*
Laurie, C.D., 307, *323*
Lazreg, M., 329, *358*
Lee, J., 11, *17*, 43, 44, *62*
Lehman-Wilzig, S., 122, *137*
Lerner, D., 26, *37*
Lévi-Strauss, C., 199, 205, *208*
Levy, M.R., 6, 7, *17*, *18*, 44, *62*, 144, 145,
    158
Lewin, J., 284, 288, *302*
Lewis, J., 343, 344, 346, 350, 351, *353*
Lewis, N.A., 292, *302*
Lichtenberg, J., 162, *181*
Liebes, T., 11, *18*, 46, 53, *63*
Lifschultz, L., 83, *96*
Lifton, R.J., 84, 89, 93, 94, *96*
Littleton, M.J., 272, *302*
Livingstone, S., 43, 61, *63*
Lobe, J., 333, *338*

LoTempio, A., 125, *139*
Lowry, D.N., 9, *19*, 44, *64*
Lule, J., 12, *18*
Luter, A., 122, *137*
Luthra, R., 329, *338*

M

Mahmood, S., 328, 329, *338*
Malek, A., 120, 123, 131, *139*
Malik, L., 332, *339*
Maney, G.M., 9, *18*, 47, 60, *63*
Mantilla, K., 332, *339*
Martin, L .J., 9, *18*
Maxwell, R., 346, *353*
McChesney, R.W., 26, *37*
McCluskey, M., 163, *182*
McCombs, M. E., 119, *139*, 349, *353*
McLeod, D., 163, *182*
McLuhan, M., 357, 369, *372*
McQuail, D., 120(*n*1), *139*
McVey, R., 203(*n*20), *208*
Meiners, E., 331, *339*
Mennell, S., 67, *78*, *79*
Mermin, J., 33, 34, *38*, 122, *139*
Mernissi, F., 334, 335, *339*
Merrill, J., 122, 126, *139*
Miller, J., 286, 288, 289, *300*, *302*
Miller, T., 346, *353*
Mitchell, A., 171, *181*
Mitchell, G., 84, 89, 94, *96*
Mitchell, H.T., 4, *18*, 46, *63*, 277, *301*
Mitchell, W.J.T., 364, *372*
Moallem, M., 329, *337*, *339*
Moeller,S.D., 68, *79*
Moody, M., 332, *339*
Morin, R., 123, *137*
Morley, D., 332, *339*
Morrison, D., 23, 24, 26, 27, 28, 30, 32, 33, 34, 35, *38*, 97, *117*
Morrow, Capt. J.M., 308, *323*
Morson, G.S., 189(*n*6), *208*
Mosco, V., 26, *38*
Moskos, C. C., 119, *139*
Mouffe, C., 214, *244*
Mowlana, H., 25, 26, *38*, 98, *117*
Mueller, J.E., 98, *117*, 123, *139*
Murdoch, G., 29, 30, 31, *38*, 163, *181*

N

Nacos, B.L., 28, 29, 30, 31, *38*, 270, 275, *302*
Naisbitt, J., 133, *139*
Nandy, A., 250, *266*
Narayan, U., 326, 331, 333, 336, *339*
Naveh, H., 122, *139*
Newman, K., 83, *96*
Nieves, E., 285, *302*
Ninan, S., 254, 257, *266*
Nir, R., 126, *139*
Nordland, R., 330, *339*
Norris, P., 4, 8, *18*, 122, *139*, 270, 274, 275, 285, 287, 290, 293, 297, 299, *302*, 349, *353*
Nossek, H., 4, 9, 11, 12, *17*, *18*, 28, *38*, 41, 42, 43, 44, 46, 48, 50, 52, 54, 56, 58, 59, 60, *62*, *63*, 119, 122, *139*, 162, 163, 164, 165, *182*, 272, 279, 281, *302*

O

O'Hanlon, M., 125, *137*
O'Heffernan, P., 33, *38*
Oliver, P. E., 9, *18*, 47, 60, *63*
Olivera, A., 30, *38*
O'Neill, D., 5, *18*, 44(*n*1), *62*
Osborne, C., 336, *339*
O'Sullivan, G., 30, *37*

P

Padgaonkar, D., 258, 260, 262, *266*
Page, B. I., 123, *139*, 344, *353*
Paletz, D.L., 8, *18*, 119, 121, 122, 123, 126, *139*
Palmer, J., 351, *353*
Park, M.J., 43, 61, *62*
Parmeswaran, R., 326, *339*
Patel, A., 258, 260, 262, *266*
Paterson, C.A., 7, *18*, 44, 60, *63*
Payne, A., 10, *17*, 43, *62*
Penhallurick, J., 146, 147, 148, *158*
Peterson, T., 120, 120(*n*1), 121, *140*
Pew Research for the People and the Press, 273, *302*
Phillip, A.J., 256, *266*
Phillips, N., 122, *139*
Picard, R., 4, *19*, 46, 50, *63*
Piqué, A., 99, *117*

Powaski, R.E., 91, *96*
Power, S., 122, 123, 125, *139*
Powlick, P., 123, *139*
Pratt, M.L., 227, *244*
Prerna, R., 262, *266*
PUCL, 261, *266*
Purdum, T.S., 168, *182*
Putnam, L. L., 122, *139*
Putnis, P., 146, 147, 148, *158*

R

Raban, J., *358*, *372*
Rajagopal, A., 252, 254, *266*
Ranger, T., 65, *78*
Rashbaum, W. K., 173, 176, *182*
Reese, S., 99, *117*
Renuart, Major General V., 315, 317, *323*
Reuters, 126, *139*, 215, 218, 219, 220, 221, 222, 223, 225, 229, *244*, 318, *323*
Rhine, S.L., 125, *137*
Rhodes, R., 91, *96*
Ricks, T.E., 119, *139*, 316, *322*
Rivenburgh, N., 121, *139*
Robins, K., 332, *339*
Roeh, I., 6, 7, 12, *17*, *18*, 44, 46, 51, 52, *62*, *63*, 123, 126, *139*, 144, 145, *158*, 164, *181*
Rogers, E. M., 123, *140*
Rojecki, A., 35, *38*, 122, *138*
Rorty, R., 76, *79*
Rosen, J., 98, *117*, 310, *323*
Rosenbaum, D.E., 287, *301*
Rosengren, K.E., 44, *63*
Rubin, A.J., 331, *339*
Ruddock, A., 119, 120, *140*
Ruge, M.H., 5, *17*, 59, *62*
Rule, J.B., 24, *38*
Russett, B., 121, *140*

S

Sadkovich, J.J., 110, *117*
Said, E.W., 214, *244*, 326, *337*, *339*, *358*, 368, *372*
Saideman, S.M., 125, *140*
San Antonio Express-News, 331, *339*
Sanders, M.L., 307, *323*

Sanger, D. E., 171, 173, 174, 175, 176, 177, *181*, *182*
Santamaria, L., 100, *117*
Sardesai, R., 256, 258, 259, 260, 263, *266*
Sarkees, M. R., 125, *140*
Satloff, R., 317, *323*
Scheufele, D.A., 122, *140*
Schiller, H., 98, *117*
Schlesinger, P., 23, 24, 26, 27, 28, 29, 30, 32, 33, 34, 35, *38*, 98, *117*, 275, 291, *302*
Schmemann, S., 170, *182*
Schmid, A.P., 8, *18*, *19*, 30, 31, *38*
Schmitt, E., 312, *323*
Schnell, F., 122, *137*
Schramm, W., 26, *38*, 120, 120(n1), *140*
Schudson, M., 121, *140*, 163, *182*, 281, 282, *302*
Schwartz, Y., 272, 273, 299, *302*
Seelye, K.Q., 171, *181*, 283, *302*
Seib, P. M., 125, *140*, 247, *266*
Sennett, R., 77, *79*
Serfaty, S., 121, *140*
Servaes, J., 52, 53, *63*
Shah, G., 251, *266*
Shamir, J., 61, *64*
Shanker T., 312, *323*
Shannon, C.E., 233, *244*
Shapiro, R. Y., 123, *139*, *140*, 344, *353*
Sharma, K., 262, *266*
Shaw, D.L., 119, *139*
Shaw, M., 97, 99, 111, *117*
Shevy, M., 163, *182*
Shoemaker, P.J., 6, *19*, 44, *64*, 99, *117*, 144, *158*
Showalter, E, 189, *209*
Siebert, F.F., 120, 120(n1), *140*
Simmons, B.K., 9, *19*, 44, *64*
Simon, A.F., 113, *117*, 122, *138*
Simpson, C., 308, *323*
Singer, D.J., 125, *140*
Smith, A., 249, *266*
Smith, C., 177, *182*
Smith, D., 10, *17*, 45, *62*
Smith, J.Y., 126, *140*
Sobel, R., 123, *140*

Sontag, S., 213, 240, *244*, 358, 360, 361, 363, 365, 366, 367, 370, *372*
Sonwalkar, P., 4, *19*, 247, 248, 250, 256, 258, 260, 262, 264, *266*
Sparks, C., 99, *117*, 123, *137*
Sperber, D., 205, 209
Spillius, A., 237, *244*
Spivak, G.C., 329, *339*
Splichal, S., 99, *117*, 123, *140*
Sprintzak, E., 50, *63*
Sreberny, A., 11, *19*, 42, 43, 44, 49, 60, *64*, 66, 148, *158*, 214, *244*
Stanley, A., 172, 174, 177, *182*
States News Service., 333, *339*
Stein, S., 163, *182*
Stevenson, R.L.,11, *19*, 43, 44, 49, 60, 62, *64*
Stevenson, R.W., 173, *182*
Stolberg, S.G., 288, 289, *300*, *302*
Straits Times, 225, *244*
Suara Merdeka, 238, 239, *245*
Sweeney, C.W., 83, *96*
Sydney Morning Herald, 225, 228, 229, *245*

T

Tankard, J.W. Jr., 122, *140*
Tarde, G. de, 119, *140*
Tarrow, S., 50, *64*
Taylor, P., 27, *38*, 355, 356, *358*, 360, 362, 364, 366, 368, 370, *372*
Taylor, P.M., 307, 308, 310, 312, 314, 315, 316, 318, 320, *323*, *324*
Taylor, Phil, 363, *372*
Tehranian, M., 34, *38*
TerKeurst, J., 162, *181*
The Telegraph, 257, *266*
The Times of India, 249, 255, 257, 258, 262, 263, *266*
Thobani, S., 325, 327, 332, *339*
Thompson, H.S., 361, 363. *372*
Thornton, P.T., 270, 298, 299, *302*
Thorson, E., 122, *137*
Tifft, S. E., 122, *140*
Tomlinson, J., 35, *38*
Toner, R., 168, *182*
Tuchman, G., 98, *117*, 150, *158*, 350, *353*

Tuman, J.S., 8, *19*, 30, 31, *38*, 164, *172*, 270, 275, 297, *302*
Tumber, H., 23, 24, 26, 27, 28, 30, 32, 33, 34, 35, *38*, 351, *353*
Tunstall, J., 51, *64*
Tyler, P.E., 291, 292, *302*

U

Ullman, R.H., 125, *140*
UNESCO, 26, *38*
U.S. Department of State, 347, *353*

V

Valdivia, A., 329, *339*
Van Belle, D.A., 5, *19*, 44, *64*, 124, *140*
van Ginneken, J., 183, 196, 201, *208*, 215, 227, 229, 231, *243*
Varadarajan, S., 252, 256, 259, *266*, 267
Varis, T., 26, *39*
Varshney, A., 251, 253, 267
Verghese, B.G., 258, 260, 262, *266*
Vickers, A., 194, 209, 223, *245*
Viera, J.D., 276, *302*
Vincent, R.C., 126, *140*
Vuckovic, G., 125, *140*

W

Waisbord, S., 121, *141*, 282, 299, *303*
Wald, M.L., 291, 292, 293, *303*
Walker, R.B.J., 68, 74, *79*
Walkerdine, V., 70, *78*
Walzer, M., 271, *303*
Wanta, W., 43, 62, 349, *353*
Wardlaw, G., 272, 277, 299, *303*
Washington Post, *358*, *372*
Waugh, P., 317, *324*
Wawrzyniak, M., 12, *18*, 46, *63*
Wayman, F. W., 125, *140*
Weart, S.R., 83, 84, 94, *96*
Weaver, D.H., 6, *19*, 45, *64*, 99, *117*
Weaver, W., 233, *244*
Webster, F., 13, *19*, 35, *36*, *39*
Webster, R., 35, *38*
Wei, W., 6, *19*, 45, *64*
Weimann, G., 4, 8, 9, *19*, 33, *39*, 44, 46, 275, 277, *303*
Weiss, T.G., 125, *141*
Welsh, I., 362, 363, 365, 366, *372*
Westerståhl, J., 44, *64*

White House, 311, 319, *324*
Wilhoit, G.C., 6, *17*, 99, *117*
Wilkenfeld, J., 124, *137*
Wilkinson, P., 4, *19*, 50, *64*, 272, *303*
Windmiller, M., 264, *267*
Winn, C., 8, *19*, 44, *64*, 275, *303*
Winnicott, D.W., 67, *79*
Winter, G., 289, *303*
Wolfsfeld, G., 25, 33, *39*, 122, *141*, 278,
    303
Wright, S., 10, *17*, 45, *62*
Wu, H.D., 44, 49, *64*

Y

Yardley, J., 286, 288, *300*, *303*
Youichi, I., 7, *19*, 44, *64*
Young, O.R., 124, *141*

Z

Zaller, J.R., 98, 111, *117*, 119, 122, 124,
    141, 350, *353*
Zelizer, B., 74, *79*, 121, *141*, 212, 214,
    215, 240, *245*
Zernike, K., 169, *182*
Zizek, S., 211, 240, *245*, *371*, *372*

Subject Index

A

Aaj Tak, 258
Abu Ghraib prisoner abuse, 16
    branding *vs.* branded, 363-364
    obscene image, 364-365
    photographic images, 364-365
Abuse
    prisoner, 16
    vs. torture, 360
Addressivity, 14
Advani, L.K., 257
Advertiser
    Bali bombs photographic supple
        ment, 228
Afghanistan, 2
    framing gender, 325–337
    Spanish humanitarian aid mission,
        102
    Taliban victimization of women,
        326–329
    wars, 15–16, 23
Aglionby, John, 198
Aircraft
    Hercules EC 30E, 313
Al-Jazeera, 317, 320
Allied journalists, 89
Al-Qaeda, 67, 351
Al-Sahhaf, Mohammed, 315
American. *See* United States

Amis, Martin, 71
Anthrax, 282
    vs. dirty bomb incidents, 295t, 296-
        297
    experts, 285
    first person reports, 286
    government reports, 286–287
    identification of, 287–288
    media criticizing government, 286
    New York Times, 284–289, 295t,
        296–297
    practical solutions for, 288
    readiness for, 288–289
    September 11, 2001, 281–283
Antinuclear protests
    Australia, 50, 145
    Japan, 145
Arab world
    photographic images of Abu Ghraib
        prisoner abuse, 358
Armed conflicts
    Spanish perception, 102
Asian Age
    Gujarat 2002, 257, 262
Assassination
    of Indira Gandhi, 253
Associated Press, 86
    Spanish news, 105
Athletes
    Iraq, 331

Atomic bomb
    flash-boom, 91
    rationalizations, 94
Atomic plague, 84-89
Attachment
    journalism, 69-70
Attitudes
    journalists, 6
Audience
    involvement in distant violent
        conflicts, 99
Austin, Mark, 191-192
Australia
    antinuclear protests, 50, 145
    reporting on French nuclear tests in
        Pacific, 143–157
    vs. British reporting, 148
    country prominence measure,
        147*t*
    vs. United States in international
        news, 148
Australian
    Bali bombs photographic supple-
        ment, 228
    reporting on French nuclear tests in
        Pacific, 145–147, 149–156
    European perspectives, 151
    named actor appearances, 150, 151*t*
    Pacific representations, 153–156
    sources, 151, 152*t*
    story type, 149, 150*t*
Authoritarian approach, 136
Axis of Evil, 370
Ayodhya
    Gujarat, 251-253

B

Babri mosque
    Hindu-Muslim clashes over, 253,
        257, 262
Baby Boom generation
    humanitarian frame, 131
Baghdad
    Abu Ghraib prisoner abuse photo-
        graphic images, 16, 356–362
    branding *vs.* branded, 363-364
    obscene image, 364-365
Baghdad blogger, 2

Balance, 165
Bali bombs
    British television news, 15, 189-193
    British *vs.* Indonesian news, 190
    CNN, 227
    earliest online report, 241
    eye witnesses, 224–226, 226–227
    framing, 215–216, 223
    history/culture
        privation of, 199
    identification, 199–200
    images, 211–243
        we defined, 213–216
    inoculation against Islam fanatics,
        199
    Kuta, 216–218
        imagery, 218
    mythmaking, 198–201
    neither-norism, 200
    perpetrator, 197–198
    Philippine Consulate in Manado,
        216
    photographic supplement, 216,
        228–241
        imaging al-Qaeda, 235–239, 236f
        provisional labels, 230–233
        text loading image, 233–234
    quantification of quality, 200
    Reuters *vs.* CNN, 221–223
    similar news everywhere, 201–205
    statement of fact, 200–201
    tautology, 200
    U.S. Consulate in Renon, 216
    video, 216
    visual importance, 216–227
    visual representation, 216
Balinese shadow theater, 202-203
Bali Post
    Bali bombs photographic supple-
        ment, 229
Balkans wars, 1
Banal journalism, 247-265
Basque
    terrorist acts of, 101
Baudrillard, Jean, 357, 366
BBC. *See* British Broadcasting
    Corporation (BBC)

BDA. *See* Bomb Damage Assessment
(BDA)
Bharatiya Janata Party (BJP), 250, 251
  disciplining media, 258
Bias
  built into foreign news reporting,
  6–7
Bikini Atoll
  Marshall Islands
    hydrogen bomb testing, 95
hydrogen bomb testing, 95
Bin Laden, Osama, 31, 368, 369
Bioterrorism, 282
BJP. *See* Bharatiya Janata Party (BJP)
Blair, Tony
  political pressure upon, 356
Blogger
  Baghdad, 2
Bomb Damage Assessment (BDA)
  Iraq, 315
Bombs. *See also* Bali bombs; Dirty
  bomb scare
  atomic, 91, 94–95
  Jewish school in Lyon, France,
  49–50
  M129 leaflet, 316
  shock and awe, 311, 315
Bosnian crisis, 14
  historical context, 131
Bosnian policy (United States)
  elite *vs.* popular press coverage of,
  119-137
  findings, 127-131, 128t, 129t, 130t
  framing, 121-122, 128t, 130
  government, 124-125
  methodology, 126-127
  press types, 122-124
  research design, 125-127
  theoretical framework, 120-121
Bosnian War, 1, 14
  cruelty, 125
  NATO bombardment, 28, 49, 53–55
  in Spain, 97–116
    distant and remote, 108-109
    divergent editorial lines, 111-114
    news reinforcing audience's atti-
    tude as spectator, 106-111

Boston Herald
  twin towers images, 213*f*
Brainwashing, 308
Branding, 371
  vs. branded
    photographic images of Abu
    Ghraib prisoner abuse, 363-364
  disciplining media, 258-259
Breaking news, 225
Brennan, Donnie, 371
Britain
  excess military spending, 341
  newspapers, 51
  photographic images of Abu Ghraib
    prisoner abuse, 358
British Broadcasting Corporation
  (BBC)
  Bali bombs, 190
  bomb explosions
    Srinigar, Kashmir, 50, 59
British media coverage
  Iraq war, 16
British news
  Christian world view, 195
  vs. Indonesian news
    Bali bombs, 190
British television news
  Bali bombs, 15, 189-193
Broadcast sports commentary
  nationalism, 66
Buffalo News
  Iraqi women, 332
Bumfights, 361, 365, 371
Burchett, Wilfred, 84, 87-89, 94
Burqa, 328
Bush, George, 66
  Abu Ghraib prisoner abuse, 358
  Iraq War, 173–176, 311
  military spending, 345
  political pressure upon, 356
Bush, Laura
  radio address on Afghan women,
  329
Byrne, Andrew, 155

C

Calvino, Italo, 367

Cameras
  digital
    pervasiveness, 23-24
"Cares of the World-How Should
  Individuals Respond At A Time of
  Crisis?", 73
CDI. *See* Center for Defense
  Information (CDI)
Celebrity democratization
  Reality-TV formats, 366–367
Celebrity Detox, 361
Center for Defense Information (CDI),
  342
Channel Surat, 258
Cheap newspapers, 123
China, 2
Chiniwala, Raju, 262
Chirac, Jacques, 145
Christian world view, 195
Chronotope, 190, 194, 207
Classical approach
  to mass media relationship to terror-
    ism, 274–276, 280, 296–297
Clawback, 194
Clinton, Bill, 345
Closed construction, 165
CNN
  Bali bombs, 221, 225, 227, 232, 232f
  banned, 258
  effect, 2, 35, 43
  vs. Reuters, 221–223
  Taliban victimization of Afghan
    women, 327–328
CNO. *See* Computer Network
  Operations (CNO)
Coercion
  effectiveness on political decisions,
    98
Cold War, 308, 327
Colonial feminism, 329
Combat propaganda, 307
Commando Solo, 313, 315, 316, 317
Communication
  changes, 29–30
  facilitation among antagonists, 24–25
  global technological changes, 61
  international

approaches, 25
  idealistic-humanistic approach,
    25–26
  technologies, 8
Communication dialogue
  terrorism defined as, 269–270
Communication maps
  ethnocentric
    local editing, 11
Composite images
  Bali bombs photographic supple
    ment, 231
Computer Network Operations
  (CNO)
  Operation Iraqi Freedom, 312
Conflict
  conventional categorization, 27
  internal *vs.* external, 46
  international, 23–36
  media's central role in management,
    25
Conflict mediators
  vs. journalists, 34-35
Congo, 2
Contagion effect, 274
Contagion theory, 274
Contractors
  vs. mercenaries, 360
Contributions to Analytical Psychology,
  369
Conventional terrorism
  defined, 272
  vs. unconventional terrorism, 273
Cook, Alistair, 71
Covert PSYOPS, 309
Crimes
  secrecy, 24
Critical approach
  to mass media relationship to terror-
    ism, 276–277, 280–281, 296–298
Critical-radical approach
  to mass media relationship to terror-
    ism, 276–277
Cruelty
  Bosnian War, 125
Cultural myths, 12

D

Daily Express (London), 84, 87
Daily Mirror, 358, 365
Daily News (Chicago), 89
Daily Telegraph, 228, 236, 237, 239
Deictics, 65-78
  analysis, 14
  reestablishing commonality, 68
Deixis, 65
  global power relations, 66
Digital cameras
  pervasiveness, 23-24
Dimbleby, Jonathan, 66
Dirty bomb scare
  government reports, 290–291
  professionals, 290
  public, 290–291
  vs. anthrax, 295t
Dirty tricks, 308
Disasters
  foreign news, 5
Discourse
  double-voiced, 189
Distance
  death of, 68–69
  types, 68–69
Distant violent conflicts
  audience involvement, 99
  media's representation of, 97–116
Domei, 88
Domestic editing
  foreign news, 43
Domestic news
  vs. foreign news, 9
Domestic terrorism, 44
Double-voiced discourse, 189
Dutt, Barkha, 256, 263-264

E

Economic power
  information as, 26
Ecstasy of Communication, 366
Editing
  foreign news, 43, 44
Editors
  foreign news, 43–46

Editors Guild of India
  Gujarat 2002, 260
Elite *vs.* popular press coverage
  of American policy in Bosnia,
  119–137
  findings, 127-131
  framing, 121-122, 128t, 130
  government, 124-125
  methodology, 126-127
  press types, 122-124
  research design, 125-127
  theoretical framework, 120-121
El Mundo, 100, 106-115
El Pais, 100, 106-114
E-mails
  PSYOPS, 310
Embedded journalists, 2
Emotion
  journalism, 69–70
Empire of Evil, 370
Encoding/decoding model, 269-270
England, Lynndie, 366
English-language *vs.* non-English lan-
  guage press
  Gujarat 2002, 249, 255
Entertainment media
  fascination with terrorism, 31
ETA. *See* Euskadi Ta Askatasuna (ETA)
Ethics
  Gujarat 2002, 255–257
Ethnocentric communication maps
  local editing, 11
EurAm news media, 227
Eurocentric standards
  local editing, 11
Euskadi Ta Askatasuna (ETA)
  terrorist acts of, 101–102
Evacuation
  Bali bombs photographic supple-
  ment, 230
Excess military spending
  Britain, 241
Experts
  anthrax, 285

F

Fact, 165
Falklands War, 45

False photographs
    Daily Mirror, 358, 365
Fangataufa, 145
Farrell, Thomas D., 86
Feminism
    colonial, 329
Feminist Majority Foundation, 328-329
Financial Times, 346, 347t, 348t
Flak
    disciplining media, 257–260
Fog of war, 352
Foreign news
    defined by local angle, 12
    disasters, 5
    domestic editing, 43
    vs. domestic news, 9
    globalization, 42–43
    journalists and editors as gatekeep-
        ers, 43–46
    local angles, 43
    local editing, 44
    national perspective, 143–157
    political violence, 46–49
    reporting bias, 6–7
Foreign news coverage
    convergence and divergence, 144
    cultural filtering, 44
    domestic bias, 44
    domestic context, 144
    local character, 143–144
    national identity, 41–61
        findings, 53-58
        media selection, 50-51, 51t
        methodology, 49-50
        qualitative content analysis
            method, 52-53
    selection, 5
Forgers
    modern media techniques, 24
Fort Bragg, North Carolina
    4th Psychological Operations
        Group, 309
Framing
    American policy in Bosnia, 121–122,
        128t, 130
    Bali bombs, 215–216, 223
    gender

Afghanistan, 325-337
    Iraq, 325-337, 329-333
    humanitarian, 131
    national, 59, 60
    of the oppression of Afghan women
        by the Taliban, 326
    Washington Post, 132
Franco, 101
Franks, Tommy, 177, 316
Freedom of the press
    vs. social responsibility, 45
Free press theory, 120
French nuclear tests reporting
    Australia, 143–157
        vs. British reporting, 148
        country prominence measure, 147t
        vs. United States in international
            news, 148
    Australian, 145-147, 149-156
        European perspectives, 151
        named actor appearances, 150, 151t
        Pacific representations, 153-156
        sources, 151, 152t
        story type, 149, 150t
Frequent-flyer journalists, 203
Fujii, Masakazu, 90, 91, 93
Functional-professional approach
    to mass media relationship to terror-
        ism, 277–278, 280–281, 296, 298,
        300

G

Galpin, Richard, 190
Gandhi, Indira
    assassination, 253, 265
Gatekeepers
    decision-making process, 47–48, 48f
    editors as, 43–45
    journalists as, 7
    local glasses worn, 6–7
    media, 99
Gender
    framing, 325-327
        Afghanistan, 325-337
        Iraq, 325-337
Geneva convention
    permissible vs. prohibited weapons,
        271

Ghetto Brawls, 361
Glasgow University Media Group, 6,
    44-45
Global communication
    technological changes, 61
Globalization, 1
    negative effects, 13
Global military threat
    military spending, 345
Global news room, 6-7
Global power relations
    deixis, 66
Global television
    affect foreign news definition, 60
Godhra station mob attack, 252-253
    retaliation for, 253
Godse, Nathuram, 265
Gonzo porno, 360, 361
Gonzo TV, 361
Government
    anthrax, 285, 286–287
    anti-terrorist measures, 279
    dirty bomb scare, 290–291
    initiating political violence, 10–11
    as initiators of political violence,
        10–11
    mass media as watchdog on, 120–121
    New York Times coverage of anthrax
        vs. dirty bomb incidents, 295*t*
    relationships with press
        libertarian philosophy, 120
    secrecy, 24
Greater Serbia
    Milosevich's attempts to rebuild, 112
Guardian (UK), 70
    Bali bombs, 198
    international terrorism coverage,
        346, 347*t*, 348*t*
    reporting on French nuclear tests in
        Pacific, 146–147
Gujarat 2002, 15, 247–265
    English language *vs.* non-English
        language press, 249, 255
    ethics, 255–257
    Hindu-Muslim clashes, 251
    Hindutva, 251–252
    India's first television riot, 254–263

    journalists' experience, 262–264
    medium as message, 255–257
    press objectivity and bias, 260–262
Gujarat Samachar
    Gujarat 2002, 255, 260–262
Gujarat Today
    Gujarat 2002, 261
Gulf War, 1
    American network coverage of, 46
    news coverage differences, 11
    second, 355, 370–371

H

Ha'aretz, 51
    BBC explosion in Srinagar, Kashmir,
58
    French nuclear test in Pacific, 57
    Jewish school bombing in Lyon,
        57–58
    NATO bombardment of Bosnia,
        54–55
Hannah, Rufus, 371
Hardball with Chris Matthews, 229
Hard news, 122
Hegemony
    syntax, 66
Hells Angels, 361
Hercules EC 130E aircraft, 313
Herizons
    Iraqi women, 332
Hersey, John, 84, 90, 94
Heteroglossia, 189
Hindu-Muslim clashes
    Gujarat 2002, 251
    over Babri mosque, 253, 257, 262
Hindutva
    defined, 265
    disciplining media, 257–260
    Gujarat 2002, 249, 251–252
Hiroshima, 83–96
    radioactivity, 86–87
    September 11, 2001 comparison to,
        202
    WTC compared to, 186
Historical experiences
    influencing society's stance on
        political violence, 101
Historical references, 165

Holbrook, Richard, 49
Holland, Fern, 331
Homecoming
    Bali bombs photographic
        supplement, 230
Horror and conflagration
    Bali bombs photographic
        supplement, 230, 240
Hospital
    Bali bombs photographic
        supplement, 230
House of Sand and Fog, 362
Human-interest genres, 123
Humanitarian aid mission
    Spanish, 102
Humanitarian frame
    Baby Boom generation, 131
Human rights, 36
    before and after the Cold War
        American foreign news coverage,
        10
Humiliation ritual
    Iraqi prisoners, 360–361
Hussein, Saddam
    capture, 356
    Iraqi women, 330, 332
    Iraq War, 161, 173–177, 309–322
    military spending, 345, 351–352
    toppling statue, 355–356
Hussein, Uday, 331
Hydrogen bomb testing
    Bikini Atoll of Marshall Islands, 95
Hyperreal
    postmodern concept of, 358

I

IAMCR. *See* International Association
    for Media and Communication
    Research (IAMCR)
Idealistic-humanistic approach
    to international communications,
    25–26
Images
    Bali bombs, 211–243
    displacing ideals, 368
    mass mediated, 215
    obscene, 364–365
    twin towers, 213*f*

Independent on Sunday (London)
    Bali bombs, 222
    Iraq, 321
Indexing hypothesis, 33
India, 2
    English language *vs.* non-English
        language press, 249
    Gujarat 2002, 254–263
    mass killings, 253–254
    political process, 249–250
Indian Express
    Gujarat 2002, 255, 257, 260, 262–263
Indian news media
    ban on naming communities,
        255–256
Indonesia, 2
    Bali bombs, 189–196
    media freedom, 186
    September 11, 2001, 15, 186
    television, 185–186
    terrorist attacks coverage, 183–208
    Trade Towers attack coverage,
        185–187, 189, 202
Information
    as economic power, 26
    sources, 165
Information Operations (IO)
    Operation Iraqi Freedom, 311–312
Information Radio, 313, 314
Information Warfare (IW)
    Operation Iraqi Freedom, 311–312
Infotainment, 123
Inside-outside spatial metaphor, 68
Insurgent terrorism
    against western democracies, 8
International Association for Media and
    Communication Research
    (IAMCR), 49
International communication
    approaches, 25
    idealistic-humanistic approach,
        25–26
International conflict, 23-36
    conceptual approaches, 24–26
    sources, 32–35
International media, 43
International news

media as gatekeeper, 99
Spain, 103, 104–105, 105
International terrorism
  coverage
    Financial Times, 346, 347t, 348t
    Guardian, 346, 347t, 348t
    Mail, 346
    Mirror, 346, 347t
  reaching diversified audiences, 270
  Soviet Union, 29
Internet
  affect foreign news definition, 60
  national ties, 61
Intifada
  American network coverage of, 46
  Middle East, 1, 2, 11
Investigation
  Bali bombs photographic
    supplement, 230
IO. *See* Information Operations (IO)
Iraq, 2
  athletes, 331
  beheading hostages, 31
  Bomb Damage Assessment, 315
  framing gender, 325–337
  sexual violence against women, 332
  Spanish humanitarian aid mission,
    102
Iraqi prisoners
  ritual humiliation, 16, 360–361
Iraqi soldiers
  instructions on surrendering, 316
Iraqi women
  Buffalo News, 332
  Herizons, 332
Iraq War, 15-16
  British media coverage, 16
  public support for, 352
  security, 23
  telling their news as our news,
    172–178
    balance, 172-173
    fact/commentary, 174-175
    historical references, 175-176
    information sources, 176-177
    story location, 177-178
  us *vs.* them, 161-180

conceptual foundation, 162-164
  ideological shaping, 163
  localization, 163
  method, 164-166
Iron Curtain
  media, 1
Islamics
  attacking Madrid on March 11, 2004,
    101
  inoculation against Bali bombs, 199
Islamophobia, 69
Israel
  newspapers, 51
  Operation Defensive Shield, 61
Israeli journalists, 45
IW. *See* Information Warfare (IW)

J

JackAss, 361
Japan
  antinuclear protests, 145
  news agency, 88
Javanese, 201
  shadow theater, 202–203
Jawa Pos, 229
Jerry Springer, 369
Jewish school bombs
  Lyon, France, 49–50
  national frame, 59
Joshi, Parish, 263
Journalism
  after September 11, 69–70
  complexity of public role, 121
  distrubing banality of, 247–265
  emotion and attachment, 69–70
  self-mobilized, 121
Journalism of convenience. *See* Banal
  journalism
Journalistic conventions, 179
Journalists
  Allied, 89
  attitudes, 6
  becoming third parties, 34
  bypassing
    Osama bin Laden, 31
  vs. conflict mediators, 34-35
  embedded, 2
  frequent-flyer, 203

as gatekeepers, 7, 43–46
Gujarat 2002, 262–264
Israeli, 45
perceptions, 6
personal opinions influencing
  approach, 99
professional attitudes vs. domestic-
  cultural attitudes, 45
as professionals or patriots, 5–6
role perceptions, 45
universal professional perspective *vs.*
  domestic national perspective, 47
Jung, Carl, 369

K

Kar sevaks, 250-252
Keating, Paul, 154
Kellog, Sonal, 262
Khomeini, Ayatollah, 16, 369
Killings
  India, 253–254
King, David, 349
Kleinsorge, Wilhelm, 90, 93
Kompas, 224, 229
Kosovo war
  NATO intervention, 27
  news coverage of, 10–11
Kuta
  Bali bombs, 216-218
    imagery, 218

L

Laptops, 24
LA Times, 236
Laurence, William, 95
Lawrence, W.H., 86
Le Figaro, 105
Legislative issues
  protests, 9
Le Monde, 105
"Letter from America," 71
"Letter from London," 71
Letterman, David, 370, 371
Liberation, 105
Libertarian philosophy
  of government/press relations, 120
Lieberman, Joseph, 358
Limbaugh, Rush, 361, 363

Literature review, 42-49
Local editing
  foreign news, 44
Local-ethnic media, 43
Local gatekeepers
  editors as, 43–45
Local (domestic) terrorism, 44
Logocentrism, 227
London
  terrorist acts, 2
Long-distance nationalism, 251
Lynch, Jessica, 333
Lyon, France
  Jewish school bombing, 49–50

M

Madrid
  March 11, 2004 terrorist attack, 2,
    101
Mail, 346, 347t
Manhattan Project, 85, 86, 95
Maps
  Bali bombs photographic
    supplement, 231
  ethnocentric communication, 11
Marshall Islands
  Bikini Atoll
    hydrogen bomb testing, 95
Mass killings
  India, 253-254
Mass media
  relationship to terrorism
    classical approach, 274-276, 280,
      296-297
    critical approach, 276-277, 280-281,
      296-298
    critical-radical approach, 276-277
    functional-professional approach,
      277-278, 280, 296, 298, 300
  as watchdog on government,
    120–121
Mass newspapers, 123
Mass-popular newspapers, 123
McGuiness, P.P., 156
McLuhan, Marshall, 357, 369
Media. *See also* News media
  altering behavior of conflicting
    parties, 34

changing responsibilities, 24
classical approach, 280
coverage of anthrax vs. dirty bomb
    incidents, 295t, 296
covering violent events, 2
criticizing government, 286
entertainment
    fascination with terrorism, 31
as gatekeeper, 99
    international news, 99
international, 43
Iron Curtain, 1
local-ethnic, 43
mass
    as watchdog on government,
    120–121
national, 43
shaping public opinion, 98
terrorist violence, 8–9, 280–281
Media coverage
British on Iraq War, 16
groups with no states, 13
impact on types of weapons used by
    terrorism, 269–300
of political violence, 98–100
psychological goals served by terror-
    ists, 278–279
shooting down planes, 10
terrorist events, 8
unconventional weapons, 15
Media Dependency Theory, 279
Media elites
    cooperation, 8
Media freedom
Indonesia, 186
Media-government, 120-121
Media Indonesia editorial, 187-189, 202
Media levels, 43
Media shock, 185
Media tautology, 366-367
Mediated violence, 65-78
Medium as message
Gujarat 2002, 255–257
Mega-terrorism
defined, 272–273
Memories
frequent-flyer journalists, 203

Mercenaries
    vs. contractors, 360
Metaphysics of presence, 227
METN. *See* Middle Eastern Television
    Network (METN)
Middle East
    Intifada, 1, 2
Middle Eastern Television Network
    (METN), 317
Military elites
    cooperation, 8
Military might
    war on terror, 341–352
Military spending
    around the world, 342
    credible global military threat, 345
    from defence to attack, 342–346
    excess, 341
    myth, 342
    popular opinion, 344
    shifting rationale for, 342–346
    underestimating, 345
    U.S. vs. potential adversaries, 343
Military threat
    global, 345
Milosevic, Slobodan, 49, 112, 345
Mirror, 346, 347t
M129 leaflet bombs, 316
Mob attack
    kar sevaks, 252
Mobile phones, 24
Mobilization, 121
Modi, Narendra, 253, 254, 259, 260
Moggach, Deborah, 73-74
Morgan, Peter, 193
Morgan, Piers, 358
Mosque, 252, 253, 257, 262
Mourning, 231
MTV Cribs, 361, 365
Mujahedeen, 327
Multiculturalism, 1
Mururoa test. *See Australian,* reporting
    on French nuclear tests in Pacific
Muslim and British, 70
Muslims, 69-70. *See also* Hindu-Muslim
    clashes

Islamic fundamentalism victimization of women, 326–329
rampage against, 248
women as abject victim, 328
Mythical news work mode, 161
Myths, 204-205
Bali bombs, 198–201
cultural, 12
military spending, 342
news as, 12
power of, 341–352
South Pacific paradise, 153
MY TV, 258

N

Nagasaki, 85, 202
September 11, 2001 comparison to,
186
Nakamura, Hatsuyo, 90, 91, 93
National framing
explaining domestication and localization, 60
Jewish school bombing, 59
National identity, 43
foreign news coverage, 41–61
findings, 53-58
media selection, 50-51, 51t
methodology, 49-50
qualitative content analysis
method, 52-53
Nationalism
broadcast sports commentary, 66
long-distance, 251
vs. professional values, 45
National media, 43
National newspapers
divergence in definition of politically
violent events, 28
National Resources Defense Council
(NRDC) ad
in *New York Times,* 212
National state
media, 13
NATO. *See* North Atlantic Treaty
Organization (NATO)
Neo-Orientalism, 368
Netherlands, 2
News. *See also* Foreign news

breaking, 225
British, 190, 195
British television, 15, 189–193
domestic vs. foreign, 9
global vs. local definitions, 7–8
hard, 122
as homogenized product *vs.* local
inflections, 6–7
and ideology, 44
international, 99, 103, 104–105
localization, 7
as myth, 12
on-line, 103
ownership drives coverage consonant with American values, 15
Spain, 103, 105
television
Bali bombs, 15, 189–193
social conflicts, 11
News agencies
Japan, 88
Spain, 103
News coverage
differences in Gulf War, 11
television
of social conflict, 46
News cultures
English-languagevs. non-English
language, 15
News framing
of the oppression of Afghan women
by the Taliban, 326
News gatekeepers
local glasses worn, 6–7
News media
EurAm, 227
fascination with terrorism, 31
Indian ban on naming communities,
255–256
Newspapers
affective writing, 70
Britain, 51
cheap, 123
Israel, 51
mass, 123
mass-popular, 123
national, 28, 59

yellow, 123
yellow-sensational, 123
News pools, 2
News room
GLOBAL, 6-7
News stories
open *vs.* closed, 52-53
Newsweek
Iraqi women, 330
twin towers images, 212
women, 334
New Yorker, 84, 90
New York Herald Tribune, 86
New York Times, 51, 84, 85, 86, 89
anthrax, 284–289
vs. dirty bomb incidents, 295*t*,
296-297
Bali bombs photographic
supplement, 228
BBC explosion in Srinagar, Kashmir,
58
covering non-conventional terrorism, 283–284
dirty bomb scare, 290–294
legal process, 292
political focus, 291-292
threat, 292-294
French nuclear test in Pacific, 56
human rights before and after the
Cold War, 10
ignoring international terrorism, 10
Iraqi women, 330
Iraq War, 161–180
Jewish school bombing in Lyon,
57–58
NATO bombardment of Bosnia,
53–54
NRDC ad, 212
September 11, 2001, 161–180,
294–296
Spanish news, 105
twin towers images, 212, 212f
New Zealand
antinuclear protests, 145
protesting French nuclear tests in
Pacific, 50
9/11. *See* September 11, 2001

Noiseless flash, 90-93
Non-weapon
defined, 273
Noriega, Manuel, 345
North Atlantic Treat Organization
(NATO), 28, 49, 53-55, 99
Kosovo war intervention, 27
Norway, 2
Nuclear consensus, 84
Nuclear tests, 14. *See also* French
nuclear tests reporting

O

Obscene images, 364-365
Observer, 70, 75-76
Old school terrorism
defined, 272
On-line news, 103
Open construction, 165
Operation Defensive Shield
Israel, 61
Operation Iraqi Freedom
collateral damage, 320
Computer Network Operations, 312
vs. Desert Storm PSYOPS, 310
integrated campaign, 311–313
Iraqi soldiers surrendering, 310
psychological operations in, 307–322
strategic information war, 318–320
tactical PSYOPS, 313–318
tale of two conflicts, 309–311
white and black PSYOPS, 308–311
Oslo peace accord, 2
Overt PSYOPS, 309

P

Pacific. *See* French nuclear tests
reporting
Pacifism
Spain
increased by terrorist attack on
March 11, 2004, 101
Pakistan, 2
Parachute and pack journalism, 196, 203
Paradise Lost, 194
Parikh, Bhargav, 262
Partido Popular (PP), 102

Partido Socialista Obrero EspaÒol
(PSOE), 102
Patriotism, 45
coping with threats, 282
Peace accord
Oslo, 2
Peaceful visions, 1
Pennsylvanian National Guard
193rd Special Operations Wing, 313
Perception Management, 13-14
Operation Iraqi Freedom, 312
Perceptions
journalists, 6, 45
Perfect Tense, 363
Permissible *vs.* prohibited weapons
Geneva convention, 271
Personal opinions influencing approach
journalists, 99
Peru, 2
Philippine Consulate in Manado
Bali bombs, 216
Phones
mobile, 24
Photographic images
Abu Ghraib prisoner abuse, 356–362
branding *vs.* branded, 363-364
obscene image, 364-365
Photographic supplement
Bali bombs, 216, 228–241
imaging al-Qaeda, 235-239, 236f
provisional labels, 230-233
text loading image, 233-234
Photographs
Daily Mirror, 358, 365
Photography
commentary on 9/11, 215
denotative *vs.* connotative associa-
tions, 234
PIPA. *See* Program on International
Policy Attitudes (PIPA)
Planes
shooting down
media coverage, 10
Political contest model, 33
Political context, 9-10
Political decisions
coercion effect on, 98

Political elites
cooperation, 8
defining news agendas, 350
Political messages
political violence communicating,
28–29
Political power of information, 26
Political proselytization, 26
Political terrorism
defined, 272
Political violence
case study, 46–49
communicating political messages,
28–29
consensual operational definition,
3–4
defining as ours or theirs, 42
defining to type, 42
definition of, 46
as foreign news, 46–49
government as initiators of, 10–11
media coverage of, 98–100
message, 3–4, 46
newsworthiness, 4–5
social concept, 100–102
South Asia, 3
Spain, 100–102
Popular opinion
military spending, 344
Popular press coverage
vs. elite press coverage
of American policy in Bosnia,
119-137
Porn
social, 357, 361, 369
Porno, 362
Pornographic barbarism
of self-reflecting sign, 355–371
Pornographic society, 360-361
Pornographic zeitgeist, 362-363
Post-Cold War era
terrorism, 29
Post-Kleinian school of Object
Relations, 67
Postmodern terrorism
defined, 272–273
Post 9/11 war images

geopolitical consequences of,
368–369
Power, 202
PP. *See* Partido Popular (PP)
Press
English-language vs. non-English
language in Gujarat 2002, 249
freedom of vs. social responsibility,
45
Spain, 14
Press Council of India, 255, 262
Press coverage. *See* Elite *vs.* popular
press coverage
Press objectivity and bias
Gujarat 2002, 260–262
Prestige press, 122
Prisoner abuse photographic images
Abu Ghraib, 16
Prisoners
ritual humiliation (Iraqi), 16,
360–361
Pro-constitutionalist parties, 102
Professional attitudes *vs.* domestic-
cultural attitudes
journalists, 45
Professionals
dirty bomb scare, 290
Professional values
vs. national interest, 45
Israeli journalists, 45
Professional viewpoint
vs. national interest, 45
Israeli journalists, 45
Program on International Policy
Attitudes (PIPA), 344
Pro-independence parties, 102
Pronoun-ciation, 71–78
Propaganda
combat, 307
Propaganda model, 45
Protest, politics and media triangular
coverage, 47
Protest movement, 9
Protests
about French nuclear tests in Pacific,
50

PSOE. *See* Partido Socialista Obrero
EspaÒol (PSOE).
Psychological operations (PSYOPS),
307
Cold War, 308
covert, 309
e-mails, 310
Operation Iraqi Freedom, 313
overt, 309
SMS text messages, 310
Psychological warfare, 307
in Afghanistan, 307
American use in Second World War,
307
British use in First World War, 307
in Desert Storm, 307
in Kosovo, 307
in Operation Enduring Freedom,
307
PSYOPS. *See* Psychological operations
(PSYOPS)
Public
anthrax, 285
dirty bomb scare, 290–291
media impact on, 279–280
New York Times coverage of anthrax
vs. dirty bomb incidents, 295t, 296
Public debates
newspapers, 70
Public intellectuals, 65-78
Public opinion
media shaping, 98
war, 28
Public support
for Iraq War, 352

Q

Quality press, 122

R

Rabin, Yitzchak
murder, 1–2
Radical-democratic critique, 45
Radioactivity
in Hiroshima ruin, 86–87
Radio address on Afghan women
by Laura Bush, 329
Radio Baghdad, 315

Radio Nahrain, 318
Radio telephones, 24
Radio Tikrit, 309, 317
Raja, Javed, 263
Rarotonga Treaty, 145
RAWA. *See* Revolutionary Association
   of the Women of Afghanistan
   (RAWA)
193rd Special Operations Wing
   Pennsylvanian National Guard, 313
Reagan, Ronald, 370
Reality-TV formats, 361
   celebrity democratization, 366–367
Regional press
   Spain, 103
Rescue
   Bali bombs photographic supple-
   ment, 230
Reuters
   vs. CNN
      Bali bombs, 221-223
      Spanish news, 105
Revolutionary Association of the
   Women of Afghanistan (RAWA),
   327, 328-329, 334
Riot
   television, 254–263
Ritual humiliation
   Iraqi prisoners, 360–361
Robbins, James, 191
Rumsfeld, Donald H., 168, 311, 319,
   358, 367

S

Sabeeh, Iman, 331
SalamPax, 2
Sandesh, 255, 259-262
San Francisco Chronicle, 331
Sangh parivar, 250, 251
   mob attack, 252–253
   replacing mosque, 252
Sarajevo
   cosmopolitan culture, 125
   NATO bombardment, 99
Sardesai, Rajdeep, 256, 263
Sasaki, Terufumi, 90, 91, 93
Satellite television, 254-263
Sati, 329

Scissors-and-paste, 225-226
Screen
   West's narcissistic obsession with,
   368
Second Gulf War, 355, 370-371
Security
   Bali bombs photographic supple-
   ment, 230
   September 11, 2001, 23
Self-mobilized journalism, 121
Self-reflecting sign
   pornographic barbarism of, 355–371
September 11, 2001, 2, 8, 13, 15
   American perceptions of terrorism
   changing after, 273–274
   anthrax scare, 281–283
   comparison to Hiroshima and
   Nagasaki, 202
   Indonesian media, 15, 186
   national security vs. professional
   values, 281–282
   over-identification with New
   Yorkers, 70
   security, 23
   telling our news as really our news,
   166–172
      balance, 166–169
      historical references, 169–170
      information sources, 170–171
      story location, 171
   us *vs.* them, 161–180
      conceptual foundation, 162–164
      ideological shaping, 163
      localization, 163
      method, 164–166
Sexual violence
   against women in Iraq, 332
Shadows of Hiroshima, 89
Shadow theater, 202-203
Shalett, Sidney, 85
Shock and awe bombing of Baghdad,
   311, 315
Shubert, Atika, 221, 227
Siddiqui, Tanvir, 263
Sierra Leone, 2
Sikh guard assassination
   of Indira Gandhi, 253, 265

Simpson, John, 316
Sissons, Peter, 191
Smith, George, 316
Smith, Rob, 191-192
SMS text messages
  PSYOPS, 310
Social actors
  swaying balance of coverage,
    179–180
Social analysis
  deconstructing public private
    boundaries, 3
Social consensus
  influencing society's stance on
    political violence, 101
Social porn, 357, 361, 369
Social responsibility, 121, 136
  vs. freedom of the press, 45
Society
  political violence concept, 100
Soldiers
  Iraqi
    instructions on surrendering, 316
South Asia
  multiple overlapping taxonomies,
    201
  political violence, 3
South Pacific paradise myth, 153
Soviet Union, 29
Spain
  Bosnian War
    distant and remote, 108-109
    divergent editorial lines, 111-114
    news reinforcing audience's
      attitude as spectator, 106-111
  humanitarian aid mission, 102
  international news, 103, 104–105,
    105
  Madrid
    terrorist attack on March 11, 2004,
      2
  news, 105
  news agencies, 103
  on-line news, 103
  pacifism increased by terrorist attack
    on March 11, 2004, 101
  perception of armed conflicts, 102

political violence, 100–102
press, 14
regional press, 103
reinforced positions towards the
  United States and the European
  Union, 104
status as significant Euro-Atlantic
  nation confirmed, 104
television, 103
television stations, 103
Spanish Civil War, 101
Sports commentary
  broadcast, 66
Srinigar, Kashmir
  BBC bureau bomb explosions, 50,
    59
STAR News, 254-258, 263, 265
State terrorism, 4
Story location, 165
  influencing news ownership, 180
Suara Merdeka, 239
Sudan, 2
Suharto, 185-186, 202, 203
Sunday Times (London), 222, 225
Sydney Morning Herald
  Bali bombs photographic supple-
    ment, 229
  reporting on French nuclear tests,
    145–147, 149–156
  named actor appearances, 150, 151t
  Pacific representations, 153-156
  sources, 151, 152t
  story type, 149, 150t

T

Tahiti, 50, 144
Taiwan, 2
Taliban victimization
  Afghan woman, 325–329, 335
Tanimoto, Kiyoshi, 90, 92, 93
Technology
  problems, 23
Telegraph (UK)
  Bali bombs, 225
  reporting on French nuclear tests in
    Pacific, 146–147
Television, 317
  Bali bombs, 15, 189–193

global, 60
Indonesia, 185–186
riot, 254–263
satellite, 254–263
of social conflict, 46
social conflicts, 11
Spain, 103
Tempo News Room
    Bali bombs, 216–219, 223–224
Terror attacks
    list of, 238–239
Terrorism, 2. *See also* International
    terrorism, coverage; Unconventional
    terrorism
    from above, 30
    from below, 4, 30
    conventional
        defined, 272
        vs. unconventional, 273
    coverage differences, 12
    defined, 27–28, 30, 269, 270
        as communication dialogue, 269-
        270
    entertainment media fascination
        with, 31
    Indonesian and Euro-American
        media coverage of, 183–208
    international
        coverage increase, 346
        reaching diversified audiences, 270
        Soviet Union, 29
    legitimacy, 30
    vs. legitimate warfare, 271
    linked with military spending,
        350–352
    local (domestic), 44
    London, 2
    longitudinal analysis, 3
    mass media relationship to
        classical approach, 274-276, 280,
        296–297
        critical approach, 276-277, 280-281,
        296–298
        critical-radical approach, 276–277
        functional-professional approach,
        277-278, 280, 296, 298, 300
    mass mediated images of, 215

media coverage, 8
media coverage impact on types of
    weapons used, 269–300
    methodology, 283-284
news media fascination with, 31
old school
    defined, 272
post-Cold War era, 29
reciprocal relationship to media,
    269–270
studying, 274-281
state, 4
symbiotic relationship with mass
    communication, 31
symbolic dimensions, 4
threat of, 346–349
traditional
    controlling media's coverage of,
    279
using non-weapons, 271–272
using unconventional weapons,
    271–272
using weapons of mass destruction,
    271–272
vs. war, 28–31
against western democracies, 8
Terrorism-media symbiosis, 275
Terrorist organizations
    modern media techniques, 24
    targeting American organizations,
    270
Terrorists
    communication strategies employed,
    278–279
    New York Times coverage of anthrax
        vs. dirty bomb incidents, 296
    psychological goals served by media
        coverage, 278–279
Terrorist violence
    media, 8–9, 280–281
Text messages
    PSYOPS, 310
Theater
    shadow, 202–203
Theoretical framework, 42-49
Third parties
    journalists becoming, 34

Thompson, Hunter S., 361
4th Psychological Operations Group
    (4POG)
    Fort Bragg, North Carolina, 309
Threats
    conventional terrorism vs. uncon-
        ventional terrorism, 273, 296–297
    patriotism coping with, 282
Times, 51
    BBC explosion in Srinagar, Kashmir,
        58
    French nuclear test in Pacific, 56
    ignoring international terrorism, 10
    international terrorism coverage,
        346, 347t, 348t
    Iraq, 318
    Jewish school bombing in Lyon,
        57–58
    NATO bombardment of Bosnia,
        54–55
    Spanish news, 105
    Taliban victimization of Afghan
        women, 327
    women, 333, 334
Times of India, 249, 255, 257, 262-263
Totalitarian approach, 136
Total war, 27
Towards Freedom TV, 317
Traditional terrorism
    controlling media's coverage of, 279
Truman, Harry, 84
Twin towers images, 213f
Two Rivers Radio (Radio Nahrain), 318

U

Unconventional terrorism
    controlling media's coverage of, 279
    vs. conventional terrorism, 273
    defined, 272–273
Unconventional weapons, 279
    media coverage impact, 15
United Press, 86
United States
    Consulate in Renon, 216
    countervailing forces during post-
        Cold War era, 125
    excess military spending, 341

foreign news coverage of human
    rights before and after the Cold
    War, 10
foreign policy, 336
    invasion of Iraq, 326
    military spending, 343
    network coverage of Gulf War, 46
    newspapers, 51
    perceptions of terrorism changing
        after September 11, 2001, 273–274
    power collapsing, 188
    soldiers torturing Iraqi prisoners, 16
    Strategic Bomb Survey, 86
    women's rights violations, 336
Universal professional perspective *vs.*
    domestic national perspective
USA Today, 126, 133
USS Abraham Lincoln, 318

V

Vajpayee, Atal Bihari, 252, 258
Veil, 328-329
Video
    Bali bombs, 216
Vietnam War, 32
Violence
    effectiveness according to media
        treatment, 98
    mass mediated images of, 215
    mediated, 65–78
    negativity, 5–6
    redefining, 359–360
    sexual, 332
Violent conflicts
    distant
        audience involvement, 99
        media's representation of, 97-116
Voice of Iraqi Liberation, 317
Volant Solo, 313
Vyas, Sudhir, 263

W

Wall Street Journal, 126, 134-135
War
    defined, 27–28
    fog of, 352
    ours vs. other people's, 27

radical shift between previous and
        contemporary, 35
War on terror, 2
    and military might, 341–352
Washington Post, 126, 132
Washington Times, 126, 133-135
"We," 65-70
Weapons
    unconventional, 279
        media coverage impact, 15
Weller, George, 89
Welsh, Irvine, 362
Western democracies
    insurgent terrorism against, 8
    narcissistic obsession with screen,
        368
Women
    ideological work, 333–337

Iraqi, 332
    Muslims as abject victim, 328
    sexual violence against in Iraq,
        332
World Trade Center attack, 15, 99
    compared to Hiroshima, 186
World view
    Christian, 195

Y

Yellow newspapers, 123
Yellow-sensational newspapers, 123
Yugoslavia
    NATO, 27

Z

Zee News, 258, 262

Printed in the United States
200197BV00005BA/64-78/A

9 781572 737297